Intimate Friends

MARTHA VICINUS

Intimate Friends

WOMEN WHO LOVED WOMEN, 1778–1928

THE UNIVERSITY OF CHICAGO PRESS ⤚ CHICAGO AND LONDON

Martha Vicinus is the Eliza M. Mosher Distinguished University Professor of English, Women's Studies, and History at the University of Michigan. She is the author or editor of numerous works, including *Hidden From History: Reclaiming the Gay and Lesbian Past, Lesbian Subjects: A Feminist Studies Reader,* and *Independent Women: Work and Community for Single Women, 1850–1920,* the last published by the University of Chicago Press.

The University of Chicago Press, Chicago 60637
The University of Chicago Press, Ltd., London
© 2004 by The University of Chicago
All rights reserved. Published 2004
Printed in the United States of America
13 12 11 10 09 08 07 06 05 04   1 2 3 4 5
ISBN: 0-226-85563-5 (cloth)

Library of Congress Cataloging-in-Publication Data

Vicinus, Martha.
    Intimate friends : women who loved women, 1778–1928 / Martha Vicinus.
        p.   cm.
    Includes bibliographical references and index.
    ISBN 0-226-85563-5 (cloth : alk. paper)
    1. Lesbians—History. 2. Lesbianism—History. I. Title.
HQ75.5.V53 2004
    306.76′63—dc22   2003017510

♾ The paper used in this publication meets the
minimum requirements of the American National Standard
for Information Sciences—Permanence of Paper for
Printed Library Materials, ANSI Z39.48-1992.

FOR NANCY JORDAN SIMONDS

CONTENTS

ILLUSTRATIONS

ACKNOWLEDGMENTS

I have incurred many debts during the years of research and writing. I began this project, in a very different form, as a Steelcase Fellow at the University of Michigan Institute for the Humanities. Time to research and to write the initial drafts of several chapters was made possible by fellowships from the National Endowment for the Humanities and the Humanities Research Centre, Australian National University. Later an LS&A Michigan Humanities Fellowship and a Delta Delta Delta/National Endowment for the Humanities fellowship at the National Humanities Center gave me essential time to complete the book. The University of Michigan research fund for Distinguished University Professors made possible additional archival research. I am grateful to each of these funding agencies for underwriting the long process of research and writing. During my tenure as chair of the Department of English Language and Literature, Dean Edie G. Goldenberg encouraged me to continue my work in spite of the heavy administrative workload.

Archivists and librarians are the indispensable friends of the scholar. My work took me to many different collections, and I met everywhere unfailing enthusiasm and interest. My thanks go to the following libraries and their staffs, as well as those mentioned below under permissions: The University of Michigan Library, especially the Interlibrary Loan services; Australian National University; the Australian National Library; the Bodleian Library; the Miller Library, Colby College; the Harvard University Theater Collection; I Tatti, the Renaissance Center, Harvard University, Florence, Italy; the University of Reading Special Collections; the Walter Jackson Clinton Library, University of North Carolina—Greensboro; the Sheffield Public Archives; the Schlesinger Library; and the Harry Ransom Humanities Research Center, University of Texas, Austin. The librarians at the National Humanities Center found little-known citations and privately published materials for me with unfailing good will during my year as a fellow.

I am grateful to the following institutions for permission to quote from un-published materials in their collections: the Bodleian Library, University of Oxford, for the Mary Benson diaries and letters; Colby College Special Collections, Waterville, Maine, for the Vernon Lee Collection and for the letters of Vernon Lee to A. Mary F. Robinson Duclaux held at the Bibliothèque Nationale; Lord Ashburton, for the letters of Louisa Ashburton and Margaret Trotter in the Ashburton Collection, National Library of Scotland; the Schlesinger Library, Radcliffe Institute, Harvard University, for the Harriet Goodhue Hosmer Papers, and for the Hosmer letters held in the Ashburton collection; I Tatti, the Renaissance Center, Harvard University, Florence, Italy, for Mary Berenson's memoirs; the Manuscript Division, Library of Congress, Washington, D.C., for the Charlotte Cushman Papers; Leonie Sturge Moore/Charmian O'Neil, for Katharine Bradley and Edith Cooper, "Works and Days," at the British Library, and the letters held at I Tatti; Special Collections, University of Michigan, Ann Arbor, for the notebooks of Christopher St. John and the diaries of Ethel Smyth; The Master and Fellows of Girton College, Cambridge, for the Bessie Rayner Parks Collection and Emily Davies's "Family Chronicle"; The Master and Fellows of Magdalene College, Cambridge, for the diaries of A. C. Benson; the Fawcett Autograph Collection, Women's Library, London, for Emily Faithfull's letter; the Historical Society of Pennsylvania, for Frances Power Cobbe's letter; and Naiad Press for the use of its published translations of Renée Vivien.

The following photographs are reproduced by kind permission: 1, The National Library of Wales; 3, © Calderdale Museums and Arts, Shibden Hall, Halifax, England; 4, Photo Collection, Library of Congress; 5, Schlesinger Library, Radcliffe Institute, Harvard University; 6, © 2002 Museum of Fine Arts, Boston (*Sleeping Faun*, after 1865. Harriet Hosmer 1830–1908. Marble; 87.63 × 104.14 × 41.91 cm [34½ × 41 × 16½ in.]. Gift of Mrs. Lucien Carr, 12.709.); 7, 11, 12, by courtesy of the National Portrait Gallery, London; 9, by courtesy of Leonie Sturge Moore/Charmian O'Neil; 10, by kind permission of the National Trust; 16, ©Tate, London 2003; 17, Colby College, Waterville, Maine; 18, Bibliothèque littéraire Jacques Doucet, Paris; 19, by courtesy of George Wickes; 21, Smithsonian American Art Museum, Gift of the artist; 22, Mary Evans Picture Library, London (Graphic Photo); 23, Hulton Archive by Getty Images, New York. All other photographs are out of copyright or owned by the author.

Parts of chapter 2 were published as "Laocooning in Rome: Harriet Hosmer and Romantic Friendship" *Women's Writing* 10, no. 2 (2003): 353–66. Parts of chapter 3 were originally published as "Lesbian Perversity and Victorian Marriage" *Journal of British Studies* 36, no. 1 (Jan. 1997): 70–98; copyright 1997 by the North American Conference on British Stidies, all rights reserved. Parts of chapter 3 were also published as "Lesbian History: All Theory and

No Facts or All Facts and No Theory?" *Radical History Review* 60: 57–75; copyright 1994 by MARHO: The Radical Historians Organization, Inc., all rights reserved, used by permission of the publisher. Parts of chapter 4 were originally published as "The Gift of Love: Nineteenth Century Religion and Lesbian Passion" *Nineteenth Century Contexts* 23, no. 3 (2001): 241–64; see http://www.tandf.co.uk. Parts of chapter 7 were originally published as "The Adolescent Boy: Fin de Siècle Femme Fatale?" *Journal of the History of Sexuality* 5, no. 1 (1994): 90–114; copyright 1994 by the University of Texas Press, all rights reserved. Parts of chapter 7 were also published as "Turn-of-the-Century Male Impersonation: Rewriting the Romance Plot" in *Sexualities in Victorian Britain*, edited by Andrew H. Miller and James Eli Adams (Bloomington: Indiana University Press, 1996). I am grateful to the editors and publishers for permission to reprint.

Students in my graduate seminars on Victorian sexuality, as well as the participants in the "New Woman and the New Man" NEH seminars of 1992 and 1996, have been an ongoing source of intellectual delight. I have learned more from them than they know. I owe a debt to specific individuals who shared research materials, willingly read drafts of various chapters, and who then cheered me on. Sharing gossip about "our women" over the years has been a great pleasure. The following generously shared research materials with me: Virginia Blain, Jean Borger, Andrea Broomfield, Barbara Caine, Marion Diamond, Nancy Erber, Melanie Hawthorne, Ann Holmes, Kali Israel, Ellen Jordan, Jill Liddington, Sally Mitchell, Alan Munton, Alison Oram, Nancy Jordan Simonds, George Robb, Laurence Senelick, and Ivor C. Treby. Thanks also to my superb research assistants: Mary Catherine Harrison, Michele Herrman, Frauke Lenckos, Bea Nergaard, and Ji-Hyae Park. Many friends listened patiently as I tried to unravel inchoate ideas: Leonore Davidoff, Richard Dellamora, Cynthia Dessen, Laura Doan, Ginger Frost, Troy Gordon, Catherine Hall, Margaret Harris, Louis Kampf, John Kucich, Karin Lützen, Jill Julius Matthews, Lisa Merrill, Billie Melman, Lesley Milroy, Claire G. Moses, Bea Nergaard, Helmut Puff, Meri-Jane Rochelson, Ellen Ross, Michael Schoenfeldt, Eva Stehle, Pat Thane, Thea Thompson, Chris Waters, and John Whittier-Ferguson. Everyone who studies the lesbian past owes special thanks to Jeannette Foster, Lillian Faderman, and Marie-Jo Bonnet, each of whom mapped the literary history of the lesbian before such work was fashionable.

I wish to thank the following who so generously read drafts and shared their expertise with me: Virginia Blain, Barbara Caine, Laura Doan, Melanie Hawthorne, Susan S. Lanser, Jill Liddington, Deborah T. Meem, Lisa Merrill, Alison Oram, Yopie Prins, Suzanne Raitt, and Ivor C. Treby. Barbara Mnookin was the best of copy editors. Julie English Early and John Gagnon read an early version of the book. Their penetrating questions, distaste for jargon, and queries about my assumptions have made this a much better book. Julie's sympathetic engagement with my argument, as well as her astute comments, went far beyond academic friendship. Judith Bennett's detailed critique of a later version was invaluable; I have benefited for many years from her keen editing skills and her knowledge of lesbian history before 1778. I owe much to my friend and colleague John Kucich, well beyond his intellectual rigor, good food, and fine conversation. My greatest debt is to Nancy Jordan Simonds, who thoroughly critiqued each chapter and read every version of the introduction, whether fat or slim, numerous times. Her loving support has meant more than words can say.

INTRODUCTION

In gathering materials for his influential *The Friendships of Women* (1867), William Rounseville Alger declares that he was "often struck both by the small number of recorded examples of the sentiment among women . . . and by the commonness of the expressed belief, that strong natural obstacles make friendship a comparatively feeble and rare experience with them."[1] He modestly hopes that those who had been "denied the satisfactions of impassioned love" will be "grateful for a book which shows them what rich and noble resources they may find in this widely different, though closely kindred, sentiment."[2] Over ten full chapters, he evades the issue of erotic friendship—how and why a woman might choose to love another woman. This erasure from the public record has helped historians of today to argue that the lesbian did not exist in the past. Yet the surviving evidence is far richer and more complex than I had imagined when I began my research years ago. Why, then, have women's erotic friendships seemingly disappeared from history? And why have they been consistently marginalized as "second best" to heterosexual marriage? What are the "natural obstacles" to friendship between women? This book traces these debates between the year 1778, when Lady Eleanor Butler and Sarah Ponsonby ran away from Ireland to settle together in Wales, and 1928, when Radclyffe Hall's courageous book on lesbian sexual love, *The Well of Loneliness*, was published and then banned in Great Britain.

The chief obstacles to women's friendships during this period were surely obvious to any woman who did not wish to marry. Whatever her social class she and her beloved usually lacked the economic means to establish a home together, and all social and familial structures discouraged such arrangements. Unmarried women frequently had family responsibilities that made it difficult even to visit a special friend. Charlotte Brontë, who had to care for her aging father, never ceased to lament the distance separating her from her friend Ellen Nussey. Intimate friendships often terminated when one woman married, and loyalty to her husband and his wishes became paramount. Informal liaisons, formed out of necessity as well as love, could be sustained for a period of time. Working-class women, whose wages often left them on the edge of poverty, sometimes clubbed together to survive. But the unsteady nature of poorly paid work made it difficult to manage a more permanent relationship. Isolated reports of women who passed as men and took wives appear in newspapers, but we know little about these couples unless they ran afoul of the law; their personal lives remain largely unknown. Women from all social classes had to balance economic necessity, family obligations, and personal wishes. Not surprisingly, this book depicts the lives of those most likely to leave documents for the future historian: white, educated Anglo-Americans. Class privilege, family support, and education fostered opportunities to live sexually independent lives. Through representative examples I consider the richly diverse modes of sexual self-fashioning adopted by these privileged women, focusing especially on the varied constructions of gender inversion. Although necessarily few in number, they were often influential and admired figures. I also explore the changing boundaries between the acceptable and the unacceptable display of same-sex love, including both popular commentary and medical debates.

FEMALE FRIENDSHIP

Education and family money might free women, but these advantages also imposed respectability. Throughout the nineteenth century the educated classes were increasingly vested in maintaining the dominant discourses in regard to women's place and behavior in society. These discourses were never without contradiction or opposition, but incentives to marry for social and economic security ensured the continued marginality of women's friendships and their construction as second best to heterosexual marriage. But widespread debates about deviant sexuality, ranging from prostitution to homosexuality, never halted unacceptable erotic feelings and acts. The great popularity of Alger's compilation is symptomatic of a pervasive concern about women's friendships and their place in everyday life; an outpouring of printed matter testifies to the hard work needed to keep same-sex erotic love marginal. Heterosexuality was under many pressures. Controversial agitation both for and against prostitution, raising the age of consent, divorce, birth control, male friendship, and other issues called both the naturalness and the moral superiority of normative heterosexuality into question. The result of these public debates was to press heterosexuality to accommodate and explain its social effects and failures. Women's friendships were an integral part of this public conversation about sexual behavior and desires. As long as sexual categories remained fluid and largely undefined, responses were also largely unpredictable and incoherent. An easy historical trajectory would trace a course from invisibility and ostracism to visibility and ostracism. But the position of women who loved women during the years 1778–1928 was far more complicated.

During the second half of the eighteenth century, women's intimate friendships were divided into two types, sensual romantic friendship and sexual Sapphism. Numerous eighteenth-century poems, novels, and treatises praised the fidelity and beauty of women's friendships, in contrast to a quickly ignited, but quickly burnt out, heterosexual passion. The rise of sentimentality and then Romanticism was the inspiration for this idealization of friendship. Educated women were encouraged to keep diaries, to examine their personal experiences (and consciences), and to empathize with others. Jean-Jacques Rousseau's ideas about the importance of feeling over reason were very popular among the bourgeoisie throughout Europe. In his novel *Julie, ou la nouvelle Héloïse* (1761), female friendship epitomizes pure feeling. Claire loves Julie more than her fiancé. She tells Julie that she cannot marry M. d'Orbe because she cannot distinguish her love for a man from her love for a woman. She asks plaintively if the soul has a sex, hoping perhaps that she can have a spiritual marriage with Julie. In turn, M. d'Orbe loves Claire because she loves Julie; Claire's love is evidence of her natural goodness.[3] An eroticized same-sex friendship is transmuted into an opportunity for the personal edification of both women and men. Rousseau in this novel and other writings articulated the Romantic belief in a true self that is hidden beneath social convention, just as the body is hidden beneath layers of superfluous clothing. By the early twentieth century, the concept of one's true nature concealed by social custom had been subtly altered, so that sexuality replaced natural feeling as the defining core of a person's identity.

Eighteenth-century pornography confirms this fascination with romantic friendship by dwelling on the scenario of a man watching women make love to each other. Denied the opportunity of emotional closeness without aggression, the male viewer observes through a peephole or closet door or window the gentle tenderness of the two women.[4] The extra, unexpressed affection of nongenital intimacy gives their relationship something unnamed that is missing from the driven, though naturally superior, sex of the man. The Sapphic contained the romantic, and vice-versa. Those who knew Greek or were familiar with the works of the Roman satirist Juvenal could find a very earthy, sexual basis for women's friendships, but this information was cordoned off and rarely applied to respectable women.[5] Men made a vigorous effort to marginalize women's sexual love, even as they relished a hidden underground knowledge of alternative sexual behaviors.

Among the educated English classes, Rousseau's version of romantic friendship was widely lauded and contrasted with the scandal that swirled around the French court. During the years leading up to the French Revolution, rumors reached England of alarming sexual freedoms, including Queen Marie Antoinette's purported Sapphic orgies. Her activities became a prime subject for pornography. Female modesty, marital hierarchy, and religious authority all seemed undermined by the extraordinary behavior of the dissolute aristocracy. The outpouring of virulent antiroyalist pamphlets and the misogyny of the French revolutionaries briefly "outed" lesbian sexuality as a chosen perversity among the titled.[6] At the same time the bourgeoisie became more cautious about the open expression of same-sex love. Descriptions of the beloved's body in poems about female friendship declined during the latter half of the eighteenth century in both England and France.[7] Middle-class women were expected to keep their love for another woman emotional and not physical. Sentiment meant viewing but not touching. Thinking, writing, and confessing one's love heightened its importance, as well as one's own self-control.

This tradition of sentimentalized romantic friendship continued into the nineteenth century, which saw a concerted effort to spiritualize all love, partly in reaction to the sexual disorder of the French aristocracy and the horrific consequences of the French Revolution, and partly in response to Romanticism's veneration of feeling. Desire was not denied, but it was deemed morally superior if its bodily nature was subsumed to its spiritual potential. In Alger's words, friendship was a union of "soul and life." Both women and men idealized their same-sex friendships, making them simultaneously more and less important. A friendship could be more important than a heterosexual love because it was considered less sexually driven and more self-sacrificing. But it was also more subject to circumstances. Friendship was a phase, an education in feelings for the young, like Claire's love for Julie. After marriage its intimacy had to be put aside, and new priorities acknowledged. A good friendship changed from love to liking. As Alger carefully explains, "In the lives of women, friendship is,—First, the guide to love; a preliminary stage in the natural development of affection. Secondly, it is the ally of love; the distributive tendrils and branches to the root and trunk of affection. Thirdly, it is, in some cases, the purified fulfilment and repose into which love subsides, or rises. Fourthly, it is, in other cases, the comforting substitute for love."[8] Alger assumes that love is heterosexual. He agrees with Rousseau that friendship is always a means and never an end. Such strenuous efforts were made to define and delimit the bodily nature of female friendship that the barrier between admired romantic friends and excoriated Sapphists must have seemed permeable. Only by constant reminders would women, and men, distinguish between friendship and love.

This book traces how women took elements from two separate categories, romantic friendship and Sapphic sexuality, to fashion something new—

a personal identity based upon a sexualized, or at least recognizably eroti-cized, relationship with another woman. Even though they did not use the word *lesbian*, women self-consciously sought to understand their feelings, their actions, and their relationships apart from men. A few women fully ac-knowledged and acted upon the sexual basis of their deep love for another woman. Others controlled their erotic desire in order to win a higher love. Physical consummation was less important than the mutual recognition of passion. The intricate interplay between the spirit and the body is central to any understanding of women's intimate friendships. A sexual love might not achieve physical consummation for a variety of reasons, including social cir-cumstances, religious scruples, a belief in the superiority of nonfulfillment, or a preference for the erotic pleasure of unfulfilled, idealized love. Some women were terrified of the consequences of their desires, yet unable to countenance heterosexuality. Willed ignorance or disavowal kept passion at bay; Eliza Lynn Linton could admit her love of women only in cross-gendered fictions. Regardless of their circumstances, for the women discussed here, same-sex love was their primary emotional bond. Women then, as now, however, could live long and emotionally complicated lives that changed over time. One woman, one kind of love, did not automatically exclude other lovers or kinds of love. Several of the women discussed here had serious flirtations with both women and men, and some were married.

As Harriette Andreadis has pointed out, we have too long assumed that women in the past *could not name* their erotic desires, rather than recognizing their *refusal to name* them.[9] Because of this, it remains difficult to trace same-sex love among women. Women have always had reasons to be secretive about their sexual desires. Given the long-standing belief that sexual rela-tions between women were limited to foreigners in hot climates and, at home, to prostitutes and other marginal groups, it is hardly surprising that educated women valued discretion. The consequences of speaking or acting too openly about physical desire could be dangerous in a world that insisted upon women's respectability. Women wrote in code, warned each other to conceal or burn letters, and used metaphors or allusion. Far better, most women felt, to remain quiet or to speak only to trustworthy allies.

Loving women brought into question beliefs about virginity, monogamy, and fidelity. If active sexuality was defined wholly in heterosexual terms,[10] a woman could be sexually involved with another woman and still remain a virgin. If fidelity was defined as heterosexual monogamy, then a woman might flirt with another woman without losing her respectability. Indeed, several chapters unravel complicated same-sex flirtations that undermined various forms of fidelity. Since men continued to gather in all-male clubs, cafés, and other venues throughout the nineteenth and early twentieth cen-turies, women were often left alone in the company of other women; erotic play was an integral part of their lives. Homoerotic teasing and touching were welcome among the bored, who sought to break the monotony of waiting to marry, or to escape a disagreeable husband, or to add excitement to widowhood. Among the women discussed, Anne Lister, Charlotte Cushman, Ethel Smyth, Natalie Clifford Barney, Renée Vivien, and Radclyffe Hall were unfaithful to their partners. These women crossed many boundaries in the pursuit of love. They usurped male prerogatives by appropriating attention in their social circles. They finessed or ignored family ties for love. Exceptional women, they believed, could behave with exceptional freedom. Surviving documents point to few feelings of guilt, except when an affair or relationship went awry. Failure, not success, aroused remorse.

Throughout the book I draw attention to the representation of many varieties of erotic love, ranging from the openly sexual, to the delicately sensual, to the disembodied ideal. Lister, a charming female rake, wrote in her diary, "I love, & only love, the fairer sex & thus beloved by them in turn, my heart revolts from any other love than theirs."[11] She also recorded her successful "grubbling" (necking) and the number of orgasms she and her lovers had. But most women were more circumspect. They used natural images that mimicked or drew attention to the desiring female body; opening flower buds, smooth, rounded jewels, tidal oceans, and lush gardens, all expressed an unnamed but not unknown sexual desire. To give but one example, Mary Benson joyfully wrote a new friend, "how could I dare to hope that the life (that I knew was there) would ever bud a blossom for me—"[12] They exchanged jewelry as love tokens, so that when apart each would feel the touch of the other. Only much later, when Benson struggled to spiritualize her earthly love, could she touch upon its sexual roots, writing cryptically in her private diary of "carnal affections" and "when I went to bed the fall came."[13] Women's intimate friendships included an acknowledged erotic component, and some were fully physical, though few women could admit this even to themselves.

DEFINING THE LESBIAN

In the past twenty years lesbian history has focused on the confusing issue of what constitutes lesbian sexuality. Scholars have disagreed about chronology, terminology, and categories. These arguments have led to further divisions, vocabularies, and debates, but to no clear resolution. Categorizing continues, exclusive or inclusive, depending upon one's political agenda. Some historians seem determined to erase the lesbian as a subject, and others want to define her so narrowly that she risks disappearing. Characteristically, biographers deny that a woman loved another woman, or claim that they could not have been sexually involved because lesbians did not exist at the time, or argue that women in the past would not have known what to do in bed with each other.

This posthumous protection of a reputation has seriously distorted women's history for years, as lesbian historians have documented.[14] For example, Blanche Cook's 1992 biography of Eleanor Roosevelt was the first serious treatment of her friendship with Lorena Hickok. Sometimes the task of silencing has been made easier when the woman in question has destroyed all compromising evidence. Jennifer Terry points out that impersonal medical records have a better chance of surviving than the personal, and possibly more revealing, diary or letters of the so-called deviant woman.[15] Yet all historians must deal with incomplete documentation and confusing chronologies.

What kind of ahistorical presumption is it to speak of "lesbians" before the formation of either communities or individuals who used this word? How can one write a book about lesbian identities when most women defined themselves by the men they married? To date many historians have been overconcerned with finding that invisible moment in the past when "the modern lesbian identity" came into being. Randolph Trumbach, for example, dates the rise of the lesbian to the end of the eighteenth century, when he finds communities of women similar to the "male-mollies" of the early eighteenth century.[16] Carroll Smith-Rosenberg sees the development of a language of sexual practices in the early twentieth century as a turning point.[17] Elizabeth Lapovsky Kennedy and Madeline D. Davis, in their book *Boots of Leather and Slippers of Gold*, focus on the formation of public communities; for them "community is key to the development of twentieth-century lesbian identity and consciousness."[18]

In discerning surveys the Medievalist Judith M. Bennett and the Americanist Leila Rupp have each argued against using the word *lesbian* for women who did not use the word themselves. Bennett suggests the use of "lesbian-like" as more fluid and flexible for the historian. As she points out, sexual practice may well have been less important in the past than "desire for women, primary love for women (as in 'women-identified-women') or even political commitment to women (especially as manifested in resistance to 'compulsory heterosexuality')."[19] Her term helps to destabilize the notion of a single sexual identity, but refuses the implicit homophobia of historians who deny the existence of lesbian-like women and behaviors in the past. It also avoids an ahistorical focus on identity and instead prioritizes behavior. But Bennett shifts the focus from a noun (*lesbian*) to an adjective (*lesbian-like*), uncomfortably concentrating on the unknowable, rather than the knowable. Rupp uses the phrase "same-sex sexuality" for many of the same reasons that Bennett coins "lesbian-like." In her survey of the global history of same-sex sexuality, she points out that "there are various ways that sexual acts involving two genitally alike bodies may in fact not be best conceptualized as 'same-sex.' In some cases, what is more important than the fact of genital similarity is the fact of some kind of difference: age difference, class difference, gender difference . . . are far more important to the people involved and to the societies in which they lived than the mere fact of the touching of similar bodies."[20] Rupp implicitly confirms how Western, modern, even *odd* it is to privilege same-sex sexuality as the determining factor in an individual's personal identity. She also reminds us that we have considerable evidence about what women thought about each other (Alger quotes reams of verse), but little evidence of what they did with each other. Rupp is more confident speaking of same-sex sexuality, rather than using the overly narrow and defining word *lesbian*. Yet this preference forces her to leave vague what constitutes sexuality and under what circumstances.

Rupp and Bennett both have good reasons to seek a different, more general vocabulary. They draw attention to the historically situated nature of sexual desire by stressing the changes in language, actions, and attitudes that have occurred over time. Nevertheless, I have chosen to use both "lesbian" and "same-sex sexuality," admittedly sparingly, to highlight the sexual nature of my topic. These terms are a convenient linguistic reminder that sex matters. In doing so I do not wish to detract from the overarching argument of this book that attitudes toward and behaviors by lesbians show a rich combination of change and continuity, as well as containing an unknowable core that is intrinsic to any history of sexuality. I also examine a number of nineteenth-century concepts and words used to describe women who seemed too interested in a particular friend, including man-like, mannish, morbid, intense, sentimental, languid, and dangerous. They served as code, alerting the sophisticated, while ensuring the innocence of the naïve. As John Stokes points out, by the 1890s the word *morbid* had become a provocative euphemism for homosexuality.[21] This key word, indicative of physical disease, tied an emotion (same-sex desire) to a bodily condition (sickness). The slipperiness of vocabulary has contributed to our own confusion about how to define women's intimate friendships without demeaning them and their erotic content.

Given the range of activities and identities that can come under the category of lesbian sexuality, the natural desire to create coherent narratives has encouraged the careful construction of distinctions among women. Judith Butler has suggested that all sexual roles are just that—roles that we perform, but that we perform under constraints constructed by a whole range of social and cultural effects.[22] For her nothing can be more falsifying than a simple label, such as "lesbian." Under her influence the instability of identification—the queerness of sexual identity—has dominated literary debates. *Intimate Friends*, however, reveals a more embodied history, in which educated women who loved women fashioned recognizable sexual identities, reached out to other women, flaunted their love in heterosexual society, and created richly varied art to showcase lesbian sexual love. Rather than speaking of unstable identities, we should think of complex identifications, embedded in class, national, and racial associations.

Judith Halberstam emphasizes the gendered elements that define the sexual self. She redraws the map of lesbian history, creating new categories for women who wanted to be men, who were seen as men, and who successfully passed as men. Such distinctions, however, would have been meaningless in the past, when several different labels might be assigned to a "gender-inverted" woman, positive and negative. "Mannishness" had as many different meanings as "effeminacy."[23] It could mean, for example, an estimable power of reasoning, or remarkable learning and knowledge, or an assertive patriotism in defense of one's country, or a dangerous aggressiveness in defying male privilege, or a too-overt interest in pursuing women as erotic objects. Halberstam speaks categorically of the "collective failure to imagine and ratify the masculinity produced by, for, and within women."[24] The key term here is *ratify*, since for centuries Eurocentric cultures have recognized and imagined the masculine woman. Indeed, they have often ratified aspects of this figure, especially in regard to her man-like intellect, reason, and assertiveness. Cross-dressed women who successfully passed as men were admired for their ability to take on higher-status masculine roles. As Dianne Dugaw has documented, throughout the eighteenth and early nineteenth centuries, female soldiers were celebrated figures in ballads and folklore.[25]

Not surprisingly, there has been a backlash against this parsing and defining of who was a lesbian and who should have a different label. As Katherine Raymond explains, "I don't look like a lesbian. Maybe this is a politically incorrect statement to make, but it is an honest one. It seems to me that the more emphasis queer theory and politics place on the endless multiplicity of sexual personae, and the more well-meaning postmodernists problematize what exactly a gay man, lesbian, or bisexual 'is,' the easier it gets to describe what one looks like"[26] She concludes, "I want to be a sexual being without defining myself solely or primarily on the basis of my sexuality."[27] Her salutary reminder that an acknowledged sexual identity is not all a woman can be confirms my sense that lesbian history is best understood as part of a larger history of women. Moreover, identity history can be limiting: more interesting and difficult questions can be asked about friendship, intimacy, sexuality, and spirituality than who had what kind of identity when. In researching some one hundred and fifty years of same-sex relations among women, I am convinced that all categories and definitions must remain provisional.

In this book I argue against transformative moments, or a linear history, or even the necessity of a shared community of lesbians for the history of the lesbian. Although the chapters are largely chronological, the organization of the book emphasizes different types of relationships. I stress continuities rather than radical changes or dramatic moments. A multiplicity of same-sex desires has always existed, and the task of the historian is not to simplify, but to illuminate the complexities and contradictions in the various texts and documents that have survived. A progress narrative is detrimental to a full understanding of personal relationships; we gain a better sense of intimate friendships by tracing repetitive patterns.[28] This is not to say that no changes occurred—clearly a great many did. The nineteenth century saw the first women's movement, the rise of educational and professional opportunities for women, major legal reforms for married women, and the creation of elaborate taxonomies of sexual behaviors. The various *representations* of same-sex love exhibit significant continuities throughout the period under discussion, but their *significance*, as well as *attitudes* toward them, show considerable variation.

Depending upon one's point of view, the title of this book, *Intimate Friends*, is an enabling metaphor, capacious enough to embrace a very wide range of erotic behavior and self-presentation. Or it is an obfuscating term that conceals sexuality and over-privileges emotional compatibility. For me, however, it embodies the indeterminacy inherent in any study of sexual behaviors and beliefs. In this book intimate friendship is an emotional, erotically charged relationship between two women. I focus on the vocabulary, metaphors, and descriptions used by women themselves in court transcripts, autobiographies and biographies, journal articles, letters, diaries, fiction, and poetry. Given the fragmentary nature of the evidence and the danger of exposure, silence becomes as important as the written word. I emphasize the representation of experience rather than the (ultimately unknowable) experience itself. As well, I discuss how others, including friends, family, and the public, interpreted a woman's refusal to marry and her passion for another woman.

Speaking and seeing raise the difficult issue of how and whether language is necessary for constructing what the body feels and desires. Whether women flaunted their sexuality or hid it, they could not control the wider response to their nonnormative behaviors. Outsiders looked for visible signs of deviance on the female body, determined to give an ocular definition of the essentially unknowable: the unmarked, invisible sexual practices of an individual. Lesbians themselves, however, struggled with both their sense of being physically different and their need to explain this deep-held belief. A language, literal or metaphorical, may be necessary to imagine an identity, but not to act upon a sexual desire. As late as 1921 an attempt to make lesbianism (like male homosexuality) illegal in Great Britain was defeated for fear that women might learn something they knew nothing about.[29] Politicians assumed that the unspoken would remain the unknown. Historians cannot accept so simple an equation. Yet self-fashioning involves self-knowledge. This inevitably grounds sexual desire in a language. The women I study were enormously inventive in creating a satisfactory language, spoken and bodily,

for their own desires that bears little resemblance to the elaborate terminology of the post-1928 period. Without fixed categories or a fixed vocabulary,
desire could and did take many forms, some visible to the public, others
known only in private.

REPRESENTATIONS OF LOVE

I believe that historians have neglected the ways in which women themselves described their intimate friendships and desires. Neither a pornographic nor a scientific vocabulary provided women with the language of
love, so nineteenth-century educated women fashioned their sexual selves
through metaphor. Women who loved women created metaphoric versions of
the heterosexual nuclear family. Change, especially personal change, depends
in part on an imaginative reworking of the known. The nonnormative is in
dialogue with the normative. The family was (and still is) the single-most-
important place where a child learns about love, authority, and power, followed by the church or temple and the school. To oversimplify, the family
teaches intimacy. It also serves as a model for how to (or not to) create a home.
Each generation repeats and alters the emotional mistakes and strengths of
its parents. Throughout the book I consider a range of familial dynamics, including those played out in public and those confined to the home. I also examine the role of religion and education in sustaining or condemning same-
sex love. These two institutions encouraged self-examination, providing a
woman with a fresh understanding of her emotional needs.

Drawing upon the rich associations of family life, nineteenth-century
women called each other by every conceivable kin relation, but rarely father.
They subtly altered the meaning of mother, aunt, daughter, niece, sister,
cousin, and even son. But "father" was almost always reserved for male parents and God. For a woman to construe herself as a father-figure meant that
she aligned herself with patriarchal rule. The feared figure was not the young
suitor, but the father. Virginia Woolf's creation of Shakespeare's sister, driven
mad by the thwarted desire to create, offers one compelling explanation for
why the father was so unattractive a role. In *A Room of One's Own*, Woolf
vividly pictures how a loving father could stifle female genius by insisting
upon heterosexual marriage. She imagines how the father might shame, beat,
and beg his beloved daughter into marrying, asking, "How could she disobey
him? How could she break his heart?"[30] Loving another woman could be construed as the ultimate act of disobedience to the father. Indeed, same-sex love
was most likely to come under attack when patriarchal authority was threatened, ranging from a poor woman caught with a dildo to a middle-class
woman refusing to marry her father's choice.

Literature provided eloquent warnings against adolescent same-sex desire as a threat to paternal control. In both Samuel Taylor Coleridge's 1816 poem, "Christabel," and in Sheridan LeFanu's 1872 novella, "Carmilla," a mysterious stranger leads a motherless girl astray. In each work a pubescent girl, waiting for she-knows-not-what, generously welcomes a sorceress into her home and nearly destroys the patriarchal household. Christabel and Laura transfer their primary love from their fathers to their guests and in the process become damaged goods, less valuable property on the marriage market. The fathers cannot protect their daughters against sexual depredation; the incest theme is trumped by the lesbian narrative. Coleridge and LeFanu titillate the reader about the degree of complicity involved. Laura is "conscious of a love growing into adoration, and also of abhorrence" for the "languid" Carmilla. At night she discovers "certain vague and strange sensations" visiting her in her sleep: "The prevailing one was of that pleasant, peculiar cold thrill which we feel bathing, when we move against the current of a river. . . . Sometimes there came a sensation as if a hand was drawn softly along my cheek and neck. Sometimes it was as if warm lips kissed me, and longer and more lovingly as they reached my throat, but there the caress fixed itself."[31] Just as the vampire Carmilla visits Laura at night to drain her blood, Geraldine poisons the mind of Christabel when they sleep together. These preternaturally innocent girls serve as warnings to fathers: pretending to maternal love, a sexually experienced woman can steal a girl's affections and destroy her appetite for marriage.

Women frequently referred to each other as "sister," the most egalitarian relationship they had in a nuclear family. As Carol Lasser has pointed out, nineteenth-century American women called a best friend sister with the expectation of lifelong emotional and financial support. Political women of many different persuasions spoke of each other as sisters united in a moral struggle.[32] The widespread use of the sororal metaphor may have been a cover for something more intimate.[33] Several nineteenth-century literary works, including Jane Austen's *Sense and Sensibility* (1811) and Christina Rossetti's "Goblin Market" (1862), portray intensely eroticized sisterly love.[34] But my own reading of the sources suggests that the sister metaphor, although crucial to female friendship, was not commonly used by women when they wished to indicate something deeper than an equal friendship. Intimate friends were not united by sisterly ties, but by a stronger emotion. Neither patriarchal superiority nor sororal equality carried the appropriate feeling, for one signified too much power and the other too little. One implied sexual suffocation, the other sexual insipidness.

The family metaphor implies a controversial point of view: in theory we can imagine innumerable sexual scripts, but historically we possess fewer than we might expect. The two most common models for the successful intimate friendship were fundamental to the heterosexual family: the wife-husband couple and the child-mother bond. A same-sex couple could either emulate and rival heterosexual marriage or repeat and replace the idealized relation-ship of childhood. A same-age same-sex relationship could be a permanent proto-marriage; a cross-age same-sex relationship promised the seamless lov-ing acceptance of mothering. Potentially either relationship might be more satisfying than the dangerous inequalities of heterosexual marriage or the sti-fling love of one's birth mother. Within these two compelling scripts women assumed many roles and behaviors. But they still struggled with issues of un-equal power and knowledge. Lacking the obvious differences between a man and a woman, women had difficulty acknowledging their own power. Who had power over whom, when and how, became vital issues for the sexologists when they began to identify and define lesbian relationships.

Same-sex partnerships between two older unmarried women were safely defined, in Alger's words, as "the comforting substitute for love." But as this book documents, women themselves did not think they had chosen a second-best alternative to heterosexual marriage. They were in love and had no difficulty distinguishing their intimate relationship from ordinary friend-ships. They openly spoke of a partner as "husband," "wife," "sposa," "better half," and so forth. Letters among women friends include fond references to "your better half" or "your beloved." These middle- and upper-class couples insisted on the validity of their relationships against strong folk traditions. When two women seemed to be totally involved with each other, some on-lookers did not see a noble, spiritual love, but rather a risible erotic relation-ship. "It's found out a woman has married a wife," a mid-1830s broadside jok-ingly declared:

> Then they laid all the night, and no doubt they both sigh'd,
> For a good strapping drayman their charms to divide;
> 'Twas very provoking it so did befall,
> That one for the other had—Nothing at all.[35]

Although both women might sigh for a penis, in satire the so-called mascu-line woman was often attacked for stealing a pretty girl. The metaphor of husband and wife might give an aura of stability to a lesbian marriage, but it also drew attention to impossibilities most women wished to keep hidden in the bedroom. A respectable female couple could be "married" in the eyes of the public only if no one looked too closely at either one or both. When people did so, they saw one woman aping the role of the man and the other sadly denied children. Like all metaphors, this one failed when subjected to literal interpretation.

The mother-daughter metaphor was more common than the husband-wife metaphor, in large part because it seemed safer than the obvious eroti-cism of a figurative marriage, but also because it implied a temporary stage. Just as a child grew up and left her natal home, so too would a young woman grow up and leave her older, maternal friend. Indeed, pedagogic eros was admired as an ennobling love between an older teacher and a younger pupil. Letters home from besotted daughters speak of their pleasure in a particular aunt, friend, or teacher, but well after adolescence women continued to use the language of the nurturing surrogate mother and the inexperienced, vulnerable child. For example, in 1911 the twenty-three-year-old medical student Octavia Wilberforce wrote her friend, the actress Elizabeth Robins, "Since I have you, nobody is more satisfied up to the hilt, more lavished in affection, more continuously pouring at your feet every drop of love in my whole being as this your devoted child. So see how completely blessed am I. And in consequence what a good doctor I will be."[36] On another occasion she mentions asking Robins "if she would allow me to look upon her as my adopted mother."[37] The child, daughter, little love, sweetheart, devoted one, worships the mother, Madonna, Madre, adopted mother, spiritual mother, beloved. Words fail to express what is clearly intended as something more than simply an intense cross-age friendship. As I discuss in chapter 8, by the early twentieth century sexologists had defined this culturally sanctioned form of same-sex love as potentially dangerous to vulnerable young women. The vampire story returned in scientific guise, warning against the danger of an adolescent girl prematurely fixing her sexual desire on a woman.

The younger woman in the mother-daughter relationship was often a tomboy. The label "tomboy," dating from the sixteenth century, implies an immature girl eager to seize some of the freedoms of the liminal adolescent boy. It also captures the combination of arrogance and fragility that often characterized the young lesbian who struggled against the accepted norms of society. Girls who might have enjoyed fatherly approval when they were intrepid young tomboys became outcasts when they reached adolescence and would not or could not become womanly. Numerous nineteenth-century stories, including most famously Louisa May Alcott's *Little Women* (1868–69), describe the necessary steps toward mature femininity every tomboy must take. The surrogate mother could be a reparative figure, giving public affirmation and love to a boyish girl in danger of thinking herself unlovable. She did not ask the tomboy to change, even when she continued her unfeminine ways into adulthood. Several of the women I discuss here were tomboys who then moved into other roles, such as husband or surrogate mother. Charlotte Cushman felt she had been born a tomboy, but she soon took on the more masterful role of husband. Others found the shift difficult to manage. An aging tomboy might continue to demand maternal love, as Ethel Smyth did, but to most observers she seemed a strange anomaly.

Where does the woman who refused the family metaphor fit in the world of intimate friendships? The available scripts for women who rejected normative heterosexuality, but also did not wish to lose respectability, were very

few indeed. The female rake was an acknowledged eighteenth-century theater figure, but her nineteenth-century history is not easily recovered. Virtually all of the synonyms for rake are male, including womanizer, philanderer,
Lothario, Don Juan, seducer, and lecher. Since sexual aggression was defined
as a quintessentially male characteristic, masculinity was attributed to the
sexually independent woman who showed no interest in men. Thanks to the
survival of her extraordinary diary, the early-nineteenth-century Anne Lister
is probably the best known example of a sexually assertive woman. But she
distinguished herself from men, declaring, "my manners are certainly peculiar, not at all masculine but rather softly gentleman-like. I know how to please
girls."[38] The female rake was manly, gentle, and emotionally open. Class privilege and wealth certainly played a strong part in freeing women to be sexual
aggressors, with examples ranging from the masculine Anne Lister to the
feminine Natalie Clifford Barney. Throughout the book I will examine the
ways in which the female rake opened social space for sexual exploration,
expanding and even crossing beyond the boundaries of respectability.

The metaphoric language of the family, so frequently used by nineteenth-
century women, is a clue to how women defined their intimate friendships.
By configuring their same-sex love in terms of husband-wife and mother-
daughter couples, lesbians linked their love to psychologically and socially
important ties. This vocabulary also reveals aspects of the complicated power
dynamics among women-loving women. Throughout the years 1778–1928,
within the gender-divided world of the bourgeoisie, a woman had a series of
predefined relationships with men, those of daughter, sister, wife, or mother.
With a woman friend, however, she could not only experiment with other
roles, but also change roles in different relations or over time. Daughters turn
into nurturing mothers, mothers into needy children, back and forth, re-
questing, demanding, coercing, then giving, bestowing, blessing. The female
rake acted like an adolescent boy or a brash wooer of married women, but
she could become a faithful husband. "Wives" loyally supported and nurtured
the genius of their partners or moved (reluctantly or with relief) into a heterosexual marriage. A cross-age relationship might become a marriage. Even
though the *structures* of intimacy remained in place, their *meanings* changed
over time. For example, gender inversion was the most important signifier of
same-sex desire, but interpretations of the so-called mannish woman varied
considerably. Throughout the book I will draw attention to continuities, as
well as important changes.

THE STRUCTURE OF THE BOOK

The eight chapters of *Intimate Friends* are divided into four parts, each emphasizing different family configurations. An introduction to each part describes

the main subject and examples. The conclusion explores the metaphors used by women to express erotic desire. Intimate relations are linked with public issues, including the law, religion, education, work, art, and money. In order to highlight different aspects of lesbian life, I have focused on specific women or couples in each chapter, but some of the women could also have played a starring role in a different chapter. Virtually all of the women I discuss worked at some time in their lives. A few made a great deal of money (Charlotte Cushman, Rosa Bonheur); others had more modest careers (Geraldine Jewsbury, Eliza Lynn Linton); some had family money but still worked (Emily Faithfull, Edith Simcox, Vernon Lee, Radclyffe Hall). Very few were as poor as Marianne Woods and Jane Pirie or the illegitimate Mary Ann Dods, but even fewer were as wealthy as Natalie Clifford Barney and Romaine Brooks. Class and race mattered—these educated, white women had the privilege of self-fashioning at a time when most women were economically and socially dependent upon male relations. I have generally referred to the women by their last names, except when discussing family members who share the same last name. The appendix gives a brief summary of the principal women discussed.

Part I focuses on the husband and wife roles in same-sex marriages. Chapter 1 examines three examples of isolated couples drawn from the late eighteenth century to the mid-nineteenth century. In their own day these exceptional women were publicly known for their freedom and daring. The chapter also includes a consideration of the female rake Anne Lister and her complicated love life. Chapter 2 looks at a community of American and English artists and writers who lived in Rome from the early 1850s to the 1870s. Although observers found the obvious masculinity of Charlotte Cushman and Harriet Hosmer disquieting, they admired their purity and independence. The chapter examines such issues as fidelity, open marriage, and the public display of same-sex love.

Part II considers same-sex love in the male worlds of the law and religion. I look at two court cases in chapter 3, one involving the relationship of two schoolteachers and the other involving a cross-age friendship between an unhappily married woman and her young companion. I conclude the chapter with a brief discussion of the ways in which men responded to same-sex love. Chapter 4 analyzes two different uses of religion, focusing first on lesbian love as a path to God and then on the love of God as an alternative to earthly love. These chapters each explore the intersection of powerful institutions and powerful emotions. Chapters 3 and 4 include examples of a husband forced to recognize his wife's erotic interest in another woman. I call these relationships "queer triangles" to draw attention to the awkward place of men in same-sex relations.

Part III investigates the psychological difficulties of same-sex love. Unlike the first two chapters, which investigated long-term commitments, chapters

5 and 6 look at the pleasures and pains of falling in and out of love. Chapter 5, focusing on the mother-daughter bond, considers three examples of an adult woman in love with an older, married woman. I explore the pain of rejection or unrequited love. A final section of the chapter examines the difficulties of a nineteenth-century lesbian mother and her biological daughters. Chapter 6 looks at how masculine women constructed their sexual personae. I contrast attitudes toward gender inversion by two women born a generation apart. Both believed they were born inverts, but Eliza Lynn Linton imagined herself to be a man, whereas the younger Vernon Lee promulgated a third sex, "not woman, not man."

The last part looks at the possibilities available to women who openly declared their preference for women. Chapter 7 focuses on a community of wealthy expatriate American and English women living in Paris in the early twentieth century. They disdained bourgeois notions of marital fidelity and maternal nurturing, and returned to the mores of the late eighteenth century, delighting in the female rake and her sexual freedom. I examine the multiple meanings of playful cross-dressing among this coterie of friends. Chapter 8 explores the impact of the early sexologists in defining the mannish lesbian or congenital invert. I focus on the creation of the ambitious, predatory woman as the socially dangerous lesbian. The self-fashioning of an earlier generation of women-loving women became more difficult after the dissemination of the new taxonomies of sexual behavior. What had previously been left undefined now had a label that could shape both individual behavior and expectations.

Finally, a word about the sources used. This is not so much a book revealing surprises, recovering unknown or forgotten women, as an exploration of neglected or denied aspects of well-known women. It provides a mapping of lesbian desire among educated women during a period of one hundred and fifty years. In each chapter I discuss the interpretive difficulties involved in using the available sources, ranging from court cases to art and poetry. We are fortunate to have such rich collections of private material by and about these women, despite the inevitable depredations of time, familial fears, and traditions of personal privacy. Harriet Hosmer's undated letters to Lady Louisa Ashburton are an unsorted jumble at present. Much of Lister's diary remains unknown, in spite of the efforts of several scholars to decipher her difficult handwriting. One's heart sinks when reading E. F. Benson's description of burning family papers.[39] Nevertheless, he ensured that his mother's love of women would remain well documented. Ethel Smyth gave a "huge box" of letters and files to her first biographer, Christopher St. John. But little seems to have survived. Did St. John, a lesbian writing in the 1950s, destroy material Smyth wanted to preserve? The poet Mary Robinson saved all of Vernon Lee's letters from the years 1881–87, but none survives from the period of their painful breakup. Creative work can reveal passions impossible to articulate in letters or journals. Emily Faithfull, Matilda Hays, and Eliza Lynn Linton recreated their tumultuous relations with women in fictional disguise. Vernon Lee's travel writings were often veiled descriptions of her relationships with a series of different women. Musicologists have helped us to understand the lesbian underpinnings of Ethel Smyth's music. Other women, other examples, await discovery and analysis, adding to our understanding of women who loved women in the past.

PART I

Husband - Wife Coupling

The women discussed in the following two chapters attempted with varying success to control the public discourse about their romantic friendships; they wanted them to be acknowledged as marriages. By highlighting their various intellectual and artistic achievements, they turned a refusal to marry a man into a unique advantage. None of the couples escaped gossip and innuendo, but all managed to present their relationships as admirable, even enviable. They did so by remaining discreet, never quarreling in public, and rarely confiding in others. The absence of a respectable vocabulary to describe the erotic liberties they took protected them from intrusive questioning by friends, family, and neighbors. For many single women they became living proof that women could be happier and better off unmarried.

Chapter 1 begins with a survey of the rituals of courtship and commitment that confirmed an intimate friendship. It then considers two well-publicized romantic friendships—between Lady Eleanor Butler (1739–1829) and Sarah Ponsonby (1755–1831), who settled in the remote Welsh village of Llangollen, and between Rosa Bonheur (1822–99) and Nathalie Micas (1824–89), who lived in rural Fontainebleau. The fame of these two couples ensured the association of same-sex marriage with "rural bliss," far from corrupt society and prying eyes. To outsiders "the Ladies of Llangollen," as Butler and Ponsonby were called, were fascinating eccentrics. Living in harmony together for half a century, they triumphantly negated the stereotype of women's friendships as shallow and changeable. Bonheur, a successful painter of animals, lived with

Mme. Micas and Nathalie Micas, the widow and daughter of her first patron. She boasted about the fidelity and respectability of her love for Nathalie in comparison with that of male husbands. Bonheur's siblings were always deeply suspicious of her masculine appearance and her relationship; they felt her money should go to them, and not to her women friends. Bonheur vigorously defended her lifestyle against both her family and public gossip.

The second part of this chapter focuses on Anne Lister (1791–1840), a Yorkshire gentrywoman who epitomizes the female rake longing for marriage to a feminine woman. Drawing upon the published transcriptions of her diaries, I trace Lister's efforts first to keep and then to replace Mariana Belcombe (1790–1868) who, despite their pledges of eternal fidelity to each other, was forced by economic necessity to marry Charles Lawton. They nevertheless continued to be lovers for many years, though Lister flirted with various women (including Mariana's sisters) and had several affairs. The most serious was with a widow, Maria Barlow, in Paris. After years of self-education and travel, Lister found Mariana Belcombe Lawton too unsophisticated and Maria Barlow too poor for her taste. In the 1830s, following an unsuccessful affair with an aristocrat, she became involved with a neighbor, Ann Walker (1803–54). Lister successfully played the role of husband to Walker, protecting and encouraging her, while also making use of her considerable inheritance. After giving up the possibility of a love match, the marriage to Walker gave Lister the means to strengthen her local political and social power.

Chapter 2 traces a women's community living in Rome at mid-century. The acknowledged leaders of this group of artists, writers, sculptors, and journalists and their supporters were two Americans, the actress Charlotte Cushman (1816–76) and the sculptor Harriet Hosmer (1830–1908). Both Cushman and Hosmer were markedly independent and forthright. Hosmer initially presented herself as an asexual, boyish American, untouched by European (and Catholic) corruption. Women journalists wrote about her as both an exceptional individual and a model for unmarried educated women. Hosmer scorned the petty jealousies of the other Rome women, preferring an open relationship with one of her patrons, the widowed Louisa, Lady Ashburton (1827–1903). She negotiated this marriage by creating an elaborate fantasy of familial relationships with Ashburton and her daughter. By the time Hosmer was in her forties, however, artistic taste had changed, and she faded from public view, her boyish glamor gone and her sculptures unsold. She became economically dependent upon her fickle lover for the remainder of her life.

Cushman, like Bonheur, had been the chief supporter of her family from a young age. When she settled in Rome in 1852, she decided to form her own self-chosen family of women friends. Cushman's remarkable self-confidence and theatrical fame drew many admirers to her salon. She mothered young women artists, including Hosmer, and acted as husband to a series of special friends. She carefully concealed the erotic content of her relationships; Cushman was more frequently attacked for her masculine style than for her intimate friendships. Within a decade she found herself entangled in a difficult set of familial negotiations. As a distinguished actress Cushman had always attracted women fans; surviving letters document several intense flirtations. In 1858, however, she fell deeply in love with the young Emma Crow, even though she considered herself married to the sculptor Emma Stebbins. Fearful of losing her young admirer, Cushman persuaded Crow to marry her adopted son, Ned Cushman. The metaphoric family roles she embraced became impossibly complicated and contributed to the breakup of her lesbian community.

Well before the late eighteenth century, it was widely accepted that some women were born more masculine in appearance and aptitude. Same-sex sexual desire was associated with gender inversion. The five principal women in these chapters, Lady Eleanor Butler, Rosa Bonheur, Anne Lister, Harriet Hosmer, and Charlotte Cushman, were all openly masculine in appearance and behavior. Even though they chose to fashion themselves as manly, they considered it instinctive. Butler was renowned for her intellectual pursuits. Bonheur regularly wore trousers and a smock. Boys and men ridiculed Lister for her stride and manner. Hosmer went about Rome at night unaccompanied. Cushman wore tailored jackets and ties and spoke in what critics called a "man-ny voice." These women believed that their attraction to women was as natural as their appearance. Throughout her diary Lister explored her innate sense of masculinity; she also studied classical and medical texts for validation. She proudly declared to her lovers that her behavior was not learned, but natural. The letters of Hosmer and Cushman also articulate a clear sense of their natural difference from feminine norms. To be true to one's inner nature fully justified their lives and loves.

The historical retrieval of early examples of female couples has depended upon these bold women who refused to conform to society's edicts. Although some couples strove to look alike, observers turned one of them, usually the elder, into the manly, assertive partner. It is she who is remembered, rather than her more outwardly conventional and feminine partner. The latter were literally less visible because they so often looked like the stereotypical spinster—or they married. These two chapters can only partially correct this imbalance because much of our surviving evidence is by and about the masculine women. Sexuality was gendered, forcing difference upon same-sex partnerships.

1   *"A Scheme of Romantic Friendship"*

LOVE AND SAME-SEX MARRIAGE

In the late eighteenth century, a dowry-less orphan and an aging youngest daughter startled their respective families by declaring their determination to live together. Sarah Ponsonby came from an impoverished wing of a distinguished Irish Protestant family. Only her father's cousin, Lady Betty Fownes, took an interest in her, and sent the thirteen-year-old orphan to Miss Parke's School in Kilkenny. During her five years in boarding school, she was befriended by Eleanor Butler, sixteen years older than she. The shy, lonely adolescent opened her heart to the brilliant, French-educated Roman Catholic. The older woman was bored and sensitive about remaining an unmarried burden on her family. They exchanged books, wrote frequently, and discussed the current fashion for rural simplicity as the epitome of spiritual refinement.

After Ponsonby returned to her relatives, the two continued secretly to correspond. Ponsonby adored her adoptive mother, Lady Betty, but to her dismay, Sir William Fownes, with an eye to the possible death of his wife, began to woo her. Caught in an impossible situation, she wrote anxious letters to Butler and other friends. At about the same time, Butler's mother became insistent that she join a French convent; her satirical, overeducated daughter should return to the community where she had been so happily educated twenty years earlier. The friends' letters took on a new urgency: they must run away together to that idealized rural retreat. On the cold rainy night of 30 March 1778, the two women, now twenty-three and thirty-nine, disguised themselves as men and fled to Waterford, planning an escape to England.[1] They were caught and returned to their separate homes in disgrace. Sarah Ponsonby hovered near pneumonia, anxious for news about her beloved Eleanor, who had been locked up by her family in a final effort to persuade her to enter a convent. The horrified families initially consoled themselves. As Lady Betty's daughter wrote, the conduct of the pair, "though it has an appearance of imprudence, is I am sure void of serious impropriety. / 5 /

There were no gentlemen concerned, nor does it appear to be anything more than a scheme of Romantic Friendship."[2]

During the desperate days when both families tried to persuade the two women to follow a more moderate path, friends and relatives spoke frankly about a passion that they could not quite name. Although precise words might fail, something was clearly wrong with this extreme form of friendship. Lady Betty kept circling the question of why the gentle and retiring Ponsonby would commit herself to her friend. "'I hear they say these two friends must not live together,' she wrote, 'I cant help thinking as they do.'"[3] Her more worldly ally Lucy Goddard felt obliged to speak plainly to the seemingly deluded Ponsonby—"to discharge my conscience of the duty I owed her as a friend by letting her know my opinion of Miss Butler and the certainty I had they never would agree living together. I spoke of her with harshness and freedom, said she had a debauch'd mind, no ingredients of friendship that ought to be founded on Virtue."[4] Contemporaries found Butler too blunt, too masculine in her style of speech, dress, and general appearance. Perhaps she had also been too masculine in her behavior, too openly seizing the role of husband? Gender inversion awoke suspicions of Sapphism, or at least of something foreign. "Debauch'd" was the word used to describe Marie Antoinette and her women friends; it also implies a sophisticated knowledge of sexual behavior, of vice, not virtue, on the part of Lucy Goddard. But Ponsonby and Butler still insisted on living together. Fearful of publicity and probably glad to be rid of them, both families soon agreed to provide financial help. This time the two aristocratic ladies traveled modestly but correctly to rural Wales, where they settled into their role of being "the Ladies of Llangollen," the model Romantic Friendship.

For over a century their experience of family disapproval, a dangerous escape, and then rural bliss on a narrow income was the paradigmatic narrative of intimate female friendship. Sarah Ponsonby and Lady Eleanor Butler became almost mythic figures who had courageously challenged patriarchal authority in order to live independent lives. Theirs was a triumphal plot, for personal happiness overcame social ostracism and led to fame and widespread acceptance. Single women revered a romanticized version of the Ladies; under the right circumstances, they too could live with a beloved friend in blessed retreat from social and familial responsibilities. But why did "they" say that the gentle Ponsonby should not live with the witty Butler? What was it that Lady Betty Fownes could not name to her own satisfaction? This chapter looks not at the rise of sentimentality and romantic friendships—these were both established during the eighteenth century—but rather at the rituals, private and public, of romantic friends who celebrated a commitment to each other. It also considers how far a couple could go in presuming marital privileges, in order to address the question of how "they," gossiping friends and neighbors, defined same-sex erotic love.

THE RITUALS OF FRIENDSHIP

Romantic friends who fell in love, courted, and then confirmed their love with declarations of marriage adapted familiar heterosexual rituals. A same-sex marriage could look remarkably similar to the ideal companionate heterosexual marriage, reflecting many of its characteristics, including a more powerful, intellectual, "masculine" partner and a milder, more feminine, soul mate. Judith Butler has vigorously repudiated the idea that homosexual practices are a pale imitation of the heterosexual. She is especially opposed to the notion that butch/femme role-playing mimics the husband/wife of heterosexual marriage.[5] I must disagree. Lesbians do imitate the rituals and behaviors of the dominant culture—how can they not, surrounded as they are by powerful normative codes? Moreover, established religious ceremonies have traditionally provided the most meaningful and effective way to honor earthly love. Women who wished to celebrate their commitment to another woman borrowed from these traditional religious rites. They also carefully distinguished between friendship and love; ideally, their "marriage" combined reason and passion without the liabilities of heterosexual marriage.

Romantic friendships began as a series of steps leading to emotional intimacy. As in heterosexual love, these included gifts, letters, and long private conversations. Vernon Lee and Mary Robinson exchanged long letters about how to dedicate their books to each other without offending their male patrons. Elma Stewart never counted the cost in time and labor for the numerous hand-carved wooden objects she gave George Eliot as tokens of her adoration. Rings, necklaces, and lockets with a strand of hair or a picture were the preferred gifts, although Bibles, prayer books, and silver crosses were popular among the religious. Anne Lister gave her pious friend Ann Walker a gilt-edged prayer book. Mary Benson, the wife of a clergyman, gave her lover "Chat" a copy of the *Book of Common Prayer,* entreating her to keep it by her bedside at all times; she also wrote special letters to Chat at Easter and Christmas. They had first exchanged jewelry, photographs, and nicknames; each gift involved detailed letters of explanation and pledges of love.[6] Because these gestures were so conventional they did not necessarily indicate an exclusive interest, and so could serve as a cover for deeper intimacies.

Lady Betty, puzzling over Ponsonby's uncharacteristic obduracy, recognized one key element in women's friendships when she sighed, "Poor Soul, if she had not been so fond of her pen, so much would not have happened."[7] A special friendship almost seemed to demand secret notes, along with the lending of books and the sharing of favorite poems, passages, and authors. Young men also participated in this ritualized sharing of knowledge, but for women it took on an added meaning, for few families encouraged learning in their daughters.[8] The written word, whether one's own or that of a current favorite author, became an emissary, a means of indirectly declaring one's love, and then of explaining a whole range of new, tumultuous feelings. Intellectual curiosity stood in for sexual curiosity: "we two" want to learn more about a favorite author or artist, and in the process of doing so, we will learn more about our feelings for each other. A love of learning strengthened a friendship, drawing two women into a world marked by serious spiritual and intellectual concerns, rather than the frivolity of heterosexual courtship or the dull routine of family duties. The intimate companionship between Butler and Ponsonby began with and then was sustained over a lifetime by their shared intellectual interests.

Secrecy often signaled a change in feeling. Parents, suspicious of a daughter's undue interest in another woman, might forbid meeting or corresponding. If they were readers they knew that clandestine correspondence and secret meetings (preferably at night) were virtual clichés in fiction. Amanda Vickery suggests that sometimes a young woman purposely created obstacles for a man in order to create opportunities for secrecy and assignations; a prolonged courtship heightened the thrill of temporary power.[9] A woman in love with another woman drew delicious pleasure from the same kind of practices. A close friend of Butler and Ponsonby, the poet Anna Seward, frequently wrote about her various romances with other women. For Seward, unable to leave her father, such entanglements increased her importance in her own eyes and those of her friends. When Elizabeth Cornwallis's father forbade romantic friendships, she and Seward still continued to correspond. After a brief meeting Seward deliciously confessed, "Our interview was stolen and dangerous." She half-lamented on another occasion, "It is hard that our attachment to each other should be a secret . . . the disclosure of which must involve as much distress and misery to both of us as if we were of a different sex, and our intercourse guilty."[10] Mr. Cornwallis, however, had confidently defined their intercourse as guilty, perhaps because it seemed too passionate, too all-encompassing, or perhaps because it took his daughter's attention away from him.

After the initial confession of love, friends fell into planning, combining fantasies of running away together with a playful bandying of nicknames. Some women enjoyed calling each other masculine or androgynous names, perhaps as an escape from patriarchal authority and its claim to the naming of women in marriage. Lister was called Fred by her lover. Among her friends and lovers, Isabella Norcliffe was the androgynous Tib; and Miss Pickford was shortened to Pic, but some knew her as Frank. Mary Benson, the wife of the Archbishop of Canterbury, was called Ben. Katharine Bradley and Edith Cooper, the aesthetic fin-de-siècle aunt and niece who wrote under the pen name Michael Field, were Michael and Henry, respectively; they engaged in elaborate play with pronouns and pet names for themselves and their friends. Radclyffe Hall was known to all her friends as John. The writer Vernon Lee and the poet Mary Robinson engaged in an orgy of renaming. Mary was Molly, Mollikins, Molchino, Mouse, and Mowk, as well as Princess Quesara. Vernon was Vernie, Vernoncina, and Vrenko, but never her actual name, Violet. Such nicknames not only implied woman-to-woman intimacy, but also created a self-sufficient world where masculinity could be assumed with the ease of a change in clothing. The casual familiarity of nicknames both amused and put off friends and relatives, judging from the little evidence that survives in letters and diaries. Naming, like so many other rituals, could slide into the assumption of male privileges within a homosocial world or it could remain an unthreatening expression of female camaraderie.

Once established as a couple, women frequently called each other husband and wife. The Ladies of Llangollen referred to each other as "my Better Half," "My Sweet Love," "my Beloved" (later shortened to "My B."), and other terms of marital endearment. Their friend Harriet Bowdler teasingly referred to Butler, the older and more outspoken, as "my *Veillard*" (my old man) and "him." She so admired their relationship that she sighed, "I wish I knew where to get another Husband."[11] Lister's first lover, her schoolmate Eliza Raine, commemorating their sexual union, noted in her diary entry of 17 August 1810, "my husband came to me & finally a happy reunion was accomplished."[12] At mid-century the American sculptor Harriet Hosmer called herself "hubby," and her lover "my sposa." Katharine Bradley and Edith Cooper sometimes referred to each other as "Fellow" to their friends instead of using their masculine nicknames. Una Troubridge and "John" Radclyffe Hall were known as wife and husband by their friends.

It is striking how insistent women could be about signaling their same-sex desires. When settled in Wales, the Ladies of Llangollen ordered identical Irish riding habits with cravats; long after it was fashionable, they powdered their hair. Their few portraits (see fig. 1) exaggerate their masculine clothing and physical similarity, but contemporaries always noted their odd appearance.[13] In the 1840s, when a Bradford admirer offered Charlotte Cushman a bolt of fine woolen cloth, she asked for double the quantity. She had a matching suit of clothes made for her then-partner, the poet and journalist Eliza Cook, giving their marriage a visible, sartorial representation.[14] When the famous poet Elizabeth Barrett Browning met Cushman and her next partner in Paris in 1852, she wrote, they have "made vows of celibacy & of eternal attachment to each other—they live together, dress alike . . . it is a female marriage. I happened to say, 'Well, I never heard of such a thing before,' to a friend

Fig. 1. The Ladies of Llangollen by Lady Leighton, ca. 1813. Courtesy of the National Library of Wales.

who answered, 'Oh, it is by no means uncommon.'"[15] For sympathetic observers dressing alike was the visible sign of a successful female marriage.

Androgynous or masculine nicknames, affectionate terms of endearment, and similar dress were each important indications of a lesbian marriage. Being a "husband" carried positive connotations within the intimate circles of women's friendships. The adroit, such as Butler and Cushman, successfully exploited admiration for a masculine mind to overcome the negative implications of a masculine appearance. The mid-nineteenth-century novelist Diana Mulock Craik endorsed gender difference in romantic friendship, arguing that one partner must be masculine in style or manner, because "their mutual feminine weaknesses acting and reacting upon one another, would most likely narrow the sympathies and deteriorate the character of both."[16] For her, reason and intellect, as opposed to emotion, were always already masculine; for a successful relationship, at least one partner had to possess qualities other than such traditional "feminine weaknesses" as emotionalism and sentimentality. Female masculinity was not so much a representation of maleness as a statement about a set of positive characteristics customarily assigned to men. Women did not ape masculinity, but appropriated its terms to create a new kind of manly woman, or according to Lister, to be "softly gentleman-like."[17]

Well into the twentieth century, no distinction was made between sex and gender. Gender inversion, whether it was effeminacy in a man or masculinity in a woman, had long been an identifying characteristic of same-sex desire. People wanted visible distinctions to explain the behavior of an assertive, intellectual woman who might fascinate and repel. If she showed undue interest in a more feminine, passive friend, then the label "masculine" stuck. Both same-sex couples and those who observed them may have exaggerated gender differences in order to signal the nature of their relationship. Yet definitions and expectations were slippery and cannot be reduced to simple binaries or to role-playing. Conspicuously masculine attributes and behavior might make visible the erotic component of the friendship, but then again it might not. Elizabeth Mavor speaks of a Miss Kirkham who was considered "too free and masculine" until she married and became the highly respectable Mrs. Chapone.[18] Both Ponsonby and Butler, like the late-nineteenth-century couple Bradley and Cooper, appeared masculine on occasion to onlookers because of their dress or behavior; on other occasions they appeared disarmingly feminine. The sex/gender system did not fit any neat paradigm, but rather was adapted and altered by both observers and participants as circumstances warranted. Contradictory beliefs and behaviors about same-sex relationships coexisted, but the principle of visible difference, gendering one woman as masculine, remained constant.

Lesbian courtship might begin as a series of private, even secretive rituals, but once established as "romantic friends," many couples chose a path of self-advertised commitment and happiness. If they refused the heterosexual norm, then their lives had to be better than those of their married sisters. Criticism, disagreements, and the normal tensions of life together were rarely made visible even to close friends. The sheer weight of being a nontraditional couple must have borne heavily upon some, but fidelity, especially long-term fidelity, remained a powerful ideal. Women's friendships might be fraught with jealousies, impossible demands, and self-doubt, but even more than heterosexual marriage, their outward face was one of devoted faithfulness. Companionate relationships, since they were freely chosen, were expected to be personally fulfilling. To admit failure was therefore more humiliating than was the case with heterosexual marriages based on convenience, economics, or family pressure.

LOVE AND PUBLIC MARRIAGE: THE LADIES
OF LLANGOLLEN AND ROSA BONHEUR AND
NATHALIE MICAS

Once settled in the Welsh village of Llangollen, Sarah Ponsonby and Eleanor Butler self-consciously set about proving themselves to be a model couple. Their family backgrounds may have prepared them for living a public life, since the aristocracy had long used conspicuous display to enforce its power over the surrounding populace. By fostering a combination of public show and polite exclusiveness, the two women won for themselves the position of leading family in Llangollen. The simplicity of their lives encouraged upper-class visitors to idealize essential economies that involved no loss of class privilege. The French animal painter, Rosa Bonheur, also used self-display to prove the superiority of romantic friendship over traditional heterosexuality. Born into a very modest artist's family, she quickly realized that a combination of outward respectability and artistic eccentricity would win her attention and commissions in the highly competitive art world. It was a model that the American sculptor Harriet Hosmer also exploited brilliantly, as will be discussed in the next chapter. Like the Ladies Bonheur faced family opposition, but unlike them she held the purse strings.

The great achievement of the Ladies was to combine rural innocence with an equally venerated ideal, that of genius. As Andrew Elfenbein has documented, an individual, mysterious, aberrant psychic characteristic, genius, has often been aligned with homosexuality.[19] Any woman of genius was automatically suspect, because too much intelligence unsexed a woman and made her incapable of fulfilling her maternal duties. For a woman in love with another woman, however, this disparaging attitude could be turned into a positive reason for refusing to marry. Early visitors to Llangollen ascribed "genius" to Butler, thereby excusing her unsuitability for heterosexual marriage, as well as her unladylike curiosity about all manner of things. Ponsonby gradually assumed similar "mannish" characteristics as the Ladies honed their public role. Their genteel eccentricity became a mark of their genius.

But true genius required invention. The Ladies set about creating the ideal friendship, complete with an ideal setting. They poured money and time into adding Gothic additions to their house, Plas Newydd, and turning their backyard into an elaborate garden. The feminine activity of homemaking personified the special genius of a romantic friendship. Both women repudiated the traditional view of women as undisciplined and uncontrolled; perhaps their continued popularity into the twentieth century can be traced to their rigorous self-discipline in an age that often seemed to believe women were incapable of reason and self-control. The Ladies were a team who exacted praise from a willing public for their unique kind of genius: they were a symbol of perfect friendship. A relationship begun as a romantic scheme came to epitomize rational living. In effect the Ladies created a work of art, their life.

The couple's life also incorporated two other favorite eighteenth-century aesthetic qualities, the sublime and the beautiful. By means of a natural metonymy, the Welsh countryside, wild and untutored, embodied the sublime, and Plas Newydd and its garden the beautiful and the cultivated. But irrational behavior was only partially transferred away from them and onto Wales. Their eccentric riding habits, practical for so untamed a country, invariably reminded visitors that their lives were somehow unnatural. If the Ladies had worn the normal attire of their social class and followed its usual lifestyle of travel to Bath and London, they would have risked being ordinary, unstylish, and scarcely worth visiting. Those two cities were filled with poor spinsters and widows, many of whom lived with a friend on the edge of society. They appear and reappear in fiction and fact, serving as warnings against either a hasty marriage or an ill-considered romantic friendship. Hester Thrale Piozzi admired her friends the Ladies, but suspected all women who lived together in these stylish urban centers, commenting in her diary, "Bath is a Cage of these unclean Birds I have a Notion, and London is a Sink for every sin."[20] But the Ladies, buttressed by remoteness and class distinction, were publicly envied and admired.

The Ladies, although rooted in Llangollen, were highly sophisticated and well educated. They could not pretend to conventional innocence and so presented themselves as models of how the refined could enjoy rural simplicity. Their garden, which many more visited than were ever permitted to meet the choosy aristocratic ladies, was much admired for its combination of beauty and practicality. A wild "male" nature might rage outside, but within the confines of their home and garden, tranquil femininity reigned. They created a female pastoral in which nature did not have to be conquered, but was instead supportive of human endeavors, boasting docile animals, rare vegetables, and tamed brooks. And like a true pastoral, the emotional weather never seemed to change as the days passed in "delicious and exquisite retirement."[21] Newspapers described Plas Newydd as "the Fairy Palace of the Vale," "that rural and sylvan like retreat of those Ornaments of their Sex."[22] One admirer concluded a versified hymn of praise, "With tranquil seclusion, and friendship your lot/How blest, how secure, and how envied your cot."[23] The Ladies carefully copied out the poem and sent it around to valued friends. External praise confirmed their decision to advertise themselves as the embodiment of the female pastoral. Rural seclusion remained a lesbian ideal into the twentieth century. The heroine of *The Well of Loneliness* (1928), for example, longs to settle with her lover on her country estate. For lesbian culture, unlike gay male culture, urban life was not a haven for the formation of a strong subculture, but instead a realm of potential isolation and anomie. In the city, as Hester Thrale Piozzi's comments suggest, a woman who loved her intimate friend risked potential exposure and the loss of respectability.

Visitors who came to admire this ideal friendship were sometimes let down. The Ladies seemed altogether too eager to learn the latest gossip. As Piozzi, exclaimed: "The unaccountable knowledge those Recluses have of all living Books and People and Things is like Magic; one can mention no one of whom the private History is unknown to Them—What they told me of Doctor Maclean's Brother was very curious and Interesting—and from them I borrowed the books I had so long searched London and Bath for—in vain."[24] Sir Walter Scott, noting this hunger for gossip, was less impressed. He remarked rather sharply to his daughter, "Great romance (i.e. absurd innocence of character) one must have looked for; but it was confounding to find this mixed up with such eager curiosity, and enormous knowledge of the tattle and scandal of the world they had so long left."[25] By the time Scott visited, the Ladies had been entertaining visitors, or coyly refusing to do so, for over thirty years. It no longer mattered who found their appearance bizarre or who distrusted their guise of noble rustication. But undoubtedly visitors sometimes found genius rather earthbound. Plas Newydd was not a secular convent; what it might have been instead was better left unmentioned.

Single women had a different view of the Ladies from other visitors. They cherished their story of running away and living happily ever after. Fidelity to each other was seen as fidelity to a cause, the freedom to choose with whom to live. The poet Anna Seward is only the most famous bluestocking who poured out her admiration in verse and letters, celebrating their home as an earthly paradise. Long after their deaths, the Ladies remained a byword for simple conjugal happiness. When the feminist journalist Frances Power Cobbe with her partner Mary Lloyd moved to Wales in the 1890s, she wrote a friend that they had become "The Ladies of Hengwrt."[26] In the 1930s the French writer Colette lavished praise on the "magic of this radiant friendship," writing in awestruck terms of its unchanging nature as "Beyond time, beyond reach . . ."[27] The Ladies had succeeded brilliantly in presenting themselves as exemplars of female fidelity. Even their most recent biographer describes "their quiet and enviable life" as changing only with the seasons.[28] Their continual pleas to friends and relatives for more money, their tightfisted treatment of hired help, and their paltry charity are all forgotten. Unlike heterosexual marriage, romantic friendship was held to an impossible standard, if we are to believe the fantasies woven around the Ladies. Women who loved women were capable of living lives untouched by real life, time, and strife, whether between themselves or with their servants, relatives, and families, or with larger society. Myth also acted to desexualize the couple, making them a safe symbol upon which to weave fictions.

But some were more prying. In 1822, only two years after the actor

Charles Mathews had dismissed the Ladies as "a couple of dear antedeluvian [sic] old darlings,"[29] Lister made a pilgrimage to their home, and even though Ponsonby struck her at first as "altogether a very odd figure," she was thoroughly impressed, because "she [Ponsonby] had no sooner entered into conversation than I forgot all this & my attention was wholly taken by her manners & conversation. The former, perfectly easy, peculiarly attentive & well, & bespeaking a person accustomed to a great deal of good society. Mild & gentle, certainly not masculine, & yet there was a *je-ne-sais-quoi* striking."[30] Lister was always on the lookout for signs of lesbian affection and aristocratic manners. She found both in the elderly Ponsonby, who also revealed something about her marriage to the curious visitor. Ponsonby and Butler had never quarreled, but "when they differed in opinion, they took care to let no one see it."[31] No wonder the Ladies became a byword for happy female friendship. Ponsonby and Lister exchanged opinions on books they had read or hoped to read. The intrepid Lister wanted more; she asked, "if they were classical." The older woman proudly told her she had never learned Latin or Greek. Probably Ponsonby never knew the Latin and Greek passages on lesbian sex that so fascinated the younger woman. Afterward Lister and her lover, Mariana Lawton, concluded that all those years together must have been cemented by "something more tender still than friendship."[32]

Others who shared Lister's suspicions were more willing to publicize their views. As public figures the Ladies could not control how they were interpreted. For example, after a decade of quiet, they were startled to read a garbled account of their elopement in the local *General Evening Post* of 24 July 1790. It concluded with a description of each. "Miss Butler is tall and masculine, she wears always a riding habit, hangs her hat with the air of a sportsman in the hall and appears in all respects as a young man, if we except the petticoats which she still retains." And "Miss Ponsonby, on the contrary is polite and effeminate, fair and beautiful."[33] At the time Butler was fifty-one, short and dumpy, but as the more assertive of the two, she was reconfigured as a tall masculine woman. The sophisticated Ladies probably knew something of the nature of the gossip about them, for they chose to write Edmund Burke about their plight; he had earlier suffered from journalistic innuendo about his effeminacy. He recommended icy silence in the face of slander. The public version of romantic friendship was less sympathetic and more knowing than the ebullient praise of literary friends. Like the masculine-appearing Lister, the Ladies could suffer indignities uncommon to their social class.

If the Ladies epitomized fidelity and rural happiness, the artist Rosa Bonheur represented the successful career of a self-made lesbian genius. Bonheur came from a poor artist's family made poorer by her father's pursuit of Saint-Simonian beliefs. All her life Bonheur was convinced that her adored mother's premature death stemmed from overwork and neglect. Her father's unconventional "religion" included gender equality; Raimond Bonheur encouraged his tomboy daughter to excel, though he warned her against becoming a professional painter. But she triumphed as the most successful animal painter of her day. It was widely believed that only a man could be an original artist; if a woman aspired to this role, she possessed something of the masculine. Bonheur, who wore trousers and had short hair, confirmed the assumption that genius was male, although she also insisted, "my gruff disposition, which is even a bit uncivilized, has never stopped me from always staying perfectly feminine."[34]

When still a teenager, Rosa met her beloved, Nathalie Micas. Some time around 1841, M. Micas, a successful investor, hired Raimond Bonheur to paint his daughter's portrait. The Micases encouraged the talented young Rosa to rent her own studio, and they helped her find commissions. According to Bonheur's autobiography, Mme. Micas came to replace the mother she had lost at eleven. On his deathbed the forty-six-year-old M. Micas arranged the union between his daughter and his protégée, telling Raimond Bonheur:

> "Let our two children stay together always. You see how much they love each other. Rosa needs Nathalie to love and protect her. Come, children, I want to give you my blessing!"
>
> We were both deeply moved and knelt down by his bed. Good father Micas placed his hands on our heads and said: "Never leave each other's side, my dear children, and may God keep you!" Then he kissed us. A few days later he was dead. Nathalie and I were always together after that.[35]

Here was a public ceremony proclaiming the marriage of the two young women, complete with a patriarchal blessing to confirm its naturalness. Soon after M. Micas's death, Bonheur moved in with her surrogate mother and her lover. Like Sarah Ponsonby's, Nathalie Micas's love confirmed Rosa's genius: "Her ambition was not to become my equal. The thing that she wanted, that satisfied this devoted heart, was to be useful to me."[36] As in a heterosexual marriage, equality of souls, not equality of intellect, was the ideal.

Bonheur erased all disagreements in describing her marriage to Micas (fig. 2), but friends remembered them affectionately as more quarrelsome and more interesting. Both women were decidedly eccentric, and each proudly displayed her individuality. One friend wrote, "Nothing was more comical than seeing this couple together, Rosa Bonheur, who, in her blouse, looked like a lad, and that tall, lank, pale woman, with her head crowned by a big hat with black and red plumes, who pronounced with a prophetic and dramatic tone pompous periods which had neither head nor tail."[37] Admiration for the way Micas catered to Bonheur jostled with bemused remarks about her ama-

Fig. 2. Nathalie Micas and Rosa Bonheur at Nice, ca. 1882.

teur scientific pursuits, garish clothing, and air of self-importance. Bonheur's early biographer, Theodore Stanton, admitted Micas's jealousies, which combined with "the very decided character of Rosa Bonheur sometimes strained the relations between the two friends to the point of an open rupture."[38] The role of wife to a genius is never easy under the best of circumstances. Colette, after quoting at length from Butler's diary, speculated on what the unwritten diary of the "blissful and mute Sarah Ponsonby" might be like.[39] We are left to speculate about Micas's feelings in regard to her role as helpmate. After her death in 1889, Bonheur gave her a "blissful" voice that contradicts friends' memories of her as lively and cantankerous. She did so to honor her friend and her relationship, but the result was merely to mute her friend.

The gentle M. Micas may have seen nothing odd about his daughter's choice of a life partner, but Bonheur herself remembered every rebuff they suffered. In her memoir she defended the Micases' respectability and insisted that she had always paid her own way. She protested so often and was so protective of her privacy that she seems to the modern reader to be concealing something more tender still than friendship. The death of her beloved Nathalie was one more occasion to attack society: "she had borne, with me, the mortifications and stupidities inflicted on us by silly, ignorant, low-minded people, who form the majority on this terrestrial ball, called the earth. She alone knew me, and I, her only friend, knew what she was worth. We both of us made ourselves humble, so as not to hurt the feelings of other people, while we were too proud to seek the confidence of idiots who doubted us."[40] Bonheur's protests had their effect. Stanton concluded his chapter documenting her complicated partnership by piously declaring, "Several letters . . . will be found in this volume . . . which place in a still stronger and nobler light the deep and pure attachment which these two women had for each other."[41] In spite of ample evidence to the contrary, he and other friends were deeply invested in defining the Bonheur-Micas relationship in the same language as an earlier generation had favored for the Ladies of Llangollen.

A few years after Micas's death, Bonheur, then in her late seventies, openly admitted loving the forty-three-year-old American artist Anna Klumpke. Already bitter toward anyone who questioned the perfection of her relationship with Micas, she anticipated trouble when she decided to marry Klumpke. Bonheur told Klumpke, "most people take a pretty dim view of women who live together, and that may influence your family. I've been battling that prejudice my whole life long." More ominously for Klumpke, she placed her in the position of wife to a genius, adding, "Happily, I've found in you the interpreter I need to get a fair trial in the future."[42] Bonheur and Klumpke lived together for a little over a year before Bonheur's death. Although Klumpke faithfully published her version of Bonheur's memoir, she could not halt the dramatic decline in Bonheur's status as an artist. Thanks to that act of devotion, as Bonheur might have predicted, her eccentric love of women became better known than her art.

As symbols of sexual and social independence, Bonheur and Micas and the Ladies of Llangollen lived on, touchstones for a future generation of romantic friends. This is what both couples would have wanted—to be symbols of the perfect romantic friendship, without the messiness of daily life and its trials, jealousies, and gossip.

LOVE AND SECRET MARRIAGE: ANNE LISTER, MARIANA LAWTON, AND MARIA BARLOW

As the examples in the previous section document, intimate friends faced numerous economic and social difficulties if they dared to establish a separate home together. This section explores the efforts of Anne Lister (fig. 3), a Yorkshire gentrywoman, to sustain a committed romantic friendship after her beloved, Mariana Belcombe, had married a man. Anne was the daughter of an impecunious younger son, Capt. Jeremy Lister. She and her sister started

Fig. 3. Anne Lister, by Joshua Horner (ca. 1830). Copyright Calderdale Museums and Arts, Shibden Hall, Halifax, England.

life with few prospects, but the untimely death of her younger brother, the heir to the Lister estate, and then the decision in 1815 of her unmarried eldest uncle and aunt to adopt her, dramatically improved her insecure social status and economic future. She immediately distanced herself from her gauche father and sister, and began a strenuous program of study, including Greek, Latin, French, mathematics, geometry, history, and the flute (considered a male instrument at the time).[43] Her Uncle James and Aunt Anne gradually turned over much of the management of the Shibden Hall estate to their energetic, capable niece. She became heir to the estate in 1826 (her elderly aunt and father each retained a one-third life interest) and was soon involved in developing the property to extract more money for travel and additions to the hall. She also became an active figure in Tory-Anglican local politics and Halifax cultural affairs in the 1830s.[44] The last fifteen years of her life she traveled widely on the continent.

Lister began to keep her diary in 1806, soon after she left school in York, where she had her first affair with a woman. The diary continues until her death from fever in the Caucasian mountains in 1840. The total is an estimated four million words. Its importance rests not only in her remarkably full and candid account of her sexual adventures, but also in her shrewd, detailed comments on the affairs of the times. Immensely attracted to Rousseau's ideas about love and self-development, Lister modeled her frank and self-searching diary on his *Confessions* (1781). From an early age she saw herself as different from other women, in her masculine temperament, her intellectual and social ambitions, and her lesbian passions. By 1821 she could declare: "Burnt . . . Mr. Montague's farewell verses that no trace of any man's admiration may remain. It is not meet for me."[45] Lister searched with an intensity worthy of Rousseau for romantic love; at the same time she pursued women with great success, carrying on numerous flirtations and affairs. She lived in a vibrant homosocial world, interacting with friends as a fascinating female rake.

Lister thought she had found a wife in Mariana (or Mary or Marianna) Belcombe, the daughter of a York doctor, whom she met through her then-lover Isabella (Tib) Norcliffe around 1812. One of five daughters, Belcombe was forced by economic necessity to marry the widowed Charles Lawton of Cheshire on 9 March 1816. Both women were determined to continue their relationship. They candidly thought the fifty-three-year-old man would die within a decade. Before Mariana's wedding Lister replaced Charles's ring with a similar one in which she had inscribed her initials in place of his. She then wore Charles's ring as a sign of her undying pledge to Mariana. This private ritual, Lister hoped, would strengthen Mariana's love, even when they were miles apart. The young, then-penniless Lister had encouraged the marriage, but she found the separation emotionally devastating. A little over a year later, she recorded, "I am often miserable & often wish to try to wean my heart from her & fix [it] more propitiously. There seems little chance of our ever getting together. Tho' I believe she loves me as yet exclusively, the misfortune is, my confidence is not invulnerable."[46]

Not surprisingly, Charles Lawton was furious when he discovered a letter from Lister in which she spoke of plans to live on his money after his death. After he refused her access to Lawton Hall and reviewed her letters, the two women began writing each other in code. Later he softened his edicts against Lister, but whenever the two women took a holiday, their time together was fraught with the fear that Mariana's husband would forbid them meeting or corresponding. During the long years of waiting, Lister repeatedly assured herself that they were fully married. But secret rituals could not expurgate her belief that she and Mariana were guilty of adultery. When she met with her lover, she sadly noted, "I felt that she was another man's wife. I shuddered at the thought & at the conviction that no soffistry could gloss over the criminality of our connection." Significantly, she added, "It seemed not that the like had occurred to her."[47] Even though Charles, Lister's aunt and uncle, and the Belcombe sisters all knew about her liaison, Mariana feared social opprobrium. Lister too wanted respectability, but she was more willing to push the limits of the acceptable, more confident in how far she could go without forfeiting her good name. Away from their families, Mariana Lawton wanted secrecy, whereas Lister wanted an acknowledgment of her position as "first husband." Unable to receive this she pondered the relationship between her religious scruples and Mariana's attachment to social respectability. Both served to weaken their love for each other.

In the meantime Charles Lawton, born in 1771, behaved more like an eighteenth-century squire than a Victorian paterfamilias. After nearly a decade of marriage, no children were born, and his wife remained indifferent to him. He took the sexual privileges of his social class and made his housekeeper his mistress. He left his wife free to develop a social position among the Cheshire elite, and he no longer protested against her frequent meetings with Lister. Yet, as Helena Whitbread has pointed out, this greater freedom to see Lister was accompanied by Charles Lawton's refusal to buy an annuity for Mariana; she had married for financial security only to find herself economically vulnerable.[48] Meanwhile Lister's emotional fidelity was wearing thin. She began to suspect that Mariana was keeping up their relationship mainly as a kind of insurance against the possibility of being left without money upon Charles's death.

Like Charles, Lister accepted sexual philandering as one of the privileges of a squire, whether male or female. She also increasingly fashioned her public appearance into the familiar figure of the masculine woman, even though it exposed her to ridicule.[49] Arguing that her behavior was "natural," she flirted and wooed women in both her own social class and lower ones with relative impunity. She lived in a world where men openly kept mistresses and treated her oddities with bemusement.[50] As long as there was no scandal and no risk to heterosexual marriage, friends enjoyed Lister's flirtations. For example, in December 1820 two of Mariana's sisters, Anne (Nantz) Belcombe and Harriet Belcombe Milne, visited Langton Hall, where Lister was renewing her sexual relationship and friendship with Isabella (Tib) Norcliffe. Mrs. Norcliffe, Charlotte Norcliffe, and a Miss Vallance completed the party of seven women. Lister seems to have flirted with everyone except Mrs. Norcliffe. By 20 December she records new intimacies with Nantz Belcombe: "Talking, at first, much in the same style as in the evening, just before, but then got more loving. Kissed her, told her I had a pain in my knees—my expression to her for desire—& saw plainly she likes me & would yield again, without much difficulty, to opportunity & importun[ity]."[51] Two days later Lister paid special attention to the other sister, Harriet, creating fresh jealousies. On a later visit to the Norcliffes, Lister renewed her flirtations with the unhappily married Harriet, drawing a pointed sexual proposal from her. In the published excerpts of her diary, Lister does not mention what Tib— her original lover at Langton Hall—thought of her flirtations, though she complains sadly of Tib's excessive drinking.

Lister tested the boundaries of sexual decorum, knowing that she could amuse a woman who avoided men for fear of losing her reputation. The ease with which she engaged in same-sex petting may be evidence that women knew and enjoyed sexual pleasures with each other on a scale heretofore ignored. The activities of Lister's social group closely resemble traditional practices of noncoital heterosexual teasing and flirting; they certainly moved in a society that accepted sexualized play between women.[52] Over the years Lister's gender inversion roused as much comment as her pointed interest in attractive young women. The widespread belief that male penetration constituted "sex" and "the sexual" gave Lister what we would now see as remarkable freedoms. Aside from the unfortunate Tib Norcliffe, none of the women with whom she flirted wanted a permanent liaison with Lister (or another woman), but they clearly found her sexual attention gratifying. Only as their hopes of marriage faded did the various Belcombe sisters become interested in the possibility of replacing Mariana in Lister's life. But as her financial situation improved, Lister looked abroad for new friendships.

In 1824, during her first extended visit to Paris, Lister was guilty of another kind of adultery: she was emotionally as well as sexually unfaithful to Mariana. The English pension where she stayed seems to have been a hotbed of lesbian intrigue. After flirting with several women, Lister became deeply involved with the widow Maria Barlow. Although Barlow obviously enjoyed their sexual games, she had practical and religious scruples. It is difficult to estimate how much her guilt might have been assuaged if Lister had committed herself fully. Barlow alternated between hoping that Lister would become her "husband" and dolefully calling herself Lister's "mistress."[53] After the two women left the pension to rent an apartment together, Barlow worried that gossip among the women there might damage her daughter's chances on the marriage market. For three years Lister attempted to sustain her marriage to Mariana Lawton, whom she could see only at infrequent intervals at home in England, while keeping her mistress, Maria Barlow, whom she could see at will but only when she was in Paris. In the process she knew she was doubly guilty of adultery, first to Charles Lawton and then to his wife—or *her* wife, if we remember their exchange of wedding rings.

Maria Barlow, like Mariana, was both attracted to and fearful about Lister's masculine appearance. Lister forthrightly responded that she did not want to be a man because, "I could not have married & should have been shut out from ladies' society. I could not have been with you as I am."[54] Whereas Mariana Lawton wanted her lover to look more feminine, Barlow sought respectability by turning Lister into a man, telling her, "it would have been better had you been brought up as your father's son" and "if I wore men's clothes she should feel differently."[55] At times Barlow verged on asking Lister to cross-dress so they could go through a public marriage ceremony. The widowed and rapidly aging Barlow longed for the facade of a heterosexual marriage, even if the substance was otherwise. Her repeated hints that Lister could pass as a man reveal a common knowledge of cross-dressing as an option for women. Barlow could not lure her lover away from Lawton nor could she undergo a mock marriage with a passing woman. Like many a betrothed woman who gave in to her young man, Barlow found herself compromised without achieving her ultimate goal, a secure marriage.

In September 1825 Mariana Lawton met Lister in the northern spa town of Buxton for a kind of second honeymoon, in which they gave each other special gifts and kissed their wedding rings.[56] Lister was feeling disillusioned with her longtime wife, especially when she compared her with the more sophisticated women she met in Paris. Nevertheless she was still determined to stand by her first love. Their time together culminated in a ceremony: "Mariana put me on a new watch riband & then cut the hair from her queer [genitals] & I that from mine, which she put each into the little lockets we got at Bright's this morning, twelve shillings each, for us always to wear under our clothes in mutual remembrance. We both of us kissed each bit of hair before it was put into the locket."[57] When Mariana quizzed her about whether she had ever given her pubic hair to anyone else, Lister barely avoided mentioning her sister Nantz.

Lister sent a tear-stained letter to Barlow in December 1825 about her recommitment ceremony, just before leaving for Langton Hall for another round of flirtations with Tib Norcliffe and the Belcombe sisters. Deeply distressed, Barlow replied, "There is no other form left to adopt but that of friendship. . . . I have received my divorce!"[58] Her words echo the widely accepted belief that love and friendship could not be combined. However much sexual intimacy might be concealed beneath the phrase "romantic friendship," for women who had committed themselves to each other, love and marriage were the preferred language. Once Barlow had moved in with Lister, they were no longer friends but publicly declared lovers. She had hoped they would become husband and wife and now she faced divorce. Later in this letter Barlow veered away from her marital vocabulary and vented her disappointment in the exaggerated language of adultery. She begged Lister to keep their affair secret: "In charity to my deserted state, bury my error in your own bosom. The loss of my self-esteem is sufficient punishment. If our secret was ever divulged, the tie which did exist would become perfectly hateful to me & have I not suffered enough?"[59] In spite of the high drama of their letters, Lister continued her relationship with Barlow off and on for several more years, even introducing Mariana to her.

Women's relations did not end in the legal finality of divorce, but rather tapered off into a series of recriminations, reconciliations, and disappointments. Only after Lister became involved with an aristocratic woman did she break with Mariana Lawton. When Ann Walker moved into Shibden Hall in

1834, Lawton finally admitted that Lister was lost for good. She wrote Lister in the same terms that Maria Barlow had used a decade earlier: "*Your* having taken another to your bosom has not left vacant your place in Mary's heart. . . . 'If the sunshine of love has illuminated our youth, the moonlight of friendship may at last console our decline.' . . . ever affectionately Mariana."[60] Lawton divided herself in two, using her more formal name, Mary, but signing herself Mariana. The division is emblematic of her situation, married to a man, but in love with a woman. Unable or unwilling to play the role of the deserted wife with Lister, Lawton returned to the language of romance—of feeling, rather than rights. Indeed, she knew she had no rights and could only appeal to emotion, the unstable core of all same-sex marriages. Yet she did not confuse love and friendship—the two were distinct. Her hackneyed metaphor underscored the belief that love was passionate, hot and dangerous, whereas friendship was cool and rational. At the same time it freed her from naming the actual nature of their relationship. That they had been "married" lovers for some twenty years could not be named, but the love itself could be euphemized into sunshine.

Maria Barlow's proposition that Lister dress as a man and that they undergo a legal wedding may have been wishful thinking or a real possibility. We know little about women who successfully passed as men in order to woo and/or marry a woman. Throughout the eighteenth and nineteenth centuries, newspapers record men who were arrested for drunk and disorderly behavior and then found to be cross-dressed women. In most cases the woman gave an alias, embarrassed authorities released her, and she disappeared. But hardly any examples of women living as men among the educated classes have survived, other than a few exposed by cases of blackmail and fraud in the mid-eighteenth century.[61] One exception is Mary Diana Dods (1791?–1830?), who remains tantalizingly beyond full historical reconstruction. Betty T. Bennett, editor of *The Letters of Mary Wollstonecraft Shelley* (1980–88), discovered that Mary Shelley had befriended Dods in London in the 1820s.[62] Mary Diana and her sister, Georgiana, were the illegitimate daughters of the fifteenth Scottish earl of Morton. Educated but unemployable, the two sisters suffered numerous indignities at the hands of their father's employees. As with the aristocratic Ladies of Llangollen, money was scarce and came irregularly and with disdain. Georgiana married a poor military officer, and Mary Diana turned to writing to earn a little extra. Despite her odd appearance as "some one of the masculine gender" who might have "indulged in the masquerade freak of feminine habiliments," Dods was briefly known in London's literary circles as an erudite author.[63] She had already taken on several male pseudonyms (an unusual action in the 1820s) before she emerged publicly as Walter Sholto Douglas and married her pregnant friend, Isabella

Robinson. Mary Shelley helped the two women to hide from society until the baby was born and then to escape to Paris with false passports.

We cannot know why Dods married the "false yet enchanting" Isabella.[64] Perhaps they loved each other, as onlookers noted when they first arrived in Paris. The international elite of Mary Clarke's salon, which included Claude Fauriel, Stendhal, Mérimée, and Hugo, readily accepted the Douglases. Dods's physical appearance was noteworthy in London, but she easily passed as a man in sophisticated Parisian circles. Within a short time Dods/Douglas succumbed to an unknown disease and died in debtors' prison. Isabella covered all traces of her irregular past, broke with Mary Shelley, and married a wealthy clergyman in Italy.[65] This example, as well as Maria Barlow's hints, indicates a subterranean knowledge of transvestite marriage. Rather than imitating heterosexual marriage rituals, necessity could drive the daring into a heterosexual marriage.

Both Dods and Lister were in Paris in the 1820s; each was involved to varying degrees in fake marriages, adultery, and homoerotic relations. Both were highly educated and discontented with their economic and social status. Both charmed friends into silence, even as they acted with extraordinary audacity. If Lister had met Walter Sholto Douglas, would she have recognized him as a woman? Society generally accepted what it saw, looking more closely only when forced to do so. Neither homosexual fidelity nor heterosexual marriage was a stable category for these two women. By the mid-1820s Lister could afford to set up a household with Barlow, whereas the Douglases appear to have been utterly dependent on whatever money friends could send them. Their place in a glamorous intellectual world was precarious. They lacked funds, *and* Isabella had an affair with Fauriel. Barlow's hope of a public marriage to cover the sexual secret at the heart of her relationship with Lister makes absolute sense in a world where respectability was a fragile commodity that required both proper behavior and an adequate income. Barlow was ready and able to guarantee her sexual fidelity in return for economic security. Unfortunately, Lister's social ambitions took her away from Barlow's sphere.

LOVE AND MONEY: ANNE LISTER AND ANN WALKER

In the late 1820s Lister dallied with several aristocratic women, but found she could not afford their lifestyle. She could squeeze only some £1,500 a year out of the small Shibden Hall estate. The Ladies of Llangollen had lived on less than £500 a year, composed of government pensions, gifts, and loans from relatives and friends.[66] Unlike them Lister was a keen traveler and social climber, as well as ambitious to improve her property and status. When Mariana asked to live with her in 1826, the new heiress insisted that she return to

Charles Lawton, fearful that scandal might limit her local influence. By 1832 Lister returned to Yorkshire, determined to consolidate her income and power as a landowner. She decided to take up with Ann Walker, whose property abutted hers. By becoming intimate with Walker, whose annual income was between £3,000 and £4,000, Lister could siphon funds into her own ambitious projects. Had she been a man, Lister's liaison with Ann Walker would have been seen as an ideal marriage, uniting properties and politics to form a powerful Tory gentry base at the edge of industrializing Halifax.

Lister vigorously wooed and kissed the lonely, isolated heiress. Walker sized up their growing intimacy to be "as good as a marriage," and Lister replied "Yes . . . quite as good or better." When Walker worried about the morality of their relationship, the experienced Lister insisted that they make their vows on a Bible. She also proposed that this private vow be confirmed by "taking the sa[c]rement with me at Shibden or at Lightcliffe church."[67] Taking communion with Walker the day after they had made love was important to both women. Even if neither priest nor public knew about their special relationship, God did. But Walker still vacillated, while enjoying (like Lawton and Barlow) Lister's sexual favors. As a woman Lister had greater access to Walker than if she had been a man. Any man would have been subject to very close scrutiny, for tradition and the law protected women against male fortune hunters.[68] After much dithering and sex, the two women at last had a ring ceremony and agreed to remake their wills, adding a codicil giving each other life interest in their estates. Lister "sold" Walker a ring for sixpence, which Walker then put back on Lister's finger.[69] This folk ceremony was a far cry from the solemn 1816 exchange of rings between Lister and the as-yet unmarried Mariana or the expensive lockets they had bought each other in Buxton in 1825.

Nevertheless Lister took her marriage to Walker very seriously and embarked on a series of maneuvers to ratify her position as a landowning husband. As with Barlow, the act of living together both cemented their relationship and drew attention to it. No one could quite understand why Walker should leave her own palatial home to live at Shibden Hall. Unvoiced concerns struggled to the surface. If Walker did not marry and bear a legitimate male heir, the young Sutherlands, her married sister's sons, stood to gain all of her considerable income. Lister worked hard to disarm Walker's sister and brother-in-law, reminding them of how much Walker gained by associating with the socially superior Listers and even suggesting that the friendship might lessen Walker's chronic depression and shyness. Walker's sister was flattered, but her husband, Captain Sutherland, never dropped his suspicions that any friend of his sister-in-law was a danger to his future financial gain.[70] He was, of course, right to be wary. An added complication was Lister's decision to send the melancholic Walker to Mariana's brother, a York specialist in

mental diseases. We have no record of what the still-married Mariana Lawton thought of this situation. Although the vigorous Lister and the depres-
sive Walker were not well matched, one can argue that Walker had made a
better bargain than her frequently pregnant sister, married to a suspicious,
greedy husband.[71]

Lister began to manage parts of Walker's estate, quietly using its income
for her own projects. Like a husband, she gained access to Walker's income
in return for emotional support and social cachet. Rather than continuing to
worship at the Halifax church, Lister rented a pew in both their names at the
Lightcliffe church, closer to the Walker properties than hers. She also had
Walker lay the cornerstone in 1835 for one of her investments, a new casino
and hotel in Northgate, Halifax.[72] This public gesture—Lister called Walker
"her particular friend" in front of the assembled dignitaries—was scarcely
likely to allay the suspicions of Walker's sister and brother-in-law, or of the
trustees of the Walker property, or of those eager to attack the Tory landown-
ers. But Lister already had plenty of experience with male responses to her
lovemaking, and so was well prepared to outfox Captain Sutherland and the
lawyers, even if she could not stop gossip and innuendo in the local taverns
and newspapers.

Still, the two women lived in a homosocial world, and stopping the
tongues of the Halifax women took all of Lister's social skills and self-
confidence. As Jill Liddington and Helena Whitbread have documented, Lister was more open about her "oddity" among her old friends in York and in sophisticated Paris than in Halifax. The key local figure was Mrs. Priestley, wife
of William Priestley, Walker's cousin and one of the two male trustees appointed to oversee the Walker estate. As long ago as 1824, the normally secretive Lister had admitted to Mrs. Priestley that she had chosen a woman
companion rather than a man. Probably Mrs. Priestley's shrewd guess that she
would never marry had elicited this uncharacteristic confession; their friendship was further deepened in intimate conversations. Lister luxuriated in the
rare opportunity of describing Mariana to a sympathetic woman friend:

> I declared her less commonplace than I & more singular than Miss
> Pickford &, in reality, tho' without appearing so, the most singular per-
> son I had ever met with. I twirled my watch about, conscious of occa-
> sionally bordering on a rather gentlemanly sort of style. She seems to
> feel but not quite understand this. She would prefer my society to that
> of any lady, perhaps scarce knowing why. She pondered over my hav-
> ing chosen a lady for my future companion.[73]

Mrs. Priestley was one of Lister's chief defenders in Halifax during the 1820s.
As the gratified Lister noted, "she always told people I was natural, but she
thought nature was in an odd freak when she made me."[74] Imagine, then, Mrs.

Priestley's astonishment when a few years later she watched Lister vigorously woo the reclusive Ann Walker. On one occasion she surprised Lister and Walker kissing: "I had jumped up in time and was standing by the fire but Ann looked red and I pale and Mrs. P- . . . looked vexed, jealous and annoyed, [and left] in suppressed rage."[75] Their seventeen-year friendship never recovered, understandably so from Lister's perspective, for Mrs. Priestley appears to have warned her husband about Lister's possible motives. Although other Halifax women gradually accepted the situation, given the power and status of the two heiresses, the Priestleys remained cool and distant.

Lister and Walker made and remade their wills to reflect their marriage. Traditional property rights held sway. Walker never gave Lister the legal management of her estate, as her sister had done for Captain Sutherland, but she did cede life tenancy to her share of the properties. Lister, fearful of the Sutherland family, in turn left Walker life tenancy in her properties and kept them entailed to a distant Lister relative. After she unexpectedly died before Walker, it took the Walker family less than two years to declare Ann mentally unstable and incompetent to manage the two estates. When his wife died prematurely, Captain Sutherland, not even a blood relative of Walker's, ended up living and dying at Shibden Hall. For a time he controlled both the Lister and the Walker properties. A distant Lister cousin did not inherit the estate until 1854, upon the death of Ann Walker, still in a mental asylum, but legally the life-inheritor. Property and male property rights had been temporarily subverted by the entrepreneurial Lister, but the most obvious beneficiary of her stratagems was neither a Lister nor a Walker nor a woman.

Romantic friends struggled to establish the legal priority of their chosen friend as a recipient of their income over blood kin. Anne Lister was fortunate in some ways, because she knew that Mariana Lawton, Maria Barlow, and Ann Walker had money from other sources. But many women faced the dilemma of how to protect a partner without an income. Lady Eleanor Butler, the elder of the Ladies of Llangollen, fretted about money her entire life. She could not forget that upon her brother's marriage to a wealthy heiress, she had not received her legal share of the family inheritance. She was never reconciled with her parents; her father failed to mention her in his will. Butler kept hoping that friends would help her gain her due. In 1784 she noted in her diary a conversation with "the Talbots," who "agree in thinking I have been barbarously Cheated." Confident of their support, she made her will, "That I might Secure all I am possess'd or Entitled to to the Beloved of My Heart—They will See Justice done her when I am no more."[76] But she never came into her entitlement, and upon her death in 1829, "the Beloved of her Heart" faced near-penury. Fortunately, Ponsonby had friends in the right places, and the Duke of Wellington was able to transfer Butler's Civil List pension of £200 to her. In effect, after nearly fifty years of life together, Butler and Ponsonby had won their goal: their romantic friendship was recognized as a marriage. But most women did not have influential male friends.

Throughout the nineteenth century family ties were considered stronger than same-sex marriages. Rosa Bonheur was completely self-made; her first earnings had paid her father's debts, and she had supported her two brothers and sister off and on all her life. Nevertheless she shrewdly guessed that her brothers would be outraged at her decision to leave everything to her new and much younger partner, Anna Klumpke. After making her will, she added a letter, warning and needling her family, who, she claimed, had "always taken a dim view of my right to live as I please. Having done my duty by my family, I was entitled, like any adult earning her own living, to my independence."[77] Her letter again emphasized the respectability of her life with Nathalie Micas and Anna Klumpke, and her determination never to sully their reputations. Bonheur fashioned a new definition of individual honor, arguing that just as she had protected the "material interests" of Mlle. Micas and her mother, she now had every right to do the same for Mlle. Klumpke. Bonheur suspected that her brothers would attempt to evict Klumpke, leaving her "not even being entitled to take away her personal belongings and losing the benefit of her financial investments in my property."[78]

Klumpke generously offered to share half the estate with the Bonheurs, but as Rosa had foreseen, her brother Isidore wanted more than that and unsuccessfully sued. Rosa Bonheur spent a lifetime fearful that her brothers would try to cheat her lovers, should she die before them. Fortunately she knew the law well enough to stop their efforts. But her actions made even the adulatory Theodore Stanton ashamed. In his *Reminiscences of Rosa Bonheur* (1910), he frequently apologizes for the rift her intimate friendships had caused with her family. His uneasiness weakens both his own and Bonheur's claims to the respectability of romantic friendship: if a woman quarreled with her family, something must be wrong; kin came before love. In effect her will spoke too loudly against convention and drew attention to something society deemed disreputable.[79]

Nevertheless contemporaries admired the Ladies and Bonheur because they placed love above security. They put romance back into romantic friendship. But they also brought reason to love. The Ladies had the advantage of aristocratic family ties, and Bonheur that of artistic freedom. But both the shadowy Mary Diana Dods/Douglas and the widowed Maria Barlow remind us of why money and connections were essential for a respectable woman. The extraordinary successes and occasional failures of Anne Lister make her exceptional in many ways. Her intelligence, drive, and ambition are rare at any time, but far rarer in the early nineteenth century, when few women could survive without male protection. Yet in each of her relationships, creating a home together was a difficult social and economic task. The next chapter explores how women might balance the claims of respectability and intimacy when under public scrutiny. In Rome artistic genius, rather than class privilege, freed women to love and live with other women.

2   *"Emancipated Females"*

THE ROME COMMUNITY

Chapter 1 considered the privileges and liabilities of the exceptional independent woman. As well-born eccentric (Butler), or heiress (Lister), or artist (Bonheur), with sufficient courage she could fashion her life as she pleased. But finding a supportive community was more difficult. This chapter focuses on a group of respectable, and respected, English and American women who lived in Rome during the years 1852–75. The Rome community serves as a microcosm in which to examine the variety of erotic options available to single women at mid-century. The group, composed of women artists, writers, sculptors, and journalists and their supporters, centered on two Americans, the actress Charlotte Cushman and the sculptor Harriet Hosmer, who arrived in Rome in 1852. Unlike many homosexual men who went to Italy looking for the classical tradition of homoerotic love, single women were in the process of making their own traditions.[1] On foreign soil these women could safely do many things that would have shocked the sensibilities of a narrow New England village or a small British town. Although those who violated the standards of female heterosexual purity were expelled, the homosocial women artists flourished for all to see. Indeed part of their attraction to bourgeois commentators was their willingness to live in public, to foreground their daily lives as models for the future. Unlike their contemporary Rosa Bonheur, they did not suffer from social and familial ostracism, nor did they choose, like Butler and Ponsonby, rural isolation. Instead, they challenged men on their own terms, forming an independent society of women.

Both Cushman and Hosmer became skilled purveyors of their public images, employing their status as artists to press beyond the permissible. Situated on the borderline of femininity, they mastered how and when to pass outside it. Their acceptance depended upon a carefully constructed asexuality; as Cushman's letters reveal, discretion was essential for maintaining respectability. But erotic passion cannot always be controlled. Rumors, gossip, jealousy, and anger flourished in and around the small, highly visible all-female Rome community. Female-to-female eroticism was an increasingly familiar aspect of nineteenth-century mainstream artistic life. Even if sophisticated Victorians lacked a fully developed medical discourse with which to define and label lesbians,they certainly knew, recognized, and talked about same-sex love between women. Although one may agree with Jeffrey Weeks that the Victorian belief in female sexual passivity may have limited any scientific effort to define lesbianism,[2] public discussion of "mannish women" was widespread, and fathers were anxious about daughters who refused to marry because they preferred their female friends. Precisely because there was no separate subculture similar to the wealthy Parisian lesbians of the early twentieth century, we can see more clearly the efforts of women to emphasize their same-sex erotic relationships without excluding heterosexual friendships, flirtations, and social privileges. Money, love, and reputation were entangled in complex ways, as women competed with each other and male artists for public attention and commissions. Unpublished letters, articles, reviews, and gossip provide substantial, if partial, information about the Anglo-American community. Without clear categories and defined labels, women tested the boundaries of friendship. But what happened when, in Anne Lister's words, a woman went "beyond the utmost verge of friendship" and revealed the sexual nature of her love?[3]

TABLEAU VIVANT: THE INDEPENDENT WOMAN

Rome had long been the final destination on the Grand Tour of the European continent for well-to-do English and American travelers during the eighteenth and nineteenth centuries. By the 1850s an estimated ten thousand to eleven thousand British and American tourists were visiting Florence and Rome each year; and the numbers began to increase significantly in the 1880s, when train travel improved.[4] But even then it was a long and expensive trip between London or New York and the heart of Italy. Visitors stayed as long as they could; the small resident English-speaking communities were welcoming, and the cultural riches unrivaled. Venice, Florence, and Rome dominated the itinerary. Unlike the growing number of Francophiles who prided themselves on their language skills and cultural knowledge, Italophiles responded to a distant past. Italy was a cultural mecca for men trained in Greek and Latin and for women eager to experience great art. Classical ideals held sway. The stunning Baroque art that surrounded them was universally decried as lacking an essential serenity and morality. Although a few foreigners were swept up in the movement for Italian unification, most found it hard to meet upper-class Italians and harder still to understand their politics. Instead, the contrast between industrializing northern Europe and America and the decaying and divided peninsula provided ample opportunity to philosophize about the fall of the Roman Empire and the corruption of the Roman Catholic Church, as well as the ugly materialism of life back home.

Generations of northern artists had settled in Italy because of its low cost of living, ready access to informal apprenticeships, ample workshop space, skilled Italian workmen, and inexpensive art supplies. The acknowledged leader of the Anglo-American artistic circle in Rome was William Wetmore Story, son of a U.S. Supreme Court judge and himself a lawyer, who had forsaken his country and his profession to become a sculptor.[5] Members of his circle included the poets Robert and Elizabeth Barrett Browning when they visited Rome; one of Robert's close friends, the writer Isa Blagden; and Anna Jameson, separated from her husband, and earning her living writing and lecturing on Italian art. Other expatriate artists included the singer Adelaide Kemble Sartoris and her sister; the actress Fanny Kemble; the Welsh sculptor Mary Lloyd, special friend of the journalist Frances Power Cobbe; Kate Field, an American woman of letters; Grace Greenwood, an American journalist and writer of popular fiction; and a variety of supporters, such as Lady Marian Alford (1816–88), and Louisa, Lady Ashburton. Other artists and sculptors moved in and out of the inner circle, including the Americans Louisa Lander, sculptor of neoclassical busts, Edmonia Lewis, the first African-American-Indian woman sculptor, and Margaret Foley, a cameo cutter.

Enthusiasm for the American women artists was disproportionate to their numbers or their artistic influence. Comments about them proved that the informant not only understood great works of art from the past, but also could recognize modern genius. This novel band of self-reliant women, it was widely asserted, were uniquely capable of competing with European artists on European soil; they were exciting examples of America's new cultural maturity. Journalists, aided by the women themselves, created a single image of these women. They were not penurious artists suffering in Romantic isolation, nor had they given up the essential womanly traits of kindness and service to others. Ambition, competition, and envy were banished from the public eye and replaced with tales of hard work, cooperation, and good spirits. Descriptions of the artists' works, homes, and studios confirmed a sense of individual self-fulfillment within a happy community. The exceptional woman artist was transformed into a symbol of personal achievement; her life, rather than her artistic accomplishments, represented her genius. In effect the American women became artworks, to be viewed and shown off as national trophies. Like tableaux vivants, the artists and their community were caught as still lifes that portrayed a single triumphal story.

An invitation to one of Charlotte Cushman's soirées was essential for a successful visit to Rome. At the height of her fame as America's first internationally renowned Shakespearean, Cushman, only thirty-six, decided to go into partial retirement, and to spend the winter of 1852 in Rome with her partner Matilda Hays, the Englishwoman whom she had trained as Juliet to replace her newly remarried sister. Cushman specialized in roles demanding powerful emotions. She was best known for her trouser roles, creating what was universally regarded as the best Romeo of her generation, but she was also applauded on both sides of the Atlantic for her Lady Macbeth, Queen Katharine, Meg Merilees, and Bianca. Both the British and the American press praised Cushman for the heterosexual purity of her personal life and for the effectiveness of her acting.

A combination of high fees for her acting in England and shrewd invest-ments in America had left Cushman a wealthy woman. She spent some six-teen winters at two different Rome apartments, where she entertained lav-ishly, presiding over a heterogeneous mix of visitors, expatriates, and women friends. For over six years, while learning her craft, Hosmer lived in the Cushman apartment rent-free. As an actress Cushman had suffered numer-ous social slights, but in Rome she found "much nicer opportunities of social enjoyment than I could have anywhere else, with people who come to me, who seek to know me, of a better, more highly cultivated class than I could get anywhere else. . . . Society is on a broader plain—wider, jollier, happier."[6] She herself was instrumental in creating this society, especially through her encouragement of single women writers and artists.

Cushman's open community of friends meant that many visitors could move in and out of homosociality—and homoeroticism—experimenting emotionally before settling either with a woman friend or into a heterosex-ual marriage. The British feminist Bessie Rayner Parkes had a series of pas-sionate friendships with other feminists, including Matilda Hays, whom she visited in Rome. She deeply admired the "genius" of Cushman. Only in 1867, at the age of thirty-eight, did Parkes marry the crippled Frenchman Louis Belloc. By then she had converted to Roman Catholicism and had drifted away from her original radicalism. The English journalist Frances Power Cobbe visited Italy six times between the years 1857 and 1879. She made her first trip following the death of her father; after years of caring for him in an isolated Irish country home, Cobbe felt lonely and purposeless. She found in Italy the kind of all-female circles she had longed for, where "young women in Florence and Rome [were] admirably working their way: some as writers, some as artists of one kind or another, bright, happy, free, and respected by all."[7] Sally Mitchell suggests that the Rome women taught Cobbe how a single woman could live a happy, full life without enduring modest self-effacement or undertaking self-sacrificing good works.[8] Cobbe's happiest memories were of the "merry parties" held at Charlotte Cushman's, where dinners consisted of "American oysters and wild boar with agro-dolce-sauce and déjeuners including an awful refection menacing sudden death, called

'Woffles,' eaten with molasses (of which woffles I have seen five plates divided between four American ladies!)."[9]

Cushman's circle also attracted lonely young men of uncertain sexual orientation. Flirtations and attention were freely undertaken in a world where the unspoken understanding was heterosexual indifference. The elegant artist Frederick Leighton, known among his close friends as Fay, enthusiastically wrote home that Hosmer was the "queerest, best-natured little chap possible."[10] They became staunch friends for life. Shakespere Wood ran errands for the inhabitants and escorted them about town. William Wetmore Story could not resist commenting, "W.'s harem (scarem) as I call it . . . —live all together under the superintendence of W., who calls them Charlotte, Hatty, and so on, and who dances attendance upon them everywhere, even to the great subscription ball the other evening."[11] Indeed, so familiar was Wood with this homosocial circle that at one juncture his presence threatened their vaunted heterosexual purity. When Hosmer's father suffered financial reverses, she turned to Wood to help her sort out her always chaotic finances. Elizabeth Barrett Browning wrote Isa Blagden, then in Paris, that "Mrs. Sartoris hears through a reliable person that Hatty is compromising herself more & more with Shakespeare [sic] Wood—What a pity!"[12] But no one could make heterosexual romance stick to the boyish Hosmer.

Cushman loved to help friends and family—and to be the center of attention. For a growing audience she read or performed portions of her most famous roles, Shakespeare's soliloquies, and poetry by contemporary women, including that of her former partner Eliza Cook. Although Cobbe "greatly admired and respected" her hostess, she thought that Cushman had, "like all actors, the acquired habit of giving vivid expression to every emotion, just as we quiet English ladies are taught from our cradles to repress such signs."[13] Story, unhappy that Cushman's evenings were upstaging his own, grumbled to his old friend James Russell Lowell: "The Cushman sings savage ballads in a hoarse, manny voice, and requests people recitatively to forget her not. I'm sure I shall not."[14] Onstage Cushman's characters displayed their dangerous passions. Offstage her theatricality, when combined with an open preference for women, touched a raw nerve among respectable men.

Cushman represented the pinnacle of American achievement in drama in the 1840s and 1850s.[15] Given the nineteenth-century American and British infatuation with self-help, the tomboy Harriet Hosmer, all potential, was a less controversial subject. Hatty, as she was known, was the only surviving daughter of a tubercular mother; her physician father, it was said, had given her complete freedom, hoping that an outdoor life would build a strong body. She was a vigorous horseback rider and walked the streets and ate in cafés unaccompanied at all hours. She captivated contemporaries by her independence and artistic self-confidence, and perhaps most of all, because she exuded a safe adolescent asexuality.[16] But the cautious Fanny Kemble wrote a mutual friend about a year after Hosmer had arrived in Rome: "Hatty's peculiarities may stand in the way of her success with people of society & the world & I wish for her own sake that some of them were less decided & singular but it is perhaps unreasonable to expect a person to be singular in their gifts & graces alone & not to be equally unlike other people in other matters too."[17] Hosmer, perhaps taking a cue from her mentor, Cushman, knew the value of dramatic self-presentation; her boyishness attracted much needed publicity and patronage. Americans and English visiting Rome soon put her studio on the list of required places to visit, as an example of the superiority of American independence and womanly purity over decadent European confinement and hypocrisy.

The poet Elizabeth Barrett Browning was fascinated by Hosmer's impetuosity and marked individuality. Seeing the numerous disreputable hangers-on who surrounded George Sand had dampened her admiration for French freedom; the decorous English poet could not ignore the famous writer's unconventional sexual arrangements. But mannish women struck her as attractively original. Only a year after she had met Cushman and Hays in Paris, she was gossiping familiarly with her sister:

> Oh—there's a house of what I call emancipated women—a young sculptress—American, Miss Hosmer, a pupil of Gibson's, very clever and very strange—and Miss Hayes [sic] the translator of George Sand, who "dresses like a man down to the waist" (so the accusation runs). Certainly there's the waistcoat which I like—and the collar, neckcloth, and jacket made with a sort of wag-tail behind, which I don't like. She is a peculiar person altogether, decided, direct, truthful, it seems to me.[18]

Hosmer and Hays, known among her friends as Max, did not leave any explanation for their unconventional dress, but surely it went beyond either professional necessity or comfort—Barrett Browning, after all, met them at a party. Her husband Robert had more doubts about the Rome women, but he too admired their intelligence and informality. Female emancipation could be interpreted not simply as economic and social freedom, but also as freedom from heterosexual desire—something that the happily married Barrett Browning did not wish for herself, but that seemed a wonderful alternative to the heterosexual freedom of Sand. In her eyes the decidedly masculine Hays and Hosmer managed to be both free and pure, hitherto defined as an impossible combination.

Women journalists were eager to assign "genius" to Hosmer. Grace Greenwood, probably one of the four "woffle" eaters, confirmed her reputation among appreciative Americans in her 1865 travel book, *Haps and Mishaps:*

"She is thoroughly original and independent, without extravagance or pretension of any kind—a simple, earnest, truthful girl, whose strong and cheerful heart is the peer and ally of her active and comprehensive intellect."[19] The British feminists Matilda Hays and Emily Faithfull wrote novels that extolled the virtues of the Rome community. In *Changes upon Changes* (1868), Faithfull's flighty heroine reads Madame de Staël's *Corinne* and admires Hosmer's statues. Matilda Hays, in *Adrienne Hope* (1866), describes Hosmer as "winning," with a "trim little figure [and] eyes and face that danced and glowed with fun and fire."[20] Her fictional characters become friends with the "charming" artist and spend many "pleasant evenings . . . in that freedom of intercourse peculiar to artist society," an allusion to Hays's happy days as Cushman's partner, living with her and Hosmer. When Hays repeated her flattering portrait of Hosmer in the new feminist publication, *Englishwoman's Journal,* the elderly Anna Jameson warned Bessie Rayner Parkes, the editor, that such praise might win friends in America, "but among judges of art it will injure her—I am anxious that women should not make your journal a vehicle for bepraising each other."[21] Jameson's advice was ignored, however, and Hosmer suffered all her life from immoderate praise for who she was, or more precisely, who she was seen to be, rather than what she had accomplished.

Like the women journalists, Nathaniel Hawthorne was both intrigued and defensive about what he saw in Rome. The combination of heterosexual purity and physical independence seemed to open dazzling possibilities. The artist-heroine Hilda in his *The Marble Faun* (1860) is supposed to be modeled upon a combination of Louisa Lander (for whom he modeled) and Hosmer.[22] When he visited Hosmer's studio in 1858, he commented in his journal that he admired her "frank, simple, straight-forward and downright" manner:

> She had on petticoats, I think; but I did not look so low, my attention being chiefly drawn to a sort of man's sack of purple or plum-colored broadcloth, into the side-pockets of which her hands were thrust as she came forward to greet us. . . . There never was anything so jaunty in her movement and action; she was indeed very queer, but she seemed to be her actual self, and nothing affected or made-up; so that, for my part I gave her full leave to wear what may suit her best, and to behave as her inner woman prompts.[23]

It is easy to mock Hawthorne's refusal to look below Hosmer's waist. But he looked where Victorian men *could* look, and he did not see that essential attribute of the mature woman, her breasts. Hosmer's jacket covered her bosom; combined with her short hair and cap, she looked like a boy. Since he admired her, Hawthorne fell back on a familiar excuse—her behavior was not made up, but natural. Hosmer fearlessly exploited her "natural" androgyny, turning it into a sign of her artistic genius. But women writers took a different tack;

they rushed to defend Hosmer's womanliness by integrating her into the ranks of respectable middle-class womanhood. Mrs. E. F. Ellet, writing in 1859, admitted that "at first glance" Hosmer gave "the impression of a handsome boy," but she insisted upon noting her "trim waist and well-developed bust."[24]

In a world that permitted the display of shoulders and bosom but insisted on covering the bottom half of a woman down to her ankles, erotic desire—and artistic taste—focused on breasts. Contemporary artists recognized their importance and candidly wrote to friends about the economics of depicting female breasts. Sculptors early discovered that busts of women sold better if both breasts were exposed.[25] The cleavage of the breasts could, indeed, stand in for an unseen cleavage, the vagina or buttocks. Portraits of contemporary bluestockings, such as Margaret Fuller Ossoli and Anna Jameson, exaggerated their femininity and full breasts to counter any negative criticisms of their intellectuality. Hosmer's concealment of her breasts symbolized a refusal of mature heterosexuality. Yet her teacher, John Gibson, considered Hosmer to be exceptionally skilled in sculpting breasts, praise that Hays and other friends repeated. Her early busts of Hesper, Daphne, and Medusa expose both breasts in loving detail; perhaps she examined the breasts of her models with special acuity.

Hawthorne's picture of Hosmer and her world was virtually identical to that of the four women journalists, Hays, Faithfull, Greenwood, and Cobbe. Hosmer and Cushman had become objects to view while on tour in Italy. As with famous artworks, everyone already had an opinion about them. For public consumption they came with a prepackaged story, one as the spirited boyish genius, the other as the accomplished manly actress. Yet discrepancies were too obvious to ignore. How much leeway could society give the mannish, eccentric woman in her emotional and erotic life? Cushman seemed to demand acceptance of her acting genius *and* of her intimate friendships. The tomboy Hosmer seemed to defy time and refuse to grow into womanly behavior and appearance. The tableau was always in danger of moving, of breaking the illusion of propriety. Although Hawthorne approved of Hosmer following what the "inner woman prompts," he wondered how she could mature if she had rejected womanliness. He concluded, "I don't quite see . . . what she is to do when she grows old; for the decorum of age will not be consistent with a costume that looks pretty and excusable enough in a young woman."[26]

MA, LADIE LOVE, AUNTIE, BIG MAMMA: CHARLOTTE CUSHMAN, EMMA STEBBINS, AND EMMA CROW CUSHMAN

Charlotte Cushman's father disappeared soon after his bankruptcy in 1828; within a few years Cushman was the main support of her mother, brother, and sister. Like Rosa Bonheur's family, they always disapproved of her independence, and they especially disliked her open affection for women. In old age the writer Geraldine Jewsbury still remembered that Cushman's "mother had the faculty of being *always discontented* & Miss Cushman had much to bear from her."[27] At an early age Cushman turned to others for emotional sustenance. Cushman's biographer, Lisa Merrill, describes how Cushman made the biological relatives of her lovers into her own relatives to authorize and reinforce the homoerotic bonds she had established.[28] As a young woman, she called the father of her first lover, Rosalie Sully, "Father," and wrote of their home as her home. But she soon outgrew this model and preferred to be the head of her own household. By 1852, with her sister safely remarried and her mother settled, she decided to spend her money as she wished, on her own friends, and not kin.

But in Rome Cushman did not wish to imitate bourgeois domesticity. For years infatuated novice actresses and young women fans eagerly entered into flirtations with her. Cushman responded warmly, writing long letters of advice and love that rarely mentioned her current partner. Even semi-retired, Cushman looked for the excitement of multiple devotees. But though Cushman's home in Rome was the site of many happy gatherings of single women, those closest to her often found her love too demanding. Matilda Hays felt trapped in the unwanted role of wife to an international star. She first retaliated by engaging in an extended flirtation with Hosmer. But after a particularly stormy battle with Cushman in the spring of 1857, she left Rome for London, joining Bessie Rayner Parkes and her friends to fight for women's rights.[29] At the time Cushman was already wooing the wealthy and highly respectable American sculptor Emma Stebbins. Unfortunately no documentation survives about this courtship, but Cushman may have been looking for a more refined and sophisticated partner than Hays. With Stebbins, her dress and manners became more subdued, perhaps in response to Stebbins's distaste for the stage. Cushman had learned from Hays the emotional cost of letting a partner give up her career: she spent the remaining twenty years of her life furthering Stebbins's work. Publicly, friends and admirers believed that Stebbins and Cushman were an ideal romantic friendship, "two as firm in their friendship as the Ladies of Llangollen."[30] But Cushman was never happy with a monogamous marriage.

Within months of vowing fidelity to Stebbins, Cushman left for the United States on an acting tour. Hosmer suggested that she stop off to see her benefactor, Wayman Crow, and ask his advice about her investments. During her two-week engagement in St. Louis in early 1858, his nineteen-year-old daughter, Emma, was smitten with this powerful Romeo. Cushman reciprocated, and the two were soon exchanging passionate letters. She warned Emma, "Do you not know that I am already married? I wear the badge

A.L.B? S.G.D.G.

Fig. 4. Emma Crow Cushman and Charlotte Cushman, ca. 1865. Courtesy of Library of Congress, Washington, D.C., photo collection.

on the 3rd finger of my left hand?"[31] even while she encouraged the young woman. Cushman had long managed to negotiate numerous cross-age love affairs while married to a woman her own age. But now she was head over heels in love. What began as a familiar offstage dalliance soon escalated into something much more serious. For the remainder of her life, she juggled two competing emotional claims, her publicly acceptable marriage to Emma Stebbins and her passionate erotic relationship with Emma Crow (fig. 4).

Emma Crow kept all of the letters she received from Cushman. None of her letters to Cushman survive. Nor, for that matter, does much of Cushman's correspondence with such intimate friends as Eliza Cook, Matilda Hays, and Emma Stebbins—a fact that makes the letters to Emma an all-the-more-valuable, if necessarily one-sided, source. In regard to all of her intense friendships, Cushman exercised caution, warning lovers to be careful about her letters, while also reassuring Emma Crow, for example, "Write to me quite freely. My letters are quite safe from observation," and "I am very careful about my letters. I have them always about with me, those I keep."[32] The letters that Emma Crow so carefully preserved are one of the few examples of an older woman wooing a younger. As chapter 5 documents, virtually all our knowledge of cross-age love is from the perspective of the younger woman. In the many letters that Cushman wrote to her "dear child" whenever they were apart, we can trace the extraordinary effort Cushman made to meet the demands of her newest conquest.

For Crow, as with many other young female admirers, Cushman seemed to combine the maternal and the powerful, the bountiful and the manly. The forty-two-year-old Cushman was delighted with "the dear 'little love' I have inspired in my 'old age' . . . it is very sweet to be loved by a young, fresh heart."[33] During the early stages of their love affair, Cushman seemed to control its pace and parameters. She complimented Crow on the "womanly & *dignified* way" in which she had blushingly confessed her love, but reminded her of the necessity of discretion. Soon they were exchanging pictures, jewelry, nicknames, locks of hair, and other love tokens, as well as making elaborate plans to meet. A few weeks before Cushman sailed back to Italy, she wrote Crow: "I love you dearly, my own darling. Darling mine, the hard words must be said. They would have been softened by me had I been allowed to press them upon your lips. *I love you! I love you!* Goodbye, I kiss your pretty soft loving eyes and hands."[34] As the young Crow pressed for more signs of affection, Cushman replied with words of warning. Without specifically mentioning Emma Stebbins, she told Crow, "You know, love mine, that I am not mistress of myself always—that I have everywhere, many many calls upon my time & patience & care & protection."[35] Cushman also had a reputation to protect. As a well-known actress, she feared scandal, and she cautioned Crow to burn her letters and to be careful when they were in public together.

At first Cushman tried to play a maternal role, advising "my darling" that her father "did not find you *persistent,* in giving yourself a *purpose* in life."[36] In response Emma Crow made it her life's purpose to be Cushman's greatest love. She offered to stay the night with Cushman at her hotel when she returned to St. Louis. On another occasion she suggested a tryst in another city.[37] Cushman found her assertiveness strikingly attractive but also feared its consequences. And the Crow family worried about their eligible daughter's undue interest in an older woman. Hosmer wrote a teasing letter to Wayman Crow: "She is a noble woman and as much a mother to me as you are a Father. . . . I perceive that she and Emma are what we this side of the ocean call 'lovers'—but I am not jealous and only admire Emma for her taste."[38] A few months later she offered to "keep a sharper lookout at Miss Cushman and not allow her to go on in this serious manner with Emma—it is really dreadful and I am really jealous."[39] Hosmer was not jealous of the relationship, but she clearly felt the need to protect her patron's interests by alerting him to a dangerous friendship. The Crow family paid the consequences of their support of independent women artists: their daughter, a wealthy heiress, the pride of her father, was slipping from under his protection and into that of an all-too-powerful mannish woman.

Emma Crow persuaded her father to send her and a sister with a chaperon on a tour of Europe. They stayed for three months in Rome as the guests of Cushman and Stebbins. The more time they spent together, the more passionate the two women became. On 9 March 1860, two days after Crow left Rome, Cushman wrote her a long, almost incoherent letter, telling her that their love was breaking their health. The young Crow's hands trembled, and she, Cushman, could not sleep or concentrate: "I am going to beg you, by your love for me, which my heart cannot doubt or question, to leave my spirit more calm through that which you will strive to cultivate in yourself." At the same time that she begged for emotional distance, she promised future intimacy, declaring that her wish to "have you ever with me is as great as you could desire it to be, " and that "much can be accomplished by a steadfast determination to affect our future union." As difficult as the three months together had been, Cushman assured Crow, "our ultimate & entire union can never be far off" because "we are needful to each other & God in his infinite goodness does not interfere with our souls' needs."[40] Desire repeatedly overcame prudence as Cushman plotted to keep Crow in her own household.

Cushman's solution was simple: Emma Crow would marry her adopted son. She had habitually turned her partners' families into relatives; now she would turn her young lover into a relative by means of heterosexual marriage. Cushman had adopted Edwin (Ned), the son of her sister's first marriage, after her sister remarried. The boy had spent a good deal of time in boarding schools without gaining any particular skills, except a love of riding and playing cards. He was conveniently at hand during those fateful three months in Rome. We cannot reconstruct what happened, but a young man without much purpose was easily bent to the will of a strong-minded woman. By the time Emma Crow left Rome in early March, she was tentatively engaged to Ned Cushman. Throughout the spring Charlotte's letters pursued Crow across Europe, mingling plans to meet in Paris, tourist notes, and jocular comments about Ned, with passionate declarations of love: "I am not whole without you! Does it make you happy darling? Are you content that I go about the world *un*whole? & if fate intervenes as I fear it will—I am never to be an entirety again?"[41]

Crow agreed to tell her sister and their chaperon that she needed to go to Paris for a week to buy new clothes for the season; she and Cushman could then rendezvous at the same hotel and find longed-for privacy. In a letter describing how Ned "lives & breathes only in & for you," Charlotte finalized their meeting, with a warning: "Yes darling, there are people in the world who could understand our love for each other. Therefore it is necessary that we should keep all expression of it to ourselves—& not demonstrate too clearly our great devotion to each other: we only excite observation & envy & jealousy & this is best avoided. *I love you as you love me* & will seek every opportunity of being with you—when I do not seem to *you* to do so."[42] Cushman speaks bluntly about the social opprobrium women faced if they showed erotic love. In particular, like a married man, she wanted the affair kept from her wife, Emma Stebbins: "Remember we cannot be too guarded, for you have very jealous eyes upon you & I have escaped so well this winter from Miss Stebbins' jealousy that I should be pained to awaken it."[43] Paris was to become a touchstone of happiness and intimacy for each woman, a reminder that in spite of all, they were meant for each other. Cushman wrote to Crow with remarkable frankness a month later: "ah what delirium is in the memory. Every nerve in me thrills as I look back & feel you in my arms, held to my breast so closely, so entirely mine in every sense as I was yours. Ah, my very sweet, very precious, full, full of extasy."[44]

This erotic ecstasy was mingled with Cushman's delight in turning her beloved into a family member. Cushman assured Wayman Crow that she would be leaving her fortune to the young couple, and he acquiesced in the marriage. Emma Crow married Ned Cushman on 3 April 1861 in St. Louis. Cushman eagerly imagined the many roles the newly married Emma Crow Cushman would play, each of which would tie them closer together: "Dearest and Sweetest daughter[,] niece, friend and love, only think how many things combined in any one of these words—for surely *any* one in *our* case comprehends the whole! . . . I could never have hoped to combine in one person so many happy relations as come to me through you my darling—who never fails me."[45] She soon added "baby's Mamma" to this list, as she eagerly anticipated seeing her name carried on to the next generation. She turned the forthcoming baby into *their* baby, a product of their love for each other. Yet none of her new familial roles could compensate Emma Crow Cushman for her continued separations from her beloved; moreover, she did not like being a daughter, with its connotations of asexuality.[46] By 1869, only eight years after the marriage, Charlotte was rebuking her daughter-in-law for considering her life wasted and for complaining about Emma Stebbins's jealousy.[47]

Ned seems to have submitted happily enough to his adopted mother's plans, but he sometimes complained about his role in the Cushman-Crow affair. As early as June 1860, nearly a year before the wedding, he told Charlotte that Crow did not seem to "love him as a woman should love a man to marry him." In her letter to Crow relaying this statement, she explained, "He thinks you feel yourself superior to him—& though he acknowledged that you are so, he thinks that if you love him you would not show it."[48] Cushman smoothed matters over and was soon writing to Crow about Ned's improved appearance and manners since falling in love with her. After their marriage

Ned reverted to tactics used by his birth mother and grandmother. He criticized his aunt for spending her money on women friends, rather than on her family. If he and his new wife were to command respect, they needed a large house and servants. His kinship claims coincided with Cushman's own desire to give Emma Crow Cushman more signs of her love. Stebbins had her own money, but she might have noticed this shift in priorities away from supporting women artists. A lack of money had dominated Anne Lister's love life; now access to money began to dominate Charlotte Cushman's. It was Ned's only weapon.

Given the one-sidedness of the extant letters, it is hard to reconstruct how Emma Stebbins felt about the intrusion of Emma Crow into *her* marriage. Cushman wrote reassuringly to Crow that "Aunt Emma," as Stebbins was now denominated, "felt a little play of jealousy as she saw me holding your hand," but "I very soon settled Aunt Emma, who is as sweet as a summer morning."[49] Cushman repeated so often how "high, true, noble & self-sacrificing" Aunt Emma was in order to reassure herself as much as her young lover. Stebbins must have dreaded the marriage that brought Crow permanently into her life. Just as Emma Crow Cushman had never bargained on being called niece and daughter, so Emma Stebbins had never chosen to be called aunt. Metaphoric family names tightly bound the women into roles each found false to her true feelings. Cushman seemed unwilling to understand the painful positions into which she had forced the two women. Cushman was *not* the young Emma Crow Cushman's mother, Stebbins was *not* Crow Cushman's aunt, and Crow Cushman was *not* the daughter and niece of the couple; instead of encoding intimacy these words served to cover a much more difficult reality. They were lovers caught in a painful triangle. Only a few years earlier, the volatile Matilda Hays had angrily exploded at Cushman, bringing their relationship crashing down. Stebbins chose the more genteel option of illness, forcing Cushman to delay seeing Emma Crow Cushman and to admit "she [Stebbins] cannot bear to be separate from me."[50]

Stebbins continued to pursue her career, but she found work an insufficient anodyne in the face of Cushman's increasing involvement with her new biological family. Matters reached a crisis in the spring of 1865, just before Ned and his family joined them in Rome. Cushman had successfully lobbied friends in Washington to have Ned appointed to a government post in Rome, and she looked forward to their reunification. Stebbins's father arrived in Rome, furious with the way Ned and Emma Cushman had treated his family. Charlotte Cushman ruefully wrote Emma Crow Cushman on 11 May 1865 that Stebbins's "whole family utterly disapproved of her life with me—that they felt she was morally, socially, spiritually, physically injured by it, that *my* family, all of them, resented her being with me & did not hesitate to express themselves with regard to it in such a way that *they* had been obliged to give up going to see Mr & Mrs Edwin Cushman."[51] The wealthy Stebbinses were outraged that their daughter might be seen as taking Cushman's money, as Ned had implied to them. Their belief in the immorality of the theater mingled with these money matters. Cushman feared that her partner might suffer a permanent breakdown under the strain, and that she might "lose her if [she was] not careful to keep her mind free from anxiety & disturbances & the mortal terror of this possesses me as I see her pale wasted cheeks."[52]

Emma Stebbins's emotional and physical collapse forced Cushman to evaluate the damage she had done her partner and herself by trying to orchestrate the lives of her two lovers. In the same 11 May letter to Emma Crow Cushman, she further explained:

> When I first knew her & took the obligations of her life & future upon me I did not *know* of other cares which were to fall upon me—*of other loves & affections which were in store for me*—I was then free to promise—I have not kept my word too well—for I have had to reconcile too many things, trusted too much to others, & not preserved my life as much intact for her as I had promised to do when I took the responsibility of her life upon myself![53]

Cushman pleaded, "My darling child is coming to *help* me, is she not?" Now that Emma Crow was married to Ned, Cushman could no longer choose to give her up, even if she had wanted to (and there is no evidence that either woman ever seriously contemplated breaking off their relationship). And Emma Stebbins probably felt she could not return to her vindictive family. They were stuck with each other (and Ned was stuck with them). But Cushman could not play with familial roles as freely as she had thought. None of the three women could manage to sustain so many conflicting identities: mother–husband–ladie love–grandma; aunt–wife–spinster daughter; wife–little love–daughter–niece–little mother. The price Cushman paid in keeping two lovers was the loss of intimacy and confidence with both. Her genuine enthusiasm for the role of "Big Mamma" to her grandchildren may have been a welcome substitute for other, deeper emotional losses.

In the spring of 1869, Cushman was diagnosed with breast cancer. The next year, after surgery at Edinburgh failed, she left Rome permanently and returned to America with Emma Stebbins. By that time she had quarreled with Hosmer,[54] and many of her artist friends had left Rome to pursue their careers elsewhere. Ned and his family returned to St. Louis and the Crows; the Republicans were out of office, and he was unemployed. Even then Cushman did not choose her partner over her family. She built a summer home in fashionable Newport, Rhode Island, large enough for all of them. Sick as she was, Cushman returned to the stage, finding that it alone kept her mind off her advancing cancer. Neither Stebbins nor Crow Cushman ac-

companied her. As she ruefully wrote her friend Mary Lloyd, "a healthy pros-
ecution of my profession and I should have been saved all the pain mental
and bodily which I have ever known."[55] The pain of living with the two Em-
mas and an unsympathetic nephew could be admitted only obliquely. Acting,
which earned vast sums for Ned and his growing family, was a welcome escape from her difficult family situation. In Cushman's final months acting
once again became her one true love; she died in 1876. Emma Crow Cushman achieved her goal of living with her beloved "Ladie love"; she also had
five sons to carry on the Cushman name. But Emma Stebbins had the final revenge. In her book on Cushman, she mentions Hosmer only once in passing,
and the fervent passion of Emma Crow Cushman is reduced to the affection
of a daughter-in-law. Stebbins's memoir focuses on how Cushman had raised
the moral tone of the theater; ironically, it was a profession Stebbins had always disliked.

FROM "WORSHIPPER OF CELIBACY" TO "LITTLE HUBBY": HARRIET HOSMER AND LOUISA, LADY ASHBURTON

Harriet Hosmer's appearance and behavior drew attention, positive and negative. If a woman artist was always defined by her sex, Hosmer would exploit
this liability. The more unlike a woman she was, the more like an artist she
must be. Her near-contemporary Rosa Bonheur had built her career on this
strategy. But unlike Bonheur, Hosmer did not set up a model same-sex marriage. The young Hosmer distrusted any entanglements that might detract
from building her career. She may also have distrusted the dynamics between
the powerful, controlling Cushman and her partners. Hosmer presented
herself as a different kind of genius, a free spirit wedded to her art but ever
ready to participate in fun. Chaste flirtation with influential women and men
was her chief stratagem. She also professed to be immune to jealousy and refused to participate in the deeper emotions that swirled about the Rome community (fig. 5).

When she arrived in Rome, Hosmer quickly discovered that artistic success depended upon social contacts. But she also discovered that it took
money to maintain the social position she needed to win the attention of the
wealthy. Cushman thought Hosmer's father did not send her enough money
to maintain her foothold in the snobbish art world of Rome. She estimated
that Hosmer needed $1,500 a year. Half-fearful, half-bragging, the finan-
cially prudent Cushman worried that she might have to lend her friend
money that she would never see again.[56] Fortunately, Hosmer had a loyal patron in Wayman Crow, a St. Louis businessman and father of her school
friend, Cornelia, and of Cushman's admirer Emma. During her time in Eu-

Fig. 5. Harriet Hosmer, ca. 1867. Courtesy of the Schlesinger Library, Radcliffe Institute, Harvard University.

rope, Hosmer regularly wrote to Crow, whom she called "Pater," and to Cornelia, describing her life and artistic goals. She concluded one letter to Crow: "however successful I may become in my profession, it is to you that I owe all. . . . Every successful artist in Rome, who is living, or who has ever lived, owes his success to *his* Mr. Crow."[57] Many of her letters advised him on how best to forward her reputation in America. Crow responded by underwriting her first full-size statue, *Beatrice Cenci* (1856), ordered by the Mercantile Library of St. Louis. He also used his political influence to help her win her first public commission, a larger-than-life statue of Thomas Hart Benton, Missouri's famous senator (1860).

Commissions could be slow and erratic, but fortunately purchasing replicas was popular. Artists exhibited plaster models and works in progress in their studios, inviting visitors to order copies or commission an original work. Hosmer's best-loved sculpture was her 1855 *Puck*, a thirty-inch baby sprite that appealed to the contemporary taste for Shakespearean art and humor. With copies selling at first for $500 and later at above $800, Hosmer made an estimated $30,000 on that work alone. In 1859 the young Prince of

Wales bought a *Puck* for his rooms at Oxford, adding to her fame among the British aristocracy.[58] In 1860 Hosmer met Lady Marian Alford, who not only commissioned works but also became a close friend. Elizabeth Barrett Browning deliciously gossiped, "She knelt down before Hattty the other day & . . . placed on her finger . . . the most splendid ring you can imagine—a ruby in the form of a heart, surrounded and crowned with diamonds."[59] An expensive gift to an artist can be interpreted in many ways. Hosmer would be expected to see the ring as a form of insurance; when and if she needed money, she could sell it. Valuable jewelry was a more discreet means of supporting an artist than outright cash. Although Alford, who signed one letter to Hosmer "mother mentor," may have intended the ring to be an act of homage to a genius, the shape of the gift bespeaks something more intimate. Unfortunately, little information about Alford's personal life survives.

Hosmer's high spirits, practical jokes, and eccentric appearance gave her entrée into some of the best homes in England, where she summered in the 1860s and 1870s. Like a latter-day jester, she set about making dull house parties lively; admiring hostesses, including Alford, indulged her boyish antics and American ingenuousness. The role also protected her against possible allegations that she was husband-hunting among the wealthy and well born. Cornelia Crow Carr filled her biography with topical verse that Hosmer wrote for charades, plays, and other productions that whiled away the long evenings in an English country home. Hosmer reveled in her social success, writing back to the States, "I often say I am the richest woman in England without any trouble, for I have only to say, 'I am coming,' and all is ready."[60] Aristocratic friends continued to order replicas of her most famous statues and to house her during her longer and longer visits to England as her career began to fade in the 1870s.

Hosmer forestalled discussions of her sexual status by insisting on the priority of her career, on her genius. Early in her stay in Rome she wrote Wayman Crow:

> I am the only faithful worshipper of celibacy, and her service becomes more fascinating the longer I remain in it—even if so inclined, an artist has no business to be married—for a man it is all well enough, but for a woman on whom matrimonial duties and cares weigh more heavily, it is a great moral wrong, I think, for she must either neglect her profession or her family, becoming neither a good wife or a good artist. My ambition is to become the latter, so I wage eternal feud with the consolidating knot.[61]

Hosmer readily admitted to her friend Cornelia that she preferred open-ended flirtations, for "the pleasantest time after all is when lovers are howling for you."[62] "You are wicked," her teacher, John Gibson, teased her, in regard to her trifling with a Miss F——.[63] While living with Cushman and Hays, she began a flirtation with Hays. In the fall of 1854, Hays left Cushman in England to join Hosmer in Rome, but after four months she returned to London to patch up her relationship with Cushman.[64] Hosmer's very openness seemed to play with the public acceptance of women's homoerotic friendships, as if she were daring her friends to name something deeper than an entertaining dalliance. By drawing attention to the innocence of her flirtations, she deflected potential criticism. She readily told men and women that she was a flirt and not to be taken seriously, unlike her friends who were too involved with each other. Hosmer's easy manner defused censure that fell upon the notably more intense Hays and Cushman.

Hosmer kept her reputation as a free flirt until 1867, when at age thirty-seven she met the widowed Louisa, Lady Ashburton. Louisa was the youngest daughter of James and Mary Stuart Mackenzie. On both sides of her family flowed aristocratic Scottish blood. As her biographer wryly comments, "On their own territory the Mackenzies were omnipotent and Mary retained and passed on to her daughter the quite unconscious tendency of expecting others to submit readily to her wishes."[65] Louisa had a series of passionate friendships with women, as well as several unsuccessful heterosexual courtships, before marrying at thirty-three the elderly widower William Bingham Baring, the second Baron Ashburton. He died within five years, leaving her with one daughter, some 33,000 acres, and a title. Lady Ashburton spent the remainder of her life avidly collecting art and artists for her four homes. Her money and position freed her to do as she pleased, and the love of women pleased her, especially if they obeyed her behests. "Generous, violent, rash, and impulsive," was how a contemporary remembered her, and

> ever swayed by the impression of the moment, she was necessarily under the thumb of somebody. Bevies of impecunious artists hovered about her like locusts, trades-people made fortunes out of her and adventurers found her an easy prey. Everybody thought her enormously rich, because, with princely generosity, she threw large sums away for any object that caught her fancy. Though she not infrequently offended, she always fully and graciously retracted, and her smile, with the light in her dark eyes, under the straight brows, put me in mind of lightning amongst thunderclouds.[66]

For both Hosmer and Lady Ashburton this was the longest and most important relationship of their mature years. But they eschewed many of the conventions of a romantic friendship, preferring a hectic lifestyle, filled with travel, unfulfilled promises to meet, passionate encounters, and protestations of eternal love. They rarely lived together and seldom let their relationship interfere with other engagements. It was a pattern that a later generation of professional women such as Ethel Smyth adopted, but quite different from that of Cushman, who counted on the loyal presence of her partner whenever possible.

Through the late 1860s and 1870s, Lady Ashburton became Hosmer's major patron. As their personal relationship grew, so did their financial entanglements. Hosmer quickly assumed the role of "hubby" in her letters to "my *sposa*," advising Lady Ashburton on everything from the purchase of furniture and paintings to the payment of various servants. Both seemed very happy in their friendship, which included, as far as one can tell, a good deal of sexual pleasure. Hosmer speaks of folding her arms around Lady Ashburton and of hoping she will soon "tumble into my arms." She repeatedly sends her "a thousand kisses," signs her letters "Thine," and thinks often of sharing a bed, commenting on one occasion, "My beloved . . . I hope [you] will hereafter never take anything to bed with you in the shape of a hot [water] bottle except the zinc one—or me."[67] Other letters imply a long-standing practice of sleeping together, contrary to the aristocratic tradition of separate bedrooms: "My darling I embrace you—and whisper in your ear—you know what—and love me as I love you . . . I am off to bed, I wish I could take you with me. . . . What would I not do to have you in my arms to kiss you and tell you how dearly I love you."[68] Hosmer, deeply invested in her reputation for "merriment" and "good spirits," could even confess, "I must never tell you when I am a little off balance because the loving little heart always exaggerates my melancholy."[69]

Hosmer reworked family relationships to suit her new situation. She had long referred to her sculptures as her children. Around 1872 she proudly announced to her "sister" Cornelia Crow Carr that Lady Ashburton and her daughter were to winter with her: "I am about to prepare for an increase in family. You will be startled at that piece of news, which must be unexpected to all my friends: however there are various constructions to be placed upon these words."[70] Just as she called Cushman "Ma," Hosmer referred to the imperious Lady Ashburton, only three years older than herself, as "the dear mother," as well as wife and *sposa*. She did not call her "sister." She was self-conscious about the artificiality of gender roles in a lesbian relation, wooing Lady Ashburton with the promise, "when you are here I shall be a model wife (or husband whichever you like)."[71] Hosmer became practiced in the art of humorous cajolery, writing her: "Now I wonder what my Beloved is doing & where she is—& how she is. I thought the last letter sounded as if she wanted her Hubby to bully her a little. How I wish we could be together for a little coze just now & talk instead of writing."[72] Hosmer constructed a joking persona in her frequent references to herself as Hubby, perhaps to pretend she had more control over Lady Ashburton than she had or that she cared less about their relationship than she did.

Keeping Lady Ashburton's attention involved the creation of a closer family tie than marriage. Hosmer also pretended that she was the twin of Lady Ashburton's beloved daughter, Mary Florence, or Maysie (1860–1902). She staged a mock scenario in which she and the young girl shared equally in the worship of "the dear mother." Hosmer addressed Maysie as "Twinnie" and "Twinniekins," and signed letters to her "Your Twinnie" or "ever thy loving sister." She never failed to send her love to Twinniekins, but she reserved her most ardent expostulations for Ashburton, offering, for example, "Hugs to my Twinnisma. Kisses ever Thine," or "Give many hugs to her & keep the sweetest of kisses and the tightest of hugs for yourself."[73] This fantasy of being both hubby and daughter was perhaps meant to force her capricious lover to acknowledge their special connection. It also brought a witness, Maysie, into the relationship, as if to ratify their commitment. Moreover, Maysie accompanied her mother everywhere, and perhaps Hatty hoped to share this privileged position. No letters from Maysie to Hatty have survived, so we cannot know what she thought of being twinned with a middle-aged woman.

The fantasy of twinning with Maysie reached its apogee in a letter written in the mid-1870s. Hosmer happily announced that they would have more time together before she sailed for America: "This will enable us all to do Laocoon even more & now you must shape your plans to get here in time, for that is my very last chance of seeing you. . . . Are you better, busy & well enjoying your selves? I hope so & will fancy when you get this that we have already begun Laocooning & will feel my arms around you."[74] One of Rome's most famous late-Hellenistic statues seems an odd choice for Hosmer's impish allusion to sexual play. The large writhing figure of the dying priest Laocoön, strangled by an enormous snake, with his two much smaller sons caught in its sinuous grasp, has generally been read as a compassionate sculptural interpretation of pain and death. Hosmer's contemporaries recognized its greatness, though they worried about its lack of classical repose and the father's failure to help his sons.[75] But precisely because it lacked a clear moral and was so charged with energy, the *Laocoön* could symbolize Hosmer's sexual frustration, as well as dramatically illustrate the interdependence of "we three." The statue served to express and conceal a double love, her sexual love for Lady Ashburton and the twinned asexual love for Maysie. The two references to *Laocoön* refer both to "us all" and to a "you" that seems to include only herself and Lady Ashburton. Hosmer's ambiguous phrasing underscores the homoerotic play mid-Victorian women were free to indulge in. The all-female Victorian world did not separate close family relations and their potential for incest from flirtatious kissing and romping with friends. Intimacy, like sensuality, worked on an undefined continuum.

The acknowledgment of Lady Ashburton's maternal responsibilities helped Hosmer to deny any possible conflict between a private sexual love and a public friendship. Lady Ashburton presented a more circumspect version of their relationship. She wrote their mutual friend Lord Houghton in 1873: "We have had a most delightful winter with dear Miss Hosmer. . . . We three were made to live together. She is the kindest sister to me and is a charming friend."[76] But they lived together only intermittently after this halcyon winter. The implicit contradictions of Hosmer being a sister publicly and a daughter and a husband privately were never openly acknowledged in the surviving Ashburton-Hosmer correspondence. Hosmer's slangy, familiar style kept the assumption of a blood tie as fantasy. It also assumed an extraordinary class privilege for an American middle-class artist writing to a member of one of the oldest lineages in Britain.

At the time Hosmer met Lady Ashburton, she had recently completed her first male nude, *The Sleeping Faun*, in which a mischievous satyr ties the ends of a tigerskin loincloth to a tree trunk, capturing a beautiful sleeping young man with delicately pointed ears (fig. 6). It was one of the most admired works at the Dublin International Exhibition of 1865.[77] An American visitor commented: "If the chisel of Praxiteles has not been forever lost, Harriet Hosmer has found it. Under her hand the beautiful old myths live again."[78] Frances Power Cobbe, eager to help a friend, wrote of its "pure, sensuous, delight-brimming existence" as characteristic of work by a New World artist.[79] The narrative is overexplicit, but the compositional unity and sculptural finish are highly effective, and Hosmer's technical mastery helps to explain the praise the statue received. The faun's body is polished to a burnished smoothness, enhancing its youthful, even effeminate, appearance. *The Sleeping Faun* exemplified the ideals of neoclassicism in its combination of classical repose and sensual innocence. Although it would be an exaggeration to call the statue a self-portrait, it seems a summation of Hosmer's early role as a boyish scamp. Like a faun, she had successfully avoided heterosexuality for years by assuming the persona of the androgynous artist. But after 1867 she called herself hubby and seemed to acknowledge new, adult emotions and responsibilities. Could she make the shift?

At the height of her career, Hosmer seemed to lose her way. Lady Ashburton purchased a replica of *The Sleeping Faun* and paid for its promised companion, *The Waking Faun*. But Hosmer never finished that statue or several others her beloved commissioned. Was it because she partied too much, as Cushman thought, or had she outgrown the role that had initially brought her fame and fortune? Andrea Marini proposes that Hosmer could not finish *The Waking Faun* because she could not integrate the spiritual and the animal, and so created a "rather lazy young man" who breaks the illusion of sensual beauty created in the first statue.[80] There were also numerous technical problems. Hosmer wrote Wayman Crow in October 1866 that her workmen had placed the braziers too close to the drying plaster cast, so that the support-

Fig. 6. Harriet Hosmer, *The Sleeping Faun* (1865). Copyright 2002, Museum of Fine Arts, Boston.

ing framework burned, and "down came my statue and broke into I don't know how many pieces."[81] Fourteen months later, after a long hiatus in England with Lady Ashburton and other friends, she returned to work on the statue. She complained to Crow in December 1867 that she could not send the two Fauns to an exhibit in Paris because *The Waking Faun* was still unfinished, explaining that "somehow or other there are certain things that will take their time to grow and blossom, just like the trees and flowers."[82]

Hosmer's artistic problems only multiplied. She was especially proud of the larger-than-life-size *Pompeiian Sentinal*, exhibited in plaster in London during the summer of 1867, but she received no orders for marble versions. A few years later Hosmer again undertook the expense of sending a plaster statue to London. In the 1870s she entered an unnamed contest, telling Lady Ashburton, "I think I am an utter fool—an utter utter fool for taking all this trouble for it will come to nothing at all . . . I wish I knew whether Lord Houghton was on the committee for he would protect my interests if the model were selected." But the letter indicates real problems with her work, for Hosmer also told her, "I want Adolfo to print this note: 'The principal figure much injured in transmission,'" adding, "The fact is it was injured in the studio, but it sounds better as I have written it & will explain its spotty nature—will you see that it is done my darling?"[83] Hosmer also was unable to finish work for which she had been partially paid.[84] During the 1870s Hosmer wrote Lady Ashburton for substantial advances to pay her marble workers, and mentioned an Amazon and a Psyche soon to be turned into marble. Neither appears to have been completed.

In the meantime Lady Ashburton had her own concerns. Although her emotional life centered on women, Lady Ashburton could not resist bringing famous men into her orbit. She was quite successful in wooing Thomas Carlyle, who had adored the first Lady Ashburton. Robert Browning reluctantly accepted her Scottish hospitality on two occasions, in 1869 and 1871, only because his son liked deer hunting. Biographers differ in their interpretations of events, but sometime around 1871 either Browning suggested marriage to her because of its advantages for his son and he hoped for greater financial security or she suggested marriage in order to consolidate her reputation as a leading patron of the arts.[85] Whatever the case Browning quickly felt he had been imprudent and wrote to Lady Ashburton disavowing any marriage plans. It is difficult to separate facts from gossip because so many letters were destroyed, but it seems that Lady Ashburton would not give him up, and Browning became implacably opposed to her. The matter simmered for months, drawing the attention of Hosmer and other friends in Rome.

Hosmer decided that Browning had insulted her special friend and roundly vilified the man to their many acquaintances in Italy. But in doing so she "outed" her intimacy with Lady Ashburton by claiming a greater voice in Lady Ashburton's personal life than was thought proper. Hosmer's self-righteous anger stepped beyond the bounds of a respectable romantic friendship; she was guilty of publicly expressed jealousy, the very emotion she had earlier ridiculed in her friends. The Victorians were masters of the unspoken and the unsaid, happy to let odd sexual relations flourish as long as no one spoke openly about them. Browning was furious and blamed Hosmer for being a "cat's paw of Lady A." He indignantly defended himself to the Storys, his closest friends in Rome:

> Does Hatty instantly practise impertinence on any friend of hers who intends to make an ambitious or mercenary marriage? As for her devotion to Lady A: begetting this chivalrous ardour in her,—Lady A. has got plenty of friends quite as intimate, who never fancied for a moment that they were called on to fight her battles. . . . So, now, I have done with Hatty, for once & always. Had I believed stories about *her*, many a long year ago, and ordered her away from people's houses on the strength of them, I should have lost a friendship I used to value highly.[86]

Browning half-confesses that he had insulted Lady Ashburton. Probably, as biographers suggest, he felt guilty about his behavior and shifted the subject to Hosmer's social solecisms.[87] In the end Hosmer failed to convince the Storys and other friends who liked Browning that Lady Ashburton had been harmed. Her actions pushed an intimate friendship into sexual possessiveness—and no one would listen. The only result of her interference was a permanent rift with Browning and a humiliating sense of how limited her influence in the Rome community had become.

Hosmer was exceptionally fortunate that her personality, noted for its bluntness, coincided with the contemporary fascination for the eccentric artist. But a career built upon boyish independence and the patronage of well-placed friends, as Hawthorne had predicted, could not be sustained once tastes changed and she aged. In her forties Hosmer reminds one of nothing so much as Maisie Ward's description of the middle-aged son of Robert and Elizabeth Barrett Browning, who had grown "from Ganymede to Punchinello."[88] Although no photographs survive of the aging Hosmer, she herself complains of growing fat and indolent. The young Henry James commented as early as 1873 that Hosmer looked like a "remarkably ugly little grey-haired boy, adorned with a diamond necklace."[89] A stocky plump woman with short hair and pronounced mannerisms was far less attractive than the lively Ganymede that had burst upon the mid-Victorian scene. Hosmer continued to rent a studio in Rome for many years, but by the late 1870s she spent most of her time in England, working on a perpetual motion machine. The project was to consume the last thirty years of her life.

❋ Self-chosen communities have a limited life. For many years after the breakup of Cushman's home and Hosmer's departure for England, women continued to visit Rome as a special place that nurtured talented artists. But none made a mark in the Anglo-American art world. Women sculptors were no longer a novelty, and the romantic neoclassicism of Hosmer, Stebbins, and their contemporaries, including the snobbish William Wetmore Story, was dismissed as a product of a bygone, prudish age. The tableau of female independence, created by women journalists and essential to the fame of Cushman and Hosmer, became as obsolete as their art. They were dubbed ugly mannish women, dressed in outmoded mores. Although both Cushman and Hosmer courted negative gossip, they never pretended to be other than women who loved women, and they were accepted as such. Despite snickering comments about their "not niceness," these lesbians were among the most widely known and respected women artists of the nineteenth century.

PART II

Queer Relationships

Chapters 1 and 2 examined the lives and loves of very public women. The next two chapters cover much the same period, but deal with four examples of private lives affected by the law or religion. The women presented here had a limited public presence and little power. Yet they left evidence of how intimate desires may clash with social expectations, and so affect both heterosexual marriages and outwardly respectable same-sex friendships. The women of chapter 3 found themselves thrust under the eye of the law, their personal language and behavior subject to searching interpretation. What had seemed like a familiar romantic friendship looked different, suspect, even sinful in court. Although the legal testimony included detailed descriptions of intimate acts, no one could or would define what was amiss. The women discussed in chapter 4 chose to live under the eye of a male God, seeking divine acceptance of their intertwined spiritual and erotic love. Friends and family recognized and accepted these women and their complicated emotional lives. But no one looked too closely; even in the confessional, lesbian sexuality remained an elusive concept. The language of religious love concealed as much as it revealed.

Chapter 3 dissects two legal cases, one for libel and the other for divorce, each of which exposed the possibility of sexual improprieties. No laws constrained women's love for each other, but social mores could not be flouted by those who needed the wealthy and powerful. In the first case, *Miss Marianne Woods and Miss Jane Pirie against Dame Helen Cumming Gordon* (1811–19), allegations of "venereal practices" between two teachers destroyed their school and their intimate friendship. The source of these accusations was Jane Cumming, the illegitimate half-Indian granddaughter of Dame Cumming Gordon. Her foreign presence encouraged everyone in the school to scrutinize the teachers' relationship, turning the seemingly natural into the unnatural. In order to keep the public ignorant, the case was tried in secret; fortunately the printed trial transcripts survive. The early-nineteenth-century Scottish judges were baffled by the unexpected possibility that women together in bed might mean more than a warm friendship. Working from the accepted models of male homosexuality and "Oriental practices," a majority concluded that Englishwomen could never have committed the alleged offense.

The second case, *Admiral Henry Codrington against Helen Smith Codrington and Colonel David Anderson* (1863–64), casts a light on a cross-age friendship involving a high-spirited wife and an overardent tomboy. In 1857 the admiral expelled his wife's friend Emily Faithfull (1835–95) from the house and gave his brother a sealed packet explaining why. Helen Codrington (1828–?) responded in 1863 by claiming her husband had entered her bedroom six years earlier and attempted to rape Faithfull. This allegation took center stage, rather than her possible adultery with Colonel Anderson. The trial forced observers to consider homoeroticism within the context of heterosexuality, raising the possibility of female sexual pleasure independent of male initiative. The contents of the sealed packet were never revealed, leading observers to speculate about the women's friendship, based on the appearance, behavior, and reputation of Faithfull. As in the earlier case, no conclusion was possible about precisely what had happened between two women. In a final section I examine Faithfull's defense of her love for the "wayward" Helen Codrington in her novel *Changes upon Changes* (1868), in which she cast herself as a respectable, poor man. This gender inversion normalized their passion and yet revealed her masculine role in their friendship. By the mid-1860s the public had become increasingly aware of and interested in the conditions that led women to deviate from gendered norms. I briefly conclude with an examination of how sophisticated men and women at the end of the nineteenth century discussed lesbianism, in contrast to the willed silence of an earlier generation.

Chapter 4 turns to a different male institution, formal religion. It examines same-sex love within two deeply patriarchal institutions, the Church of England and the Roman Catholic Church. The women in this chapter welcomed the spiritual discipline of these institutions, as well as their promise of a divine love that made earthly love complete. The love of women, "gifts from God," sustained Mary Benson (1842–1918) throughout her unhappy marriage to Edward White Benson (1829–96). The Codrington and Benson marriages were already in trouble before each wife became involved with another woman. But same-sex friendship called attention to an unnamable threat to social norms. I call these relationships "queer triangles" to draw attention to the ways in which women eluded the power of older, patriarchal men. Helen Codrington may have been involved with Emily Faithfull only briefly to break the boredom of her life, but same-sex love was fundamental to Mary Benson's entire life. Outwardly she was the devout wife of an ambitious Anglican clergyman. She cared for six children as her husband rose rapidly in the ranks to become, in 1883, Archbishop of Canterbury, head of the Church of England. At the same time Mary Benson's emotional and erotic life centered on a series of women friends. As a devout Christian she struggled to turn these "carnal" relations into spiritual opportunities. Mary's happy love life helped to stabilize her difficult marriage, leaving both partners happier with each other.

In the second half of chapter 4, I focus on the conversion of two English-women, Katharine Bradley (1846–1914) and Edith Cooper (1862–1913), to Roman Catholicism in 1907. This aunt-and-niece couple, who wrote poetry and verse tragedies under the pseudonym Michael Field, enjoyed a brief period of fame in the 1890s. But by the time they converted, thanks to works published in small, expensive editions, they were virtually unknown; conversion further isolated them from the mainstream literary world. Although Catholicism brought the women new happiness, it broke their close intellectual and emotional harmony. They no longer collaborated in writing poetry together; each separately explored the mystery of the Crucifixion and human suffering. Throughout their lives Bradley and Cooper had created a fictive male principal to ratify their unique female unity. Their male pseudonym claimed and disclaimed the privileges of male authorship. They sought male poets and critics to endorse their creative genius, and used Cooper's father and later their dog, Whym Chow, to confirm their love relationship. These witnesses became participants in emotionally charged triangles that did not disrupt, but rather reinforced, the loving cross-age dyad of the two women. As Catholics they created their final triangle with God the Father, who symbolically crowned their spiritual unity.

3   *"They Venture to Share the Same Bed"*

POSSIBLE IMPOSSIBILITIES

In his 1811 summing-up of the Edinburgh trial, *Miss Marianne Woods and Miss Jane Pirie against Dame Helen Cumming Gordon*, Lord Meadowbank warned his fellow judges of the public's stake in their keeping the details of the case secret:

> The virtues, the comforts, and the freedom of domestic intercourse, mainly depend on the purity of female manners, and that, again, on their habits of intercourse remaining as they have hitherto been,—free from suspicion. Dreading the baleful effects on domestic morals, which even surmises of such a litigation as the present must produce . . . your Lordships . . . have taken every precaution within your power, though necessarily with small hopes of success, to confine this cause by the walls of the Court, and keep its subject and its investigations unknown to general society.[1]

In effect Lord Meadowbank argued that male experts had a special duty to preserve the innocence of white upper-class British women. Although the Scottish trial might be kept from the general public, the families (and servants) of the aristocratscy who knew Dame Cumming Gordon surely gossiped among themselves. Once the sexual grounds of the trial had been mentioned, suspicions clung to all those involved, whether guilty or innocent. Women together, especially in bed together—a crucial episode in each of the examples discussed in this chapter—were not above suspicion. The legal profession struggled to define, or to leave carefully undefined, passion between women. Recognition and denial went hand in hand.

A trial is an eruption, in which private acts become public, and witnesses are sworn to speak nothing but the truth. The truth, including the concept of female sexual innocence, proved to be exceptionally elusive in the two trials discussed in this chapter. Men in positions of authority confronted an impossible challenge: how could one know whether the purity of body and mind of young, upper-class women was unsullied? Knowledge itself could corrupt, giving innocent girls ideas that they might act upon or that might inflame latent desires. Far safer was ignorance. At the heart of each trial lies not so much a secret as an unnamable possibility. Anne Lister and Charlotte Cushman had cannily exploited the impossibility of naming same-sex erotic relations in respectable, public circumstances. Both women knew what they were after and had secrets to conceal. But what if the evidence of actual sexual practices was utterly denied or suppressed? The strategic ignorance of women such as Harriet Hosmer or Emma Crow Cushman was replaced by sworn ignorance, by an avowal of absolute innocence. Yet neither the legal profession nor observers believed the parties to these suits. Did all women have something to hide?

Testimony in both trials rested on what was heard, felt, and surmised, rather than seen—the bed containing two women became unaccountably empty whenever the legal eye gazed upon it. Ironically, in an effort to ensure the ignorance of women, men kept themselves ignorant. The lively languages of upper-class pornography and street slang were excluded from the legal debates. The conservative legal profession also disregarded medical or scientific labels in both trials. Gender inversion, hinted at by knowing friends and servants, was ignored. Only at the end of the nineteenth century did educated men and women begin to read and apply scientific and medical theories about nonnormative sexual practices. One of their principal objects of study was the innocent adolescent led astray by an older woman, the focus of these two trials. Throughout much of the nineteenth century, respectable men and women struggled to articulate in public uncertain distinctions and practices— sexual acts that were all too easy to imagine, but impossible to accept.

ROMANTIC FRIENDSHIP ON TRIAL: MARIANNE WOODS AND JANE PIRIE

The trial *Miss Marianne Woods and Miss Jane Pirie against Dame Helen Cumming Gordon* demonstrates the definitional uncertainty at the core of lesbian studies.[2] A cornerstone of lesbian history is a libel case brought by two teachers who adamantly denied any carnal knowledge—of each other, of their students, or of men. We know nothing about them beyond the bulky court documents. A few letters between them and to friends and relatives were read into their petition. We do not know what they looked like, aside from a casual remark that they were not especially good looking. Their invisibility was confirmed by the decision to hold the trial behind closed doors. Press coverage was limited to simple announcements. Of necessity, analysis of this trial focuses on male responses to inconceivable sexual allegations. There is no civic drama here, no spectacle in which the main characters publicly enact different narratives

of the events under consideration. The intricate public response to the Oscar Wilde trials that Ed Cohen has deconstructed is simply absent.[3] The lawsuit embodies the denial and silence that characterize so much lesbian history. It also illustrates the complex connections among sexual expression,
economics, and social status for single women.

The case is easily summarized.[4] Marianne Woods and Jane Pirie met in
Edinburgh in 1802 and quickly became close friends. Woods taught elocution and rhetoric, and Pirie worked as a governess. They opened a boarding
school for young ladies in 1809, hoping to unite their work and love under
one roof. Lady Cumming Gordon, heartbroken at the death of her son, had
brought his illegitimate daughter from India. At first she sent her to a school
to learn a trade, but after some eight years, she decided to acknowledge the
girl and to introduce her to genteel society. In the fall of 1809, she placed
the half-Indian Jane Cumming in the new school, so that she might gain the
appropriate manners and education. In addition, this influential noblewoman
recommended the school to her friends. Her patronage ensured the success
of the venture. Within months Misses Pirie and Woods had nearly reached
their capacity with nine boarders and five day students. But Jane Cumming
was unhappy with the school discipline; at sixteen she may also have longed
for the promised pleasures of high society. In November 1810 she accused
her teachers of having sexual relations while she shared a bed with Miss Jane
Pirie. Lady Cumming Gordon instantly removed her granddaughter from
the school and persuaded the other parents to remove their children. She
also refused to offer any explanation for her actions.

In May 1811 the two schoolteachers sued Lady Cumming Gordon for libel. In response she charged Woods and Pirie with "indecent and criminal
practices." The financially ruined teachers persisted for over nine years in
their legal efforts to receive compensation. Everyone acknowledged that neither would ever be able to teach again in Edinburgh, whatever the results of
the trial. They were found guilty by the first panel of judges by a vote of 4–
3; they appealed and were found innocent by the same margin of one vote in
1812. Lady Cumming Gordon then appealed to the House of Lords. When
she finally lost in 1819, she delayed payment of their claim. Confusion, contradictions, and vacillation among the male judges underscore their putative
legal authority and their actual weakness in enforcing gendered sexual norms.
The two women, their friendship broken, disappear from history without our
knowing if they ever received compensation. What became of Jane Cumming is also unknown.

The legal case turned on two irreconcilable questions: could an innocent
child of sixteen have imagined or seen "that very abominable crime," or could
two respectable women have committed the crime in the presence of a child?
As was common at the time, teachers and pupils slept together in dormito-

ries. Miss Pirie was head of one dormitory and slept with Jane Cumming. Miss Woods was head of the other and slept with Janet Munro, the next-oldest student in the school. Jane Cumming was very explicit about what she had heard, though she had seen nothing. She testified under oath that while sharing Miss Pirie's bed,

> She has been wakened different times by their kissing and whispering. [She] heard Miss Pirie say one night, "You are in the wrong place," and Miss Woods said, "I know," and Miss Pirie said, "Why are you doing it then?" and Miss Woods said, "For fun"; and she wakened one night with a whispering, and heard, Miss Pirie say, "O do it darling," and Miss Woods said, "Not to night," . . . and then Miss Pirie pressed her again to come in, and she came in, and she lay above Miss Pirie: Then Miss Woods began to move, and she shook the bed, and she heard the same noise [like] putting one's finger in the neck of a wet bottle. [She] asked Miss Pirie what was shaking the bed so, and Miss Pirie answered, "Nothing"; . . . and she felt Miss Woods move over to the other side of the bed.[5]

On another occasion, she claimed, Miss Woods had asked Miss Pirie to wait until the holidays to come to her bed, and Miss Pirie had replied, "O Mary-Anne don't ask me for you know I could not keep it if I were to promise."[6] The testimony of Janet Munro corroborated that of her friend. Miss Munro swore that Miss Pirie regularly came at night to lie on top of Miss Woods, and that she too had on occasion complained about the shaking of the bed because it prevented her from sleeping.[7] Her details seemed persuasive, and the convictions of the powerful Dame Cumming Gordon were not easily dismissed. The judges struggled with this shocking testimony, unable to believe that "wherever two young women form an intimacy together, and that intimacy ripens into friendship, if ever they venture to share the same bed, that becomes a proof of guilt."[8]

Everyone agreed that the women were devoted friends. In a birthday note accompanying the gift of a Bible, Pirie wrote, "dearest, *earthly* friend, never open it, without thinking of her who would forego all friendships, but her God's to possess yours."[9] Lord Woodhouselee called this *"the language of enthusiasm,* but it is the enthusiasm of a pure, a pious, and a virtuous mind."[10] His emphatic statement appears to have been as much to convince himself as his fellow judges. Just before the school broke up, the two teachers were fighting bitterly over both the running of the school and the role of Miss Woods's widowed aunt. Marianne Woods had lived with her aunt and uncle from the age of fifteen; when she opened the school with her friend, she felt obliged to house her meddlesome aunt. Jane Pirie had put up the bulk of the money, but early advertisements indicated that the school was run solely by Mrs. and Miss Woods. As Lillian Faderman notes, Janet Munro was convinced the two teachers must be lovers because they quarreled so much.[11] Lord Wood-houselee found a different interpretation: "what could be more natural, than that Miss Woods should, after parting with her aunt, endeavour to quiet those suspicions of her friend, by coming to her bed-side, lying down with her in bed, soothing her with endearing expressions, kissing and caressing her, even with ardour and fondness?"[12] Clearly upper-class men accepted a good deal of warm affection between women friends as "natural."

The judges explored virtually every reason why the women could not have had sexual relations: to do so was impossible for Christian ladies; it was economic and moral insanity; it was physically impossible because they used no "tools." Lord Meadowbank, having spent several years in Paris and India, considered himself the most worldly of the judges. He admitted that

> women of a peculiar conformation, from an elongation of the *clitoris*, are capable both of giving and receiving venereal pleasure, in inter-course with women, by imitating the functions of a male in copulation [It] is also true enough, that as a provocative to the use of the male, women have been employed to kindle each others' lewd appetite. Nor is it to be disputed that by means of tools, women may artificially ac-complish the venereal gratification.[13]

But then, through a series of torturous examples, he achieved an act of willed ignorance, denying that the events could ever have happened: "I state as the ground of my incredulity . . . the important fact, that the imputed vice has been hitherto unknown in Britain."[14] The act of identifying same-sex prac-tices did not so much distance them as make them loom in the male imagi-nation as a real possibility. In the process of insisting on the innocence of British women, Lord Meadowbank had recourse to libertine knowledge. Since the women were not tribades or prostitutes, they could not be guilty of a lesser offense, which did not exist anyway. Yet an elongated clitoris, sex be-tween women as a preamble to arouse debauched men, and the use of a dildo were all described in John Cleland's *Memoirs of a Woman of Pleasure* (1748–49), which continued to be reprinted well into the nineteenth century.[15]

Forced to explain the inexplicable, the more conscientious of the judges found themselves considering the only available sexual language, pornogra-phy. After the testimony of their key witnesses appeared inadequate, Dame Cumming Gordon's lawyers provided proof of the practice of tribadism, drawing attention to examples from the classics and the Bible, as well as from Diderot's infamous *The Nun* (1760). All their examples were left in their origi-nal tongue, as if there were no words in English to bring an acknowledged prac-tice out of the world of licentiousness and into the world of the law. In the pe-tition submitted for the appeal, the counsel for Misses Woods and Pirie spent considerable time demonstrating the differences between these examples and

QUEER RELATIONSHIPS / 66 /

the two innocent teachers. The judges were urged to dismiss evidence drawn from "obscene books" because "the human imagination" can "*invent* modes of gratifying the venereal passion, having no existence in nature."[16] As the judges struggled to name acts that no respectable woman should know about, much less practice, they dismissed bawdy literature as irrelevant to the case.

How, then, were they to understand the teachers' romantic friendship? The counsel for the defense insisted, "it was the general opinion in the school that the pursuers [plaintiffs] caressed and fondled each other more than was consistent with ordinary female friendship."[17] But what was ordinary female friendship? As we saw in chapter 1, Anne Lister took full advantage of flirting and fondling, going well beyond ordinary friendship in her caresses. Lord Woodhouselee pointed out to his fellow judges that both teachers suffered from rheumatism, so phrases such as "Do it my dear" and "You are in the wrong place" could as easily refer to massaging a painful back as it could "un-natural" and "improbable" conduct.[18] Was it possible to attribute "unnatural lewdness" if one woman asked another into her bed on a cold Scottish night so that they might discuss the day's events in reasonable comfort? To answer this question in the affirmative strained the credulity of Lord Gillies, who rhetorically asked: "Are we to say that every woman who has formed an early intimacy, and has slept in the same bed with another, is guilty? Where is the innocent woman in Scotland?"[19] As Lisa L. Moore has argued, the curious effect of insisting on middle-class women's purity and virtue made sexual agency in women utterly unnatural, complicated, and devious.[20] If sexual desire was unnatural in women, then any evidence of it became a sign of impurity. Rather than seeing women's virtue as unproblematic, the judges were forced to conclude that, like women's sexuality, it was something complicated and unreliable. Neither innocence nor knowledge could be assumed. Perhaps all women were liars.

The judges who found the teachers guilty presented shorter speeches or notes than those who supported them. They seem to have felt no need to explain their decision, however shocking its implications. Innocent girls, they believed, could never provide such precise particulars if they had not seen and heard something. Lord Robertson could not believe "that two young girls of sixteen, the age of innocence, of purity and of candour, have entered into a most abominable conspiracy, to ruin the fortunes, and to overwhelm with infamy two young women, from whom they have received no injury."[21] He concluded that no motive for revenge had been given. Moreover, Miss Munro proved her innocence when she swore she had not understood what she heard until she had spoken with her nursery maid. He found "the alleged physical impossibility of the pursuers having committed that offense" to be irrelevant, and concluded that if the teachers had "imitated . . . the action of a man and a woman *in coitu:* then, whether it was attended with complete gratification or not, it was an act of gross immorality and shameful indecency."[22] His argument, however, brought to the surface yet another potential hazard: women could give each other erotic pleasure without coming to orgasm, so perhaps their frequent and socially accepted caresses might mean more than anyone suspected.

The judges who found the teachers innocent focused on two quite distinct reasons: accepted norms of behavior and the physical impossibility of the act. Lord Woodhouselee, for example, based his argument upon the "*criterion of common sense,*" and insisted:

> It is a very improbable supposition, that two persons confessedly possessed of good sense and a sound understanding, who knew, that in the line of life they had chosen, their bread absolutely depended on their virtuous, decent, and exemplary conduct, while the slightest departure from such conduct, was utter ruin and disgrace, should blindly and madly embrace that ruin, and sacrifice their means of subsistence, their welfare, character, every thing, for some beastly sensual gratification, which must with them have outweighed every other earthly consideration.[23]

Lord Meadowbank agreed and suggested that the two teachers could easily have slept together in one bed without arousing suspicion; why then did they sleep apart with the two oldest students? Lord Gillies relied on the habits of respectable women, which included "perfectly innocent and natural, but perfectly common" intimate friendships. Like the other judges, he returned to the bed, the guilty site, and concluded, "God forbid that that time should ever arrive when any lady in Scotland, standing at the side of another's bed in the night-time, should be suspected of guilt, because she was invited into it."[24]

The judges ignored the erotic possibilities of transvestism because the information came from servants. In spite of the defense's best efforts, they also passed over the information that a pregnant servant had dressed in men's clothes "to amuse the young ladies" on the night of Miss Woods's birthday.[25] Doubtless for Dame Cumming Gordon, the event proved both the class and the sexual disorder of the boarding school. The servants suspected the teachers' friendship and defined it in terms of gender inversion. According to the three pupils who testified, the nineteen-year-old servant, Charlotte Whiffin, "spoke very often" to them about the teachers, hinting at improprieties. She told Jane Cumming and Janet Munro that once she had peeped through a keyhole at the two teachers lying side by side on the drawing-room couch. Charlotte Whiffin assumed that they could not sexually satisfy each other and suggested to one of the pupils, "They might as well take a man at once."[26] Janet Munro's nursery maid, Mary Brown, told her, "they were worse than beasts, and deserved to be burnt if it was true." When asked to elaborate, she explained, "It is a very wicked thing, and Miss Pirie certainly is a man."[27] For the two servants, passion between women was possible but depended on one of the women looking and acting like a man. However, neither teacher appears to have looked particularly masculine, though efforts were made to pin this label on the more volatile and outspoken Jane Pirie.

In the witness box Charlotte Whiffin claimed she had never seen her two mistresses doing anything improper, and that she had not spoken to any of the students about their behavior. Her testimony was so at variance with what "the young ladies" said that the judges briefly considered arresting her for perjury. They certainly were not going to take her testimony seriously. Mary Brown, in turn, was dismissed as giving hearsay evidence, filtered through the imagination first of Jane Cumming and then of Janet Munro. Neither Lord Meadowbank nor Lord Robertson, on opposite sides in the case, believed Whiffin, for "falsehood is the ordinary vice of persons in her line of life."[28] They assumed that servants lied to protect themselves, and that they could not be sexually unaware. But Miss Woods and Miss Pirie catered to an upper-class clientele, and so both they and their pupils were held to a higher standard of honesty—and of sexual ignorance.

The judges, regardless of how they voted, distrusted the instigator of the case and concluded that Jane Cumming, having spent her early years in India, was guilty of imagining practices that could only occur in a hot country. She could not be held to the same standards as a British woman and therefore might be lying. In the appeal the judges in favor of Misses Pirie and Woods resolved their difficulties over who was innocent by blaming Jane Cumming. No one, starting with her grandmother, seems to have asked whether she might have started a rumor in order to be expelled from the hated school. Jane Cumming, stereotyped as a lustful, illegitimate half-breed, provided a convenient scapegoat. The sexualized colonial body can stand in for the deviant sexual desires of British women. In this trial the judges seem to have gone further: these desires were confronted, made foreign, and then denied as existing in Britain. In effect middle-class women could not be capable of lesbian sex and remain British.

Whatever Jane Cumming may have intended when she made her accusations, she ruined an already fragile relationship. But after her detailed testimony about acts that no innocent girl could know, Cumming would forever be connected to the two teachers. All three were permanently labeled guilty of sinful sexual knowledge. This queer all-female triangle is emblematic of later lesbian situations: an all-female community, an inexperienced girl, and two seemingly respectable women.[29] Outside forces in the form of Lady Cumming Gordon lay waste the fragile institution and its network of volatile relationships. The quarreling teachers were never able to regain their reputations or their friendship; both were shattered by a case they ostensibly won. In spite of the detailed testimony, we can never know the true nature of their friendship. But what richer image do we need than an invitation to join a beloved friend in bed on a cold night?

THE CODRINGTON DIVORCE TRIAL AND EMILY FAITHFULL

The secret trial in Edinburgh destroyed three lives, but it had no impact on either the legal system or social mores. By the 1860s, however, middle-class single women were a recognized social problem. The struggle to broaden their economic opportunities went hand in hand with increased attention to women's friendships. The widely publicized 1864 Codrington divorce trial exemplifies many of the mid-century public debates about the responsibilities of marriage, conditions of divorce, and the position of single women. Because it involved a well-known feminist, Emily Faithfull (fig. 7), as well as a distinguished admiral, it drew more attention than most lawsuits. Around the same time that Emma Crow became involved with Charlotte Cushman, Emily Faithfull was involved with Helen Smith Codrington. As all four women discovered, heterosexual marriage, with its public recognition and social obligations, was a strong impediment to same-sex intimacy. But no letters survive between Faithfull and Codrington, and their friendship ended with the divorce trial. And the trial yielded only contradictory evidence, concealing their intimate friendship from the legal gaze.

Marriage represents heterosexuality more forcibly than any other public institution; support for it, as well as attacks upon it, reveals larger social concerns about masculinity and femininity. There was a lively public debate about what marriage should be throughout the nineteenth century. The problems of Caroline Norton, whose husband falsely accused her of adultery and misappropriated her money, were widely publicized by her and the press in the 1840s and 1850s.[30] The failures of the aristocracy to live up to the publicly espoused norms of domestic life became a source of embarrassment for conservatives and of ridicule for radicals. Everyone agreed that many marriages were not consonant with the professed ideals of society, but how to reform the institution was contentious.[31] Feminists thought that easier divorce would mean the loss of economic and social security for women. Clergymen feared the undermining of traditional community values if divorce was made cheap and accessible to the poor. Legislators spoke movingly of the property rights of the husband. The first Matrimonial Causes Act (1857) enshrined the sexual double standard: men could obtain divorce for simple adultery, but women could sue only for adultery combined with bigamy, incest, desertion, or cruelty.[32] If a man condoned his wife's adultery, he could not sue later for divorce, the situation of George Henry Lewes (chapter 5).

Fig. 7. Emily Faithfull, ca. 1875. By courtesy of the National Portrait Gallery, London.

Henry John Codrington (1808–77) came from a distinguished military family; his father had been an admiral in the Napoleonic Wars, and his brother was a general. The largely favorable *Dictionary of National Biography* entry describes him as an officer who spent most of his career protecting British trade in the Mediterranean. His discipline was so notorious that he was among "the most unpopular men in the service. . . . It was quite possible that tact was occasionally wanting."[33] At six foot five inches, his physical size must have been an imposing confirmation of his habits of authority, order, and rule. In 1849 in Florence, Italy, at the age of forty-one, he married Helen Jane Smith, aged twenty-one, the daughter of a gentleman long resident in that city. We know her personality only indirectly. During the divorce trial her barrister felt called upon to explain her late hours and love of entertainment as a product of her Italian upbringing: "Her manners were not formed in the school of English society; she was more lively, or, perhaps, more what might be called frivolous than most English women. She was also artless, and free, reckless of what she said or did, not sufficiently attentive to the opinion of others as to her conduct, but guileless and without deceit."[34] The middle-aged captain had probably been enthralled by her vivaciousness amidst the warmth and ease of the small English community in Florence. Since the Renaissance the

English had identified Italy with sexual disorder; in the divorce trial her reck-lessness of speech appeared to signify something more than a free manner.

When her husband was ordered to the Mediterranean during the Crimean War, Helen Codrington invited Emily Faithfull to live with her. Faithfull, the youngest daughter of a Surrey clergyman, insisted that they were friends, and that she had never been a companion, with its connotations of financial de-pendency. She was certainly from a more modest background than the Cod-ringtons, but the class difference was less than that between Lady Ashburton and Hosmer. She lived with Helen Codrington from 1854 to 1857, and their friendship continued up until the trial. Soon after leaving the Codrington household, Faithfull met several leading feminists, including Bessie Rayner Parkes, Adelaide Proctor, and Jessie Boucherett, who together founded the Society for Promoting the Employment of Women in 1859. Through these contacts she met members of the Rome community discussed in chapter 2, including Matilda "Max" Hays. From the beginning feminism was associated with close female friendships. Bessie Rayner Parkes in the 1850s had been so deeply involved with Barbara Leigh Smith that her father worried about whether she would ever marry.[35] In 1860 Faithfull founded the Victoria Press, employing women as compositors; in spite of the opposition of the printing trades unions, the press flourished. A few years later she began the feminist *Victoria Magazine*.[36] After the divorce trial she moved to Manchester and con-tinued to write, publish, and lecture on behalf of feminist issues. She visited the United States three times in the 1870s and 1880s, and wrote for the British press about American feminism; these essays were published as *Three Visits to America* in 1884.

The Codringtons' marriage seems to have been in trouble long before Faithfull moved in. According to her testimony, "Generally they did not agree—they were in the habit of quarreling. In the first week of my acquain-tance with her she said she was not happy, and sometimes they would not speak to each other for a week."[37] Henry Codrington dated his marital diffi-culties to a later period. He asserted that his marriage had been happy until he returned from the Crimea in August 1856, when "he found reason to com-plain of his wife's conduct in some small matters, and [though] some slight differences arose between them, nothing of any serious importance oc-curred, and the Admiral had not the slightest reason for suspecting her of any misconduct." But then: "Miss Faithfull, who had been his wife's companion during his absence, still continued an inmate in his house. From time to time Mrs. Codrington had proposed that she should sleep with Miss Faithfull, stating that she was subject to asthma, and in the spring of 1857, she posi-tively and absolutely declined again to enter the same bed with the Admiral, and she insisted on having a separate bed and sleeping with Miss Faithfull."[38] At this juncture Codrington had brought in his wife's parents. Faithfull was dismissed from the house with the "full concurrence of Mr. Smith," and a sealed packet explaining why was placed in the hands of General Sir William Codrington, his older brother. Although Helen sought a separation order, she found that she did not have sufficient cause. Faithfull moved on to her feminist work, but stayed in touch with her friend. Henry Codrington was still caught in a queer triangle that paved the way for further marital difficulties.

Soon after these events of 1857, Codrington was promoted and sent as admiral superintendent to Malta. His wife accompanied him. While he was busy with his administrative duties, she flirted and socialized. When the Codringtons returned to London in 1863, they were on the verge of breaking up. The admiral hired a detective to track his wife, suspecting her friendships with two officers she had met in Malta. He also stole her desk, hoping to find incriminating letters. Although his evidence was weak, he filed for divorce on 14 November 1863, charging his wife with "having committed adultery with David Anderson and divers other persons." After the usual legal skirmishing, the case came before the Court for Divorce and Matrimonial Causes on 29 July 1864. The chief co-respondent, Col. David Anderson (1821–1909), had commanded a battalion stationed in Malta.[39] Immediately after he returned from that posting, he became engaged to a Scots cousin, perhaps to protect himself from an unhappy wife. Those directly involved in a divorce case could not appear in court and be cross-examined or respond to witnesses, and only a legal summary of the court record was kept. We know about the trial through the legal summary, newspaper accounts, and gossip among friends; we never hear the voices of those most closely concerned. Nevertheless, the case provides a remarkable example of patriarchal power and the perils of women's sexual independence.

With the help of her solicitors, Helen Codrington constructed the best possible response. She began by insinuating collusion, and then accused her husband of depriving her of the household keys and of forbidding her access to her closest friends, both female and male. He had treated her "with the greatest neglect, never appearing in Public with her, prohibiting her leaving the House without his express authority and preventing her having any control or authority over her Servants and her children."[40] By denying his wife command over the domestic sphere, the admiral was guilty of breaking the protocols that underwrote the ideology of separate spheres. By refusing to escort her in public, he failed to fulfill the duties of his social class.[41] Codrington belongs to a familiar fictional stereotype: the older, despotic husband gripped by jealousy, unable to control his attractive wife. All of his actions, though unfortunate, were familiar to the divorce court.

But then Helen Codrington accused her husband of serious sexual transgressions. He had refused her access to his bed and practiced birth control: "On one occasion when she had attempted to go into the Admiral's bedroom, he had removed her to her own room and had hurt her in doing so," and on another occasion he had advised a fellow officer to "follow my example and have no more" children.[42] But most damaging was her claim that he had entered the bed of her friend, Emily Faithfull, some six years earlier: "One night in October 1856, while she was occupying the same bedroom with Miss Emily Faithfull, in the house where she was residing with her husband in Eccleston-Square, he had come into her bedroom and attempted to take improper liberties with Miss Faithfull."[43] In the spring of 1864, Emily Faithfull signed an affidavit testifying that Admiral Codrington had attempted to rape her. This accusation brought to public attention three characters: the mannish young woman, the tyrant husband, and the married woman who claimed the freedom to choose her own friends, women and men.

The admiral's prime evidence was read out in court the first day of the trial. It included the draft of an undated letter without a salutation or address that had been found in Helen's stolen desk. In the letter, seemingly written to David Anderson, Helen pleaded with him to rethink his precipitous engagement and suggested, "I can meet you at 10, Taviton-street, for I know Miss Faithfull will gladly effect anything towards my happiness and future peace of mind."[44] Faithfull in the meantime had fled to avoid a subpoena to appear as a witness. In the eyes of some of her oldest political allies, she had fatally compromised herself. They believed that she had been an accessory to an adulterous affair. Why would a respectable woman help a friend carry out a heinous sexual offense unless she was irrationally committed to that friend? Faithfull's unthinking support of Helen Codrington brought out her marginal social status as a single woman. Joseph Parkes, a lawyer and father of the feminist Bessie Rayner Parkes, passed on to her what Law Court gossip he heard, including a report "that she [Faithfull] is still in London in Male attire. I should doubt the fact, thinking her more probably abroad."[45] He was so intrigued with the idea of cross-dressing that he repeated the rumor two days later in another letter. Since the most readily available language to describe a lesbian was gender inversion, any reference to her masculine appearance contained a veiled reference to her suspect sexuality.

Evidence of folly, hatred, and revenge unfolded before the court, jury, and journalists. Faithfull's affidavit at first seemed of little interest in comparison with the salacious details of high life abroad. Former servants, brought from Malta, testified to Helen Codrington's irregular hours and questionable behavior. When she came home with Colonel Anderson in the government gondola, it listed as if both passengers sat on one side of the cabin. The boatman's testimony was typical of the web of innuendo that the admiral wove around his wife: he swore that "bad thoughts crossed his mind when the boat got out of trim, because, he supposed his mind was wicked and he was prone to evil thoughts,—not because he ever saw anything improper."[46] The only time we hear Helen Codrington's voice is in the incriminating letter. This document became the single-most-damning piece of evidence against her, but we can read it as the voice of a quite sensible, if possibly compromised, woman. She pleads for one more meeting, declaring: "I shall never forget the respect due to myself, and you may rest assured that instead of being an obstacle to any plans you may form for the future I will, on the contrary, help you, and also help you, as you desire, to let the past be forever past. . . . Believe me, I am not so dangerous as you seem to fancy. True moral courage and self-control will never fail me in my hour of need, when duty and my sense of honour support me."[47] In this letter she claims two attributes no one gave her credit for possessing: self-control and a sense of honor. But with all the forces of patriarchy ranged against her, defeat was inevitable.

Everyone had ample time to gossip about who was concealing what, for after three days the trial was delayed to gather more evidence on behalf of the accused. Four months later, in November 1864, the trial reopened. This time Faithfull was ready to testify in court. In what turned out to be a masterly performance against her onetime friend, she utterly denied the attempted rape in October 1856. Now in the witness box, she declared that she had been asleep through the whole incident and saw only a "white figure" retreating through the door when she awoke. She also denied that Helen Codrington's solicitor had asked her if "the Admiral had had connexion with you." She claimed she had signed the infamous affidavit without reading it. As *The Times* reported, faced with Faithfull's defection, Helen Codrington's barrister was forced to argue that "there was no doubt that the Admiral had gone in his night-dress into a room where his wife and Miss Faithfull were in bed, and although he [the barrister] did not contend that that was any proof of his having committed adultery with Miss Faithfull, he did contend that it was an act of great indelicacy and impropriety."[48] Joseph Parkes, however, had no doubt about Faithfull's role: "I believe the truth to be that she kept back much fact & truth of both husband & wife in her evidence, & that forced into the [witness] box she made up her tale to cut the best figure for *herself* in her painful ambiguous & contradictory relations to both. Indeed I believe never was a trial in which more falsehoods were told or more *suppressio veri* on both sides."[49] Parkes's lawyerly soul revolted against the numerous and barefaced lies told both to legal advisers and under oath.

Faithfull successfully shaped her courtroom testimony so as to present herself as someone who was sexually naïve and socially inexperienced but "high principled." This image exonerated her for the *Daily Telegraph*:

> A girl of nineteen, she clearly entertained a romantic and credulous attachment for a dangerous friend; she believed what was told her, without any stated reason for it. . . . She was wrong to trust her friend against reason—wrong to sacrifice herself for a moment for the credit

and peace of that misleading friend—and wrong to shrink at the first from an examination. . . . Her plain and simple narration once told, she had nothing more to apprehend. The reputation of this well-known lady is, then, perfectly re-established.[50]

Faithfull was transformed into an adolescent led astray by a sexually voracious married woman. Even Joseph Parkes could say, "Still one pities her as a wild girl thrown into such a society at the early made age of 19."[51] She was the tomboy daughter of a rural clergyman, new to London and aristocratic life. The price Faithfull paid for sexual vindication was to acquiesce in the representation of herself as a young and credulous girl—the opposite of her self-image as an experienced feminist businesswoman. And she never addressed the issue of why at twenty-nine, ten years after meeting Helen Codrington, she continued to be her close friend and ally.

After the jury found unanimously in favor of the admiral, both respondent and co-respondent appealed unsuccessfully. Finally, in September 1866, on summons, Colonel Anderson was called upon to pay the petitioner's costs of £943.2.4; then, in January 1867, the petitioner was ordered to pay his ex-wife's legal costs of £1,118.10.0. This unusual step was taken because the judge felt that Admiral Codrington "had suffered, if not enforced, his wife to absent herself from his bed at night, and lead a separate life by day," as well as leaving his wife to find her own way home from functions they attended together.[52] Although upper-class single women were expected to have no knowledge of their own sexual desires and needs, married women should not be forbidden access to their husband's bed. In October 1869 Henry Codrington married Catherine, widow of Admiral Aitchison. He retired in 1872 and died in 1877, leaving over £70,000, including annuities of £30,000 to each of his two unmarried daughters. Colonel Anderson must have felt the blow of nearly a thousand pounds in court costs, not to say the infamy of so notorious an affair. But it appears to have had no effect upon his career; he retired with full military honors as a major general in 1888.[53] Helen was deserted by her widowed father; she lost custody of her two daughters; her erstwhile lover had quickly married before the trial began; and her dear, mannish friend had deserted her, lest the contents of the mysterious packet be revealed. Helen Smith Codrington lost husband, lover, friend, and children—and disappears from history.

"A ROMANTIC AND CREDULOUS ATTACHMENT FOR A DANGEROUS FRIEND": THE FAITHFULL-CODRINGTON RELATIONSHIP

The troubled friendship between Emily Faithfull and Helen Codrington demonstrates the perils of loving a married woman and of indulging in lesbian passion without a supportive female community. In 1857 three powerful men—husband, father, brother-in-law—intervened to dismiss Emily Faithfull from the Codrington home. As a navy man the admiral would have been familiar with male homosexuality; doubtless as a notorious disciplinarian, he always punished such grave acts of insubordination. I suspect that on that fateful October 1856 night, he was inspecting the women's shared bed, rather than checking the fire, a task everyone agreed belonged to the chambermaid. He may have been furious at their intimacy and acted hastily against the mannish usurper. Even though the admiral had taken pains to preserve his side of Faithfull's expulsion in the sealed packet, he did not attempt to use this information in a divorce trial plagued by weak evidence (Joseph Parkes declared that "Court, Bar & Public" were convinced that only the judge's biased summing-up could make possible a conviction). The secret contents of the sealed packet tantalized onlookers, but most assumed they knew what it might contain.

The newspapers made much of the admiral's unpleasant behavior. The radical *Reynolds's Newspaper* editorialized about the "glut of profligacy" among the upper classes and sardonically concluded:

> This ancient mariner, after a certain period of married life had elapsed, withdrew himself from the nuptial couch, and never, it was alleged, entered it unless his wife was sleeping with a female friend. On such an occasion the "fatherly old man," under the pretence of poking the fire, and performing other housemaid's work, quietly walked into his wife's chamber in his night shirt, and as noiselessly slipt into her bed. Whether this nocturnal visit was paid to Mrs. Codrington or her friend, Miss Faithfull, or only for the purpose of keeping both warm by maintaining a good fire, we cannot presume to determine. We much regret that the name of a young lady who has hitherto been associated with many philanthropic projects should be mixed up in so very nasty and foul a matter. In justice, however, to the admiral and Miss Faithfull, it must be admitted that the jury has virtually white-washed them by its verdict.[54]

Like Parkes, the editor of this weekly did not believe the tales told under oath. To be whitewashed was not to be innocent. He did not question the guilt of Helen Codrington and instead focused on the queer triangle created that October 1856 night. The salacious description of the admiral poking the fire probably made the rounds in more blatant forms in Law Court and Fleet Street gossip.

Surviving private responses also focus on the unpleasant husband and his queer relationship with two women. In contrast to the Edinburgh trial, no one pretended to be ignorant of women's erotic desires. Joseph Parkes found the whole affair "dirty." He disliked the admiral's spying, the wife's guilt, and

Faithfull's lies. After Faithfull's testimony he wrote his daughter about her former political ally, declaring, "I believe nothing she said. . . . But E. F. will have her partizans, tho' I think most men & nearly all your Sex will give her up as a dangerous woman & of impure mind."[55] The young Faithfull, like the Scottish schoolgirls, had seen too much, but worse yet, she had aided her guilty friend. Parkes warned his daughter not to associate with her, lest she further damage the feminist movement: "On the whole the dirty case will take all the enamel offer [sic] E. F.'s reputation & ruin her business. If wise she will at once retire from business & her Printership to the Queen."[56] Parkes was most shocked at the unnatural behavior of Helen's father in his long-standing support of the husband against his own daughter.

Robert Browning, an inveterate gossip, went straight to the unmentionable evidence of Faithfull's lesbian sexuality—the unopened packet given to Henry Codrington's brother. But he too never names names. He wrote to his friend Isa Blagden in Italy:

> One of the counsel in the case told an acquaintance of mine that the "sealed letter" contained a charge I shall be excused from even hinting to you—fear of the explosion of which, caused the shift of Miss E. from one side to the other. As is invariably the case, people's mouths are opened, and tell you what "they knew long ago" though it seems *that* did not matter a bit so long as nobody else knew: Mrs [Anne] Procter, for instance told me of a lie she (E) had invented to interest Adelaide, about as pretty a specimen as I ever heard, though familiar with such sportings of the fancy. After all, folks are safe enough in the main—if you know a thing, and fear to be the first in telling it, all's one as if you were ignorant: you won't say—"I'll have nothing to do with him or her, *I* know why & won't tell"—because friends smile and reply "Really, you can't expect that, without a definite charge being made, I am to avoid the person you please to dislike"—that is—"I contest your superior experience, and disbelieve in your acuteness, & suppose you to be prejudiced somehow besides": then one day comes a howl & a wondering at this wicked world.[57]

For the widowed Browning, longtime friend of the Anglo-American coterie of lesbian artists living in Italy, there was no secret in the sealed letter. What was the "explosion" he suspects Faithfull wished to avoid? Was it something everyone knew about but "feared to be the first in telling"? Perhaps Emily Faithfull had made a pass at the feminist poet Adelaide Procter, a close friend of Matilda Hays in the late 1850s.

Browning's gossip corroborates Eve Kosofsky Sedgwick's argument that nothing is more open than the gay closet—everyone knows, but nobody tells.[58] His self-conscious jokiness betrays a recognition that naming names would break the decorum of his close friendship with the unmarried Blagden.

Others talk, while he is discreet. Browning's refusal to hint is, of course, more than a hint. His equivocation acknowledges without stating the sexual nature of Faithfull's relationship with Helen Codrington. He assumes that the worldly Blagden, known for her own romantic friendships, would understand how Faithfull had stepped beyond the boundaries of propriety. Her publicly recognized folly—abetting her friend's affair—hid a second folly, same-sex passion. The commonplace events of an adultery, though "dirty," were hardly worth commenting on in comparison with the titillating sealed packet. Browning justifies his own prurience with a long analysis of the ways in which the unmentionable remains unmentionable until abruptly everyone is talking. Suddenly "sportings of the fancy" are common knowledge, only to be laid aside when a new affair calls for attention.

In contrast, mid-century respectable feminists drew a veil of silence over behavior that was far more common in their homosocial circles than heterosexual peccadilloes, religious unbelief, or free love. Surviving comments are censorious without quite naming the primary issue. The wealthy Louisa Hubbard, who saw Faithfull as a rival in their separate efforts to improve employment opportunities for middle-class women, tersely commented in the margin of a letter of Emily Faithfull's to a Miss Phillips, "She took a great part at a very early period in woman's work but had considerable eccentricity and was more inclined to seek advertisement and pecuniary returns and notoriety in general than was desirable."[59] Emily Davies, in her unpublished family chronicle, briefly comments for the year 1864: "It will be seen from the references to the Victoria Magazine that things were going badly. The business side of it had all thru' been very unsatisfactory, & the situation at last became intolerable & I withdrew from it. Some months later, Miss Faithfull was obliged, owing to some references to her in reports of a Divorce case, to withdraw for a time, from society, & I, & others, ceased to be associated with her."[60] Davies' discomfort is revealed by her odd wording. She withdraws from serving as the paid editor of the *Victoria Magazine* for sound business reasons, even though it continued to be published for several more years. Then "some months later" Miss Faithfull voluntarily withdrew from society, so that Davies and other unnamed feminists cannot be held responsible if they "ceased to be associated with her." Although Davies claims her economic sagacity, she evades knowledge of, much less responsibility for, Faithfull's changed social position in the feminist movement. Indeed Faithfull's damaging courtroom testimony is reduced to "some references to her in reports of a Divorce case," as if she had never contradicted her sworn affidavit, fled a subpoena, or given suspicious testimony in a witness box. Hubbard and Davies do not define precisely what they disapproved of about Faithfull. Was it her mannish eccentricity? Her business sense? Or her complicity with an adulterer?

Yet Faithfull's reputation was not permanently damaged by the trial. She successfully brazened out her notoriety and only resigned from the Victoria Press in 1867, three years after the trial. She lived in Manchester her last twenty years, far from her former London friends, including her old ally Bessie Rayner Parkes. Among her essays describing American women is a long diatribe against easy American divorces and flirtatious women.[61] But her reputation for mannish behavior was not so easily shed. No portraits survive from the period 1854–64, but the undated Figure 7 shows that later in life Faithfull dressed in a masculine style, with short hair, brooch, and shirtfront. In 1898, three years after her death, the Lancashire feminist, Mrs. Wolstenholme Elmy, indignantly noted that Mrs. Fenwick Miller in the *Woman's Signal* had "misrepresent[ed] Miss Emily Faithfull, who, she says, was the only one of the early workers who wore cropped hair and dressed in a mannish fashion. This Emily Faithfull never did. I believe for a very short period after an illness she had to wear her hair short till it had grown again."[62] Faithfull spent the remainder of her life firmly ensconced in an all-female milieu; less cautious feminists presumably welcomed her energy and organizational skills. At her death she left her substantial estate to her female partner; her savings of £1,081.10.2 were less than what Admiral Codrington had paid for his divorce.

The silence at the heart of the Codrington trial is lesbian sex. We are not dealing with absence, but with innuendo, metaphor, allegations of transvestism, and self-censorship. We do all of the principals in the Codrington drama an injustice if we assume that because no action was named or uncovered, nothing happened. Everyone assumed something had happened—why else would Admiral Codrington have inspected the women's bedroom, dismissed Faithfull from his home, and left a sealed packet with his brother? Homosocial and homoerotic relations were most accepted among bourgeois women if they remained unmarried and within their own all-female communities; they were most threatening if they disrupted heterosexual norms of courtship and marriage. But when lesbian sex intruded into marriage, or when it seemed to prevent a young woman from marrying, or when it was linked with heterosexual adultery, it became the object of male anger, mockery, and dismissal. Emily Faithfull was saved by men, her legal advisers. But questions remained, echoing those of the earlier Scottish trial. When two women bed together, is there sexual contagion or only "ardour and fondness"? An elderly man, accused by the defense of refusing his wife's sexual overtures, is guilty of stirring a bedroom fire with a poker—what better metaphor for male interference in female warmth?

By the 1850s and 1860s, respectable women and men were trying to find a new, appropriate language to discuss nonconforming sexual desires and practices. They did not want to describe inchoate desires in words borrowed from either contemporary pornography or the obscene classical texts alluded to by the judges in the Edinburgh trial and by Anne Lister. Women self-consciously turned to well-established paradigms of visual difference, including gender inversion. The easiest way to explain same-sex desire was for one woman to cast herself as a male partner. For example, Harriet Hosmer always used a male pronoun when she called herself "hubby," and Anne Lister repeatedly defined herself as a naturally masculine woman. Some women, however, found fiction a safer venue in which to explore their erotic feelings for another woman. By imagining herself as a male hero, a woman might safely investigate, even give voice to, her unmentionable desires. The impossible could be imagined and acted upon within the safety of fantasy. Eliza Lynn Linton, discussed in chapter 6, created versions of herself in male guise in her novels. Emily Faithfull did so in her only novel. Both wrote novels in which class, money, and privilege block a poor, gentle man from marital happiness. In a world where homosexual desire cannot be acknowledged, homophobia cannot exist. But society can still be the enemy of true love.

However cool Faithfull may have been on the witness stand, she was clearly obsessed with Helen Codrington. In 1868 she published *Changes upon Changes,* in which she justified her love for and then repudiation of her friend. In the preface to the American edition (retitled *A Reed Shaken in the Wind: A Love Story*), Faithfull admitted: "I have seen with my own eyes the curious combination of intellectual power and instability of purpose portrayed in Tiny Harewood; I have watched with an aching heart the shifting weaknesses and faint struggles for redemption described in these pages."[63] Tiny Harewood, frivolous, artless, and extravagant, replicates Helen Codrington as described by her barrister. Further clues to Tiny's true identity are buried in the text. At one juncture she acts the part of Helen in an amateur production of Sheridan Knowles's play, *The Hunchback.* Her family lives on Grosvenor Crescent; Helen Codrington had met Anderson at the Grosvenor Hotel upon their return from Malta. Early in the novel Tiny claims to love her staid cousin, Wilfred, and she agrees to a secret engagement. But we know from the beginning that the relationship is doomed because of her "warm, subtle, half-perverse nature" and "an innate wildness" that "was not very far from developing into wickedness."[64] When her widowed mother, a hypocritical society woman, insists that the cousin is neither distinguished nor wealthy enough to marry her, the right-minded Wilfred suggests a six-month trip to Rome to test their love. This gives Faithfull the opportunity to have Tiny write ecstatic letters about the novelist George Sand and the sculptor Harriet Hosmer.

But their example of female independence is not enough. When a further year of testing is demanded by her mother, Tiny weakens and flirts with a series of handsome men she meets in country houses. In the meantime Wilfred wrecks his health earning extra money at the Naval Office (of all places) to impress Tiny's family. His only solace is smoking large cigars. Inevitably the time comes when Tiny writes from Scotland (Anderson's home) that she has accepted Lord Lothian's hand. Wilfred cannot resist telling Tiny, "you are utterly unstable; and I am powerless to save you, because the feeling of love and honor which you ought to have is wanting."[65] Faithfull then abruptly reveals that Wilfred too is guilty, for he once loved a married woman. The novel ends melodramatically, with Wilfred declaring, "I have deserved this bitterness— you are simply the instrument of a just retribution; nothing short of having my own happiness torn up by the very roots would ever have punished me as I *deserve*."[66] Wilfred bears God's punishment for the sin of Colonel Anderson, and of Emily Faithfull: loving the married Helen.

Most readers by this juncture would wonder why this pious sobersides had ever fallen for the absurd Tiny (or vice-versa). The answer is the pleasure of combining sexual attraction and moral reform: "Wilfred, fascinated by her childish grace and apparent frankness, believed in the ultimate development of the beautiful qualities which existed in rare profusion among the baser elements of this peculiarly gifted being. . . . He believed that all Tiny really wanted was wise guidance."[67] Faithfull appropriated the convention of courtship as the education of a young woman who learns to be worthy of the hero. Masquerading as Wilfred, Faithfull turned herself into a moral guide, whereas at the trial she looked like either a pander or a naïf. *Changes upon Changes* unfolds not as a conventional romantic story, but as a struggle within the lovelorn Wilfred: can he reform Tiny or will she elude his grasp? Wilfred, as the morally complete figure, passively waits for Tiny to return from her many tempting balls, house parties, and travels. He seethes with well-controlled passion, hoping that fidelity will prove sexy enough to hold the wayward Tiny. The result is a story that lacks the familiar triangle of desire, in which either two men struggle for the hand of one woman or two women love the same man. Nor could it be a tale of lesbian self-discovery, in which one character discovers her true self by falling in love with a woman. Faithfull did not recreate the painful triangle she had experienced in which the powerful admiral defeated her. Rather, all her sympathies lie with poor, passive Wilfred; those many cigars bolster his masculinity, even if they do not alter his social status.

As the instigator of a doomed love story, Tiny is not a heroine, but a fickle, perverse cheat. I think that Faithfull wanted to write a story of lesbian love that was also a retribution tale. The tyrannical, dominating male, reminiscent of the admiral, must be absent from Faithfull's scenario, because he would turn Tiny into a sexual object, whereas she must retain her erratic, impulsive subjectivity in order to demonstrate the dangers of undisciplined sexual privilege. Even Tiny's mother is not an adversary, in spite of her vanity. She too fears that Tiny will not "abstain of her own free will from actions which the commonest sense of right and wrong condemned."[68] By denying Tiny a father, Faithfull places Wilfred in that role. Tiny repeatedly confesses to him her flirtations with other men, her need for excitement, and her emotional infidelities. Each time Wilfred forgives her because he gains moral and emotional power over her. Whatever Tiny does, Wilfred cannot stop loving—and correcting—her. Patriarchy does not disappear from the novel, but is reinscribed onto the good hero. Faithfull had to portray her own love as pure and self-disciplined. But in doing so she moved Wilfred into the position of male authority, even as she tried to define him as a sympathetic casualty of society's prejudices.

Faithfull faced another textual difficulty. Her virtuous hero is hemmed in by the secrecy of their engagement, a secrecy that replicates her relationship with Helen. At one juncture Wilfred pontificates, "lacking as we do the public acknowledgements and safeguards which such ties as ours generally receive in the world, we are doubly bound to cherish our private position."[69] Read as a lesbian novel, *Changes upon Changes* underscores the difficulties of winning even private recognition for a romantic friendship between women. Secretly exchanging rings and vows, Faithfull seems to admit, cannot bring stability to an inherently unstable love relationship. Public acceptance and the rituals of betrothal and marriage stabilize passion, but they are denied to two women. Without public acknowledgment, Wilfred's passion distorts his senses and reason. The last-minute revelation that he has loved a married woman makes sense only as a comment on Faithfull's own devastating love for Helen Codrington. Her novel is a masochistic reworking of an obsessive love. Besotted with Helen Codrington, in the guise of Wilfred, Faithfull revisited her failed efforts to reform Helen's errant ways with emotional entreaties and prayers. Yet both before the divorce and in the novel, a loyal friend becomes a boring catechist.[70] In the witness box Faithfull saved her own reputation by destroying Helen's. Their friendship was as irretrievable as that of Marianne Woods and Jane Pirie half a century earlier.

Emily Faithfull explored her painful passion for Helen Codrington by transforming herself into a feminized, morally upright man. Hers was one of several options this generation of mid-century women chose in an effort to define themselves sexually. Other women comfortably explained their sexual attraction to women as a phase, as part of growing up. Unmarried older women used the culturally acceptable appellation romantic friendship. Many probably avoided articulating their desires, lest they be wholly defined by their words. Numerous contradictory behaviors and definitions coexisted, though the most common identifying mark of the woman who loved women was still gender inversion. In the 1880s and 1890s, the elderly Faithfull lived happily with a female partner in a romantic friendship that, for her, needed minimal justification.

But the young tomboy Ethel Smyth (chapter 5) felt compelled to explain her complicated sexual needs. She never referred to relationships with older mothering women as romantic friendships, nor did she try to cast herself in the role of a man. What, then, was the source of her profound desire for women? I conclude here with a brief analysis of Smyth's letters to Harry Brewster in order to reprise two ongoing issues addressed in this chapter, the difficulty of finding a respectable language in which to discuss same-sex desire and the odd role played by men in this effort. I turn away from the legal evasions and gossip that marked the two court cases, and consider instead how a late-nineteenth-century woman and man discussed their sexual needs with each other. A full generation after Faithfull, they focused on psychological and social, rather than physical, attributes in order to identify the sources of lesbian erotic desire.

Smyth loved a series of mothering women throughout her life, but she was deeply in love with Harry Brewster, an aesthete and author, with whom she discussed all manner of questions. During their long relationship, each had other serious emotional and erotic involvements that never upstaged their commitment to each other. Their relationship succeeded in part because they never lived together. Rather than openly discussing her lesbianism in her numerous autobiographies, Smyth published excerpts of letters between herself and Brewster discussing it. By the end of the nineteenth century, such matters might be broached without fear by two sophisticated people. In an 1892 letter to Brewster, Smyth alludes to the medicalization of women's friendships: "I wonder why it is so much easier for me, and I believe for a great many English women, to love my own sex passionately rather than yours? Even my love for my mother had an intense quality you can only call passion. How do you account for it? I can't make it out for I think I am a very healthy-minded person and it is an everlasting puzzle."[71]

Behind her final sentence may be her reading of Richard von Krafft-Ebing and other German sexologists who were describing lesbian love as an adolescent phase or an innate defect, leading in both cases to morbidity, nerves, and/or hysteria. At thirty-four she could no longer claim innocence or naïveté in regard to sexual matters, though she had as yet refused all sexual overtures from Brewster himself. Yet even this letter is less blunt than the legal cases: she never mentions the bedroom, much less a bed, in any of her autobiographies. "To love my own sex passionately" may be franker than past discussions of lesbianism, but it conceals as much as it reveals.

Brewster, after first describing his attraction to a young Swiss peasant woman, replied reassuringly, "You are the healthiest person I have ever met." Comfortable in his own sexual freedom, he grants her a freedom that did not alter their love. For him lesbian friendships are simply a natural reaction against the constraints of modern-day marriage: "these affections entail no duties, no sacrifice of liberty or of tastes, no partial loss of individuality; whereas friendships of equal warmth with men have that danger (and others) in the background. This can be read either as a reproach to the women who have not enthusiasm enough to consent to moral drowning, or as a criticism on the institution of marriage and the restrictions it brings to both parties."[72] When society had a more rational understanding of heterosexual relations, male and female homosexuality would naturally be less attractive. But in the meantime worldly men could dismiss affairs between women as amusing and marginal to their own heterosexual prerogatives. Indeed, in 1892, Brewster was still married, and could be seen as committing adultery physically with the Swiss woman and emotionally with Smyth. He does not overturn traditional values, but bypasses them for the benefit of those like himself, educated, tolerant, and faithful to particular ideals. For him no social norms are broken because only a few friends and family members know about their private lives. Discretion covered a multitude of sexual behaviors.

Brewster tolerated Smyth's passionate involvements with women because they confirmed his own phallic superiority. She could play the tomboy while remaining a woman; he, the true man, waited. Smyth only hints at Brewster's desire for more sex; even after she agreed to consummate their love, she had little interest in repeating the event. But one anecdote that Smyth records shows that he was still thinking about heterosexuality, even if she was not. On one occasion around 1904, when Brewster had had a fling with a mutual friend, breaking their agreement that he would have sexual relations only with women outside their social circle, Smyth retaliated by claiming to have had a brief heterosexual affair herself: "After the first moment which seemed to paralyse him as would a blow on the head with a heavy stick, came a mood that might have sat passably on an ardent young honeymooner, but not on the Harry I knew! And this mood merged gradually into an outburst of frenzied suffering such as I never would have believed him capable of."[73] Shocked, Smyth admitted that she had made up the story, only to be confronted with "an outbreak of another sort of violence that seemed to me almost insane. He threw my words back in my teeth, 'I don't believe you!' he cried."[74] His response may have been flattering, but it also revealed how irrelevant women's same-sex love was for a self-confident heterosexual man. Brewster took Smyth's sexual experiences seriously only when a man was involved. Smyth discovered, to her surprise, that she had pushed sexual frankness beyond an unstated limit. The next chapter, however, will show that men's anxieties about, as well as their acceptance of, female sexual independence, are more complicated than it might at first appear. As long as same-sex love remained unnamed, or defined by a religious language, it could flourish in unexpected places.

4   *"The Gift of Love"*
RELIGION AND LESBIAN LOVE

Relatively few women were directly involved in the law in the nineteenth century, but all were affected by religion. The Victorians lived with, in, for, and against formal religion. The women discussed in this book were brought up in the Judeo-Christian traditions of Europe and America, and although several became agnostics, and others were indifferent to spiritual claims, none escaped this dominant religious framework.[1] The various neo-Christian rituals described in previous chapters satisfied the need for some kind of formal imprimatur for many, but others grappled directly with formal religious faith, earthly love, and sexual desire. Victorian women believed profoundly that love came from God, and that it had to be honored as His gift. As Mary Benson wrote about her intimate friendships, "Ah Lord, thou has given me in some measure the gift of love."[2] Women who loved women saw no division between their love of women and their love of God. This chapter examines same-sex love within two deeply patriarchal institutions, the Church of England and the Roman Catholic Church. The liberties and sanctions of these institutions both enabled and constrained the expression of earthly same-sex love.

Not surprisingly, lesbians had as wide a range of responses to formal religion as their peers did. Until churches actively condemned homosexuality, homosexuals were comfortable in organized religion. A few followed Mary Benson's path into a devout Evangelicalism, with its emphasis on an individual relation with God. Some nineteenth-century lesbians, such as Anne Lister, embraced conservative politics and religion in order to confirm their class privilege. Eliza Lynn Linton reacted strongly against her clergyman father's faith. Vernon Lee adhered to her mother's eighteenth-century agnostic tradition. Her friend Amy Levy detested bourgeois English Judaism and adopted atheism, while writing prolifically about the ethical and spiritual issues facing her Jewish community.[3] The Americans Harriet Hosmer and Natalie Clifford Barney seemed little concerned with religious matters, simply accepting their Protestant upbringing, while finding spiritual comfort in art. Conversion to Roman Catholicism, a minority religion in Britain and the United States, gave some women a religious confirmation of their marginal sexual status. Emma Donoghue suggests that for many early-twentieth-century lesbians, it "meant becoming slightly foreign, aloof from the establishment; as a church it was associated with the rich and the poor, but definitely not the bourgeoisie."[4] Catholicism may also have seemed more forgiving, more ready to accept failings that came under scrutiny in Protestantism. As Joanne Glasgow has pointed out, a church that defined sexuality in wholly phallic terms could not imagine, much less condemn, female homosexuality.[5] Moreover, Catholicism endorsed celibacy as a higher form of spirituality than marriage, and its priests and nuns served as living examples. Single men and women felt comfortable in a milieu that put little pressure on them to marry.

The boundaries between spiritual and sexual love must have seemed naturally permeable to women who found religious meaning in their lives through the love of a spiritually wise, mothering woman. The agnostic Linton wrote about a woman she had loved as an adolescent, "when I thought of God, she stood ever foremost at His hand."[6] George Eliot attracted numerous younger women who had lost their faith and hoped to find spiritual sustenance in her religion of duty.[7] Her keenest admirer, Edith Simcox, was a devout agnostic, but she admitted, "Since I have loved her I have sometimes idly wished that there was a religious order, a cloister where one might spend one's days in worship and commemoration."[8] She joined numerous other admirers in calling George Eliot "Madonna."[9] The comparison of a beloved with the Madonna did not imply an acceptance of the thick aggregation of meanings around this figure in Catholicism. "Madonna" served as a shorthand reference for the purity of the lover's motives and the infinite spiritual superiority of the beloved to other women. It also carried a faintly illicit anti-Protestant or anti-Jewish (with their privileging of a male God) aura to the relation.

European literature from at least the Middle Ages has found one language for love, whether divine or earthly. Nineteenth- and early-twentieth-century women used the language of religious love to explain their passionately erotic and spiritual feelings. Surviving letters between women testify to a profound trust in the language and precepts of faith to express the spiritual and erotic longings aroused by human love. A spiritual language could both conceal and reveal, providing an acceptable public face, while allowing lovers to speak a private code to each other. Sometimes it hid what Mary Benson called "carnal affections." But other times religion gave meaning and structure to inchoate feelings that required no more than verbal expression. The young Louisa Stewart Mackenzie, the future Lady Ashburton, had a series of intense friendships with women before and after her marriage. Her surviving letters capture something of the delicate line trod between the erotic and the spiritual, between God's blessing and something more. In 1854 she wrote the older and more pious Jane Stirling, "Yes, love, I wd have my affection to you made 'Eternal,' sanctified & freed [of] Earthly passions—so hallowed, that it may begin here, to continue for Ever—I *do* love you very tenderly."[10] Undoubtedly many women's homoerotic relationships were not fully physical, so that they could be defined as a form of praise to God, although Ashburton seems to be shaping her passion to fit Stirling's demands, or at least to combine her erotic and spiritual ardor.

The most devout women who loved women so identified earthly love with God's love that they considered its loss to be a sign of God's wrath. All who read *Jane Eyre* (1847) knew the danger of making an idol of one's beloved. Jane is justly punished for loving Mr. Rochester too much, for making him stand "between me and every thought of religion, as an eclipse intervenes between man and the broad sun."[11] Romantic love, whether heterosexual or homosexual, was the greatest emotion a woman could feel, but it had to be kept within bounds. Margaret Coutts Trotter, unmarried and living with an indifferent brother, fell deeply in love with Louisa, Lady Ashburton. For several years in the 1860s, Ashburton responded enthusiastically to her unfeigned adoration, but she grew bored and moved on to the more exciting and demanding Harriet Hosmer. Trotter was devastated. Although she knew that her beloved was fickle, she was convinced that God had punished her for loving Ashburton more than Him. Until she could stop thinking about Ashburton, she would remain among the damned and would be denied both Ashburton's love and His forgiveness. The only sure sign of His mercy was a letter from Ashburton. As she noted in one return letter: "Last night I thanked him for [my] being less rebellious. . . . So when he had broken the will of which he saw that there was good reason to be jealous—for God is a jealous God and will be first—Then—he sent this good kind present [of a letter from you,] that assurance of your Love which I so much needed. I kneeled down and thanked God before I read your letter for easing my mind."[12] Trotter kept looking for comfort from God, whom she characterized as jealous and demanding, the very characteristics she wanted from the increasingly indifferent and distant Ashburton. She hung on for several years, living off tidbits of information, offering free child care to Ashburton's daughter, and arranging for various errands and deliveries. Time diminished her sense of desolation, and she came to accept losing her beloved as God's will.

Margaret Trotter knew her sin, just as Jane Eyre knew hers, but she did not live in fiction, and God did not bless her suffering with the return of her friend's love. She joins countless anonymous women and men who have loved an unworthy man or woman. Her emotional anguish was made intelligible in religious terms, yet when she confronted both her God and her beloved, there was no satisfactory answer for why she suffered so very much for earthly love. Other women, wracked by a sense of spiritual isolation or disbelief, rejected such stark alternatives, yet faith in divine love when human love was absent or distant was not easily achieved. This chapter looks at different definitions of how divine love shaped human love for women who loved women. The two cases, one of a heterosexually married Evangelical and the other of a lesbian couple who converted to Catholicism, reveal how religion could enable or destroy a relationship. They also demonstrate the intertwining vocabularies of religious and secular love.

"THE CONSECRATION OF FRIENDSHIP": MARY BENSON

Mary Benson (fig. 8), unhappily married to a successful clergyman, struggled to meet the demands of her husband and still maintain faith in herself and in God. She asked herself, "What, & how far, is the union of two souls in matrimony, and what is the individuality?" "What does a woman owe to her husband and family?" "To herself?" "Would God accept her as a sinner?"[13] She found the answers to these questions through her love for a series of women. A deeply religious woman, her intense evangelical belief in a personal savior began in earthly love. Benson came to understand divine love through a human love for women. Since she spent her entire life within a highly respected and respectable marriage, her spiritual and sexual negotiations offer complicated and contradictory, though inevitably partial, insights into women's religious beliefs, Victorian marital life, and women's bonds with each other.

Tracing the course of Mary Benson's life, we can see how she evolved from an unhappy wife to a powerful mother-confessor who drew women to her. We know almost too much about the Benson family. Edward White Benson, his wife Mary, and the five surviving children kept diaries, wrote letters, and published books. Arthur and Fred each wrote four memoirs of family members and themselves; only early death prevented Hugh from writing more than one autobiography. The three sons were well-known public figures in their own right, so comments by contemporaries abound. Although Fred, the last of the family, destroyed many letters and diaries, a sufficient number remains to overwhelm the historian. Mary Benson, the two daughters, and the three surviving sons all preferred members of their own sex.[14] None of the five children married, and none appears to have found the sexual happiness that their mother won for herself.[15] She forged a deeply intuitive spirituality that drew other women to her; earthly love, for her, was a sign of God's love. Religion and erotic love for women were to be "inextricably twined cords" in Mary Benson's life.[16] She remained committed to her husband's happiness, but as Fred said, "Two things only remained to her of her own which were not his: these were her personal relation to God, and her personal relation to her

Fig. 8. Mary Benson, ca. 1872.

children and friends."[17] More bluntly, the archbishop had no access to those
subjects that mattered most to her.

Mary's upbringing makes for chilling reading. The Reverend Edward
White Benson, twelve years her senior, fell in love with Minnie, as he called
her, when she was eleven. In collusion with her widowed mother, he educated her for marriage to him. She was barely eighteen when they married in
1859. She had already had several crushes on women and knew she did not
love Edward. In her poignant retrospective diary, she remembered the years
leading up to her marriage, "I was happiest when I knew E. happy and yet
wasn't with him." At other points she wrote of a "mother rather feared than
loved" and a "fatal want of confidence in my mother." She remembered their
honeymoon as a nightmare, when she

> *danced* & sung into matrimony, with a loving, but exacting, a believing
> & therefore expecting spirit, 12 years older, much stronger, much more
> passionate, & whom I didn't really love—I wonder I didn't go more
> wrong. . . .
>
> I have learnt what love is through friendship—how I cried in Paris!
> poor lonely child, having lived in the present only—living in the pres-

ent still—The nights! I can't think how I lived—I cldn't have thought so much abt myself as I do now—we prayed, but didn't come near to God. I mean I didn't.[18]

For the first ten years of their marriage, the young Minnie attempted to suppress her own needs and to obey her husband. During the very years when George Eliot was writing about Dorothea Brooke's disastrous marriage to the Reverend Casaubon in *Middlemarch* (1871–72), Mary Benson was try-ing to reconcile herself to an energetic husband who shared with Casaubon an expectation of absolute obedience. Edward was a priggish bully and manic-depressive. With maddening rationalism he supervised his wife's accounts, her expenditures, and her behavior toward him. He was also not above wounding personal comments. On one occasion he told her "that some people shrank from things of an unpleasant nature, especially if they had fat chins."[19] But the "bickering" and "jarring" as described by Mary indicate that she was no Dorothea, trusting in God to help her control her temper. In spite of her overwhelming distaste for her husband's intimacies and emotional de-mands, it was unthinkable that she should leave an ambitious clergyman.

Victorians often concealed a sexual crisis in the more acceptable terms of a spiritual crisis, but the two were inextricably mixed for Mary Benson. After the birth of her sixth child in 1871, she collapsed and went to Wiesbaden to recuperate. She stayed there longer than expected, wrestling with a crisis of faith—in God, Edward, and herself. During her dark night of the soul, she became convinced that she was unlovable as well as unloving. She simply could not turn to her strident, confident husband, who would have seen her mental state as a betrayal of both himself and God.[20] She evaded confronting doubt by falling in love with a fellow boarder:

> Then I began to love Miss Hall—no wrong surely there—it was a complete fascination—partly my physical state, perhaps—partly the continuous seeing of her—our exquisite walks. If I had loved God then *would it* have been so—could it be so now? I trust in God, NOT—Yet not one whit the less sweet need it be—I have learnt the consecration of friendship—gradually the bonds drew round—fascination pos-sessed me . . . then—the other fault—Thou knowest—I will not even write it—but, O God, forgive—*how* near we were to that![21]

Mary finally returned home, and Miss Hall briefly joined her. About these events she could only say in her retrospective diary, "I haven't gone, and I cant, fully, into the way I worried my dear ones here—I lost my head—and, blessed be Thy name, O Lord, I came to grief—The letter—ah! my hus-band's pain—what he bore, & how lovingly, how gently—*our talk*. My awful misery—my letter to her."[22] Presumably Mary told her husband that she did not love him and intended to live away from him with Miss Hall. In the end she did not desert her husband, and Miss Hall faded away. But Edward was forced to accept his wife's primary emotional and erotic loyalty to women. They had no more children.

Although the Bensons were never to have a happy marriage, their relationship improved with Mary's clarification of her own emotional and religious needs. She ran Edward's household, softened his relations with others, and successfully helped him to make his way up the church ladder, to become the first bishop of Truro (Cornwall) and then primate of the Church of England. When divorce was impossible or too socially disgraceful to contemplate, sensible men and women had to adapt to a failed marriage. As long as neither the husband nor, more usually, the wife, spoke publicly, life could go on. Helen Codrington, observers believed, had brought her disgrace upon herself. If she had been discreet, she could have continued in her unhappy marriage, flirting with men and women and possibly risking something more. Certainly many married men, including Joseph Parkes, had quiet affairs on the side. For others the solution was a whirlwind of work that we now label peculiarly Victorian. This latter state certainly characterized Edward, who thought nothing of fourteen- and eighteen-hour working days.

For nineteenth-century women, to an extent that we are only now recognizing, a special woman friend might give life fresh meaning. Children were not the be-all for every unhappy wife. Schooled in a culture that approved of adolescent crushes, many mature women turned to old or new women friends when their marriages were unsatisfactory. Documentation is necessarily scarce; even today overt criticism of one's spouse is seen as evidence of an impending breakup. Virtually every Victorian novel keeps marital misery within the family, forcing the unhappy heroine to turn either to God or to a relative for advice and sustenance. Virginia Woolf, in *To the Lighthouse* (1927), however, portrays a family reminiscent of the Bensons. In her dissection of that monster of Victorian patriarchal egotism, Mr. Ramsey, she provides Mrs. Ramsey with the adoring, albeit ineffectual Lily Briscoe. In a scene reminiscent of Edith Simcox at George Eliot's feet, Lily Briscoe imagines flinging herself "at Mrs. Ramsey's knee" to declare her love.[23] Marital misery remains unspoken, but love gives Lily insight. History provides more examples of an unhappily married woman turning to a woman confidante, but even here documentation can be patchy. Geraldine Jewsbury unfailingly supported her beloved friend Jane Carlyle, whose marriage was notoriously difficult; after Jane's death, she destroyed her letters. Kali Israel cites the example of Eleanor Smith, who provided maternal nurturing and feminist advice to Emilia Pattison during the long years of her unsuccessful marriage to the leading Oxford don Mark Pattison.[24] Mary Benson gave an unusual amount of time to her friends, but friendship was widely regarded as an important component in the lives of professional families, especially when, as was often the case, they lived far from family and kin. Her choice of religious and sexual solace in the arms of pious women was simply a more extreme resolution to the loss of faith in husband and God than that taken by other unhappily married women.

If Mary felt trapped in her marriage, Edward desperately needed her, both for his career and for his emotional well-being. In a letter of 30 March 1876, he wrote: "I have prayed for humility and sweetness always, yet I have not had before me the right ideal of character. . . . The lost ground I have to make up is aweful [sic]. It is therefore I who want your prayers, more than you mine." Aware that he was in danger of losing her, he concluded his long letter with a promise to be more mindful of her needs: "I am afraid this is all awkward—but it is a true endeavour to express how earnestly I will carry out your wishes. And *you* for me?"[25] He was caught in a marriage of his own making—his long engagement had kept him pure—but the consequences were emotionally devastating. Although Miss Hall disappeared, for the remainder of his married life, Edward Benson shared his wife with a woman; it was a queer situation he could confide about to no one. Edward was forced to accept that his personal happiness depended upon his career; he became a dedicated administrator, whose wife and children evaded his too-powerful grasp. Unlike Mary, he made few new friends as he grew in power and fame; his rare free evenings were most often spent with curates and other subordinates. As his son and biographer, Arthur, delicately explained: "Argument with him always engendered heat, and he was apt to express himself too vehemently to be agreeable. . . . He was not really at home in an atmosphere of perfect equality; [but] surround him with a certain deference and affection, and he was expansive, humorous, racy."[26]

After giving up Miss Hall, Mary Benson was saved from depression by the love of "Tan" Mylne, the wife of an older theology student. We know little about this spiritual adviser aside from Mary's diaries. Tan suggested that Mary write an account of her life, including her marriage, in order to review how she had failed to love God. She confirmed Mary Benson's sense of sin, of her lack of a consistent, unwavering faith in God, but she also showed how recognition of one's sinful nature could be the first step back to an all-loving God. Benson found her path to God arduous and exhilarating:

> I, having fallen away from good through the entire absence of personal religion, begin to seek God again by finding my growing weakness & poverty of soul; I am brought into close relations with one who tells me she finds her only strength, her fullest hope, her most ardent love in direct personal communion with this Xt [Christ]—She says "love," and she knows, I find, what it means, for she pours out to me what I acknowledge as sweetest & fullest human love—I begin to read the Bible.[27]

The married Tan Mylne, unlike the poor and unmarried Miss Hall, counseled Benson how best to cope with her husband. She both supported Mary's "rebellion" against the demands of Edward and prayed with her until her heart "was softened & turned to Thee."[28]

Tan called Mary Ben, a name that all her close women friends called her, whereas Edward used the childhood (and childish) diminutive Minnie. "Ben," a shortening of Benson, could have had the additional implication of "benison," or God's blessing. "Tan" is more difficult to decipher but may have referred to the Greek letter T (Tau), a Christian symbol for the crucifix and for life—an appropriate name for a mother-enabler. In her diary Benson calls Mrs. Mylne "my beloved helper," "beloved Tan, my Mother in Christ." Alternatively, the nickname could refer to her unfashionable skin color. Or it might imply the slang "to thrash soundly," because Mary brought her sinful nature to Tan to be scourged. But given the religious symbolism of Ben, it is more likely that Tan symbolized a Christ-given gift. Benson confidently wrote, "Thou of thine abundant, rich goodness gavest me hours with my darling Tan—hours in the fullness of the beauties of Thy creation—and she spoke of Thee—and as she spoke, the Love of Thee—I know it—filled her heart to the brim—and its peace was shed on me."[29] Since they could not live with each other, time together must have seemed like sweet stolen hours, snatched from other duties, yet blessed with a special kind of nurturing peace and understanding.

Benson ruefully admitted that when she could at last claim Christ as her Savior, she had expected "all joy & no cross," but found instead that she needed constantly to suit her ways to those of her needy husband. Her sins all circled around Edward; she could not conquer her impatience and anger. Thus, ironically, Mary needed Edward as a kind of chastisement, just as she needed her beloved Tan as a reminder that human love would bring her to God. A woman's supportive love taught her to know God's love, whereas Edward's love consumed her and destroyed her relation with God. In her struggle to find a sustaining faith, Benson repeatedly accused herself of a heart like a "rocky surface, only hardening and hardening as the years went on," and of lacking any roots to her faith.[30] When Mylne's love brimmed over she felt the water of divine peace and could then put her trust in Christ. Benson pictured her own human obduracy, her "hardness," as a problem, but God's obduracy was a source of spiritual strength and nourishment. In contrast to her husband's Establishment faith, Mary's faith was based on a loving, invisible Father who forgave sinners. As their son Fred said, she "looked on God as a Father, he as an omnipotent King."[31]

In 1876 Edward Benson was appointed the first bishop of Truro in Cornwall. He threw himself into improving the Church of England in this stronghold of Methodist dissent. He was frequently away visiting ministers in his diocese, and the children were old enough to leave Mary free of their care. Far from Tan Mylne, Mary fell in love with Charlotte Mary Bassett, who was unhappily married to an invalid. Mary's son Arthur admiringly described her as

> a woman of great character and charm, upright and handsome, silent, with big dark flashing eyes which seemed to indicate deep reserves of passionate feeling. . . . She had been in her younger days a girl of extraordinary animation and vivacity, of undaunted and adventurous spirit; but her husband's illness and other sad experiences had given her, I used to fancy, a certain aversion to life; there seemed something pent-up and thwarted about her.[32]

Fascinated by her flashing eyes and deep reserves, Mary eagerly counseled "Chat" on matters of faith and human love. Their correspondence, from 1879 to 1888, provides insight into how Benson came to see her relations with women as spiritual opportunities. Early in their relationship she wrote to Bassett, "The divine thing in the world would be to be able to heal a spirit one loved, wouldn't it?"[33] Just as Tan Mylne had brought her to see God through human love, Benson now instructed Bassett to have faith in their love for each other as part of God's plan. Earthly love made possible an understanding of God's bounteous forgiveness.

Male possessiveness had crushed Bassett, as it had Benson at an earlier juncture, but now Benson promised her a new kind of love: her God-given love would liberate Chat from a life shorn of earthly love and spiritual faith. Benson passionately argued a theme that was repeated with other women friends who entered her inner circle: "it is all of God. [Not] one whit less than *all you* will I have, in that mysterious, sacramental union where one can have all, and yet wrong no other love—"[34] She exhorted Bassett to think of their love as like the Easter Resurrection, bringing forgiveness for past sins, a rebirth in faith, and a new future.[35] The two women exchanged flowers, secret gifts, photos, nicknames (Bassett called Benson Robin), and vows of eternal love. Benson knew well the talismanic power of touching, promising Bassett, "I am going to send you a charm as soon as I can find one, so that you may from henceforth never be free from the *touch* of me, as well as my ghostly company."[36] After they had spent ten days together, Benson declared: "Besides this new welling of water in you to everlasting life, besides all that God has taught me in this, & through you, our lives have been *welded* here—fused together—united into that union which is both human & divine."[37] For Benson the erotic and the spiritual were necessary to each other; through earthly love they would together know God's love and be better women.

In both her diary and her letters to Bassett, Benson wrote of moments of "fusing," in which she achieved a very earthly spiritual union: "Did you *possess* me, or I you, my Heart's Beloved, as we sat there together on Thursday & Friday, as we held each other close, as we kissed? . . . Chat, my true lover, my true lover, see, I am your true lover, your true lover, Robin."[38] Mary/Minnie/ Ben/Robin mingled God's love and human love throughout her life. For too long the gushing affection of Victorian letters between members of the same sex has been labeled wholly asexual and without the sexual meaning that we would impute to such florid language. Indeed, there seems to be a refusal to accept sexual sophistication on the part of the Victorians because modern words are not used.[39] Rather than looking for specifically sexual language, we need to respect the self-knowledge of a woman such as Mary Benson. Christians must wrestle with the contradictions between the privileging of the spiritual and the fact that love is usually experienced most intensely through the physical. Benson recognized the potential sinfulness of sexual love, even as she cherished erotic intimacy with Bassett. On one occasion she cautioned Bassett, "When one's heart is fullest, when the physical side of Love asserts itself most, then one must *love* in mind, that things may be wholesome & well."[40] With each relationship she struggled to keep "love in mind," to control the heart and body, but in no case more so than with her final partner, Lucy Tait.

In 1883 Edward Benson was appointed Archbishop of Canterbury, head of the Church of England. Around this same time Mary, who was drifting away from the "thwarted" Chat, met Lucy Tait, the daughter of Archbishop Archibald Campbell Tait, Edward's predecessor. Little survives about Lucy, except in the numerous Benson writings. The quick-witted Benson children describe her as homely and humorless. Lucy, busy with her various philanthropic projects, was apt to be tart and self-righteous, but Mary Benson found an ongoing sustenance in their love unlike any she drew from her other intimate friendships. Edward asked Lucy to live with them in the late 1880s; she stayed till Mary's death in 1918. His invitation was an overt acknowledgment of his dependence upon his wife, but Lucy also sweetened his path by giving unfeigned homage to her father's successor in Lambeth Palace. Yet the price was high. As Fred candidly stated, Lucy Tait, "slept with my mother in the vast Victorian bed where her six children had been born."[41]

By the mid-1890s, as Edward's health weakened from overwork, Mary leaned more and more heavily on Tait for support. The sexual—and spiritual—base of their love is irrefutable. Just before Edward's death she wrote in her diary an analysis of her growing reliance upon Tait's greater faith. On the opposite page she wrote this revealing prayer:

> Once more, & with shame O Lord grant that all carnal affections may die in me, and that all things belonging to the spirit may live & grow in me—Lord look down on Lucy and me, and bring to pass the union we have both so entirely & so blindly, each in our own region of mistake, continually desired—The Desire has been fading lately, through de-

spair of each, in our own way—& despair is very near me still as I wait
& pray. I ask from thee O Lord strong & unconquerable love of the
spirit, a flame of fusing, an eternal fire that the desire which came from
thee may be accomplished for thee in us, for ever.[42]

Benson honored same-sex love. But as a Christian she could not wholly accept the desires of the flesh. She reconciled her sexual desire for Lucy Tait by
offering it as a gift to God, who had given her Tait's love. Fire, a symbol of
purification, meant a spiritual conflagration that would take their earthly love
and purify it for God. It was a goal she did not always achieve, and probably
did not want to achieve, despite bouts of guilt.

Mary Benson struggled her entire life with the sexual basis of her love for
women. Even in her private diary she found it difficult to articulate the appropriate limits for an intimate friendship. She turned to the language of spiritual longing, or she spoke elliptically of failing to keep God's love foremost
or of resting selfishly on human love. Carnal affections between women were
sinful not because she and her friends were married to men, but because a
friendship should be consecrated to God. Yet for her, kissing, touching, embracing, and sleeping together were all expressions of sacred love. Years before, she had recognized the dangers of carnality. She had refused to return
home for Christmas in 1872 because of her infatuation with Miss Hall. In her
retrospective diary she speaks of "the other fault" they nearly committed.
Here, and elsewhere, she is alluding to carnal intimacies that surpassed the
spiritual mergings she aspired to.

Benson could write about confessing her erotic desire but not about the
desire itself. Soon after falling in love with Tan Mylne, she wrote in her
diary: "Uneasiness began on Sunday, after the Circus. Somehow, I cannot
clearly see how, the suppleness, litheness, movements of the limbs stirred me
to an uneasy afternoon—a fierceness, a tingling—I came away & went to Tan,
& sitting there with her told her all—she helped me as she always does—but
the restless desire increased, and I *knew*, instinctively it wasnt good."[43] At a
later stage, she was more forthright. Ethel Smyth in her autobiography mentions how each of her new friendships began with what "Mrs. Benson used
to call the first stage, the 'My God, what a woman!' stage."[44] It is a colloquial
comment on female desire that almost startles in its bluntness, coming from a
clergyman's wife. Clearly Mary enjoyed the physical process of falling in love,
the erotic frisson of a new relationship. But then she worked hard to turn these
feelings toward God. Like so many Christians before and since, she wrestled
with the dilemma of how to transform sexual love into a spiritual gift.

Benson won her sexual independence within a socially sanctioned marriage; she never considered her love of women to be adultery. Marriage was
not a cover, as it became for many early-twentieth-century lesbians. She was

known to be markedly sympathetic to women, but she was always discreet, and contemporaries were careful not to pry into her married life. Moreover, the Victorians prized heterosexual fidelity more than emotional fidelity. John Stuart Mill's chaste love for the married Helen Taylor is the most famous example. For over twenty years the older John Taylor tolerated Mill's frequent visits to his wife as long as he did not consummate his love of Helen. Mill waited over a year after Taylor's death before marrying her. Given Mary Benson's loyalty to her husband, she had no reason to feel that she was unfaithful. Indeed, she studied hard how she might "not think of *being at my ease*, but of suiting my ways of saying things to his feelings" because Edward "thinks more of little remarks, is more sensitive, more easily wounded than I am."[45] By the 1890s the Bensons had achieved an equilibrium in their marriage, and Edward approved of Tait. For Mary Benson sexual relations with Lucy Tait were not so much an act of adultery or disloyalty to her husband as a falling away from a spiritual ideal, in which Desire rather than God dominated their love. Although she struggled to achieve the goal of spiritual rather than bodily fusing, Mary was never wholly comfortable with a bodiless affection. After Edward's death, even as she wrestled with her carnal desires, Lucy stayed in her "vast Victorian bed."

Benson was to know little happiness aside from her women friends. Edward never overcame either his depression or his domineering ways, and overwork brought an untimely death at sixty-three. Two of their six children died young. Their first-born, and Edward's favorite son, Martin (1860–78), died at seventeen of meningitis. Arthur (1862–1925), the next son, was subject to severe, disabling bouts of depression and crafted his life so as to avoid all emotional entanglements. Their youngest son, Hugh (1871–1914), converted to Roman Catholicism; he too evaded human relations as much as possible and loved only his old nurse, Beth. Their daughter Nellie (1863–90) died at twenty-seven of diphtheria, caught when caring for the poor. Maggie (1865–1916), the remaining daughter, also suffered from depression and eventually had to be institutionalized. Only E. F. (Fred) Benson (1867–1940), the popular and prolific novelist, seems to have been free from the Benson curse of depression, but he too avoided intimacy by constructing a life of homosocial bonhomie.[46]

As Mary Benson aged, friends and sons united in their praise of her loving, accepting religion. Arthur, a teacher of Greek, noted in his diary after her death: "Mama was an instinctive *pagan* hence her charm with the most beautiful perceptions and ways. Papa was an instinctive Puritan, with a rebellious love of art. Papa on the whole hated and mistrusted the people he didn't wholly approve of. Mama saw their faults and loved them."[47] Benson was not a pagan, and she would have been dismayed at the label, but perhaps her wholehearted acceptance of people made her seem free from the taint of Edward's debilitating religion. Toward the end of her long years as a confidante of women, she wrote a friend "especially to say how strongly I feel that Motherhood must be, and is, as absolutely contained in God as Fatherhood. . . . Surely it must be so, for all to take exactly what they need—from the Deep Well of Eternal Quality."[48] In her seventies, still living with her beloved Lucy Tait, Mary Benson could take her religion one step further and define God as both female and male. She came to see mothering not as an expression of spirituality, but rather as an intrinsic part of it. An all-forgiving God must, therefore, contain both the father and the mother. It is a position that only now has gained serious inroads in theological debate. Within the confines of a traditional marriage, Mary Benson found room for lesbian love and a radical conceptualization of God.

BACCHIC JOYS AND ASCETIC PLEASURES: KATHARINE BRADLEY AND EDITH COOPER

The English poets Katharine Bradley and her niece Edith Cooper present quite a different situation from that of Mary Benson. By all accounts the Bradley family was very happy and close. Katharine's father was a successful tobacco merchant in Birmingham; he died when she was two, leaving a sister eleven years older and her mother. The sister, Emma, known as Lissie, became a semi-invalid after the birth of her second child, and so Katharine and her mother moved in with the Coopers to help raise Edith and Amy. After Mrs. Bradley's death in 1868 from cancer, Katharine became a crucial mother-figure for the two girls. She early recognized the intellectual capacity of Edith and encouraged her to write poetry. By the time Edith was in her teens, maternal love had become erotic love. They were seldom apart for the rest of their lives. At sixteen Edith Cooper swore her love for her aunt for the first of many times; when she was twenty-one they appear to have consummated their love.[49] They lived at home, caring first for the ailing Lissie and then for the increasingly crotchety widowed James Cooper. The two women (fig. 9) systematically trained to be poets, reading widely, taking courses, and meeting contemporary authors. They made regular trips to London and traveled both in Britain and on the continent. Everyone noticed their intellectual intensity, emotional closeness, and social independence.[50] Only in 1899, after Amy's marriage and James's death, did they move to their own home in Richmond, where they lived out the rest of their days. Edith's father, James, played a particularly important role in their lives, for he brought new blood into the Bradley "race." This somehow exonerated their incestuous relation.

Bradley and Cooper first published poetry as Arran and Isla Leigh, but in 1884 they published two verse dramas, *Callirrhoë/Fair Rosamund*, as Michael Field. They aimed to equal or surpass the greatest poetry in English literature,

Fig. 9. Katharine Bradley and Edith Cooper, ca. 1895. Courtesy of Leonie Sturge-Moore/Charmian O'Neil.

Renaissance verse tragedy. Theirs was a very bookish world. Through thirty-three volumes of diaries, eight volumes of lyric poetry, twenty-seven tragedies, and a masque, they wrote only on artistically worthy subjects. They saw themselves as defenders of art and beauty in a materialist age. Katharine learned Greek, and together they wrote *Long Ago* (1889), a series of poems "completing" Sappho.[51] After studying Italian Renaissance art, they published a volume of verse celebrating famous paintings, *Sight and Song* (1892). Initially their work received high praise from leading men of letters, but when Robert Browning revealed the true sex and dual authorship of Michael Field, opinion turned against their work as unwomanly.[52] During the 1890s the pair seemed to know everyone and to go everywhere, but they slowly withdrew from a world that neglected their writings. The politics and economics of the literary marketplace seemed antithetical to their expressed goal of living a life dedicated to Art. By 1900 most of their work was published in fine limited editions, further contributing to a decline in their readership. With the rediscovery of Victorian women poets, Michael Field at last is gaining recognition as an important turn-of-the-century poet.[53] Critics have explored the nature of their joint authorship in detail, including their concealment behind a male pseudonym, but their conversion to Catholicism and the consequent divisions between them have been neglected.[54]

Both women adored fine apparel, elaborate manners, and the conventionalities of the times. They insisted on evening dress at dinner long after their peers had given it up. They despised Bohemianism and distrusted *The Yellow Book* and other fin-de-siècle efforts to break down traditional Victorian sexual and moral taboos. Beneath their exterior of expensive suburban respectability, however, breathed two very odd souls. Until their conversion to Roman Catholicism in 1907, they "worshipped" an amalgam of Christianity and paganism. They became connoisseurs of Love in all its ecstatic stages. Drawing from classical mythology, they defined themselves as Maenads or Bacchantes, the female followers of Dionysus.[55] The worship of Dionysus was an artistically freeing fantasy, enabling the poets to celebrate women's bodies without sentimentality. They created a shrine to Bacchus in their garden, and no higher praise could be given to a friend or animal than to call him Bacchic. Like Rosa Bonheur, the two women insisted on their unique genius and expected to be treated as a great poet, writing as a single male figure: "Holy and foolish, ever set apart / He waits the leisure of his god's free heart."[56] Unselfconsciously they referred to each other as "my dear fellow," and friends called them by their nicknames, Michael (Bradley) and Henry (Cooper, also sometimes called Field).[57] Their names flaunted their male identification, even as their dress displayed ostentatious femininity. Seemingly self-sufficient in their love, they never ceased to seek the right audience for their writing and their lives. This was almost always sympathetic but sexually unavailable men—father-figures, older writers, homosexual men, and finally, Roman Catholic priests. These men, along with James Cooper and their male dog, all served to create fictive triangles, blessing their female unity.

Edith Cooper had long been in poor health—in 1891 she had a severe case of scarlet fever; in 1900 she had rheumatic fever and a heart attack, and in the following years her heart condition was combined with gout and other unidentified symptoms. Her suffering did not immediately halt their effusive poetry, but Cooper spent more and more time writing in their shared diary, while Bradley annoyed their friends with her bitter lamentations against obtuse literary critics. Then, in 1907, they both became Roman Catholics. For almost a year Cooper had shared with Bradley her enthusiasm for the Catholic service. Nevertheless, when she secretly converted, Bradley had "hopelessly exclaimed, 'But this is terrible! I too shall have to become a Catholic!'"[58] Emma Donoghue suggests that they found a ready-made family in the Church as a replacement for the constant rebuffs and condescension they had met among the literati of London.[59] Extravagant devotion to lost causes and social marginality they already knew. Conversion gave them not only a community, but also new subject matter. What greater subject could there be than Christ's dying for all mankind? But Catholicism also brought to the fore a rift in what had been a relationship marked by almost preternatural closeness.

Where Lady Ashburton's onetime friend Margaret Trotter found earthly love to be in competition with her religious faith and Mary Benson celebrated earthly love as God's gift, Bradley and Cooper sought God's love through a passionate sacrifice of self, both bodily and intellectually. As the priest who knew them best declared: "The neo-paganism which, without their knowing it, they cherished not mainly for its culture but for its cult of sacrifice, had turned their dramatic souls toward the Sacrifice of Cavalry. . . . The step forward from neo-paganism to the Church of the Mass was but the inevitable Envoi to all they had thought and lived and sung."[60] Sacrifice became their main theme, both in their poetry and in their daily lives. They began to compete with each other for the attention of favorite priests, as well as for who could accomplish more acts of sacrificial piety. Unlike so many of their peers, they only occasionally spoke of the Virgin Mary as an intercessor, nor did they turn her into an all-loving, all-knowing Mother. They preferred to focus on Christ's sufferings, on God made incarnate. All their lives they had celebrated physical beauty. Christ in His many earthly and heavenly forms attracted their considerable emotional and aesthetic powers. But each woman approached these themes differently, making coauthorship increasingly difficult. Suffering and obedience are solitary activities; so too, it turned out, was writing religious poetry.

Bradley and Cooper were never wholly doctrinal in their Catholic worship. Both before and after conversion, they played with different genders, roles, and metaphorical guises. Even amid their most devout Catholic reflections, they never dispensed with their private trinities. Years earlier they had reconfigured their family in terms of various flexible trinities, with James Cooper, Edith's father, serving as a Godhead. They also consistently placed the masculine apart from, but in close relationship with, each of their various imagined selves. Their writing life was a trinity: Bradley, Cooper, and their creation Michael Field. After their conversion the Holy Trinity held a particular fascination because it gave a symbolic place for the masculine. Their private religious iconography united two feminized roles, the crucified Christ and the Holy Ghost, with an active, masculine God of passion and power. They could use, enjoy, and even possess the masculine without embracing the patriarchal as long as they constructed masculinity as part of a divine trinity in which they were equal participants.

Irreverent reverence had reached its apogee with the death in 1906 of their dog, Whym Chow. Previously they had turned him into a kind of male household god, with Bradley as his Mistress/Mommie and Cooper as his Auntie. He was also an essential male principle, whose vigorous brutality they adored. On one occasion he brought home the mangled remains of Rudyard Kipling's pet rabbit, an act they exulted in as having "made a man of him."[61] Bradley and Cooper found in Whym Chow a combination of mystic and wild beast, of Bacchic energy and Christian spirituality. After their conversion in 1907, they claimed his death had led them back to formal religion. Cooper boldly declared that this "Earthly Trinity of love" (Whym, Bradley, and herself) mimicked the miracle of God's triune nature. She commemorated this phenomenon by changing her birthday celebration to 27 October, the date of Whym's birth. After six years she returned to 12 January for fear of neglecting to honor her mother, another figure that moved in and out of their shared trinities. Cooper lamented that she had loved Whym too much, but pronounced it the purest love she had ever experienced.[62] She may have been obliquely commenting on her dissatisfaction with her sexual connection with her aunt. For Bradley Whym became the Holy Spirit, turning her into God the Father, and the increasingly frail Cooper into Christ the suffering Son. In 1906, even before her conversion, she wrote that "the Trinity is ever breaking forth into fresh combinations."[63] She happily created a series of elaborate but adaptable fictions that served to bless their unique love and Art.

Edith Cooper enthusiastically participated in their fantasies, but she also struggled throughout the early years of the twentieth century to regain poetic inspiration. If she had entered the Church hoping to find fresh inspiration, she discovered the opposite. The Church made no concessions to her poetic temperament, and she felt intellectually hemmed in. She relates how she almost caused a permanent rift with her confessor when she complained to him that "I had not been able to work since I joined the Church & that my Faith & my Vocation were as yet unreconciled, though I was sure some reconciliation would come." He reminded her, "It is rather difficult to make any terms between Zeus and Christ." She tried to reassure him that if she had to choose between her faith and art, she would choose her faith, but of course, "my Art is my Life."[64] Her confessor was not mollified. Two years after her conversion, Cooper had still not found her poetic voice and complained bitterly about the Church's obtuseness in regard to the poetic spirit and about its restrictions on Beauty. To make matters worse, Bradley impressed their priests with her faithful obedience, and "on every Fast-Day [she had] been inspired to do rare & wild lyrics—Catholic lyrics—choice and yet impulsive." Cooper's weeping confessions were met not with sympathy, but with instructions to "enter the spirit of the Church in her liturgies."[65] She was forced to ask herself why she, always seen as the more spiritual of the pair, found neither support nor creativity in the Church.

Cooper finally found her subject matter in her own body: the greater her physical pain, the closer she was to the power of God. Belief changed her passive acceptance of pain, especially following her diagnosis of bowel cancer, into a jubilant, active embrace of suffering. She refused all pain killers in order to remain alert and to continue writing. Like her fellow poet and convert Gerard Manley Hopkins, Cooper was fascinated with Christ's wounds, gushing blood that purified; rather than a permanent stain, His blood whitened the soul.[66] In *Poems of Adoration* (1912), a volume she had written without Bradley's assistance, she published several poems on the paradox of red blood symbolizing purity, pain bringing peace. By the time she was dying, Cooper rather relished parading her mastery of pain. When William Rothenstein drew a portrait of her a few months before her death, she wrote thanking him, "Though it is the linear music of my trial, I still look now and then with fascination at my face as it will appeal at the last judgment—at those eyes of mine you have filled with the extensiveness of pain."[67] Meditating upon the crucifixion, Cooper turned her painful dying into an acceptance of God's will, just as Christ had come to accept His own slow death on the cross.

None of their friends could understand why Bradley and Cooper practiced the strictest fasting and bodily humiliation. They had chosen the Dominican route to Christ. Atonement for sin, especially sins of the flesh, rather than redemption, as preached by the Franciscans, attracted them. They would have found Mary Benson's faith too passive. Just as the heroes in their tragedies struggled with great moral issues, they sought the drama of personal self-conquest. Although Michael Field's poems continued to celebrate the body in all its forms, especially that of the suffering Christ on the cross, the two women embraced with startling avidity the pleasures of asceticism. Like Hopkins, they discovered new satisfactions in the mortification of the flesh, in self-denial, and in total submission to God's presumed will. But they also had their backslidings. Cooper admitted in their diary to thinking only of "Tea & slices of bread & butter" during early Mass, where she had arrived "tortured with thirst, feeling in flesh like a dug-up body. . . . The Rite fails to animate a spiritual response."[68] But she so enjoyed her newfound purpose in life that her confessor warned her that her soul was a weedy garden; she was guilty of "beating about, making noise & fuss with my office & prayers & masses," rather than examining her own deficiencies and praying for them.[69] He exhorted her to guard against the sin of spiritual pride; Cooper obediently documented her lack of humility in frequent diary entries.

Bradley faced a different spiritual weakness: she was too attracted to the Church's rituals, which seemed almost pagan in their enchanting richness. "Doubtless I am too wild for the Fold," she admitted, adding, "I want to sing the bees who make the wax. I love all about the lights. It is 'Lumen Christi' that set my heart on fire. Is it that once I was a torch-bearer on the hills?"[70] In contrast to Cooper, who pursued a masochistic route of self-immolation, driving herself to undertake severe fasting and countless prayers and vigils, Bradley found her particular pleasure in the beautiful Church rituals of sacrifice. She never quite gave up her pagan past, but she found temporary peace in a renewed sense of spiritual love—for both God and her beloved niece. As Cooper noted with some surprise, Bradley had no problems with obedience, thoroughly enjoying all of her acts of contrition. But inwardly Bradley believed that she lacked simplicity—that she could not approach the Church's teachings and its services with a simple mind, but instead delighted in complexities, unforeseen beauties, and even humor. And she was overenthusiastic, advertising her newfound happiness and pushing her old friends to convert. Most of her religious poetry worked through Catholic dogma with sincerity, but the fire of passion—the old Bacchic flambeau—is strikingly absent from her volume of religious poems, *Mystic Trees* (1913).

Cooper's diary entries after 1907 have the same overinsistence as Bradley's letters to friends. Yes, they are truly happy now, she declares to herself and her readers. By this time they had decided to preserve their diary, so Cooper was writing not only to Bradley, but also to an unknown public. She redoubled her praise of her aunt at the same time that she outlined ongoing difficulties. Reading between the lines of her year-end summary for 1907, one senses a strong undercurrent of discontent: "Then the plunge into the River of the Water of Life that was to sever one from all one had been. . . . The jar between Michael & me at the broken confidence, the ragged unity at first exacted by the conditions of the initiation—the demon strife against change in oneself & another & in all one's days!"⁷¹ The 1907 volumes contain torn-out pages, leaving the reader to wonder whether descriptions of "demon strife" were destroyed. Like the Ladies of Llangollen, Bradley and Cooper were overinvested in their perfect unity. Gestures of passive-aggressive anger, nevertheless, keep cropping up in the diaries. For Easter 1911 Bradley gave Cooper a set of coarse linen nun's hoods and handkerchiefs. The ever-stylish Cooper was shocked at the gift; she wanted to choose her own forms of self-denial.⁷²

Although Bradley and Cooper, like Mary Benson and her lovers, never called themselves lesbians, they enjoyed an active sexual life for many years, based on evidence found in their early letters, numerous oblique comments in their diaries, and of course, their poetry.⁷³ But Cooper seems to have found this side of their life increasingly problematic. Virginia Blain ascribes Edith's growing antipathy toward sexual relations after 1897 to a combination of causes, including the death of her father, her erotic attraction to the art critic Bernard Berenson, and her wish for greater emotional independence.⁷⁴ Cooper herself credited her sexual distancing to religious scruples. The diary entries in the weeks leading up to her first confession half-reveal her ambivalent feelings toward her sexual past. She agonized over how to tell her unsophisticated confessor about what she called "my secret sins." She thought she might obliquely confess via Baudelaire's notorious lesbian poems, "Les Femmes damnées," a reference the priest was unlikely to understand.⁷⁵ Like Bradley at a later date, Cooper was always uncertain how much of her previ-

ous life needed to be confessed and then abrogated. But about their sexual relations she remained adamant: this must be one more sacrifice to God. The
Catholic Church honored celibacy and validated her decision to retain a kind
of bodily privacy by saying no to sex. Ironically, as her cancer grew and her
body began to disintegrate, she became intimately dependent on Bradley.

At first sex seems to have been an easier renunciation than Art. At the end
of 1907, Cooper celebrated her victory over herself—and Bradley: "A year of
strife, & over the flesh of triumph through the dedication of my will to be a
sanctuary lamp before the Real Presence of the God who dies for me. . . .
God make us one in a new tenderness of love, in a compact joy in each other
as Catholics—May we have new confidence in each other as poets."[76] The
shared forfeiture of sex for God meant, for Bradley and Cooper, in their more
exalted religious states, a uniquely beautiful sacrifice that would ensure life
together in Heaven. Margaret Trotter drew comfort from her belief that the
absence of hope in this life meant the promise of spiritual fulfillment in the
afterlife. Her desolation at the loss of Lady Ashburton's love was absolute,
whereas, even amid their disagreements, Bradley and Cooper held onto a belief in their unity of blood (as aunt and niece) and art (as Michael Field). But
conversion destroyed their union as a single poet. Although it gave them
shared delights in the Church's rituals and commands, the ensuing years did
not bring them "new confidence in each other as poets."[77]

Bradley had the strongest investment in the public myth of their unity. She,
who felt every slight and slur of her friends, now grappled with her beloved
partner cutting her out of her deepest self. By 1907 Cooper was writing virtually all of the entries in their joint diary, so we can only surmise Bradley's grief.
Somewhere around this time, Bradley wrote the sonnet "Constancy," asking
"why . . . / Hastes she to range me with inconstant minds?" Did Cooper think
Bradley had entered the Church for false reasons or had she failed in some
obscure way to love her sufficiently? The poem concludes, "I confront the
charge / As sorrowing, and as careless of my fame / As Christ intact before the
infidel."[78] The autobiographical roots of the poem are obscure, but the stress of
that year is well documented. This may be as close as Bradley could come to
begging Cooper to remember her lifelong fidelity. Bradley had not freely chosen Cooper's path into holy celibacy. However inspiring they each came to find
this state, "unity" without sex was hard on her and their poetry. Bradley's repeated recourse to Father John Gray might have had its roots in her admiration
for his sexual self-control. In the 1890s he was considered to be the model for
Oscar Wilde's anti-hero in *The Picture of Dorian Gray* (1892). His lifelong friend
André Raffalovich was presumed to be his former lover, though no whiff
of scandal touched them after Gray became a priest. More ominously for
Bradley, upon Gray's conversion he had ceased to write poetry. In the past
Bradley and Cooper had defined their sexual relationship as a mythic trinity

of body, soul, and intellect, bringing them closer together than ordinary heterosexual couples.[79] When the body was denied, they lost an essential component of their sacred trinity. Could spiritual sensuality replace the body?

In many ways Cooper's repeated protestations of love for Bradley were true. She felt closer to her because their relationship no longer included sex, but rested instead on their commitment to Catholicism. Their love could now be expressed as a shared adoration of Christ's Passion. But in all of Cooper's ruminations about Art and the Church, Bradley was conspicuously absent. After 1907 she craved the praise and reassurance of her male confessor. When at last she began to write again, her poems lacked tension in their wholesale descriptions of suffering.

> Give me finer potency of gift!
> For Thy Holy Wounds I would attain,
> As a bee the feeding loveliness
> Of the sanguine roses. I would lift
> Flashes of such faith that I may drain
> From each Gem the wells of Blood that press![80]

Bradley wrote defensively to her old friend Mary Berenson about Cooper's *Poems of Adoration*: "To me it is a great joy, I often go to it adoring. *Only some of the poems:* We shall not be angry—if you & Doctrine [Bernard Berenson] who love Cooper so dear—do not love her Catholic book. Perhaps you are lovers of the faun Cooper. I do myself prefer the faun perhaps." This intimation of trouble, however, was smoothed over by the additional comment, "Cooper writes & lives very acutely—& loves her flowers, her home, & Michael—also she is loved back."[81] Both Cooper and Bradley had written lovely celebratory poems about each other, but poems of celebratory faith proved to be more difficult to write.

Bradley too sought to express an unquestioning faith, but her best poems plumb the tensions between herself and Cooper in a religious context. She explored her sense of impending loss, as Cooper lay dying, in a troubling late poem:

> He is parting from me,
> I know not how this thing should be,
> It is as if a big bumble-bee
> Were so deep immerst
> In his honey-thirst,
> He remains a-boom
> In his foxglove tomb,
> He is lost, he cannot recover—
>   O my lover![82]

Bradley and Cooper had long used flower-and-bee imagery (and male pronouns) to describe their erotic love. They had even named their 1908 collection of pre- and post-conversion lyrics *Wild Honey*, as if to express the
sweetness of all forms of love. Men have used the flower as female genitalia
for centuries, but seldom with such variety and sophistication as these
women poets in regard to same-sex love. In lyric after lyric they depict the
physical giving of love through images of flowers unfolding, opening to the
bee, the rain, the human hand, and after conversion, to God. They understood that in opening herself, the flower was irretrievably changed—that
passion was as destructive as it was creative. But what happened when the unopened flower became a "tomb," trapping the bee? Was Cooper imprisoned,
drunk on the honey of belief? The image of the bee entrapped in the flower
is hardly one of a joyous entry into a better life.

For five years Bradley and Cooper struggled to join their deep love for
each other with their new faith. But in Bradley's untitled poem, the bee is
caught in a deep, private place where the narrator cannot follow. He does not
complete the cycle of life. The flower will not open and release the bee to fer-
tilize other plants; nor can human hand open the petals. An undercurrent of
sadness and separation runs throughout the poems Bradley wrote to Cooper
during their final years. She could not go where the bee went. Around 1912
Bradley wrote her last love poem to Cooper. She published it after Cooper's
death as the final poem in *Dedicated* (1914), a volume credited to Michael
Field, but actually composed of Cooper's early pre-conversion poems. In
"Fellowship" Bradley returns to the holy and fiery whiteness of pagan myth,
eschewing all references to blood and suffering:

> In the old accents I will sing, my glory, my delight,
> In the old accents tipped with flame before we knew the right,
> True way of singing with reserve. O Love, with pagan might,
>
> White in our steeds, and white too in our armour let us ride
> Immortal white, triumphing, flashing downward side by side
> To where our friends, the Argonauts, are fighting with the tide.[83]

Bradley had long been drawn to imagery of fire and flame to describe her
rich sexual and spiritual love for Cooper. In 1885, in what can be called their
"honeymoon days," she had written Cooper, "Love always this terrible & fiery
old Fowl, who loves not as mortals but fearfully as a god." Cooper had replied,
"your Pussy loves you deeper than anything but Art!"[84] It may have been a
warning. Thirty years later she loved Christ more, and Bradley followed her
into the Church to keep her, hiding her pagan self deeply buried within. Perhaps Bradley had always loved like a Greek god, fearlessly and passionately,
whereas Cooper had been more muted, more willing to accept her caresses,

like the Pussy of her early nickname. For her, true passion was found in art, and at the end, in God, and not in a human being.

If Cooper found some kind of serenity in religious faith, Bradley found her better self in nursing her niece. They returned at the end to what they had been at the beginning: an elaborately metaphoric mother-daughter couple that no person could penetrate. Their personal trinity changed one more time, with Christ referred to as "the Beloved," a name they continually used about each other. Now the trinity consisted of three gentle beloveds—each other and Christ, one body forever. If they depended more on their priests, what a friend had dubbed their "cher pères," for personal affirmation, they still pledged their deepest loyalty to each other. Only a few months before her death, Cooper read aloud a selection of Bradley's love poems one evening during the visit of their cousin and Bradley's onetime suitor Francis Brooks. The listening male affirmed their love for each other. Perhaps at the end Cooper accepted that their Bacchic past could not be denied. After her death Bradley lived another eight months, dying of a cancer that she had never revealed to Cooper. Alone on Easter day 1914, she put together a shrine composed of the pictures of her beloved Bradley family members, her mother, her sister Lissie, and Edith Cooper, and asked them each to bless her—but especially Cooper. Her trinity had become all-female. But she was of the earth, earthly, and no one ever spoke to her across the great divide. Fortunately she did not have long to wait to rejoin them.

PART III

Cross-Age and Crossed Love

Chapters 5 and 6 explore the deeply satisfying, and yet deeply troubling, lesbian love between surrogate mothers and admiring daughters. Each examines the eroticism of an unequal love, in which the beloved is older, wiser, and seemingly more powerful. Whereas same-sex marriages could be more equal than heterosexual marriages, cross-age love accentuated inequalities. For the women discussed in the next two chapters, disparities of age and power increased the opportunities for intense emotional dramas between women. Privately two women could rehearse emotions that might be dangerous to express in public or to a man, ranging from strong, even explosive, love to proud, contained self-control. A key emotion was anger, aroused by the desire for merger and the fear of the loss of autonomy. I also consider how a cross-age relation was attractive to older women repelled by heterosexuality and yet unable to escape its dictates. For the women in these chapters, cross-age love was not an adolescent phase, but a lifetime commitment, filled with a rainbow of emotions.

Virtually every woman discussed in this book had at one time a crush on an older woman. Some long-standing relationships began as a cross-age mother-daughter relation before they became a husband-wife marriage. For example, Sarah Ponsonby was sixteen years younger than Eleanor Butler; their relationship began as pupil-tutor. Edith Cooper was fifteen years younger than Katharine Bradley. The aunt-niece couple played almost every possible family role. Sometimes a woman found a replica of her beloved mother in an intimate friend. Rosa Bonheur repeatedly compared Nathalie Micas's nurturing love to that of her long-dead mother. Harriet Hosmer began her career in Rome not as a rival to Charlotte Cushman but as her admirer; Cushman was "dear Ma" to the motherless younger Hosmer. Other women found a better, more fulfilling surrogate than their own inadequate mother. The early feminist writer Mary Wollstonecraft never forgave her mother for preferring her brother and sought affection from a series of alternative mothers.

In chapter 5 I focus on three "daughters," the novelist Geraldine Jewsbury (1812–80), the journalist and social activist Edith Simcox (1844–1901), and the composer Ethel Smyth (1858–1943), to trace continuities and differences during the Victorian era. These three women combined adoration for an older woman with tomboyish acts that tested the boundaries of respectability. Submission alternated with erotic forthrightness and insistent demands. Jewsbury and Simcox undertook extraordinary acts of humiliation for their beloved mothers. They received little gratitude and fewer kisses, yet both found their love a transformative experience, even if never wholly fulfilling. Ethel Smyth with great difficulty forged a complex set of relationships that met her erotic and creative needs. She wanted both unquestioning love and tempestuous love from surrogate mothers; rather than settling upon one woman, she pursued several simultaneously. During the happiest period of her life, she integrated the mothering love of a man with the turbulent love of an older woman. Like Cushman, Smyth ignored whatever collateral damage she might cause in pursuing specific women. A final section examines the relationship of Mary Benson and her two adult daughters, Nellie and Maggie. It illustrates the difficult negotiations biological mothers and daughters made in constructing independent sexual and emotional lives.

The "mothers," Jane Welsh Carlyle (1801–66), George Eliot (1819–80), and the numerous older women that Smyth loved, including especially Elisabeth (Lisl) von Herzogenberg (1847–92), Mary Benson (1842–1918), and Lady Mary Ponsonby (1832–1916), all actively shaped the emotional lives and professional careers of their protégées. The younger woman symbolized hope for a different future, as well as a revolt against the social edicts to which these married women conformed. Through reprimand, discipline, or encouragement, these mothers found an outlet for their own frustrations, ambitions, and anger. Aggressive daughters met their match in aggressive mothers. Young love could also honor, without forcing into the open, deep-buried secrets. Sexual frustration (Jane Welsh Carlyle), the guilt of achieved ambition (George Eliot), thwarted passion and a distant husband (Lady Mary Ponsonby), and an unhappy marriage (Lisl von Herzogenberg, Mary Benson) gave each woman an added impetus to accept the love of an adoring surrogate daughter.

The women in chapter 5 long to merge with the beloved, but those in chapter 6 fear the loss of identity. For them the drive toward what one loves is overpowering, yet the achievement of this goal is terrifying. In sharp contrast to the women of chapter 5, who longed for the potentially suffocating embrace of mother-love, the women of chapter 6 struggled with the psychic and erotic effects of an absent mother. In their fiction Eliza Lynn Linton (1822–98) and Vernon Lee (1856–1935) created forbidden, distant or punishing mother-figures who were then rejected for a more perfect, imagined love. Each acknowledged her passionate need for intimacy, yet each felt too odd, too intellectual, to find an understanding partner. Highly self-conscious about their masculine attributes, each crafted a vocabulary to explain her sexuality. Linton's revealing fictions played with gender inversion, changeling fantasies, insanity, and fiery passion. She imagined same-sex love by turning herself into a gentle, understanding man, but throughout her life she excoriated mannish women and extolled womanly women. Lee was proud of her sexual self-control; she saw women's love for each other as superior to driven, egotistic heterosexual love. In her horror stories, however, she explored uncontrollable emotions, forbidden desires, and monomaniacal passions.

All five of the "daughters" discussed in these two chapters rejected the norms of femininity. The Victorians polarized masculinity and femininity, leaving little space for women who felt they possessed characteristics from both sexes. Any woman who actively loved another woman became unnaturally masculine and lost her passive, feminine character. Yet in spite of this dominant ideology, these women defined their feelings and behavior as natural and appropriate for them. In different ways each came to terms with her masculinity. Jewsbury refused to subdue her aggressive wooing of both women and men. Simcox's diary is the fullest and most honest surviving account of same-sex desire during the 1870s and 1880s, and is worthy of comparison with Anne Lister's 1820s–30s diaries. In it she dissected how and why she believed herself to be "half a man," and therefore unattractive to men, but powerfully attracted to George Eliot. Linton feared that her masculine desire for women was a sign of degeneracy; she made sure the public recognized her feminine skills, including housecleaning and sewing. Late in life she embraced the role of surrogate mother.

Born a generation later than Linton, Smyth and Lee struggled to articulate an alternative to gender inversion, with its focus on physical characteristics and behaviors. Without wholly dismissing past theories about masculine women, they posited the possibility of a new woman, neither feminine nor masculine. The androgynous woman united masculine creativity with feminine understanding. They did not identify themselves with or as men, but rather saw themselves as vulnerable boyish figures in relationship to maternal women. Smyth insisted that she was healthy-minded and loved a man, as well as women. Unlike Linton (or Emily Faithfull), she cast herself as a tomboy, rather than mannish. Lee admitted to "nerves," but blamed them on a combination of her odd upbringing and her overdeveloped brainpower. She championed women who had sublimated their passion for the betterment of humankind. Neither woman ever used the word *lesbian* in her writing, but each looked toward a new definition of women who loved women as members of a third sex.

5   *"A Strenuous Pleasure"*

DAUGHTER-MOTHER LOVE

The ideal mother was the essence of human divinity, for she poured unconditional, unearned love upon her children. One could take one's anger, arrogance, and folly to a good mother and expect understanding. As a paradigm
of intimacy, nothing could surpass the mother-child relationship. The assumption that mother love was the supreme form of love became both the
strength and the weakness of nineteenth-century women's erotic relationships modeled on the mother-daughter tie. When a woman fell in love with
another woman, she could justify it in terms of this formative love experience. A Victorian woman naturally defined her passion for a woman by refashioning the language of mother-daughter love. Frances Power Cobbe
concludes her autobiography, "God has given me two priceless benedictions
in life;—my youth a perfect Mother; in my later years, a perfect Friend."[1] In
a society that venerated maternal love and categorized women's sexuality as
either holy (marriage) or fallen (prostitution), women found in the idealized
language of maternal love an appropriate and highly regarded vocabulary to
describe same-sex love. But implicitly this unconditional love could never exist in real life. In actual love relations daughter-mother love was an enabling
and disabling metaphor.

    This chapter focuses on cross-age romance between a single younger
woman and a heterosexually married older woman. These relationships were
initiated not by adolescents, but by women in their twenties and thirties.
The younger woman played the child, demanding to be loved whatever the
circumstances. Enmeshed in family and spousal responsibilities, the older
woman still made time for the younger. The daughter knew from the start
that she could never live with her beloved, could never fully possess her, and
so she staged a series of dramas and interventions to cement her claim to love.
These might include fierce intellectual disagreements, jealous scenes, flirtations with other women or men, or, most effective of all, an illness requiring

the undivided attention of the beloved mother-lover. For the daughter, love's impossibilities, including the desire to be the primary interest of the older woman, fed the flames of romantic passion and idealism.

The intimate friendships described here were more profound and longer lasting than the widely accepted phase in which an older woman advised her young protégée. They cannot be easily classified as sexual. Rather, women strove to achieve a passionately spiritual intimacy that subsumed the erotic. The love of a woman, figured as either daughter or mother, became a vehicle for exploring what one's life in the fullest moral and spiritual sense should *be*, and not just what one should actually *do* with that life. This struggle to be more worthy of the wise beloved, however, could take its toll. As Edith Simcox admitted in her memorial to George Eliot: "In friendship George Eliot had the unconscious exactingness of a full nature. . . . To love her was a strenuous pleasure, for in spite of the tenderness for all human weakness that was natural to her, and the scrupulous charity of her overt judgments, the fact remained that her natural standard was ruthlessly out of reach, and it was a painful discipline for her friends to feel that she was compelled to lower it to suit their infirmities."[2] Even making allowance for Eliot's extraordinary genius, one can sense a certain weariness about living under her sun. It was strenuous work to be a good daughter when the mother offered so little in return. Simcox and the others discussed in this chapter had to come to terms with the limitations of the daughter-mother paradigm that both made possible and circumscribed their erotic love.

This chapter traces a trajectory of changing roles, oscillating power, and differing desires. Sometimes the needy daughter willingly abased herself for signs of affection. At other times the mother sought support. As we saw with Charlotte Cushman and Emma Crow Cushman, the pace and place of desire and power could shift in complicated ways. As in any love affair, at first the young lover felt vulnerable, powerless, and unworthy of the indescribable goodness of her beloved. The next stage, however, brought a shift in power, in which the beloved admitted her need for adulation and support. Geraldine Jewsbury and Jane Welsh Carlyle seem to have made this transition with less fuss than many other women who conceptualized their erotic love as a mother-daughter relationship. Unrequited love had its own power, as we will see in the case of Edith Simcox and George Eliot. To love without expectation could be transformed into a superior spiritual love, closed to those who possessed love's bounty. Once again the privileges of genius come to the fore: was the budding composer Ethel Smyth a genius who deserved the nurturing love she demanded, regardless of the pain she might cause? Or did she press mother-daughter love out of shape, damaging or destroying virtually every relationship she entered into?

A DIFFICULT MOTHER: GERALDINE JEWSBURY AND
JANE WELSH CARLYLE

Geraldine Jewsbury (fig. 10) lost her mother at six and her sister at twenty-one; she lost her faith in her late twenties. Caring first for her father's home and then her brother's, she led the life of a typical middle-class unmarried daughter and sister in the industrial city of Manchester. But she aspired to something more, and in the spring of 1840 she wrote the famous Victorian sage Thomas Carlyle. Her letter struck a responsive chord, and he replied to her rather than to the numerous others who had begged him for spiritual, emotional, or pecuniary assistance. The following March, when Jewsbury visited the Carlyles in London, she discovered a couple who could live neither with nor without each other. Jane had married Thomas convinced that he was a genius and would someday be famous. Egotistical and sexually repressed, he was a demanding, insecure tyrant. Any noise distracted him from writing his brilliant work. Jane vented her frustrations in a corrosive wit and satiric letters that led many to urge her to write fiction. They were probably the most famous unhappily married couple in London. The enthusiastic Jewsbury overstayed her welcome, talked interminably, and smoked cigarettes. At first Thomas hoped to keep the friendship to himself, but he soon abdicated to his wife the care of this demanding, volatile young woman. For Jane Jewsbury's unabashed admiration could not have been better timed.

Their friendship is not a lesbian story, but rather a narrative that makes possible lesbian understandings. It illustrates how a woman who tried and failed to win a husband, who seemed at times too assertively masculine and at others too emotionally feminine, could gain a hold on the affections of a woman who prided herself on her rationality and self-control. The surviving documentation of this intimate friendship is limited. Jewsbury destroyed her friend's letters, and the editor of Jewsbury's letters destroyed the originals. But through the letters that Jewsbury and both of the Carlyles wrote to others, indirect evidence survives of Jane's increasing dependence on the younger woman throughout the 1840s and 1850s. Only from Jewsbury could she receive a warm and unquestioning love. For over twenty-five years, Jewsbury found in Carlyle not only a surrogate mother, but also someone who listened, poured doses of salutary cold water on ill-defined schemes, and in the end, came to need her more than anyone else in her life.

Their lifelong friendship started out as a romantic friendship, giving each woman ample room to dramatize same-sex love. Could it, would it, be more successful than heterosexual passion? In an early letter, Jewsbury showered Carlyle with love:

Fig. 10. Geraldine Jewsbury, ca. 1845. Courtesy of the National Trust, London.

I think of you a great deal, and with an anxiety I cannot account for. I can't express my feelings even to myself, only by tears; but I am no good to you, and I, who wish to be and do anything that might be a comfort to you, can give you nothing but vague, undefined yearnings to be yours in some way. . . . Talk as much as I will, it's the same thing said over and over; you will let me be yours and think of me as such, will you not? How are you? Do you sleep well?[3]

Carlyle (fig. 11) was a poor sleeper, but the conjunction of the question with a declaration of love implicitly signals an unmentionable erotic component to Jewsbury's love. Jewsbury followed the conventional script of cross-age friendship, "resolving to try to be conformable and more proper-behaved in my manners and conversation, in order to be more of a credit to you!" But she did not cease declaring her passionate affection: "You know I love you as no-body else can, and everything you do is right in my eyes," and "you will laugh, but I feel towards you much more like a lover than a female friend!"[4] Carlyle, by setting the limits to their friendship, paradoxically gave Jewsbury more space in which to express her fervent love. Had she reciprocated with equal passion, they would have faced irresolvable complexities. Their intimacy rested on different grounds from that of, say, Chat Bassett and Mary Benson. The latter two women began by accepting each other's unhappy marriages and then built a relationship on their search for a more perfect religious faith. The unmarried Jewsbury based her love on Jane Carlyle's unhappy marriage,

Fig. 11. Jane Welsh Carlyle, ca. 1855. By courtesy of the National Portrait Gallery, London.

suggesting that her love might make Jane happy. She softened this arrogant assumption by declaring how much Jane Carlyle made her a better person.

An inveterate pessimist, Jane Carlyle did not initially accept this bargain. But she thoroughly enjoyed Jewsbury's emotional tempests, since they proved her superiority to the young woman. Jane, a consummate actress on her own stage, repeatedly claimed to be shocked by Jewsbury's declarations of love: what was genuine feeling in a woman who could effortlessly go from heart-rending tears to easy laughter? On a visit to their mutual friends, the Paulets, Jewsbury staged an exhibition of "tiger-jealousy" toward potential women rivals, or so Jane wrote her husband. She turned a small country-house contretemps into a drama that placed herself on center stage, with Jewsbury playing the role of forlorn suitor. The setting is that most intimate site for female confessions, the bedroom:

> Nothing but outbursts of impertinence and hysterics from morning till night—which finished off with a grand *scene* in my room after I had gone up to bed a full and faithful account of which I shall entertain you with at meeting—It was a *revelation* to me not only of Geraldine but of human nature!—such mad lover-like jealousy on the part of one woman towards another it had never entered into my heart to conceive—By a wonderful effort of *patience* on my part—made more on Mrs Paulets account who was quite vexed—than from the *flattering* consideration that *I* was the object of this incomprehensible passion, the affair was brought to a happy conclusion—I got her to laugh over her own absurdity—promised to go by Manchester if she would behave herself like a reasonable creature and with her hair all dishevelled and her face all bewept she thereupon sat down at my feet and—smoked a cigaritto!! With all the placidity in life![5]

Jane Carlyle both rejects and asserts her centrality, simultaneously diminishing the importance of this scene and promising more details (in the bedroom?) for Thomas. She is preternaturally patient, but only to maintain social courtesies. She knows nothing of such "mad lover-like" jealousy between women, but her very denial is an acknowledgment of its flattering power; it also implies that Jewsbury gave her something that Thomas did not. The two exclamation marks signal an unconscious recognition that a cigaritto might be a sexualized signifier in this new friendship. Jane frequently reworked similar scenes to entertain her husband, creating a kind of asexual intimacy with him based on mocking Jewsbury's passion. This strategy denied any possibility of a queer love triangle and reasserted her husband's primacy. Letters were Jane's safety valve, giving her an opportunity to show Thomas, rumored to be impotent, an emotional love that he had denied her.

Jewsbury created her own dramas by parading her heterosexual failure.

Her inability to secure a husband was not a bourgeois tragedy, but an especially rich comedy to share with her unhappily married friend. She asked Mrs.
Elizabeth Paulet to send Jane "a precious batch of caricatures . . . professing
to be '*illustrations of Miss Jewsbury's late matrimonial speculation*'—in my life I have
seen none cleverer."[6] By laughing at herself she avoided openly criticizing the
institutions of courtship and marriage. Her seeming humiliation gained Jane's
approbation overtly for her "good nature" and covertly for her good sense in
not marrying. Their relationship was built upon a shared recognition that
Carlyle's life was a failure—and that Jewsbury would not make the same mistakes. This bold strategy worked until 1857, when Jewsbury began a long
correspondence with Walter Mantell. Jane Carlyle was furious at being upstaged and at the possibility that her friend might desert her for a man.[7] Fortunately for her Mantell did not want to marry a strong-minded woman, and
the friendship tapered off with his return to New Zealand.

Jane Carlyle honed her role of the distrusting rationalist. She was both
captivated and shocked by Jewsbury's candor "on the passion of *Love* as it dif-
fers in Men from Women!! She is far too *anatomical* for me."[8] Throughout her
life Jane freely used excessive, even violent language to attack any unwar-
ranted show of feeling. She consciously separated herself from other women
by maintaining absolute bodily and emotional control, while indulging in
verbal histrionics. She, not Jewsbury, could use extreme language because it
was her only emotional outlet. Her letters are mini-dramas of domestic life,
turning her husband into a monster of unconscious selfishness and herself
into a captious martyr. She also belittled Jewsbury in her letters, declaring on
one occasion, "her speech is so extremely insincere that I feel in our dialogues
always as if we were acting in a play [;] . . . not being myself an amateur of
play-acting, I prefer considerably good honest *silence*."[9] Similar accounts of
Jewsbury's so-called wild behavior became opportunities to foreground Jane
Carlyle's virtues, even as she modestly denied her need for attention. A
double standard operated: Jewsbury could act in an unwomanly fashion, but
must write herself into respectability; the married Carlyle was always feminine, but could write with unwomanly force and self-aggrandizement.

Much to Jane Carlyle's distress, Jewsbury's fiction was as disreputable as her
behavior. Her first two novels, under the influence of Madame de Staël and
George Sand, were dismayingly candid about sex. Zoë (1845) combined religious doubts and sexual disappointments in a heady mixture of exoticism, with
a half-Greek heroine, a lapsed Catholic priest, and a French count. In Jewsbury's second novel, *The Half-Sisters* (1848), the illegitimate half-Italian heroine, Bianca, is partially modeled on the young Charlotte Cushman. Bianca's
goodness and economic independence contrast sharply with her dull legitimate sister, who marries for financial security. Hundreds of pages later, Bianca
marries an aristocrat, while her sister commits suicide after an adulterous af-

fair. Since Jewsbury refused to tone down *Zoe*, Jane retaliated by exaggerating the evils of the book and her own perspicuity, *"C'est assez,"* I said to myself, "if she *will* run about the streets naked it is not I who am her keeper."[10] Scenes in the privacy of a bedroom were one thing, but writing about sexual passion for the reading public was the worst kind of exposure. And Jane Carlyle was not immune from jealousy; she met Jewsbury's growing literary reputation with sardonic commentary. Jewsbury responded with more pallid heroines in later novels. Perhaps she felt Jane was right in censoring female fantasies of sexual and economic empowerment. Rosa Bonheur, Charlotte Cushman, and other independent women who lived public lives aroused misgivings mixed with admiration.

By the late 1840s the division between Thomas and Jane Carlyle had widened. As a famous writer, he was a star attraction in the homes of the aristocracy, while his wife was ignored. Thomas became infatuated with the first Lady Ashburton and spent weeks at her country home without Jane. Geraldine Jewsbury became Jane Carlyle's chief confidante. Moving away from the passionate language of romance, Jewsbury deepened their ties by becoming the stronger of the two. She now wrote Jane openly about her marriage: "The thing you intended for the best and noblest dedication of yourself has not borne the fruit you have reason to expect. Dear friend, do not let yourself be made bitter by this trial."[11] Jane enjoyed disciplining Jewsbury, teaching her to submit to respectable social mores, but she found her own self-discipline hideously difficult. Perhaps with an echo of the Ladies of Llangollen, in 1851 Jewsbury reminded the depressed older woman of their fantasy of running away together. "Do not you recollect how we settled that we 'go and seek our fortune,' that you were to defend me from all the cows we met in our way, and that we were to take a cottage in some place, either on a moor or on a mountain? What is to hinder our putting it in practice?"[12] Norma Clarke argues that Jewsbury had an investment in empowering Carlyle's suffering. If Jane needed her, that need turned the unconventional Jewsbury into a supportive, nurturing woman.[13] Ambitious and independent, Jewsbury avoided traditional femininity, while celebrating its perils and triumphs in her friend.

Most of Jane Welsh Carlyle's letters exude self-deprecating egoism, but at the end of her life a new note of sentimentality crept in. During the early years of their friendship, she had concealed her needs beneath a language of exaggeration, ridicule, and contradiction. Although she had at first reciprocated with her own dramatic scenes, by the mid-1850s Jewsbury no longer needed Jane Carlyle's attention. She enjoyed the growing recognition of her writing and a widening circle of new friends. Their friendship, still working within the confines of a mother-daughter love, had shifted from romantic love to daughterly independence to maternal dependence. They each moved beyond their initial intensities. Sensing Jane's increasing need for reassurance, Jewsbury began addressing her letters to "My dear Child"—she would care for the isolated, aging Jane Carlyle. Virginia Woolf, in her admiring essay about the two women, concluded: "Intimacy is a difficult art, as Geraldine herself reminds us. . . . The tie between them could stretch and stretch indefinitely without breaking. Jane knew the extent of Geraldine's folly; Geraldine had felt the full lash of Jane's tongue. They had learnt to tolerate each other."[14] But if all the letters had survived from this early Victorian romantic friendship, it might seem more intimate and less socially acceptable. It also might not read as a "natural" progress-narrative, from turbulent passion to mutual respect.

"OUR RELATION IS BETWEEN UNEQUALS": EDITH SIMCOX AND GEORGE ELIOT

Following the extraordinary critical and popular success of *Middlemarch* (1871–72), the novelist George Eliot (Marian Evans) received numerous admiring letters from both women and men. She counseled submission and selfless duty to all young women and men seeking an alternative to formal religion. Duty, admittedly combined with sharp resistance, had brought Jane Welsh Carlyle misery. How might it bring happiness to the women who loved George Eliot? Several of these "spiritual daughters," as they were called, struggled to keep their lover-like passion within the confines set by Eliot and her lover, George Henry Lewes, but none more than Edith Simcox. Simcox was a remarkably energetic and successful social activist and journalist. She was a partner in a model shirtmaking enterprise that paid seamstresses a living wage. She served on the London School Board, was a pioneer in women's trade unionism and the cooperative movement, and was a delegate to international trade union conferences. Simcox's diary records these activities, but its principal focus is a detailed analysis of her love for Eliot. Since her love was unreciprocated, the diary became a repository of her most conflicted, depressing thoughts. Unlike letters, which demand some restraint, a private diary permits a degree of self-pity that has led some biographers of Eliot to dismiss Simcox.[15] But this highly self-conscious and articulate spinster left an invaluable self-analysis, exploring how her sexual attraction to women, her love for Eliot, and her lack of interest in men defined her identity. Simcox knew that her love for Eliot met the very highest standards of fidelity and loyalty, so why should heterosexual love be considered superior? She responded to her erotic and emotional marginality by arguing for the spiritual superiority of unrequited same-sex love.

Throughout her life Marian (or Mary Ann, as she was baptized) Evans attracted women admirers, but she never forgot that it was largely women who had rejected her after she decided in 1854 to live with the married George Lewes. She insisted on being called Mrs. Lewes and refused all social invitations, lest she suffer further public snubbing. The couple carefully constructed an image of marital harmony; as in the case of the Ladies of Llangollen, it was born in part out of a powerful need for approbation. Although unmarried (Lewes could not divorce his unfaithful wife), they epitomized respectable bourgeois marriage. Then, following the success of *Middlemarch*, a new generation knocked on their door. Lewes encouraged this one-sided socializing because Eliot had been isolated for years. He may also have found Eliot demanding and wanted more time for his own writing.[16] Eliza Lynn Linton, who disliked them both, tartly commented that "as a lover," Marian Evans "was both jealous and exacting."[17] Those who came to worship Lewes's "wife," left admiring his "almost maternal tenderness" and "protective love" of the diffident, often depressed genius.[18]

We cannot know how Lewes selected some women to visit Eliot at their home and rejected others. They arrived as devotees whose fantasies had been fueled by a close identification with the heroines of her novels. Lewes encouraged them to call her "Madonna." As Rosemarie Bodenheimer suggests, this sobriquet not only affirmed the quasi-religious love they felt for her, but also mediated between the formality of her public name and the intimacy of Marian.[19] The sophisticated Lady Mary Ponsonby, who visited Eliot to discuss her religious doubts, found herself bowing deeply as if to royalty.[20] Elma Stuart showered Eliot with gifts, abject apologies for minor social solecisms, and an unwavering adoration. Lewes noted in his diary that when Stuart dined with them on 15 February 1875, "She showed us the handkerchief with which she had wiped the tears from Polly's [Eliot's] eyes, and henceforth has preserved as a *relic*."[21] He encouraged Simcox to sit at the Madonna's feet, a position reminiscent of the many scenes of high and low relations in Eliot's *Romola* (1863). In this suppliant position she could more easily touch her and perhaps elicit a small return of the affection she poured out. Eliot called the thirty-three-year-old Simcox "a thoughtful child" and other terms of mild endearment.

Like Jane Welsh Carlyle, George Eliot had a complicated relationship with mothering. Her own mother had withdrawn into illness and had sent her to boarding school at the young age of five. Biographers disagree about how willing or successful she was as a stepmother to Lewes's sons. As she aged, she needed and wanted these "daughters," but she also found the sexual subtext distasteful. When Eliot asked Simcox to cease calling her "Mother," she did not offer another alternative. In late March 1880 Simcox drafted a response:

> "Sweet Mother" has come a hundred times to the tip of my pen since it was told not. Do you see darling that I can only love you three lawful ways, idolatrously as Frater the Virgin Mary, in romance wise as Petrarch, Laura, or with child's fondness for the mother one leans on notwithstanding the irreverence of one's longing to pet and take care

of her. Sober friendship seems to make the ugliest claim to a kind of equality; friendship is a precious thing indeed but between friends I think that if there is love at all it must be equal, and whichever way we take it, our relation is between unequals.[22]

Simcox defines her love as consisting of all three of these "lawful" forms, namely, idolatrous worship, romance, and the child who wishes "to pet and care" for the mother. Denied one relation—mother-daughter—she feels denied the other two. Like Mariana Lawton and Maria Barlow in chapter 1, Simcox distinguishes between love and "sober friendship." Unreciprocated love cannot settle for the lesser relationship, devoid of passion. Simcox proudly refuses this kind of friendship and instead embraces her unequal love. The best she can do to tone down her erotic passion is to promise a "boundless grateful love that must still and always be yours." But gratitude, as Eliot herself had said many years earlier to Sara Hennell, is not part of true love.[23] Gratitude also excludes passion.

No paradigm of love seemed adequate to explain Simcox's exalted sense of self-fulfillment, arising out of a combination of despair, "wolfish" desire, and pride. Only gradually did she construct a powerfully redemptive self-love from her suffering. She shifted the terms of mother-daughter love away from the built-in expectation of nurturance to an implicitly superior growth in self-knowledge. Simcox asked herself, could "love prosper a whole lifetime widowed of perfect joy"?

I answer without haste and after listening to every doubtful pause—It can. Married love and passionate friendship are the first open gates; the way of salvation leads plainly through them, and the flames that dart across the portal and fasten consumingly upon the selfish lusts of those who would pass through have not much terror for the happy elect who enter hand in hand. But there is another gate, narrow, obscure, to which each one draws near alone and the path to it through the valley of the shadow of death: we tread barefoot and the stones are sharp, we fall, the ground is a flame, the air is a suffocating smoke, invisible demons ply their scourges: there is one strange pleasure in the agony—to feel sharp flames consuming what is left in us of selfish lust, there is one pain passing all the rest, to feel the same flame fasten upon our every wound, within, without, and consume the very pain as if that too was sin. The path is long: who knows if we shall live to reach the end, where is the gate of religious love—and few there be that find it. But that fierce trial can teach as much as the sacramental mysteries of double love.[24]

Simcox placed marital love and passionate friendship on an equal footing, but she had experienced neither. She painfully transformed her isolated, un-

CROSS-AGE AND CROSSED LOVE / 124 /

requited love into a form of divine suffering that left her the spiritual equal of any happy couple. She grounds her redemptive suffering in sexual frustration, in which the flames of lust scourge the unrequited lover. Neither married couples nor passionate friends have to undergo this lonely penitential journey. Ironically, her renunciation of reciprocal love turned her into a heroine worthy of Eliot. As John Kucich suggests, "Eliot sought to meliorate isolation by deepening it, in a way that might make the self into a world sufficient to itself."[25] The supreme lesson Eliot taught was not "fellow feeling," but emotional self-sufficiency—the lesson that Simcox made into a parable of her own moral growth. Simcox subtly empowered herself and all the nameless others who joined her in suffering the pangs of unrequited passion. Their "fierce trial" makes them more ready to enter the "gate of religious love" than those "happy elect who enter hand in hand." Her exalted vision places her at the center of any "scheme of salvation" and gives her life a kind of absolute spiritual meaning that, she implies, might be lost to all but the finest couples.

After Lewes's death in late 1878, Simcox's visits to her idol were greatly curtailed. But freed from his benevolent gaze, the younger woman was more daring in her affection, until one March evening in 1880:

> I kissed her again and again and murmured broken words of love. She bade me not exaggerate. I said I didn't—nor could, and then scolded her for not being satisfied with letting me love her as I did—as a present reality—and proposing instead that I should save my love for some imaginary he. She said—expressly what she has often before implied to my distress—that the love of men and women for each other must always be more and better than any other and bade me not wish to be wiser than "God who made me"—in pious phrase. . . . She said I gave her a very beautiful affection—and then again She called me a silly child, and I asked if She would never say anything kind to me. I asked her to kiss me—let the trembling lover tell of the intense consciousness of the first deliberate touch of the dear one's lips. I returned the kiss to the lips that gave it and started to go—she waved me a farewell.[26]

Simcox knew exactly what she wanted—those passionate kisses by the fire came from a pent-up fire within. But Eliot knew what she did not want, and deftly pushed her aside by telling her she wanted only her "beautiful affection." Two months later Eliot, reverting to her original name, Mary Ann Evans, married the young Johnny Cross, who had earlier called her Aunt. She left it to her stepson Charles Lewes to tell Simcox.

Following Eliot's death in December 1880, Simcox renewed the memory of her love by visiting each of the other "spiritual daughters." These intense conversations with fellow sufferers were strangely soothing. A Mrs. Congreve admitted "she had loved my darling lover-wise too."[27] But Simcox abandoned her proposed biography and returned to private self-examination. At heart hers was an isolated love, feeding on itself. Then, in July 1881, a Miss Williams "professed a feeling for me different from what she had ever had for any one." Simcox "thought of my like love" and "urged upon her that I did not deserve such love as *I* had given *to* Her, it pained me like a blasphemy."[28] Simcox was a connoisseur of unrequited love and dismissed Miss Williams's love as trifling, though with a slight regret that she might have encouraged it. A character in Eliot's last novel, *Daniel Deronda* (1876), speaks of a woman "specially framed for the love which feels possession in renouncing."[29] After Eliot's death Simcox no longer had to suffer from willful misunderstanding or grieve at her insignificance in Eliot's life. Instead, she could memorialize her love. Years of voluntary, actively pursued suffering gave her an incomparable sense of spiritual achievement. Simcox's faithful love, rather than Eliot the woman, became her ultimate monument.

Biographers have often been embarrassed by George Eliot's seemingly insatiable need for unstinting love and praise from women. The young Marian Evans, before she became an author, had at least two intimate romantic friendships. During her youthful religious phase, she had exchanged passionate letters with her former teacher, the Evangelical Maria Lewis. She then moved on in the 1840s to the more sophisticated Sara Hennell. For nearly a decade she addressed Hennell in terms very similar to those of Harriet Hosmer to Lady Ashburton. She played with metaphors of marriage, addressing Hennell as "Lieber Gemahl," "Cara sposa," and "Dearly beloved spouse," and referring to herself as "a husband" and "Thine ever affectionate Husband."[30] Like the other women in this book, Marian Evans knew the script for intimate female friends, but she broke away from it and its ties to religiosity and emotionalism. In later years she continued to vow love and gratitude in her infrequent letters to Hennell, but female friendship became associated with her unhappy days as an unknown provincial translator of German philosophy. She openly admitted to lacking faith in women and equipped none of her heroines with a woman friend (unlike Charlotte Brontë, Elizabeth Gaskell, or Margaret Oliphant, to name other contemporary women novelists).

In the 1870s Eliot seems to have placed the adulation of her spiritual daughters in another category than that of romantic friendship. She reversed the Jewsbury-Carlyle relationship, forcing her young admirers to be self-controlled in the face of her own capriciousness. She could demonstrate neediness, even selfishness. When one admirer seemed cold, Simcox noted, "the Darling, my sweet Darling rushed out of the room in tears."[31] While preaching submission, she vented unfeminine egotism that kept each worshipper returning to the shrine. She was no longer the masterful husband she had played with Maria Lewis and Sara Hennell. Instead, daughters brought comfort to her. Eliot and her admirers were locked in an intimate drama: her daughters had come to worship her perfection and instead found a "de-sponding soul" who longed for their praise as a "healing balm for a trembling sensibility."[32] It was a heady discovery that felt ennobling much of the time. But as the ruthlessly honest Simcox realized, "The *rôle* of idol is a trying one to play: granted that George Eliot's worshippers had all reason on their side at first, does not so much incense end by becoming in some sort a necessity to its recipient?"[33] After Eliot's death Simcox continued to offer incense to her beloved's memory. But when she came to write her memoir of Eliot, she sadly admitted, "I feel as if the habit of self-suppression strangled even here the ut-terance of that 'passion' she used to wish for in my writing."[34] Dutiful sub-mission had damaged her writing. Yet she never quite submerged her pas-sionate love into her assigned role of spiritual daughter. Instead, she placed herself at the moral center of her own tale, turning her hopeless desire into a memorial to same-sex love.

A DIFFICULT DAUGHTER: ETHEL SMYTH

The composer Ethel Smyth (fig. 12) was notorious for her outspoken, man-nish ways and her numerous *cultes*, as she called them, for a series of beauti-ful, older upper-class women. The details of her life are recorded with artful artlessness (and much repetition) in nine volumes of memoirs.[35] Only a few letters survive outside of those she chose to edit and publish. Her autobi-ographies are a kind of courtship in which she flirts with her reading public, refusing to commit herself to a single course of action or a single lover. Be-cause she never quite comes out as a lesbian, but instead presents her lesbian behavior as a sustained emotional experiment, she leaves room for contin-gencies, including falling in love with a man. Her repetitiousness, as well as her overobvious metaphors and overinsistent innocence, invite opposition. We dismiss her recurring themes and find her guilty of loving surrogate mothers more than her own biological mother or the patient Harry Brewster. Smyth wrote the script of daughter-mother affection not as the unequal pas-sion of Simcox or as the marital metaphor used by Cushman and others; for her it was an enabling base from which she could explore conflicting erotic and emotional needs.

At nineteen Smyth received permission from her military father to study composition in Leipzig. In 1878 she began private lessons in harmony and counterpoint with Heinrich von Herzogenberg, a leader in the revival of Jo-hann Sebastian Bach. She soon fell in love with Herzogenberg's wife, an Aus-trian aristocrat eleven years her senior. Lisl (fig. 13) fully reciprocated. This great love and its inexplicable loss became the crucial story told and retold by Smyth. For seven years she lived in blissful harmony with Lisl and Hein-

Fig. 12. Ethel Smyth with her dog Marco, 1891. By courtesy of the National Portrait Gallery, London.

rich as Lisl's surrogate daughter. Their fantasy of eroticized mother-daughter love began when the hyperactive Smyth collapsed and was nursed by Lisl:

> And there, amid the homely surroundings of a sloping roof and ram-shackle furniture, began the tenderest, surely the very tenderest rela-tion that can ever have sprung up between a woman and one who, in spite of her years, was little better than a child. . . . It was settled that though my mother must never hear of it I was really her child, that, as she put it, she must have "had" me without knowing it when she was eleven; all of this with a characteristic blend of fun and tenderness that saved it from anything approaching morbidity.[36]

Forty years later Smyth constructed this event as the epitome of nurturing love. But why not tell her birth mother, if all of this was just pretend? Why

Fig. 13. Lisl von Herzogenberg, ca. 1880.

deny that it was "approaching morbidity"? And how long could each woman sustain her role? Lisl's fantasy implies a closed system of dependency and nurturance, but Smyth was just discovering new worlds.

The only way into Lisl's thoughts is through Smyth's translations of her letters. (She wrote in German in part to conceal her intimacy from Smyth's jealous birth mother.) Fragmentary as these edited letters are, we can see that she and Smyth expressed their love through both a fictive familial relation and semiprivate musical references. Lisl cast Smyth in the role of the daring reprobate to be loved and reproved by her faithful, stay-at-home lover. She compared their situation to such famous opera duos as Tamino-Pamina, Tannhäuser-Elisabeth, and Florestan-Leonora.[37] The published excerpts reveal a shift in their roles, with Lisl becoming the needy lover who feared Smyth's many distractions, including her irrepressible same-sex flirtations.

She admonished the younger woman, "for one like me, faithful and heavy to a perhaps exaggerated degree . . . it seems hard to see *the* friend, the most cherished of all, so easy in giving and accepting affection and apparently always craving more."[38] In April 1880 Lisl pleaded: "My child, what has become of the calm steady mood of your first letters, the sense that we are together though separated, the all-round steadfastness? . . . am I to wait for ever for the pedal-point—'the note that sounds so softly, but can always be heard by those who listen for it in secret?'"[39] Secrecy is a recurrent theme in their letters, alerting the reader to the undertow of passion in their relationship.

In 1882–83 Smyth made the first of several trips to Florence. She went with an introduction to Lisl's older sister, married to an American aesthete. Although Julia and Harry Brewster were notoriously reclusive, they welcomed the outgoing Smyth. She promptly fell in love with Julia and wrote Lisl long letters about her infatuation. At the same time Harry was attracted to her. Ethel responded to this heady atmosphere by starting a flirtation with the married Adolf Hildebrand, a German sculptor and friend of both the Brewsters and the Herzogenbergs. She spoke frankly about this dalliance with Hildebrand's wife, as well as the increasingly dismayed Lisl. The open-ended nature of her activities in Florence contrasted with the closed, seemingly unshakable daughter-mother bond she had established with Mother Lisl. Then, the next winter, Harry Brewster suggested that they have an affair. Although Smyth rejected him, his offer opened new sexual possibilities. Could love and desire be separated? Could she love a man (Harry) and not desire him? And desire a woman (Julia) and not love her? Could she have them and still keep her mother-love (Lisl)?

Lisl von Herzogenberg tried to be sympathetic and understanding, but she was placed in an impossible situation. When Smyth continued to correspond with Brewster, in 1885 she broke off their friendship, abruptly and completely. Smyth was devastated. The pretend mother-daughter relationship could be sensual, even sexual, as long as only the mother was heterosexually active; when the daughter proclaimed her interest in heterosexuality, their masquerade was exposed. In her memoirs Smyth claimed she never understood Lisl's rejection. She cast herself in a new drama that partially exonerated Lisl's desertion: Ethel was a naïve Cinderella, damned by Lisl's mother, "the Wicked Godmother." Baroness von Stockhausen had hated Smyth "at first sight with a vitriolic jealousy of one who had never permitted her children to have friends, or even playmates."[40] This implacable mother's hatred predated Smyth's interference in her daughter Julia's marriage. From the beginning she had distrusted her daughter Lisl's enthusiastic attachment to Smyth. Well before the final breakup, Lisl was torn by irreconcilable loyalties. On one occasion, traveling with her mother, she awoke, frightened that she "had shrieked 'Ethel'" after dreaming that "entering our little dining room,

I saw my mother and you on two chairs, she almost swooning and you bathed in tears!"[41] Smyth insisted that her mother was not jealous and then showed her to be so. In her reconstruction of events, she was blameless. She never accepted responsibility for the damage that she had wreaked in the Herzo-genberg-Brewster families. Instead, all the mothers, her own, Lisl's, and even Lisl herself, were guilty of an irrational possessiveness, of refusing their daughters an essential independence. Smyth created an all-female world of love and hatred, turning mothers into villains and ignoring husbands. This allowed her to keep Harry Brewster, the original catalyst of the breakup, in-nocent.

The unmentionable heart of this conflict was not adultery, because Smyth had steadfastly refused Brewster's overtures. Rather it was same-sex passion. Elizabeth Wood has suggested that Lisl may well have feared that her sister Julia would retaliate by publicly "outing" her sexual relationship with Ethel. The manuscript version of Smyth's first memoir, *Impressions that Remained* (1919), reveals a distraught and frightened Lisl. Smyth deleted a key phrase in Lisl's letter: "I was never and am not unfaithful to you and our mutual past. What separates us now is stronger than you and I [and here the words 'and our passion' are heavily scored out]. . . . Don't try to make me say more I can not."[42] The potential affair with Harry Brewster became the excuse for break-ing up the two women lovers. Unlike Anne Lister, Smyth never saw her rela-tionship with Lisl von Herzogenberg as adultery. Since she did not see her-self as a husband, but rather as a child, she could proclaim its innocence. In memoir after memoir she kept shoving this deeply sensual love into a mother-daughter paradigm and celebrating her own passive surrender to it.

For some lesbians, including Smyth, the major psychic barrier to emo-tional autonomy was their passionate connection to their birth mothers. Smyth felt profoundly attached to her volatile mother and found it difficult to refuse her emotional demands. She knew that she would never fulfill her mu-sical talents if she stayed at home. Mother Lisl had performed an essential role, encouraging both Smyth's creative life and her emotional independence. Af-ter the breakup she came to represent a lost unconditional love, while Smyth's biological mother continued to exemplify voracious love. Pages of Smyth's *Impressions that Remained* are spent explaining how she *was* a good daughter, in spite of all appearances. A generation later Radclyffe Hall bitterly reacted against the tight daughter-mother bond and insisted that a lesbian naturally identified with her father and should expect maternal rejection. Smyth, how-ever masculine her appearance, did not identify with a father-figure; to her mind she was a tomboy, and as such, she resolutely demanded maternal ac-ceptance—from her birth mother and from Lisl or other surrogate mothers. Unlike Hall, who saw herself as a man trapped in a female body and accordingly wanted the privileges of a man, whether lover or husband, Smyth, wanted acceptance for who she was, a masculine woman.

In 1885 the brokenhearted Smyth limped back to England, convinced that she would never again be able to compose. She could not look to her mother for support but soon found a new source in Mary Benson, whom she met through family friends. Benson responded to her obvious needs with a combination of empathy and good humor, telling her: "I would give anything to be any good to you—but I leave that in God's hands—only if patient listening and eager desire *really to see* and understand tenderly and truly is any use I think I dare promise that."[43] Benson cajoled and exhorted, and Smyth adored the attention. Smyth, however, discovered that she had to share this mother with too many other needy young women. In her first autobiography she mocked Benson, whose "life was consecrated to her patients, as I used to call them, who when bereft of her physical presence were kept going by words of counsel and comfort written on letter paper so diminutive that it inevitably suggested a prescription."[44] Moreover, Benson urged Smyth to accept the same kind of self-denying faith that had sustained her for years. But Smyth was no Edith Simcox, just as Benson was no George Eliot. And times were changing; submission was no longer fashionable for women.

Smyth remained deeply grateful to Benson: "but for Mrs. Benson I shd never have got over one bit of my life: the few months succeeding that farewell letter of Lisl's. My whole world was shattered—Every interest of my life had I given up for music such as marriage & that necessity. . . . And in one moment music slipped so utterly out of my reach that I might be pardoned for thinking it gone forever."[45] But she needed someone who would take her seriously as a composer. For Smyth music alone gave her an identity apart from that of a "normal" heterosexual woman—she had willingly sacrificed marriage and children for it, but if she could no longer create music, she was left with no identity, no faith in herself or in life itself. In Leipzig she had experienced both love and respect in the Herzogenberg musical circle. Then she lost most of her German friends, her beloved Lisl, and, seemingly, all power to compose. Her mental and emotional health depended upon the fostering care of someone who could appreciate her ambition. She concluded that Benson did not understand "how music is my religion, my all, how love and everything else is but a superstructure."[46] Only with the help of several different women did Smyth slowly regain her creative power.

In 1890, after a five-year hiatus, Smyth ran into the still-married Brewster at her London orchestral debut, and they resumed their correspondence.[47] Benson was deeply upset, but Smyth pushed her away, convinced that she would condemn her, even if she still refused his sexual overtures.[48] Smyth gradually fashioned a new relationship with Brewster. As if to mark his new place in her life, in her numerous memoirs she published no letters from him before 1890. We have no direct knowledge of his initial response to the young Ethel or of the havoc his love created for her and his in-laws. Instead he is portrayed as the one person who always took her music seriously; she dedicated numerous works to him. And she chose him to write the librettos for her operas. (Lisl despised opera and had encouraged Smyth to continue writing quartets.) Elizabeth Wood suggests that when Smyth was unable to regain Lisl or her old Leipzig life, Brewster alone stood by her, and over the years he came to represent the lost innocence and love of those days.[49] A man became a stand-in for the happiest mother-daughter love of her life. She would never lose him, never face his desertion, as she did with Lisl. And he fully supported her musical career.

In 1892 Lisl von Herzogenberg died of heart disease without having seen her "beloved child" again, and in 1895 her sister Julia died. Smyth at last agreed to meet Harry in Paris to consummate their relationship, but she adamantly refused to marry him. As Suzanne Raitt points out, Smyth had the pleasure of recounting openly her sexual encounters with him, while censoring her sexual affairs with women.[50] But even here ambiguity remains. In 1940 Smyth published an 1898 letter in which she praises heterosexual lovemaking: "There *is* a mystery in this actual belonging to the best being you know, to the one who knows you best, which has come upon me with all my 37 years, as a surprise, a new force in life."[51] But this letter is addressed to her married friend Lady Mary Ponsonby, who had long urged the couple to consummate their love. Later, when courting the notoriously cool Virginia Woolf, Smyth admitted to visiting Versailles with Brewster, "just after the dépucelage had taken place, & I remember arguing with him beside the Grandes Eaux as to whether any, any, any woman could ever have enjoyed such an experience."[52] After their initial Paris rendezvous Smyth did not agree to routine lovemaking. Brewster had to be satisfied with occasional meetings and an intense emotional life via letters. But if we reconfigure Brewster as the mother who never deserts her daughter, then his role in Smyth's life makes sense. Smyth wanted love and not sex from this male mother; she wanted sex, love, and adventure from women, at whatever cost. She did not always get her way—Brewster sometimes got sex, and women did not always fall into her arms. Until his death in 1908, Brewster and Smyth remained true to their self-created love-narrative, fashioned into what might be called a male mother–tomboy daughter love.

Smyth found the ideal counterfoil to Brewster in the ultra-sophisticated Lady Mary Ponsonby, wife of Queen Victoria's private secretary. They met in 1891, just as Smyth was reconstructing her life to include Brewster. Mary Ponsonby supplied adventure and excitement, tolerating Smyth's emotional vagaries (including numerous flirtations with other women) with greater savoir faire than either Lisl von Herzogenberg or Mary Benson. After her husband's death in 1895, Lady Ponsonby moved almost exclusively in a world of women who loved women.[53] We cannot know whether this new relationship with Ponsonby was fully sexual, but both women found it deeply fulfilling. Brewster hated quarreling, but Ponsonby loved a good fight; and for twenty-six years she and Smyth loved, clashed, and made up. Smyth concluded: "she was dearer to me than any woman in the world, never in my life, except perhaps with my mother, have I had such elemental rows."[54] As she noted, Ponsonby liked to end their rows with the icy comment, "Pray don't let us have the *scène aux cheveux*," naming the moment in melodrama when the heroine lets her hair down to weep over her lover's betrayal. To go further risked breaking the conventions of love duets. Geraldine Jewsbury, when she was most jealous of Jane Carlyle's flirtations, had gone to the very edge of respectable behavior, tearing her hair, weeping, and smoking a cigaritto. Ponsonby, like Carlyle, thoroughly enjoyed encouraging Smyth to test these same boundaries. Dramatic scenes both acknowledged and covered emotional vulnerability. Ritualized verbal sparring also exposed a depth of feeling that could not be openly named. Forbidden sex, forbidden fulfillment, exploded into a drama that could be repeated as often as the two women wanted. And best of all, Smyth could tell Lady Ponsonby: "I can't divorce myself from vehemence toward life—If you were not the cause, something else would be, and when the tempest catches me up I am always laid low. Perhaps these things are necessary—Anyhow they are generally followed by very good work. *Every good thing I ever did was preceded by such battles.*"[55] Smyth's creativity depended upon tempestuous love; when it was lost, so too was her music. Harry Brewster saw no contradiction in loving both his wife, Julia, and Ethel Smyth. Smyth found no contradiction in loving both him (a replacement for Lisl) and Ponsonby (a substitute for her mother). Brewster supplied her with stability, and Ponsonby with passion. Together their love made possible her best work.

Within the pages of her diary, Simcox struggled to define and explain her sexual feelings; convinced they were natural for her, she refused to deny their validity in spite of Eliot's repeated disparagement. In her sixties, when Smyth began the first of her memoirs, she chose a series of metaphors to reveal her same-sex passions and to justify them. These feelings were as strong as the natural elements, she proclaimed. But given familial and social disapproval, facing them demanded courage. In the final pages of *Impressions that Remain*, under the title "In the Desert," Smyth concluded that in spite of her gift of "an almost bewilderingly rich, tender form of affection," Lisl von Herzogenberg had submitted to the demands of her mother, and that perhaps "only passionate temperaments can stand erect in elemental storms."[56] In looking back at the failure of her friendship with Mary Benson, which had begun with such promise, she commented that it was "like two trees whose upper branches, occasionally mingling, gave the illusion of one tree, whereas their roots were far, far apart."[57]

But her love for Lady Ponsonby, "the happiest, the most satisfying, and for that reason the most restful of all my many friendships with women," was "like the trees on that wild Mecklenburg coast; storms in the upper branches merely drive in the roots deeper."[58] Lesbian love was intrinsic to Ethel Smyth's very nature; her most compelling relations were with older women. Smyth, ratified by a maternal man, Harry Brewster, successfully wooed woman after woman.

"BLACK DESPAIRS AND PAINFUL PASSIONS": MARY BENSON AND IMPERFECT MOTHERING

Ethel Smyth was never afraid to revisit her erotic history. In the 1930s she began her last *engouement*, a love affair via letters with the author Virginia Woolf. Encouraged by Woolf's sympathetic curiosity, she reviewed yet again her relationships with women. Smyth suggested that an incestuous desire for her mother might fuel her love of women: "The most violent feeling I am conscious of is . . . for my mother. She died 38 years ago & I never can think of her without a stab of real passion; amusement, tenderness, pity, admiration are in it & pain that I cant tell her how I love her (but I think she knows). Now you can imagine how much sexual feeling has to do with such an emotion for one's mother!!"[59] In her seventies this highly successful composer could at last face her conflicted love for her mother. Smyth's love of difficult, quarrelsome women, her own volcanic energy, and her demanding mother were of a piece, balanced in the past by the quiet, unconditional love of Harry Brewster. This section examines Smyth's insight into the potentially incestuous roots of cross-age lesbian love within a single family, the Bensons. Mary Benson never successfully negotiated either finding husbands for her two daughters or integrating their intimate friends into her family. Unlike Smyth, Nellie and Maggie Benson were not able to balance their love of women with their love of their mother. The powerful emotions wrought by family closeness were redoubled by the sexual sameness of their erotic object choices.[60]

During the years 1885–90, in spite of her continued pain over the loss of Lisl, Smyth was emotionally involved with four women: Mary Benson and her daughter Nellie (to whom she wrote over one hundred fifty letters in a year) and a devout English Catholic girl, Pauline Trevelyan, and her mother. (Only after she met Lady Ponsonby in 1891 did Smyth briefly settle down to one love.) By all accounts Eleanor Benson ,or Nellie (1863–90), combined a bright and outgoing personality with a cheerful willingness to fall in with other people's plans. As such she was an ideal companion for so powerful a personality as Ethel Smyth. When Smyth began to shift her affections from mother to daughter, Mary Benson wrote to her about the emotional cost of this change, disclaiming intervention, yet crying out for sympathy.

Benson stood to lose both the erotic intimacy of advising Smyth and her emotional closeness with a suddenly distant daughter. She was agreeable at first, declaring: "I have always claimed both for myself and others, that when a new friendship began to blossom there should be freedom given to form it. . . . I know personally I cant form two relations worth having at once. I wanted and want you to understand how free I leave you about Nellie."[61] But Benson could not leave her protégée alone with her daughter. A month later she wrote Smyth:

> I have been pained to think that Nellie was desiring something fuller than you spoke of in your first. [I asked] to see a letter of yours, she de-murring, I asking if there was anything private, she saying yes, I going on to ask would she have any feeling of indecency in showing it to me. She saying yes, I asking if you wd feel it so, she admitting no. She is a bivalve you see, and you *do* want both her shells. . . . *Dont tell Nellie abt this letter of mine.*[62]

Clearly Benson struggled with herself, knowing she should not demand to read the letters of the twenty-five-year-old Nellie. Had Smyth stolen her daughter or had her daughter stolen her beloved? Put so starkly, this triangle becomes a rewriting of the plot of a bad novel, in which the son steals his fa-ther's mistress. If youth always trumped age in love matters, at least youth, in the form of Ethel Smyth, should have known how she was again hurting dif-ferent family members in her quest to balance maternal comfort and sexual adventure. It almost seems that Smyth understood families only as metaphors, not as real entities with their own internal dynamics.

Benson sounded the theme of a secret dialogue between herself and Smyth again in November 1889, writing to her in Munich, where Ethel was staying with the Trevelyans:

> Think over the past—we meet first, you and I—we sound depths to-gether—and out of that there grows of itself a relation—a deep rela-tion. . . . Ah, my child, you have ever half believed how I have known this, or how sacredly I have reverenced and loved it. But I am slow—and I grieve. Then there comes this new drawing of you and Nellie—I dont understand just at first. . . . But—and here we come to our pres-ent crux, your way out of it I cannot make mine. The play of nature between Nellie and me—The awful inner tie of mother and daugh-ter—and if you will, *my own limitations* speak all together in clear tones, and a most deep inner instinct bids me be still—bids *me,* so to speak "get out of the way" while this relation, which is evidently increasing more than either of you knew it would, developes [sic] itself.[63]

Was Mary Benson confusing her spiritual advising with her erotic needs? She had successfully juggled a series of lovers and ex-lovers in her own circle of intimates, but Smyth, so close in age to her daughters, occupied a different position. Perhaps Smyth had pushed for greater intimacy, Benson had drawn back, and then Smyth had turned to Nellie. Benson struggles in her letters to come to terms with what Smyth might demand of her daughter, without being able to articulate it clearly, aside perhaps from the sexually implicit metaphor of the bivalve oyster shell. She flounders for a love vocabulary outside religion, wanting to acknowledge her daughter as a desiring (and desired) sexual subject, as a mature person with her own needs, but without loosening their mother-daughter tie. Nellie marked all her private letters "Burn," so we do not know how she felt. Probably like all the Bensons, if forced, she would have sided with her family against Smyth.

As I discussed in chapter 4, Benson's language of spiritual fusing freed her to develop erotic friendships without feeling that she had sinned. Moreover she could be a loving friend to numerous women simultaneously without feeling any disloyalty to Lucy Tait. She was also on morally sure ground about Harry Brewster and the possibility of heterosexual adultery. When it came to Smyth's growing attraction for Nellie, however, she floundered, unwilling or unable to express her growing jealousy. Benson worked hard to be understanding, rather than suggesting that Smyth's erotic and emotional demands had become too costly for her and her family. The lack of precise labels and definitions freed women to explore privately many different roles, but it also left Benson without guidelines for assessing her dual maternal roles, biological and erotic. Much later, in 1930, Smyth and Virginia Woolf discussed "perversion" at length, half-surprised, half-pleased that such a word could be mentioned. Woolf acknowledged the benefits of labeling, but she concluded: "Where people mistake, as I think, is in perpetually narrowing and naming these immensely composite and wide flung passions—driving stakes through them, herding them between screens. . . . What is the line between friendship and perversion?"[64] But Mary Benson had no "screens," no categories for her "wide flung passions," and so was especially vulnerable to Smyth's enthusiastic exploration of different kinds of intimate friendships.

Nellie's premature death from diphtheria in November 1890 abruptly ended this difficult all-female triangle. It also forced the inward-looking Maggie (1864–1916) into the role of chief daughter at home. In the 1880s Maggie had been a brilliant philosophy student at Lady Margaret Hall, Oxford. Contemporaries remembered her shyness and cloistered girlish air; she was not permitted to participate in a reading party without a chaperon.[65] When she had to spend winters in a warmer climate, she became an expert in Egyptology, a subject women could make their own at a time when men controlled classical studies. During one of her winters in Luxor, she met Janet "Nettie" Gourley (d. 1912), who was to become her partner in excavating the Temple of Mut at Luxor. At about this time Maggie told a friend that she "could never

Fig. 14. Janet Gourley and Maggie Benson, ca. 1905.

conceive of meeting anyone who was 'man enough to marry and yet woman enough to love.'"[66] Friendship with Gourley resolved the issue. Later, when both were too ill to return to Egypt, they wintered together in Cornwall, and Gourley visited the Benson home for months at a time (fig. 14). In his discreet biography Maggie's brother Arthur comments with an air of masculine distaste, "her friendships, very various and far-ranging, were seldom leisurely and refreshing things. She . . . threw herself into their problems and difficulties, while her emotions were loyal and intense, so that she could not just make up a friendship and leave it to take care of itself."[67] In spite of her various responsibilities as the only remaining daughter, Maggie continued to publish, write letters, and organize religious reading groups.

After the archbishop's sudden death in 1896, the family, including Lucy Tait and Nettie Gourley, went to Egypt for the winter of 1896–97. As the person most experienced in Egyptian ways, Maggie took charge of family affairs, protecting her mother and Tait "from the beggars and importunate salesmen of fraudulent antiques."[68] But Mary, newly freed from her husband's domination, did not willingly accede to her daughter's leadership. Then Maggie came down with a fever, followed by pleurisy and a heart attack; thereafter her physical health was quite fragile. Back in England, while helping Arthur with the theological sections of his biography of their father, Maggie began to take on more and more of her father's characteristics. She seems to have been seeking some way to harness her intellect and her increasingly explosive feelings. Her only model for this combination of authority and anger was her father, who had also been subject to wide swings in mood and behavior. Looking around at her all-female home, composed of her mother, herself, Nettie, and Lucy, she announced to Lucy "that the strenuous element wd now be lacking, and that she ought to supply it."[69] As her depression deepened, Maggie was openly torn between her desire to be phallic—the masterful, intelligent imitation of her father—and her desire to regress to the dependent child, unconditionally loved by her mother.

Maggie desperately wanted her mother's undivided attention. In a long entry in her 1898 diary, Mary Benson described Maggie's insistence that no one cared for her, that "she didn't want *only Nettie*, she wanted change," culminating in terrible accusations about her mother's selfishness. Benson summarized her difficulties:

> What am I to do? Am I really very selfish? does some of the sadness come from selfishness & my desire to go away myself & get enjoyment & distractions? And yet I feel at bottom a sense that it wd be very bad for her if I had no life of my own, but lived only for her. There is in her displeasure, as there was in her father's, a power of bringing one into bondage—a dreadful fear—fear lest one should be displeasing her, while one was going along quite innocently. . . . All this *occupies* ones thoughts so—in a *horrid* relative, self conscious way that I catch myself acting as of old, in a sort of dull slave spirit—without freedom or liberty . . . also a fettered sense of a long vista of slavery, never knowing what she wd like, avoiding too much companionship with Lucy.[70]

Mary Benson may have been selfish to want her own life for the first time since she was a young girl, but she had held this remaining daughter very close. What did the thirty-four-year-old Maggie really want? Why did she not find her substantial intellectual accomplishments, her friendship with Nettie Gourley, and her church activities sufficient? Was Maggie struggling to articulate a forbidden, incestuous desire? Her anger overwhelmed both mother and daughter. Two days later Benson asked herself, "Have I given her my own company too much? & not enough realised that she wanted more variety?"[71]

For Mary the problem was what she called her daughter's "really falling in love with her father." But Maggie's self-diagnosis may have been closer to the mark: rather than falling in love with her father, she wished to replace him. Maggie, a brilliant and domineering unmarried woman, could command authority only over a few women. Other young women discussed in this chapter found a way of asserting themselves by making scenes, insisting that the mother-daughter relation be renegotiated. But they did not ask to rule. As Maggie tipped into depression, she literalized the fluid, metaphoric roles of women who loved women. Even as she vowed unwavering love for her mother, Maggie became determined to reign as her father had done. But Lucy Tait had already usurped the male role. Under no circumstances would Mary Benson either give up Lucy or return to a form of her husband's rule. As she confided to her diary,

> She [Maggie] dwelt, with great care on Lucy's influence on me—being with me *day & night*—first thing in the morning, last thing at night—& she & I were growing apart. I told her it was difficult for anyone to realize the difficulty of living these last years—she said how she wanted to help me. [She felt] the difference in my relation to Lucy now, & 3 years ago [before Edward's death]. Later she came to my room & said I had kissed her unlike any other time in her life today twice & she could not bear it—I told her how despairing I had felt & was feeling. . . . She was sure I wanted *my own kin*, and that was what she had felt when she wanted Fred & me & her to be at Brighton together, without Lucy— she got greatly agitated, but restrained herself.[72]

Benson concluded her long entry, "In a way I think the long years in which my whole desire was to soothe her, & please, and make her sad ill life as sweet & cherished as possible have hidden from her—in fact could not reveal—me, myself (if there is a me!) and now, in her renewed health this protective part almost passes from me to her, and our true relation has got to be made." They went to Brighton without Lucy Tait, but Maggie could not change. Earlier Benson had struggled to let go of Nellie; now she struggled to develop an adult relationship with Maggie. By rights as she aged, she should have been able to look to her daughter for comfort, just as Jane Carlyle and George Eliot had found comfort in their surrogate daughters. But Maggie felt Lucy Tait had usurped the care-taking role.

Maggie represents a lesbian nightmare: she literalizes the fear that lesbian sexuality is mother-daughter incest. She constitutes the visible sign of the pre-Oedipal incest desire of little girls for their mothers. By late 1899 Benson recognized that "[Maggie's] whole desire was to be reunited with me."[73] Reunification, however, could only be achieved through regression. When brought face-to-face with a mother who openly expressed her sexual desire for another woman, Maggie did not feel empowered, as Jessica Benjamin has theorized, but instead defeated.[74] Around 1905–6 Maggie made yet another bid for power over her mother: she reverted to being a child. If she could not control her mother by playing the role of authoritarian patriarch, the moral replacement for her father, then she would command her attention by becoming an invalid child. But this demand for nurturing—metaphorically speaking, to climb into her mother's bed again to be comforted from her nightmares—was balked by the presence of Lucy Tait. Maggie was surrounded by women whom she believed had failed her. Unlike Ethel Smyth she had no nurturing male-mother to rescue her.

One morning in late 1906, Maggie told her mother, "I am killing it." Then she took a horsewhip and beat herself. A few months later, the night before Mary Benson and Lucy Tait were to leave for a vacation, Maggie sent for Tait—her hated rival—and told her she was afraid that she might kill herself or someone else, and she needed to be restrained. They delayed their holiday and called in the family doctor. With a surrogate father to heed her story, Maggie proceeded, in her brother Fred's words, to become "homicidal." She raged all night long, yet seemed to seek the attention and to be proud of how many nurses it took to hold her down. Her oldest brother, Arthur, sadly commented in his diary that "she has begun to take the line of *all being over* for her—that she had misused & lost & wasted all her opportunities, & that her soul was lost."[75] Four days later, on 8 May 1907, Maggie was taken to St. George's Convent, an institution for the insane.[76] In time Maggie improved sufficiently to be moved to a home, but she never fully recovered.

At first Maggie blamed herself for her failures and begged to be punished, but within a short time she bitterly railed against her mother and Lucy Tait. Over the remaining nine years of her life, she refused to see them, convinced they were persecuting her. When her brothers visited, her early "memory was absolutely unimpaired, and by the hour we talked over detail after detail of the days when as children we made joint collections of plants and butterflies and birds' eggs."[77] In her childhood fantasies Maggie found unconditional maternal love and protective brothers. Mary, unable to see her daughter, faithfully wrote to her. A few letters survive, annotated in tiny handwriting by Maggie, declaring "not true," "wrong," and various unintelligible phrases. Maggie also wrote vitriolic letters attacking her mother, which Fred burned after his mother's death. Arthur was convinced that Maggie was possessed by the devil, given her unerring skill at hurting her family.[78] Just before her death she recovered briefly, lovingly welcomed her mother and Lucy, and then darkness closed in again.

In 1901 Maggie had published a small volume, *The Soul of a Cat and Other Stories.* Her affectionate description of her cat, a "dainty lady, pure Persian," concludes: "I would never again develop the sensibilities of an animal beyond certain limits; for one creates claims that one has no power to satisfy. The feelings of a sensitive animal are beyond our control, and beyond its own also . . . and these waked a strange conflict and turmoil in the vivid and limited nature, troubling her relations with her kind, filling her now with black despairs, and painful passions, and now with serene, half understood content."[79] Maggie Benson did not have a "limited nature," but she suffered deeply from a jealous love of her mother. She also endured deep despair, believing God had deserted her. The extraordinary understanding she had for small animals led her, when incarcerated, to "curious and beautiful fancies about birds, which she said were imprisoned spirits."[80] It was a miserable end for so bright an intellect. Only Mary Benson seemed able to believe firmly in God's goodness during the long years of her suffering.

Was too much family service expected of unmarried daughters in the upper-classes, and did the intensities of Evangelical religion contribute to the emotionalism of the Benson mother-daughter relationships? Yes, but Maggie Benson's plight was certainly not unique, if extreme. Lady Ponsonby's unmarried daughter, also called Maggie, was deeply jealous of her mother's involvement with Smyth. The married Ponsonby children "were simply amused, while Maggie was furious, when they heard 'people' say it was a pity that Lady Ponsonby let Ethel Smyth dominate her life."[81] Both the Benson and the Ponsonby daughters were intelligent, well off, and forced to be companions to their mothers at a time when less wealthy girls could be working. Tied to distant fathers and attractive mothers who preferred other women—no wonder they were angry. These unmarried daughters watched their mothers flourish under the admiring attentions of younger women as they felt their own lives wither and narrow. Each succeeding generation of educated women definitely did not have greater freedom and more opportunities. Arthur Benson glibly insisted that his sister "had of course many resources of interest and work. But she could never peacefully abandon herself to them!"[82] But work without any particular goal could seem painfully trivial. After Lady Ponsonby's death Maggie Ponsonby prepared a selection of her letters; like Emma Stebbins's memoir of Charlotte Cushman, with its calculated silences, the collection contains scarcely any mention of Ethel Smyth. Maggie Ponsonby's acquaintance Maggie Benson discovered that working on her father's life fanned her hatred of *his* sexual rival, Lucy Tait. No wonder Tait became *her* sexual rival.

Mother love was the strongest, the most troubling, and the most fundamental of all emotions for women and men of this generation. Jewsbury found strength in self-knowledge; she accepted Jane Carlyle for who she was, rather than hoping for what she could not give. If Mrs. Cross, her beloved George Eliot, had lived longer, Edith Simcox suspected that her love would have been crushed. Death ennobled her love and kept it alive as a complicated, exultant memory. Ethel Smyth found at great cost that only when disagreements—winds of jealousy, discord, and misunderstanding—swept through her intimate relations could her music flourish. In her numerous autobiographies she drew attention to the erotic force behind her stormy cross-age friendships; nuturing mother love was transferred to a man. The next chapter explores women who faced the complications of mother loss and the search for an adequate substitute.

6 *"Passion . . . Immense and Unrestrained"*

DESTRUCTIVE DESIRES

This chapter examines the demonic, voracious side of lesbian love—love that cannot be directly named because it is so fearful, so unwomanly. Educated, middle-class women had few models for irrational, overwhelming same-sex love. The opera diva and Shakespearean heroine did not translate into ordinary life. Women were expected to adapt their love to more familiar, manageable forms, such as nurturing mother or giving child or responsible wife. But not every woman who fell in love with another woman wanted her relationship to be a haven from predatory men. Tender affection between women was not sufficient. Passionate love meant inequalities of power, abasement, exaltation, desolation, and jubilation. How could a woman articulate these aggressive, even destructive, feelings? Disguise, sexual transpositions, and metaphors might express the inexpressible. In fantasy and fiction heterosexual marriage could be turned upside down. If lesbian love was natural, heterosexual marriage was an aberration. And if lesbian love was unnatural, then it was a kind of adultery—the unruly heart's refusal to remain faithful to social mores. I explore here how two women created sexual narratives that exposed feelings they both welcomed and hated—and that drew unfavorable attention to them and their fictions.

Lesbians found a language for demonic passion in the tropes of Romanticism, which often defined love as a hostile yet irresistible force. Rather than be content with the unfinished or deferred love of an Edith Simcox or a Geraldine Jewsbury, some women wanted immediate bliss or debasement. They fantasized dominating a woman and then submitting to her command. The longed-for ideal was a love so perfect that it could stop time, in an overwhelming "now," driving out personal respectability, family obligations, and social norms. The impossibility of achieving this perfect love only increased its desirability. To die—metaphorically or even literally—for another seemed entirely imaginable. Especially attractive were such Romantic characters as the hypermasculine hero who undertook highly feminine acts of fidelity and self-sacrifice and the heroine who enthusiastically embraced martyrdom to save her beloved. In the previous chapter the dominant sexual fantasy was the pleasure of merging. In this chapter it is the fear of merging. A profound yearning for love went hand in hand with a deep-seated terror of losing oneself.

In a world that construed women as innately passive, the desire to capture and dominate a woman was defined as a male attribute. We have already seen how several women felt that their masculinity was natural and empowering. Both Anne Lister and Charlotte Cushman wooed and won women because they were so attractively masterful. This chapter examines two women, Eliza Lynn Linton and Vernon Lee (Violet Paget), born a generation apart, who struggled with their gender inversion as a difficult and confusing condition. For Linton masculinity held all the virtues she admired and wished to possess; she channeled her unruly desire for women by imagining herself to be a man. But Lee was deeply suspicious of male social power and sexual freedom, and promulgated an ideal of the nonmaternal woman who would be a moral leader. Each writer in different ways advocated a feminine purity that arose from disciplined desire, rather than from either a denial or an ignorance of passion. Yet they also created explosive, irrational characters driven by uncontrollable feelings. Although they wrote deeply pessimistic tales about romance and human happiness, both were intensely receptive to love and wished passionately, too passionately, for it. Each struggled to reconcile her conflicting need to be cared for and to dominate, to be vulnerable and commanding.

For Linton and Lee the body negated the powers of the mind. Explosions of temper (Linton) or bouts of "neuropathic" illness (Lee) were signals to others and to themselves that intellect alone was insufficient. Linton resolved her psychic conflict by turning her anger outward toward the very women who most attracted her, flirtatious pretty women that she dubbed the "girl of the period" and "wild women."[1] Lee guarded her health by following a careful work schedule. In essays, fiction, and letters she lashed out at the immorality of the male-dominated literary world. Neither Linton nor Lee adopted the older, positive definition of the eccentric female genius. "Genius" was too closely aligned with madness. These well-read women recognized themselves as innately different from other women and struggled to validate themselves via intellectual and moral superiority. Linton's reading of current scientific theories, including Social Darwinism, gave her insights into herself that contemporaries like the artists Bonheur and Hosmer could avoid. For Lee the scientific thought of the 1880s and 1890s confirmed her fears about female hysteria. Max Nordau, for example, in *Degeneration* (1894), his best-selling analysis of Europe's moral and mental decay, identi-

Fig. 15. Eliza Lynn Linton, ca. 1880.

fied "highly-gifted degenerates" as characterized by a "lack of harmony, the absence of balance."[2]

Linton (fig. 15) resolved her feeling that she should have been a man in three ways: by placing a great value on such "masculine" characteristics as reason, intellect, and self-control; by creating nontraditional plots with characters who embodied gender extremes; and by writing autobiographical fantasies of boyish weakness and maternal power. All three solutions reinforced her profound sense of emotional dislocation and isolation. In contrast, the younger Lee favored a version of the German formulation of a male soul trapped in a female body. In the 1860s and 1870s, Carl Heinrich Ulrichs theorized a nonmedical model of homosexuality, in which "inverted" men had women's souls, and "inverted" women men's souls.[3] Lee believed she had been born with a divided temperament. Her whole life she struggled to combine her masculine intellect and feminine sympathy. She rebuked herself on one

Fig. 16. *Vernon Lee*, by John Singer Sargent (1881). By permission of Tate, London.

occasion for repulsing a woman's overtures, "ironically my vanity, my curious pose of manliness, & no nonsense superiority to womanish sentiment, my cursed pose to feel & act as I look in that sketch by John [Sargent], all this was silencing my goodness, & sympathy & just gratitude for profound affection."[4] (See fig. 16.) She looked to intimate friendship to help her unite these gendered halves, whereas Linton looked to friendship to confirm her masculine nature. Linton represents one strand of lesbian history that continued into the 1920s; Radclyffe "John" Hall felt that she, as a "congenital invert," was masculine. Lee represents another, in which a masculine intellect and feminine sensibility combined to create a new, third type, the spiritually pure androgynous woman.

"ONLY THE TOP-COATING . . . HAD MISCARRIED": ELIZA LYNN LINTON

Eliza Lynn was the youngest of twelve children born within fifteen years. Her mother died soon after her birth, and her oldest sister died when she was less than two. She felt especially vulnerable to the bullying of her older siblings, who incited her fiery temper. Her indolent clergyman father never hired a governess for his daughters. He disliked his tempestuous youngest child, whom he blamed for having killed his wife. From the beginning she was compared unfavorably to her blond, feminine sister Lucy. As her first biographer says, "Early in life she was looked upon by her father and others rather in the light of a naughty boy than a weak and defenceless little girl, naughty or otherwise. . . . Indeed, alluding to this, she has more than once said with something of gravity, that when she was born, a boy was due in the family, and it was only the top-coating that had miscarried."[5] She felt lacerated her entire life by a combination of guilt for causing her mother's death and anger at her mother's desertion. Novel after novel portrays selfish mothers who are unthinking worshippers of convention and feel no love for their tomboy daughters. In 1845 Linton escaped her unhappy home and went to London to try her hand as a writer. She had achieved considerable success when, in 1858, at thirty-six she married the Radical engraver, W. J. Linton, out of pity for his motherless children. Within months they were quarreling; early in 1864 they separated. His biographer speculates that the marriage may never have been consummated.[6] Linton ostentatiously adopted her married name, but since Lynn was exclusively a male name, as E. Lynn Linton she traded on gender ambiguity. One of Linton's most curious characteristics is her flaunting of her own masculinity at the same time as she excoriated it in others.

Linton never escaped from her unhappy childhood. A favorite plot included two contrasting women, one conventionally feminine but selfish and treacherous (as she remembered her sister Lucy), and the other naturally boyish, combining sexual innocence, honesty, and physical audacity (like herself). As Constance Harsh points out, these immutable stereotypes left Linton little room for character development or change.[7] But they gave her an opportunity to defend girls like herself, innately (she believed) impetuous, moral, and generous. "Natural forces" in these girls had to be tamed, but also honored. Linton's real enemy was Society, which distorted women and men, making them capricious (silly, flirtatious women), cowardly (effeminate men), villainous (sensual men), misunderstood (boyish women), or—a tiny minority—noble-hearted (manly men and womanly women). Character could not be changed, she believed, but society could be—and a better society would make it easier for the noble-hearted to find happiness. Linton filled her writing with "heretical and bold" ideas, characters, and situations.

Illegitimacy, changelings, hereditary insanity, miscegenation, concealed identity, effeminate men, and mannish women fill her novels. Add to this rich mixture her numerous attacks on organized religion, and it is easy to understand why critics found her work controversial. Even Geraldine Jewsbury dismissed her third novel, *Realities* (1851), a candid treatment of contemporary sexual mores, as a "book that makes one feel 'trailed in the mud.'"[8]

After the negative reception of *Realities*, Linton turned to honing her reputation as a hard-hitting journalist. She achieved notoriety with her antifeminist attacks on "The Girl of the Period" in the early 1860s. Then, in 1867, she brought out an ambitious novel, *Sowing the Wind*. Perhaps indirectly reflecting her own marital difficulties, the plot focuses on a deteriorating marriage. St. John Aylott, a "morbid," effeminate husband, enforces absolute obedience upon his beautiful wife. Isola is torn between "her duty to God as represented by her conscience [and] her duty to social law as represented by her wifely submission."[9] As Aylott's demands grow more importunate, Isola begins to rely on the advice of her manly cousin, Gilbert Holmes. Racial stereotypes serve as convenient moral markers. The dutiful Isola and the trustworthy Gilbert are of Nordic blood, whereas the tyrannical St. John Aylott is part Spanish, and the dangerous flirt Marcy is an octoroon.

Isola learns her husband's true worth when he runs away from a burning inn, while the strong Gilbert Holmes stays to save the trapped women. Escaping the fire is a moment of truth for Isola and Gilbert: "In the very presence of an appalling death they were neither affrighted nor discouraged, but on the contrary, filled with a strange and solemn peace, as if some great beauty were about them and some divine joy awaited. The world seemed to have gone very far off from them, as they stood hand in hand with death beside them; but God seemed very near them, and each looked wonderfully beautiful to the other."[10] They walk across a narrow ledge "from the red light of the flames into the golden light of the breaking day." Safe from the fiery dangers of passion, they hold hands and declare themselves "brother and sister for life." Isola now understands true love. Linton exploits that characteristic Victorian distinction between physical fidelity and emotional adultery. St. John Aylott's jealousy is unworthy of him, but his wife *does* love another man. He descends into madness and finally dies, permitting a final-page prenuptial reunion between the womanly woman and the manly man. Although the novel was generally well received, *The Athenaeum* complained about Isola receiving so many farewell kisses from Gilbert while her husband was still alive. It also concluded from the numerous descriptions of women's beautiful bodies that Linton's reputation as a misogynist was exaggerated, for "she has a sincere admiration for feminine grace and virtue."[11]

As Deborah T. Meem documents, Linton believed gender inversion was the worst sign of degeneration.[12] For those who feared that same-sex love was unnatural, atavistic, or degenerate, falling in love with a woman was a source of shame and concealment. Nevertheless, "manliness," regardless of gender, was superior to selfish femininity. In *Sowing the Wind* Linton is unsparing in her description of her alter ego, the "unlovely boy-woman" Jane Osborn, known among her fellow journalists as Jack. Yet Jane is the only consistently sensible woman in the novel. She takes in the Aylott family when St. John loses his money, and quietly works overtime to meet the extra expenses. But Jane is doomed to love without being loved in return. Her selfish mother barely notices her sacrifices, and Isola thinks only of Gilbert. Linton sets up a circular argument. The boy-woman is unnatural and unattractive; she cannot attract a virile man and procreate; therefore she is unnatural and unappreciated. But in a degenerate, economically ruthless world, suffering a dearth of true men, she has a necessary role in helping the womanly woman survive. Indeed Gilbert Holmes disappears for five years to make his fortune in California, so Linton can briefly limn the blessings of an all-female family. Isola's adopted son, reared by three women, is the true new man: gentle, loving, and faithful.

By the 1880s and 1890s, when fears of physical and mental degeneration among the educated classes were widely discussed, Linton's often contradictory portraits of fierce boy-women and foppish male aesthetes became common subject matter in advanced literature, scientific periodicals, and popular journalism. Linton responded with even greater exaggerations, eager to take advantage of her public role as the most outspoken antifeminist of her age. *The Rebel of the Family* (1880) was a vicious attack on gender inversion, but its inconsistencies puzzled critics and readers. The naïve heroine, Perdita, with the narrator's approval, condemns her mother's snobbishness and her sisters' social climbing. Rather than marry a wealthy ironmaster twice her age, she is drawn to the unwomanly feminist Bell Blount, "a handsome hybrid" and "petticoated bachelor." Bell is the first full-scale realistic portrait of a lesbian villain. She warmly kisses Perdita and espouses an ideology of freedom that the lonely young woman admires as superior to her mother's amoral indifference. But she soon discovers that Bell behaves like a patriarchal husband, bullying her "good little wife." The "wife" is fiercely jealous of Perdita, for she is "as much Bell Blount's creature as if she had been a man's mistress . . . giving body and soul for maintenance in the present, in the hope of a permanent provision in the future."[13] Their home is "bare, mean, unlovely, disordered," with bottles of beer, soda water, and brandy and tobacco everywhere.[14] Bell's affections and affectations leave the morally healthy, albeit undisciplined and unloved, Perdita "revolted by something too vague to name yet too real to ignore."[15] Bell's lies and mismanagement of funds further demonstrate her corrupt nature.

Small wonder that Perdita must be saved by a gentle (and as a foil for her socially ambitious mother and sisters, lower-middle-class) man. Perdita may be based on Linton's young self, but she marries the man Linton wants to be. Leslie Crawford combines the maternal nurturing Perdita so desperately needs with masculine courage and honesty. He is full of kindly actions, masculine self-control, and moral uprightness, but he is married. Several hundred pages later, the death of his mad, adulterous wife makes possible a happy ending. Although Linton avoids the crudities of the earlier novel—no sister and brother kisses—she again creates a morally awkward situation for her heroine. Moreover, her obsessive fascination with extreme feeling emerges in gratuitous comments. Perdita is repeatedly described in terms that indicate her near-madness—her brain is on fire, her cheeks burn, she feels aflame, she is a volcano. Brought face to face with the seducer of Leslie's wife, Perdita heatedly warns her mother against him, only to find herself accused of insanity. The epithets exaggerate her actual behavior but create a sense of overwrought passion tumbling out in ways that polite society could label "madness." As contemporaries noted, Linton both blames and exonerates Perdita, placing the responsibility for her follies ultimately on those who misunderstand her. And the fact remains, she loves a married man.

The central paradox of Linton's writing was her inability, or unwillingness, to imagine an asexual friendship between women. In spite of Jane's economic support of Isola, Linton subverts any opportunity for their friendship. Isola steadfastly declares that "brother" Gilbert is her only friend. No sensible girl would be friends with Bell Blount. As Meem points outs, only in one very late letter to her sister does Linton use "we" when referring to women; her infamous attack "The Girl of the Period" in the 1860s repeatedly referred to women as "them."[16] Linton's profound attraction to beautiful women, barely concealed in her fiction through gender changes, must have forced friendship after friendship into the realm of erotic tension. In fiction she could transform herself into an idealized male. Her Gilberts, Leslies, and other honorable men were spokespersons for Linton's deepest desires. The homely asexual journalist, Jane, was a safe self-portrait, but Linton's idealized self was realized in her portraits of sexually attractive, gentle men. Throughout the nineteenth century intimate friends made a distinction between love and friendship. Linton's erotic attraction to women precluded friendship, but her fear of degeneracy prohibited love.

Linton could not admit that her love of women was natural. It was instinctive and ineradicable, but unnatural. Unlike Lister and Cushman, she could not play with gender inversion as a sign of her natural self—rather masculinity was the forbidden and longed-for identity. This contradiction is illuminated in Linton's autobiographical novel, which she wrote in the voice of a man "as a screen which takes off the sting of boldness and self-exposure."[17] The cross-gendering in *The Autobiography of Christopher Kirkland* (1885) instead exposed a tangle of gender and familial transformations. Throughout Linton speaks of son-mother, brother-sister, father-daughter relations in ways that reveal rather than cover their sexual subtext. The novel is an often-poignant portrayal of frustrated passion, for it spends little time on Christopher/Eliza's quite successful writing career and a good deal on his/her unsuccessful love life. The publisher's anonymous reader complained that the "love-affairs are somewhat numerous, but in such a character the influence of passion must have been immense, and unrestrained." He went on to suggest, "we should all be content to hear less about the exact shape of ladies limbs, and the quality of their complexions!"[18] Linton's biographers, while treating *Christopher Kirkland* with care, admit that it follows her life quite closely, so we have no reason to suspect that Linton was fabricating her emotional involvements, though she may well have exaggerated her upright conduct. She certainly had many flirtations, for as Christopher admits, "I confess that I like to hear the frou-frou of a woman's dress about me. I like to hear the softer tones of her voice, and to look at her shining hair and the smooth outlines of her flower-like face."[19]

Christopher's love life reflects Linton's, including a shadowy affair in the 1870s, when she was in her early fifties. Her first biographer speaks mysteriously of "one who was very dear to her, but was not worthy of her affection."[20] Apparently Linton lent money and gave expensive gifts to a younger woman. The woman in turn may have tried to blackmail Linton because of her sexual overtures.[21] In Linton's fictional version of the event, she paints herself as injudicious but innocent. Christopher offers to help an attractive aspiring writer, Katie Pender, the daughter of his landlady. Soon he is lending her money and receiving kisses in return. Christopher disingenuously claims that he took Katie's kiss "as I should have taken it from my own daughter."[22] Then Katie steals an expensive ring, and they part angrily. Katie soon falls "into the abyss for the cursed love of gew-gaws and dissipation."[23] The inevitable deathbed scene of reconciliation between dying "daughter" and "bereaved father" completes the picture. Perhaps because of her well-known temper, Linton portrayed Christopher as a model of reason and patience, and gave Katie an uncontrollable temper. When accused of spending too much money, "Katie's face flamed, and her passion with her face," but Christopher assures the reader, "Katie's flames, though they scorched me, did not consume."[24] Just as Gilbert can safely bring Isola out of a burning building, so too can Christopher handle the fire of passionate anger. But the open secret was Linton's burning passion for pretty women that no fictional displacements could erase.

Following this disastrous cross-age friendship, Linton left England in 1876 to spend eight years on the continent. She stayed mainly in Italy, where she met and encouraged the young Vernon Lee.[25] Linton was accompanied by the recently orphaned eighteen-year-old Beatrice Sichel. After four "perfect years . . . free from clouds or storms,"[26] Sichel married, leaving Linton bereft. Linton's decision to write her autobiography in the voice of a man brought out her erotic love for this womanly woman. In a remarkably clitoral image, she describes Beatrice as a "smooth and rounded pearl," going on to say: "And for four years all went merry as a wedding-bell. There was not a hitch anywhere; not a cross no heavier than a shred of pith; not a stumbling-block bigger than a straw. We got on together in the perfect accord proper to people whose intimacy never degenerated into familiarity, and who respected themselves too much not to respect one another."[27] In her novels Linton assigned volcanic passions to characters who go insane because of a genetic regression or from sexual license, or both, as in the case of St. Aylott and Leslie's French wife or Katie Pender. They die, and the self-controlled thrive. Her ideal was intimacy that "never degenerated into familiarity," but her feared desire was for a fiery union.

Linton never ceased her fervent declarations of admiration for women. Her discreet first biographer quotes a letter written in May 1887, without revealing the name of its recipient. Linton declared:

> My dearest and sweetest woman, my most respected lady,—Your goodness to me touches me far more than I have words to adequately express. The true, pure, holy Christian charity of that white soul of yours is a living poem, an acted prayer, a warrant for the old idea of angels and seraphs. That is what I feel for you. . . . I am more lovingly grateful to you than you can possibly divine. There is no one whose love and devotion and enthusiasm go out more passionately than mine to goodness, purity.[28]

Had Linton found her Isola? Possibly this letter is only a warm response to someone who showed kindness to the aging author. The extreme emphasis on purity underscores a lifelong pattern of seeking the perfect woman, the perfect love object that, like her dead mother, was unavailable to a rough, impetuous half-man woman. The loving feminine woman lived in Linton's imagination, representing all that she was not—a Christian upper-class lady of impeccable morals, sweetness, and generosity. The agnostic Linton's life was full of battles and misunderstandings, fighting always, she thought, in a manly, honorable fashion against feminism, effeminacy—and manly women. In 1898 the *Academy's* obituary for Linton described her as "half masculine" but "not mannish."[29] She would have agreed.

"SINGED BY LOVE": VERNON LEE

No one could call Violet Paget's (Vernon Lee) itinerant childhood a traditional Victorian upbringing. She grew up on the continent, speaking English, French, Italian, and German, tutored by governesses and her capricious mother, who in her daughter's description was "passionately despotic. She could be most charming, was very pretty and most amusing, but a Tyrant."[30] Her father was largely absent and inconsequential emotionally for her and her mother. Instead her older half-brother, Eugene Lee Hamilton, took charge of her later education, writing her long letters of instruction, which their mother enforced. Intellect reigned supreme. The family settled in Florence more from caprice than any specific love of Italian culture. The decision had far-reaching consequences for Vernon Lee, much of whose best work is set in Italy. (She took on her pseudonym at an early age; close friends called her Vernon or Vernie, rather than Violet; her mother and brother continued to refer to her as Baby well into her twenties.) Mrs. Paget considered both her children geniuses, but she favored her son. In 1873 Eugene, at the beginning of a promising diplomatic career, came down with an inexplicable paralysis and returned to his mother's care. His sister, ten years younger, entertained him with gossip, books, and affection. At fourteen she published her first work in French.

Then, at twenty-four, Lee published the remarkable *Studies of the Eighteenth Century in Italy* (1880). Widely recognized for the erudition and originality of this work, she was hailed as a coming writer when she visited London in the early 1880s. She arrived already in love with A. Mary F. Robinson (1857–1944), a poet whose parents were well-known hosts to the Pre-Raphaelites and other leading artists and writers. Dressed in tailored suits, with thick glasses, and speaking high-pitched English with a slight continental accent, Lee was a fascinating novelty. She soon met all of the leading literary and critical lions of the day, including Walter Pater, Dante Gabriel Rossetti, Robert Browning, William Morris, and the young Henry James. Her arrogance and outspoken disdain for anyone who disagreed with her laid the groundwork for her later unpopularity and dismissal from these "top circles." But for a time her remarkable intelligence and ambiguous sexuality fascinated London.

Linton declared in the preface to her 1885 autobiographical novel that it traced "infinite progress, by the law of moral evolution working from within."[31] As a firm Social Darwinist, she drew comfort from a belief in social progress. Lee was less certain. Yet she refused to give up the notion of progress because she believed the world held a central intellectual and moral place for women like her. In a series of long letters to Mary Robinson (fig. 17), Lee expounded her theories about the role of the woman writer, arguing: "I feel so strong myself in the face of all the things, injustice, & death & necessary evil, which I don't shirk from recognising & calling by their names. . . . I do see the world as a great Augean stable, & that we must all unite our tricklings of good sense & good feeling into a great river to sweep it all clean. Oh dearest Mary, it is such a splendid thing to be strong, to tuck up one's mental sleeves & take up a good moral broom!"[32]

A major influence on Lee's decision to take a moral broom to society was her friendship with Mme. Anne Meyer, whose husband brought his mis-

Fig. 17. A. Mary F. Robinson, ca. 1880. Courtesy of Colby College, Waterville, Maine.

tresses into their home, forced his wife to consort with his "beastly" Russian friends, and controlled the education of their son. That all his actions were perfectly legal further horrified Lee. Several summers in England, where she encountered patronizing advice and sexual innuendo, only confirmed her sense that moral reform must come from a strong, truth-speaking woman. In 1884 she published her first novel, *Miss Brown,* a satire of her London aesthetic friends that also drew upon stories she had heard about M. Meyer's life.[33] Although she thought she was attacking the fashionable doctrine of "art for art's sake," her friends were shocked by the novel's sensuality and felt she had turned on those who had shown her hospitality.

Miss Brown reveals more about Lee and her sexuality than she may have intended. It is her first full-scale effort to create a pure, lesbian-like heroine. A morally weak artist, Walter Hamlin, educates the beautiful but poor Anne

Brown, the daughter of a Scottish sailor and an Italian seamstress. While waiting for Anne to be "finished," he satisfies his sexual needs with a manipulative Russian woman, Sacha Elaguine. The "hysterical" Sacha, constantly devising ways to attract attention, is the essence of degraded femininity. Lee shows her holding court, dressed in vaguely oriental robes, stretched out on a couch, while besotted men, unmanned by their desire, obey her slightest whims. Anne, who finds Walter's touch abhorrent, is obsessed by his mistress's touch. She feels "a vague, undefinable repulsion" when Sacha Elaguine grasps her tightly and kisses her. In one scene the coolheaded Anne helps the overheated Sacha put out a fire burning in Sacha's bed. Later, after the other guests disperse, Anne realizes that Sacha had lit the fire herself. Lee concludes the chapter with Anne recollecting "scientific books" she had read "about the connection between hysteria and monomania, about the strange passion for deceit, for hoax, for theatricality."[34] Lee simultaneously reminds her readers of contemporary theories about sexuality and insanity, while also describing Anne's intimate familiarity with the bedroom of the fascinating, duplicitous Sacha.

In reaction to Sacha's moral corruption, Anne forces herself to marry the dissolute Walter to save him, "even though the sense of Hamlin's baseness, of his selfish aestheticism and his untruthful morbidness, weighted more and more on her day by day."[35] Anne is left to suffocate rather than burn, "To become the wife of Sacha's lover . . . to give way, to dissolve[;] a horrible warm, clamminess overtook her; she could not breathe, or breathed only horror."[36] Her marital bed will always include Sacha. Lee, like Linton, concluded in a moral muddle: most readers found Anne's self-sacrifice for the moral improvement of a man a hideous crime against herself. Lee created a bizarre triangle of desire, in which same-sex passion emerges in the struggle for a man neither woman wants. In contrast to many late-twentieth-century lesbian plots, the two women do not unite against the man; rather, all three are trapped in a quagmire of sensuality. It is *not* realistic that Anne should marry Walter Hamlin, but she must escape a seemingly worse fate—the burning passion of the oriental Sacha that threatens to incinerate her.

Up until the ending the "exceptional" Anne seems to be preparing for a life of service in the slums. Throughout the book she is revolted by the sexual overtures of men and appalled at their submission to Sacha. She knows passion, but rises above it:

> Some few women seem to be born to be men, or at least not to have been women. To them love, if it come, will be an absorbing passion, but a passion only of brief duration. . . . They are indeed sent into the world (if any of us is ever sent for any purpose) to be its Joans of Arc—

to kindle from their pure passion a fire of enthusiasm as passionate, but purer than it is given to men to kindle: they are not intended to be, except as a utilisation of what is fatally wasted, either wives or mothers.[37]

Lee shifts the site of sexual self-revelation in fiction from the fiery moment of fusion (most often symbolized by the first kiss or the fire scenes discussed earlier) to a moment of triumphant refusal, of purified self-control. Fire remains the dominant image for passion, but for her it should be the crucible that creates a life-enhancing purity.[38] A special kind of woman who knew, and overcame passion, was the ideal leader to cleanse the Augean stables of society.

Well before the better-known sexologists of the turn of the century, Lee struggled to define this new Joan of Arc. In the 1870s and 1880s what definitions there were of the masculine woman-loving woman in literature were awkward and inconsistent; virtually all of them, mostly by men, were negative. Linton boldly sexualized a familiar caricature of the mannish woman in her whisky-drinking Bell Blount. She equated gender inversion with moral degeneracy, and Bell confirmed preexisting prejudices. But Lee argued that inversion was a sign of moral regeneration, and so set about creating a positive portrait of the woman "made not for man, but for humankind." In *Miss Brown* she edged toward the notion of a *superior* third sex, a concept gaining ground in England and Germany among male homosexuals.[39] For Lee the future belonged to women who refused to marry in order to improve society. These heroic women, these "masculine women," she insists, "mere men in disguise, they are not: the very strength and purity of their nature, its intensity as of some undiluted spirit, is dependent upon their cleaner and narrower woman's nature. . . . They are, and can only be, true women; but women without woman's instincts and wants, sexless—women made not for man, but for humankind. Anne Brown was one of these."[40]

Lee echoes a long-standing feminist argument that the single woman had "not fewer duties than others, but more extended [ones]." Self-sacrifice, "more entire than belongs to the double life of marriage," was "the true law of celibacy."[41] But she sexualized these clichés because she spoke out so strongly against marriage for the sexless woman. Created before the birth of the feminist New Woman, Anne Brown was dangerously close to the unnatural, the perverse. Lee's sex-hating heroine seemed scandalous, especially when combined with an attack on hedonistic men. As Kathy Psomiades points out, to be sexless did not merely connote the absence of sex; among aesthetes it included an idealized same-sex desire.[42] Lee drew attention to and then renounced the female body, covertly naming and then denying lesbianism. Readers were transfixed by her overheated descriptions of stage-managed passion and ignored her utopian pleas on behalf of "women without women's instincts."

Lee's fault in 1884 was the same as Radclyffe Hall's in 1928: both chose the novel, a popular and widely read form, in which to promulgate their vision of the place of the lesbian in modern society. Other spokespersons were far more careful and still ran into difficulties. When the homosexual Socialist Edward Carpenter published his pamphlet *Homogenic Love* in January 1895, he marked it "printed for private circulation only" and distributed it to select friends. As part of the widespread effort to create a new nonpornographic vocabulary for same-sex sexual practices, German and British theorists had coined numerous neutral words, some scientific, some neoclassical, including homogenic, meaning a love of one's own sex. After the arrest of Oscar Wilde in April 1895, Carpenter's London publisher broke his contract to publish *Love's Coming-of-Age,* even though it did not contain the homogenic essay. Carpenter found a new publisher a year later, but only in the fifth edition, in 1906, did he add a revised, less explicit chapter on homogenic love to the book. He described the new homogenic woman as a sign of progress, using eugenic terms that echo Lee's:

> What exactly evolution may be preparing for us, we do not know. . . . The women of the new movement are naturally largely drawn from those in whom the maternal instinct is not especially strong; also from those in whom the sexual instinct is not preponderant. Such women do not altogether represent their sex; some are rather mannish in temperament; some are "homogenic," that is, inclined to attachments to their own, rather than to the opposite sex; some are ultra-rationalizing and brain-cultured.[43]

Sixteen years after Lee, Carpenter was as tentative as she, unwilling to assign a single characteristic (for example, mannishness) to the new woman, yet determined to honor her place in the natural evolution of society. The same characteristics gather around his homogenic woman as around Lee's exceptional woman. He too suggested that "the other love should have its special function in social and heroic work, and in the generation [of] the philosophical conceptions and ideals which transform our lives and those of society."[44] A set of characteristics, some traditional ("mannish" and "brain cultured"), but some new (lacking maternal and sexual instincts), now clustered around certain types of women.

Soon after the publication of *Miss Brown,* Lee recorded in her journal a warning from a friend that she seemed "obsessed by a sense of the impurity of the world and that in transferring this obsession to my readers, I am really enervating them, not strengthening them."[45] Rather than writing to improve humankind, she might be unconsciously weakening it. Like Eliza Lynn Linton, Lee was accused of filling her book with sensuality; each clearly shared a compulsive fascination with clammy sex. Henry James, to whom *Miss Brown* was dedicated, pointedly suggested that she was guilty of "a certain ferocity" and "too great an implication of sexual motives." Lee's zealous attack on immorality was bound to offend James's highly refined sensibility. He advised her that, "morality is hot—but art is icy!"[46] Lee had succeeded all too well in showing "hot" sexuality chasing "icy" feminine purity, but she had not yet found a language to present convincingly the cleansing power of the lesbian heroine. Only in her horror tales was Lee able to explore in less self-revealing ways the inner workings of both fiery passion and passionate purity. But in these stories she gave up any attempt to define the nature and purpose of the new, sexless woman in the modern world.

In August 1887, while in Scotland visiting a new friend, Clementina (Kit) Anstruther-Thomson (1857–1921), Lee received news that Mary Robinson, her intimate friend for nearly a decade, had abruptly decided to marry the distinguished French orientalist James Darmsteter (1849–94). Lee had encouraged Robinson's poetry, and for years they had read and critiqued each other's writing. Lee's horror of male sexuality, as well as her consternation at Robinson's desertion, found an outlet in attacking the proposed marriage on eugenic grounds. A series of candid letters to her mother and brother reveals her tangled emotions:

> M. Darmsteter is youngish, he has a very sympathetic face. . . . But he is a dwarf, a humpback. . . . He looks as if all his stunted misshapen little body (he is the size of a boy of ten) would fall to pieces, and his hand, even on a boiling day, was cold like a snake. . . . Really, two centuries ago, this quasimodo wd have been burnt for less. Everyone feels quite useless arguing with Mary. . . . She doesn't seem to realise the deep horror which this marriage, & the mad haste in which it was decided on, *must* inspire in others.[47]

Lee felt the marriage would be a disaster for the delicate Robinson, who could not tolerate childbearing. When her male rival agreed with her, telling her that they intended a platonic marriage, her own style of platonic love was expunged. She discovered that the marriage of true minds if it consisted of two women had no place in society.

The Darmsteters' decision to have a *mariage blanc* was perhaps less extraordinary than it seems today. It coincided with numerous novels and essays about the New Woman and her alleged lack of interest in sex, her discriminating perceptions, fastidious nerves, and intellectuality. Mary Robinson resembles an upper-class version of Sue Bridehead in Thomas Hardy's *Jude the Obscure* (1895). Sue dislikes sex and considers her intellectual partnership with an Oxford undergraduate ideal, though he dies under her regime. Other 1890s novels candidly discussed venereal disease, frigidity, and other marital problems; platonic marriage was one of several solutions offered.[48] Many advanced fin-de-siècle thinkers (though not Hardy) found a spiritual marriage to be one sign of a new era of greater sexual equality. As mentioned earlier, Linton may never have consummated her marriage. If for Lee lesbian purity was ennobling, she considered heterosexual purity impossible and morally suspect. As she wrote her mother, to her dismay the newly engaged couple failed to see their plan as "false" or "difficult" or "wicked."[49]

We can never know whether Robinson consummated her marriage with Darmsteter, but as she had determined beforehand, she never had children. Soon after his death in 1894, she married a distinguished scientist, Emile Duclaux (1840–1904). Neither marriage probably demanded much sex. She continued to live in Paris, where she established herself as a *femme de lettres*, writing in both English and French. After she embraced heterosexuality, Mary tried to turn same-sex love into friendship. She insisted that her marriages made no difference to her intimacy with Lee, a position that infuriated Lee, who felt betrayed by her platitudes. In a 1907 memoir of Lee's brother, Eugene, Mary Robinson Duclaux described her first winter in Italy in 1881 staying with her new friend:

> From early dawn to dewy eve we appeared to exist merely in order to communicate to each other our ideas about things in general. . . . We were always writing in corners, Violet and I. She at a carved table on large vellum-like sheets; I huddled in a shawl on the chimney step, my inkpot neighbouring the firedogs, a blotting-pad upon my knee. I cannot say we wrote in solemn silence. Impressions, forecasts, reminiscences, quotations from Michelet or Matarazzo, subjects for ballads, problems for essays, aesthetical debates and moral discussions would burst forth. . . . We were so young, Violet and I.[50]

Her comments, with the careful repetition of "Violet and I," read like a love letter, wooing Lee to remember their happy days together. Yet the letters she carefully preserved prove that Mary Robinson had never called her "dearest Vernie" Violet, a feminine name Lee almost never used. Did Robinson feel a kind of heterosexual envy for her homoerotic past? Lee, Darmsteter, and Duclaux were all people of extraordinary intellectual accomplishments, but only Lee was a fellow writer with whom Robinson could share work. However successful her Paris salon, she may have envied Vernon Lee's freedom and network of women friends. Heterosexual envy of homosexual autonomy is often forgotten in histories of homosexual victimization and homophobia.

Lee wrote numerous horror stories about obsessive love, but few deal with marriage. An exception is "The Wedding Chest," a tale that may represent her continued anguish over the Darmsteter marriage. Troilo, the villain, brutally seizes and then disposes of any woman he finds attractive. The illegitimate but high-born Troilo is a "most beautiful youth," with skin "astonishingly white and fair like a woman's," who always seems young, "having no beard, and a face like Hyacinthus or Ganymede, whom Jove stole to be his cup-bearer, on account of his beauty."[51] Lee's heterosexual rake looks more like the object of male homosexual desire, underscoring his subversion of marriage—and Lee's own distrust of all heterosexuality. Moreover Troilo's name echoes that of the failed lover Troilus, who could not keep his lighthearted Cressida. Troilo contrives to steal the beautiful Maddalena, engaged to Desiderio, a cabinet-maker, while she is bathing nude with other women. His dalliance soon over, he returns Maddalena to the cabinetmaker, her body and dead child stuffed into a wedding chest. Desiderio, the skilled maker of the chest, is maddened with revenge. He murders Troilo, the "ferocious and magnanimous" boy, the arch-transgressor. Desiderio then "till his death" preserved "with him always the body of Monna Maddalena in the wedding chest painted with the Triumph of Love, because he considered she had died ordore magnae sanctitatis."[52] He fetishizes his unconsummated love as pure and holy via the wedding chest, which survives into the present, its true purpose forgotten.

The fable can be read many ways. Lee may have recast the boy-sized Darmsteter into the role of the sexually voracious boyish Troilo, who returned Mary only after she was erotically dead to Lee. Lee, like the craftsman Desiderio, seems on the verge of worshipping her memory. Yet perhaps Lee used the violent Troilo to explore emotions that she could not admit to, or that came out only in descriptions of figures like Sacha Elaguine. Was she, the chaste intellectual, at heart Troilo, the passionate lover who stole Mary away from heterosexuality? Lee appears to have cast herself as a passionate destroyer of heterosexual love. By creating in Troilo a villain who is partially defined by his homosexual attributes, she both conceals and reveals same-sex desire as a form of thievery, as naturally destructive. Desiderio cannot return Maddalena to her virgin state, nor can he ever marry her. Like Linton, Lee throughout her career was attracted to physical violence and inflated language as a way to express irrational passions. John Addington Symonds had early cautioned her about her writing, "your modulations are often violent,"[53] but she would not give up her exaggerations. Perhaps Lee saw herself in all three characters: the artisan lover who—like Vernon Lee—loves too strongly; the thieving Troilo who—like Vernon Lee—revenges himself upon husbands and fiancés, and fair Maddalena, the unfortunate victim, who—like Vernon Lee—cannot speak about the roots of her love or her sense of violation.

Lee returned to the theme of compulsive love in her horror stories. But after the debacle of *Miss Brown*, she largely avoided contemporary realistic fiction. Instead she concentrated on art and aesthetics, writing personal essays that revealed a deep appreciation of female beauty. Like Lee Linton enjoyed describing beautiful women and what attracted her to them; indeed she read-

ily admitted to a friend that she could not form a close friendship with anyone she did not find good-looking.[54] Lee was especially intrigued by the tall,
statuesque Kit Ansthruther-Thomson, whom she described as "a picturesque
personality, paints very well, dresses crâne [stylishly] & rather fast, drives tan-
dem & plays polo."[55] She was infatuated with Ansthruther-Thomson's outdoor life in Scotland, so different from her own continental upbringing. Her
remote beauty and intellectual naïveté seemed akin to Anne Brown's. Unlike
the delicate Mary Robinson, she was "a charming person, with that supreme
charm . . . of never having felt except for others, of being absolutely unruf-
fled, unsinged by passion."[56] After the hot pangs of disappointed love,
Anstruther-Thomson's coolness was utterly attractive.

Lee's new friend became for her a symbol of the beautiful homogenic
woman. Turning her beloved into an art object made it possible to celebrate
their love publicly. The highest compliment Lee could pay Anstruther-
Thomson was to compare her to a Greek statue. In *Althea: A Second Book of Dialogues on Aspirations and Duties* (1894), dedicated to C.A.T., she describes
Althea (Anstruther-Thomson) as "a young god," and her brother, who accompanied them on their walks in the Scottish moors, as "a little faun." At another point the statuesque Althea's head was "less like a woman's, in its large
placid beauty and intellectual candour, than like that of some antique youth's
in whose marble effigy we fancy we recognize one of the speakers of the
Phaedo or the *Eutheydemus*."[57] Anstruther-Thomson's sculptural purity makes
sex visible but without moving into the dangerous area of actual bodily contact, such as the passionate kisses of Sacha and Anne Brown.[58] Reminiscing
thirty years later, Lee recalled Anstruther-Thomson as a "Venus de Milo"
whose "virginal expression made one think rather of a very beautiful and
modest boy, like some of the listeners of Plato."[59] Lee redefines the Western
archetype of female heterosexual beauty, turning it into a virginal modest
boy—a lesbian. Like her friend the homosexual art historian Walter Pater,
Lee believed that Greek statuary was the supreme representation of sexless
beauty. Her educated audience would certainly have recognized Lee's descriptions of her intimate friend as an effort to visualize, to embody in marble, a special kind of love.

For over a decade Lee and Anstruther-Thomson successfully combined a
very close friendship with an enriching study of art and aesthetics.[60] But by
1898–99 Anstruther-Thomson came to find Lee's intellectualizing exhaust-
ing, and she fell in love with a woman who needed her care. In *Althea* Lee had
complimented her friend's emotional coolness and her dislike of hurting others. She loved Anstruther-Thomson precisely because she seemed, like Anne
Brown, a heroine who had risen above passion. Now, Lee admitted to a mutual friend, "I suspect that this is her first real, headlong & unreasonable affec-

tion for anyone—You see she looked at me as a teacher, etc. etc. etc."[61] As Lee recovered her health and intellectual self-confidence, she no longer needed nursing, and Anstruther-Thomson never pretended to be an intellectual.

I believe another element led to their breakup: even though the two women openly preserved a cool, chaste relationship, Lee was privately too passionate, too fiery, for Anstruther-Thomson. She confessed that Anstruther-Thomson disliked scenes and admitted that "in some ways I have never satisfied Kit. She despises & fears impulsive & demonstrative people; and she really doesn't give me credit for as much grit as I have."[62] Lee, always considered to be icy and brainy, may have been more like Sacha Elaguine, the "impulsive & demonstrative" Russian, in ways difficult to document except indirectly in her overwrought prose. Her surviving letters to Mary Robinson and Kit Anstruther-Thomson from the 1880s and 1890s are passionate, demanding, and intensely intellectual. Lee apologizes proudly to both for her unconditional love, confident that they will reciprocate. Her favorite descriptive term was "necessary"—each woman was *necessary* to her happiness, "the very atmosphere in which everything that I care for . . . always must grow."[63] Unfortunately, over time she was not necessary to them. Unlike Ethel Smyth, Vernon Lee never found a way to balance her need for hot love and cool beauty.

Two years after the breakup with Anstruther-Thomson, Lee confessed that she felt like an "interloper" when she turned up each summer in England. "I feel it would be a great source of strength," she told a friend, "to meet anyone who felt like myself about impersonal matters; but I fancy I am too much of an alien, a cosmopolitan, an exception, for that to be possible. . . . I am just an individual, and an individual is a weak thing! . . . I know it will cost me all my passion as a writer. & the other hazard I am getting more & more attached to my own ideas & engrossed in them."[64] Although Lee continued to spend almost every summer in Britain during the early years of the twentieth century, she increasingly avoided London. She wintered in Florence, reading, writing, and hosting women visitors. Old friends, including Lady Ponsonby and Ethel Smyth, remained loyal, but her fiction, criticism, and aesthetics lacked the originality that had attracted so many fellow writers in the 1880s and 1890s. During World War I her pacifist writings were condemned as too pro-German, and her aesthetic studies of art and music too amateurish. High-minded philosophical dialogues on art and morality had a limited readership on the brink of Modernism. Lee failed to connect with a new generation of sexual and intellectual radicals. A young confident generation of English and American women in Paris, under the leadership of Renée Vivien and Natalie Barney, flaunted their homosexuality and their internationalism.[65] Barney's openly lesbian sonnets appeared in 1900, Vivien's *Une Femme m'apparut* (*A Woman Appeared to Me*) in 1904. They, like their male counterparts, made no effort to reach a wider audience, but instead addressed their work solely to those who would appreciate a private language of desire. As the next chapter shows, they reworked many of the images and styles that character- ize Lee's stories and dialogues. Vivien shared with Lee the wish to create an imaginative world where female sexual desire could be explored. But lesbian history does not consist of clear lines of influence or long-term communities. Each generation had to rediscover its past and forge its future, recognizing only a few iconic cases, such as the Ladies of Llangollen. We can only spec- ulate how Lee might have been influenced by this daring new generation had their paths crossed.

"THE UNREAL ONE CANNOT LOSE": LESBIAN LONGINGS

At the end of the nineteenth century, sexologists looked around at the nu- merous unmarried women involved in long-term romantic friendships and identified the "true invert" as a mannish woman. But though she was a famil- iar figure, gender inversion at this point continued to be a set of fluid charac- teristics rather than a single labeled identity. Many lesbians, rather than fully embracing an impossible adult masculinity, identified with the adolescent boy who combined elements of both sexes. His liminal sexual position and appearance made him both familiar and ambiguous, within the family and yet apart from it. Unlike the tomboy, with her boisterous immaturity and uneasy, willful avoidance of sex, the androgynous boy had a long history in the arts as a symbol of a rare and delicate erotic potentiality. The boy was less a fig- ure of adventurous sexual exploration, and more one of preternatural under- standing and spiritual purity. Like male homosexuals, lesbian writers could admire the boy as a stand-in for their own adolescence or, like Vernon Lee's many references to Kit Anstruther-Thomson's boyishness, as a way to under- score an asexual, otherworldly beauty. The boy was a representative of chaste innocence, of a special, lost quality in the modern world. Alternatively, some later lesbian writers embraced the figure of the boyish (never girlish) an- drogyne as representative of their difference from other women. It did not carry the negative connotations of male effeminacy for women, but rather signified their refusal of heterosexuality.

This section looks at the adolescent boy-woman's passionate commitment to the unavailable mother. She was the woman who could love the vulnera- ble boy within Linton and Lee unconditionally—but without the danger of consummation. Judith Roof has argued that lesbians create a successful path to sexual maturity not through a return to the pre-Oedipal stage of unity with a nurturing mother, but rather through the construction of an absent, fantasy mother. They learn to desire desire itself, which remains always unfulfilled and therefore always open to negotiation.[66] But her formula may be too schematic to fit the many different configurations mother-love could take. It also seems too negative, too empty, given the extraordinarily rich fictions created by Linton and Lee. Each imagined herself as an adolescent boy in love with an older woman in order to explore a perfect love relationship. Fantasy helped to normalize a forbidden and impossible love that was fundamentally different from and yet better than all other love. But it always remains dangerous; illness and death punctuate their plots.

The single-most-revealing passage in Linton's *Autobiography of Christopher Kirkland* occurs when the wealthy Mr. and Mrs. Dalrymple come to Christopher's neighborhood. In "his" late teens he falls head over heels in love with Adeline Dalrymple, a sophisticated woman, "languid in her movements; indolent in her habits; but she had an almost feverish activity of mind, an almost dangerous energy of thought."[67] Like Sacha Elaguine in Lee's *Miss Brown*, she holds court lying on a couch, wearing flowing gowns. Christopher/Eliza passionately longs "to kneel to her, to kiss the hem of her garment, to make myself her footstool, her slave, so that I could be of use to her."[68] Christopher worships Adeline, whose pantheistic religion gives them permission to be together and confirms the spirituality of their passionate attraction:

> Did that sweet voice which always reminded me of pearls tremble, and something as tender as tears come into her glorious eyes? . . . "I am with you always—like God and with God—in the future always, as I have ever been in the past."
>
> Her hand . . . burnt like fire, and the diamonds on her fingers and at her throat flashed as if by their own internal light. . . . Something seemed to pass from her to me which thrilled me like electricity. . . . She was beyond womanhood to me—she was the casket that embodied and enclosed the Divine.[69]

Familiar heterosexual tropes of passion are subtly altered to embody a specifically lesbian desire. If Lee turned Anstruther-Thomson into a work of art, Linton turned Adeline into something timeless, a divinity bedecked with diamonds. Female passion is expressed through a series of clitoral and vaginal images. The voice, eyes, hand, all stand in for those female parts that cannot be named but are hinted at by the pearls and casket. Rather than burning cheeks, Adeline's hand burns; she is feverishly passionate, but is that hot hand a sign of something more, of a masturbatory love? Even touch is likened to electricity sending a shock through Christopher's body; this is a love so complete that it moves beyond words. Yet the double meaning of casket hints at something more frightening. Adeline embodies not only the divine, but also death.

Christopher becomes "furious and wild against the obstructions that kept us apart." Night after night he stands secretly watching her bedroom window. Inside and outside are reversed when Adeline goes out to the waiting boy and reveals her love: "Child! what have you done to me to draw me to you? What strange power have you over me?" Christopher is overwhelmed:

> I cannot describe the curious sense of inversion which these words cre-
> ated. I, who had been the slave, the worshipper, the subordinate, to be
> suddenly invested with power—to be even so prepotent as to compel
> obedience from one who had hitherto been supreme—it was a change
> of parts which for the moment overwhelmed me with a sense of uni-
> versal instability; and to the end of my life I shall never forget the
> strange confusion of pride and pleasure, of pain in loss yet joy in the
> sensation of a newborn power which possessed me, as the goddess thus
> became a woman, and made of me, who had been her slave, her mas-
> ter and a man.[70]

They spend the night holding hands. At dawn Adeline kisses him on the fore-
head and eyes, as a "seal of our eternal oneness. Overpowered by an emotion
so powerful as to be physical pain . . . I think that for a moment I died."[71] Orgasmic bliss leads to a breakdown. Christopher falls prey to brain fever and
no longer recognizes his beloved, who tirelessly nurses him. It was awkward
but not compromising for Mrs. Dalrymple to sit beside the bed of the delirious young man. Like the bond between Lisl and Ethel, their intimacy is cemented through regression to helpless childhood, though Christopher is
wholly unconscious during Adeline's ministrations.

Homoerotic passion is transformed into the longings of a sick child for
her mother—for a return to a time Linton never had, of perfect fusion with
her mother in the socially sanctioned embrace of maternal love. But Linton
did not stop there, because she wished to convey as precisely as possible the
depth of her love for this older woman. Whereas the rest of the *Autobiography*
focuses on the mature Kirkland's amorous difficulties, this first love gives Linton an opportunity to explore the pleasure of being the passive beloved, rather
than the active male-like lover. The delirious Christopher imagines that he is
nursed by his dead mother "out of heaven," or the Divine Virgin "who had made
me her second Christ," or the goddess Isis. Then the lovers become "Endymion
and Diana or Ixion and Juno." Adeline remains throughout a goddess-woman,
but Christopher is polymorphous, being first the bereft son and the crucified
savior, then a beautiful shepherd boy (with well-established male homosexual connotations), and finally the would-be seducer of Zeus's wife.[72] Seeking
to capture same-sex passion, Linton tries out a series of dissimilar images circling the figure of the vulnerable young man. None quite captures the spiritualized eroticism of the relationship. Before Christopher recovers, Adeline
and her effete husband leave for Italy. Years later he learns that the husband
became an opium addict and Adeline had died.

The fervid presentation of this relationship led Linton's first biographer to apologize: "in strict accord with the unfortunate plan of the book, the not un-usual phenomenon of a girl's infatuation for a woman of eight or ten years her senior is metamorphosed into the passionate devotion of a youth for a young and fascinating married woman."[73] But more was at stake than he admitted. Adeline's death is prefigured in the reference to her role as a divinity in a cas-ket, but also in Christopher's *petite mort* when kissed by Adeline. True love is death for Linton. The blissful merging that Smyth found with Lisl von Her-zogenberg led to a form of death for Linton. Since love threatened a loss of self, a death of one's precious, hard-won identity, she kept it at a safe moral distance by creating only impossible scenarios. A perfect but unnatural love could be described only in terms of a potentially adulterous love. And Christopher never achieves another true love, but must instead mother a se-ries of young women.

Vernon Lee repeats a garden scene of pure cross-age love in her fin-de-siècle tale "Prince Alberic and the Snake-Lady" (1896). The an-drogynous Prince Alberic is "at once manly and delicate, and full of grace and vigor of movement. His long hair, the color of floss silk, fell in wavy curls, which seemed to imply almost a woman's care and coquetry. His hands, though powerful, were . . . of princely form and whiteness."[74] He is the neg-lected grandson of the "ever-young" Duke Balthazar, who is bankrupting the Duchy of Luna in order to build a grotto filled with marble animals and a chapel for his sepulcher. The duke resembles a pantomime dame, with his heavy makeup, wigs, and pretensions to youth and sexual allure; modern readers would recognize him as a camp queen. The lonely prince is confined to his rooms in his grandfather's sterile castle. He learns about rabbits, herbs, and natural things only through the careful examination of a tapestry that portrays the tale of his ancestor Alberic the Blond and the bewitched Lady Oriana. Though she "ended off in the long, twisting body of a snake," Prince Alberic loves her. When his uncle tries to teach him heterosexual passion by replacing the old tapestry with one depicting Susannah and the Elders, he slashes it to pieces. His response is one of a series of foreshadowings that pre-dict the tragic conclusion of his love for the Snake Lady.

Alberic is expelled from the Red Castle for his destructiveness and sent to the remote Castle of Shining Waters, which bears a remarkable resemblance to his beloved tapestry. After exploring his sensuous new world, he drinks from a well. "The well was very, very deep. Its inner sides were covered, as far as you could see, with long delicate weeds like pale green hair, but this faded away in the darkness. At the bottom was a bright space, reflecting the sky, but looking like some subterranean country. Alberic, as he bent over, was startled by suddenly seeing what seemed a face filling up part of that shining circle."[75] The scene is redolent of lesbian imagery, including not only the lush vaginal-like well, but also the mirroring of two lovers. Lee leaves ambiguous whether Alberic has seen himself or someone else reflected in the deep well; the "wonderful tones" responding to his voice could be a distorted echo or a magical presence. This mysterious moment culminates with the arrival of "a long, green, glittering thing," the snake to which his future (and his past, via the tapestry) is tied. Then, at sundown, the snake disappears, but a very beautiful woman arrives, who declares herself to be his godmother, come to teach him. Every evening she brings him books, horses, and appropriate attire, so that he grows up the very model of the perfect prince.

For years Alberic lives in an isolated, self-contained idyll of sensual love that needs no sexual consummation. But upon reaching adolescence the "full-grown and gallant-looking youth" wonders about the story of his ancestor and the Lady Oriana. At the very edge of defining his own sexual desire, Alberic is "still shy and frightened," for "the greater his craving to know, the greater grew a strange certainty that the knowing would be accompanied by evil." A traveling bard reluctantly reveals to him that "the Fairy Oriana, most miserable of all fairies, [is] condemned for no fault, but by envious powers, to a dreadful fate."[76] Alberic the Blond and a second Alberic had both failed to remain faithful for ten years to the Snake Lady in order to free her of the curse of being half-snake. This knowledge makes the prince gravely ill, and he falls into a delirium. Once again sickness is the sign of overwhelming erotic desire.

Then, on a moonlit night, Alberic rises from his sick bed to follow a nightingale to the well, for "it was, he knew, the hour and place of his fate." As Jane Hotchkiss notes, it is a moment of clitoral unveiling, as "a quiver came through the grass," "a rustle through the roses," and "on the well's brink, encircling its central blackness, glided the Snake. 'Oriana!' whispered Alberic. 'Oriana!' She paused and stood almost erect."[77] Nature stops, silent, as he "pressed his lips on the little flat head of the serpent." So traumatizing is this orgasmic moment that Alberic falls unconscious. Like Christopher Kirkland, he is initiated into sexual maturity by the kiss. "When he awoke the moon was still high. The nightingale was singing its loudest. He lay in the grass by the well, and his head rested on the knees of the most beautiful of ladies. She was dressed in cloth of silver which seemed woven of moon mists, and shimmering moonlit green grass. It was his own dear Godmother."[78] Bathed in moonlight, the preeminent symbol of the feminine, Alberic submits to his fate. His godmother changes from being his mother and teacher to being his love object. Lee brings together every explanatory model for the boy's passion: he is fetishistically attached to the tapestry and its narrative; he is a direct descendant in blood and appearance to the previous two Alberics; he has loved the snake since it first slithered into his pocket. Nature, nurture, and maternal care have all conspired to commit Alberic to an unnatural love. The sheer lush *jouissance* of life at the Castle of Shining Waters expresses vividly a natural delight in the senses. Sexual pleasure is not a narrow drive toward consummation, but rather an integral part of the happy life of learning, love, and companionship. Prince Alberic and his godmother possess these rare gifts briefly but completely, until the outside world destroys their happiness.

The tale moves swiftly to its inevitable conclusion. His grandfather discovers that Alberic has "no eyes, let alone a heart, for the fair sex." Desperate for money to complete his art projects, he imprisons his grandson in order to force him to marry a rich tradesman's daughter. On Friday the 13th of August 1700, in the midst of a thunderstorm, Duke Balthasar, "of enlightened mind and delicate taste," visits his stubborn grandson with three advisers; when he spies the snake, they instantly kill it. The old duke recovers from his fright, kicks the "mangled head with his ribboned shoe," and laughingly comments, "Who knows . . . whether you were not the Snake Lady?" Alberic refuses "all nourishment" and dies "a fortnight later." His grandfather goes mad, haunted by the rumor that when the prison room was cleaned, "the persons employed found in a corner, not the dead grass snake, which they had been ordered to cast into the palace drains, but the body of a woman, naked, and miserably disfigured with blows and saber cuts."[79] Phallic swords destroy the good fairy godmother. Yet her magic implicitly remains in art, for "certain chairs and curtains in the porter's lodge" are made from "the various pieces of an extremely damaged arras, having represented the story of Alberic the Blond and the Snake Lady."[80]

Just as Linton's first biographer had squirmed at her sensual prose, Lee's first biographer called the story a specimen of "unwholesome weirdness . . . loaded with an unhealthy excess of color and jewelled ornament" that must be "evidence of a diseased sensibility."[81] Even when they disguised their fiction as heterosexual passion, both women had written altogether too overtly lesbian narratives. Erotic pleasure is displaced onto rich descriptions of natural objects that mimic the female body—pearls, diamonds, a mossy well, the moon, and verdant gardens conspire to reveal a highly wrought sense of the female body. Fulfillment is so overwhelming as to be almost unsupportable: a kiss leads to deathlike fever or fainting. Perhaps like Anne Lister, Linton and Lee employed the kiss as metonymy for an orgasm. Each writer presented youthful passion as so utterly pure that the corrupt world will inevitably destroy it. Their fiction does not conceal a deviant desire, but rather celebrates its absolute rightness—and inevitable destruction.

Linton and Lee obsessively revisited lost loves and lost opportunities. Remaking their past experiences, they could relive the intensities of passion but alter the conclusions to fit desired ends. Even early in life Lee meditated on how she remade relationships, turning the beloved into a work of art. In

1883, while Lee was involved with Mary Robinson, Anne Meyer unexpectedly died. Lee was devastated at the loss of an early love. In a revealing diary entry in 1884, Lee examined her relationship with the dead woman. She saw in herself

> a growing desire for artificial ideal beings . . . who can never shift the moral light in which we see them, who can never turn round in their frames and say "see, we are not what you imagined.". . . Accustomed to see everywhere the unreal, accustomed to hanker even for the absolutely imaginary as the one and only certainty, I feel as if I had lost nothing or but little in the possible loss of the real Mme. Meyer, for does there not remain, unchanged and unchangeable, the imagined one? [The] creature born of one's fancy and one's desires, the unreal, one cannot lose. She remains and remains to me a certainty.[82]

As with Linton's Adeline, death robs Lee of her beloved. But the relationship could not have gone further. Lee transformed their transitory moment of intimacy into a work of art, commemorating what was and what might have been. Nothing could sully Linton's memory of that night in the garden or Lee's memories of Anne Meyer, even as she admitted to herself, "whenever the feeling of being misunderstood or misappreciated came over me, [I] used to seek comfort in the thought of A.M., who very likely, had she been alive, would not have been particularly comforting."[83]

Vernon Lee knew no fairy godmother would comfort her, so she created one out of Anne Meyer, just as Eliza Lynn Linton constructed an idealized erotic mother out of Adeline Dalrymple. This chapter has emphasized the similarities between the two women, but they differed in one major respect: Linton made peace with herself only by imagining herself as a man. It was always a tenuous solution, because the very object she most attacked—the feminine woman—she most desired. Her narrators can never make up their minds whether to sympathize with or admonish her women characters. Coming of age a full generation before Lee, she could not contain her passionate feelings within any contemporary definition of femininity. Only by rewriting herself into the character of a nurturing man did Linton find a role, yet even then she barely stayed within the boundaries of respectability. Reviewers repeatedly noted that Linton's heroines (including "Christopher") had, in the words of one, an "instinct for forming undesirable acquaintances."[84] It may be our key to her passionate love-hate relationship with women. Lee, on the other hand, never wanted to be man; as she put it in *Miss Brown,* she wanted the world to honor "women without woman's instincts and wants, sexless—women made not for man, but for humankind." The disastrous response to this ideal led her to concentrate on writing art essays and horror stories. Rather than promulgating ideals for the future, Lee looked to the past for inspiration. In recreations of a long-gone Italy or classical statuary, she transposed same-sex desire onto art objects. She may have intellectualized her feelings about women, but she did so in some of the most passionate prose of her generation.[85] Lee took comfort in imagining women she loved as the "unchangeable . . . one cannot lose," but her writing reveals a far more complex, more ferocious love that never stands still. Desire was fulfilled by remembering, describing, and writing about a beloved woman—this was as sensual and loving for her as any lovemaking. Indeed, it was lovemaking.

PART IV

Modernist Refashionings

The final two chapters trace how lesbians themselves contributed to the construction of the modern lesbian. I consider four case studies, drawn largely from literary sources; each represents a particular Modernist slant on the lesbian and her relationship with contemporary ideas about same-sex sexual desire. Chapter 7 focuses on a group of wealthy Anglo-American expatriates, led by Natalie Clifford Barney (1876–1972). Beginning in the early twentieth century, Barney made her home in Paris a center for the literary avant-garde. By that time she had had several well-publicized lesbian affairs and had no intention of hiding her sexual interests. Barney created a *parallel society* to the mainstream cultural institutions of her day. She kept her women-only events and her sexually mixed salon free from political and social debate; she was not interested in overthrowing contemporary values. Rather, her social occasions functioned as independent entities, unconcerned with public opinion. The codes of upper-class polite behavior and intellectual discourse reigned, but without the moral judgments that Barney felt characterized other Parisian salons. The most radical among this Modernist generation of lesbian writers was Renée Vivien (1877–1909), Barney's onetime partner. Vivien imagined *an entirely new society,* apart from and in opposition to the existing world of heterosexuals. She rewrote well-known myths, populating her stories and poems with idealized androgynous women. She also explored the extremes of sexual feeling, including not only a desire for complete union with the beloved, but also its violent opposite, the desire to hurt or destroy the beloved. Vivien knew that her utopia could not exist in the present society, but without such imagined possibilities, she felt women would always remain chained to existing conventions.

In contrast, the novelist and playwright Winifred Ashton (1887–1965), who wrote under the pseudonym Clemence Dane, used contemporary psychological theories to construct her conservative solution to the problem of lesbianism. She believed that the power dynamics in cross-age friendships between teachers and students were especially dangerous. Dane recommended *expulsion from society* of the power-hungry, sexually frustrated spinster who preyed upon innocent younger women. This solution agreed with the current thinking of medical and legal experts. The second half of chapter 8 examines the alternative proposed by Radclyffe Hall (1880–1943), who wrote *The Well of Loneliness* (1928) to win sympathy for the born invert. She argued that the invert's instinctive revulsion toward heterosexuality was natural. By creating an honorable, socially and mentally superior invert, she hoped to persuade *society to change* its attitudes toward the homosexual. Responses to her novel ranged from outrage to support, but few saw the need for society to change; rather, the lesbian should either give up her adolescent love and turn to mature heterosexuality or accept a lifetime of celibacy. Ironically, both Dane and Hall encouraged the widespread belief that the true lesbian was a neurotic, lonely *femme damnée*.

Throughout this book I have argued that the lesbian was *an integral part of society*: even if she was not always recognized, she was an essential presence. She might be an unacknowledged minority, to be condemned or ignored, but she could not be eradicated. In the early years of the twentieth century, the lesbian seemed to be increasing in numbers and visibility. What had previously been recognized, but left undefined, was now a known figure in sophisticated circles in London and Paris. In the 1920s the woman-loving woman of past centuries, stereotyped as an asexual spinster, or an oversexed vampire, or a masculine invert, stepped forward in all her complexity. The fact that a small coterie of wealthy women chose to live outside traditional family structures ensured the greater visibility of the self-confident, privileged lesbian. But most educated women and men ignored these initiatives and chose instead to dismiss all forms of same-sex love. They were not willing to accept the ethical or emotional validity of lesbian desire. Thus, in the early twentieth century, we can trace an erratic, although largely unsuccessful, effort to cordon off the nontraditional woman.

For early-twentieth-century Modernists, the old metaphors of the lesbian "family" were no longer useful. The women discussed in chapter 7 revolted against the bourgeois family and championed instead an informal network of friends, including lovers and ex-lovers. But this deliberate rejection of familial metaphors was also an acknowledgment of their continuing importance for defining intimate relations. Vivien replaced the powerful mother with a mysterious, charismatic goddess, free of all human responsibilities. In some circles the female rake, typified by Natalie Barney, possessed exceptional power. She who refused jealousy and fidelity achieved a unique authority over other mortals. Chapter 8, in contrast, analyzes two efforts to revivify family metaphors. But what had earlier been nurturing and positive constructions became dangerous and destructive. "Daughters" and "wives" were infantilized, and "husbands" were driven, domineering personalities. Inequalities of age, knowledge, and experience dominate the fictional portraits of lesbians during the interwar years; indeed the negative treatment of the teacher-student relationship became a literary cliché. Dane identifies the evil lesbian by her lack of maternal feeling. Hall contrasts the bad families of the upper classes with the painful efforts of lesbians to create their own good families. She assumes that without social acceptance, these proto-families are doomed, but for good measure, she dooms them by giving each character a fatal weakness.

By the late nineteenth century some number of social commentators, political and sexual activists, and sexologists were struggling to define both heterosexuality (and its essential social corollary, marriage) and homosexuality (and its presumed loneliness). Their unattainable goal was a stable sexual identity for everyone. Their psychomedical discourse gave lesbians a wider choice of vocabulary but a narrower choice of roles. My four case studies reveal a mixture of the old and the new, in which gender inversion continued as the major visible sign of lesbian desire. Self-chosen cross-dressing (chapter 7) and the born mannish invert (chapter 8) were fresh adaptations of familiar cultural stereotypes. An earlier model of marital equality (previously considered a happy substitute for heterosexual marriage) was dismissed as obsolete. Instead both professional and popular discourse focused on unequal relations and power differentials. The repeated connection of lesbian sexuality with relations of domination and submission led to its association with a perversion, sadomasochism. Thus, in spite of the efforts of well-meaning sexologists to normalize homosexuality, it became entangled with suspect practices. Lesbian self-fashioning, combined with the scientific language of the late-nineteenth-century sexologists, brought into the open the richly symbolic figure now called the modern lesbian.

7 *"Familiar Misquotation"*
SAPPHIC CROSS-DRESSING

Western societies have a long tradition of women passing as men—of successfully imitating male dress and behavior in order to join the military, find
better jobs, or travel more freely.[1] The history of passing women runs parallel to the history of the lesbian, but as earlier chapters have documented,
women who passed as men or looked masculine or wore masculine-style
clothing were often assumed to be sexually interested in other women. I
focus here on a group of Anglo-American women living in Paris during the
years 1890–1930 who chose theatrical cross-dressing as one means of
affirming their belief in the artistic and cultural superiority of women who
loved women. Dress was both a literal trying-on of different roles and a
metaphor for that elusive, still emerging figure, the self-identified lesbian. I
begin by discussing the creation of a variety of theatrical roles designed to
foreground lesbian erotics, including the reworking of the *travesti* roles of the
French superstar Sarah Bernhardt. I next focus on Natalie Clifford Barney and
how some of her contemporaries responded to her and the salon she created.
The following section examines the sadomasochistic life and writings of Barney's onetime lover, the poet Renée Vivien. I conclude more briefly with Barney's longtime partner, the painter Romaine Brooks, to suggest how a woman
might participate in and yet reject the playful possibilities of cross-dressing.

In order to differentiate these women from those who passed as men, I
draw on one of Natalie Clifford Barney's own epigrams. Like her gay male
predecessor Oscar Wilde, Barney raised verbal and visual misquotation to a
high art, insisting: "To mis-quote is the very foundation of original style. The
success of most writers is almost entirely due to continuous and courageous
abuse of familiar misquotation."[2] The cross-dressing discussed in this chapter
can be compared to a series of misquotations—a layering of meaning, drawn
from a variety of sources, to create an independent, self-sustaining lesbian literary and social culture. For the members of Barney's circle, unlike the many

women who passed as men to go into battle or to go on the road for better jobs, or the trousered Bonheur, boyish Hosmer, and elegant Hall, cross-dressing was a playful assertion of gender instability. Equally important for these women was the conscious misquoting and reworking of traditional beliefs about virginity, purity, and female sexual desire.

Rather than depending upon the theorizing of medical men, lesbians could partially control preexisting sexual scripts through imitation, parody, and play. Some historians have assumed that the sexologists' definitions of so-called deviant sexuality became increasingly dominant during the years 1880–1930. But in fact many homosexuals remained impervious to the medicalizing of desire. Those who read the sexologists, as I discuss in the next chapter, tended to pick and choose information that suited their needs. Women could select their own fashion, masculine or otherwise. Clothes have always been the vehicle for women's self-expression, but among a new generation of lesbians, they took on an added importance. Illustrations of turn-of-the-century New Women show many, like Ethel Smyth and Vernon Lee (Figs. 12 and 16), wearing tweed jackets with a tie or brooch. These fashionable signifiers could be worn with flirtatious dash among friends, but still pass as the practical garb of the educated working woman. For some women their clothing became an expression of their lesbian identity—to wear a tie and jacket was a revelation of self. Like Anne Lister, who carefully fashioned her attire to match her masculine desires, Lee, Smyth, Hall, and others wore mannish, but not masculine, clothes. Alternatively, as I discuss here, one could dress quite conventionally, but use special occasions to masquerade, to try on different sexual and psychological states. "Mannishness" was only one of several options. For some women a boyish androgynous appearance was more popular than ties, tweeds, and short hair; for others an elegant, cool femininity expressed their distance from men. By performing—costuming—gender difference, erotic desire became visible.

Recent work in performance studies and queer theory has put cross-dressing at the center of debates about sexual preference and sexual object choice. The works of Sue-Ellen Case, Jill Dolan, and Marjorie Garber have been influential in their suggestive interpretations of cross-dressed men and women.[3] The metaphor of performance has attracted queer theorists over the past twenty years; a definitional instability and rich complexity of interpretive possibilities have adhered to the cross-dressed woman or man. To cross-dress is always a self-conscious act, and whether temporary or permanent, it indicates a chosen public identity in opposition to one's biological sex. Cross-dressing symbolizes sexual fluidity, an assertion that what is seemingly natural and immutable is socially constructed.[4] By highlighting the disjunction between the body and clothing, a woman can draw attention to the rigidities of both female and male sex roles. Perhaps the opposition of male and female is false, and we are all more polymorphous, more perverse, than our socially assigned roles. But as Kaja Silverman has argued, clothing serves to define the body culturally, to affix sexual identity and to give it meaningful form so it can be seen.[5] However much cross-dressers may construct their clothes to speak of a particular self, they are subject to interpretation and its consequences.

In *Vested Interests* Garber argues that critics "look through rather than at the cross-dresser, to turn away from a close encounter with the transvestite, and . . . instead to subsume that figure within one of the two traditional genders."[6] Her insistence forces us to look directly at what we see, rather than comfortably remaining within the conventional categories of male and female. But her focus on the "reality" of the third gender downplays the complex responses to and uses of cross-dressing. The Parisian lesbians believed that they were never less than women, whatever their outward appearance. Their androgynous and masculine costumes embodied a desire that found no viable expression within the narrow confines of upper-class femininity. By making visible this desire, whether in their private theatricals or in their public jackets and ties, they insisted upon their own sexual self-fashioning. Their adaptation of various male symbols was a means of self-representation, rather than any exclusive embodiment of a third gender. Although Garber privileges the transvestite's own interpretive strategies, I focus here on the strategies of a subculture keenly aware of the need to create and sustain a mythos of female power. In their theatricals, writing, and painting, the Parisian lesbians played with gender instability in order to showcase their sexual objectives.

HOMOSEXUAL THEATRICS

Nothing can quite prepare us for the extraordinary flowering of lesbian culture at the turn of the twentieth century in Paris under the leadership of the remarkable American Natalie Clifford Barney. Born in Cincinnati, Ohio, the granddaughter of a railroad magnate, Barney learned French as a child from her Louisiana-born grandmother as well as from governesses. Later she studied French prosody and systematically read French literature; everyone speaks of her extraordinary command of the language. At eleven the family moved to Washington, D.C.; they summered in Bar Harbor, Maine, and regularly visited Europe. Alice Pike Barney's flamboyance shocked the staid society of the nation's capital and encouraged her daughter's independence. As her parents' marriage deteriorated, Natalie's father spent more and more time with his mistress and alcohol in London, and her mother went to Paris with her two daughters to study painting under Whistler and Duran.

From an early age Barney knew she was attracted only to women. When her father died in 1902, she inherited a very large fortune and a taste for social freedom. Fortunately, neither her mother nor her sister interfered with her life. Confident, intelligent, attractive, and willful, she spent her long life wooing women, supporting writers, and hosting one of the most famous salons of the twentieth century.[7] She lived her life in direct opposition to the definitions of the sexologists discussed in chapter 8. For her the lesbian was not psychologically abnormal, did not ape men, and was not sexually estranged from her body. Barney's most original contributions toward the emerging modern lesbian identity were not only her unabashed and guilt-free flaunting of her sexuality, but also her consistent refusal to accept the sexologists' definition of the true lesbian as a mannish woman. She pioneered a stylish feminine and feminist lesbianism.

Barney and her lover, Renée Vivien (fig. 18), systematically set about creating their own version of lesbian culture. Both women were free of most familial obligations, and both despised bourgeois respectability. Unlike the other women discussed in this book, they self-consciously broke away from, rather than rewriting, family roles. Although they could not ignore who had power (Barney's father bought up all the copies he could find of her first volume of openly lesbian poetry), money and class privilege insulated them from conventional proprieties. In their self-fashioning they also repudiated Anglo-American culture and modeled themselves on Parisian high society. Both chose to write in French rather than English. Their early introduction to French literature included the works of that notorious independent-minded cross-dresser George Sand (1804–76). Like Radclyffe Hall and Una Troubridge, they read all the French and English texts they could find that featured lesbian characters. French writers, including Diderot, Balzac, Gautier, Baudelaire, Zola, and Verlaine, characterized lesbians as ravishingly attractive or demonically tormented female rakes.[8] Barney and Vivien met Pierre Louÿs, author of *Les Chansons de Bilitis* (1894), poems purportedly written by one of Sappho's women lovers; he gave each a signed copy of the deluxe edition. They learned Greek in order to read Sappho in the original, and in 1904 they visited the isle of Lesbos. Vivien kept a villa there and returned numerous times. Like all upper-class girls, they relied on books for most of their information, but Barney fearlessly sought out sexual experience. She demanded that one of her mother's women models introduce her to the demimonde and explain birth control. Unlike her friend the French writer and performer Colette, Barney never actually lived in the marginal worlds she wandered through. Vivien sought more spiritualized experiences, through travel, alcohol, and drugs. She also sailed the rough seas of her own psyche, finding fulfillment in self-inflicted death, summarized in her epitaph, "Here then is my ravished soul . . . / For the love of Death, having / Pardoned this crime of Life."[9]

Fig. 18. Renée Vivien and Natalie Barney, ca. 1900. Courtesy of Bibliothèque littéraire Jacques Doucet, Paris.

In the 1880s and 1890s in Paris, homosexuality was fashionable among the intelligentsia and aristocratic elite. Unlike the English press, which fed on the occasional sex scandal, a raft of French journals, such as *Le Gil Blas*, *L'Assiette au beurre*, *La Comédie humaine*, and *Le Petit Parisien*, specialized in publicizing sexually scandalous events connected to the theater, the literary world, and the aristocracy. Their satiric commentary kept the *grandes horizontales* and their friends in the limelight and fed Paris's reputation as the most tolerant city in Europe. Over a dozen novels about lesbians were published during the 1890s and 1900s.[10] Obviously not all lesbians were affected by this loosening of sexual mores. Francesca Canadé Sautman has traced the difficulties working-class women who loved women faced; the police and pimps harassed them, feminists and the left despised them, and upper-class men assumed they were prostitutes.[11] We have already seen how threatening the intensely intellectual Vernon Lee could be, and how the openly married Katharine Bradley and Edith Cooper were marginalized. Their Paris was earnest and learned. The younger Barney, Vivien, Colette, and other women friends operated in a rarified atmosphere, but one that benefited from the fin-de-siècle fascination with homosexuality. By the 1920s, after this moment had passed, they were so famous that negative commentary could have little effect on their behavior.

At a time when the theater was the single-most-popular form of entertainment, it was hardly surprising that young women turned to theatrical costuming to act out their ambitions and desires. By temporarily assuming a different character, a woman could express her discontent with women's traditional social position, experience the erotic pleasure of "dressing up," and, in the case of Barney, embody same-sex courtship and love. Natalie Barney and her artistic mother adored private theatricals and staged presentations that included music, dance, and mime in both Washington and Bar Harbor. The young Barney continued this tradition in Paris, encouraging her friends to dress up and role-play.[12] Long after these events, a lover wrote to her asking about her "inexplicable love of bals masqués."[13] Theatrical display was both a passionate pleasure and a portrayer of the pleasures of passion. Barney and her various lovers celebrated lesbian erotics by photographing themselves in costumes that ranged from nudity in the woods of Maine to the britches and ruffles of eighteenth-century pages (fig. 18) and the flowing gowns of Sappho's Greece.[14] They created their own self-image out of a *bricolage* of reworked classicism, popular theater, decadent art, and poetry. They fancied a feminized male beauty or classical androgyny, rather than the military uniforms favored by some lesbians of the time. For Barney cross-dressing was an erotic embellishment of lesbian play, not the embodiment of her special nature. Like Bradley and Cooper she could not understand why anyone would want to resemble a man. Her onetime lover Liane de Pougy roundly declared in her memoirs, "I shall never understand that kind of deviation: wanting to look like a man, sacrificing feminine grace, charm and sweetness. . . . And cutting off one's hair when it can be a woman's most beautiful adornment! It's a ridiculous aberration, quite apart from the fact that it invites insult and scandal."[15]

Something of Barney's theatricality can be gleaned from her many nicknames. Friends called her Natty, Netty, Net-Net, and, more colorfully, Moonbeam (for her long blond hair, as well as her inconstancy). She also appears as seductress and hostess extraordinaire in numerous novels. She is Emily Florence Temple Bradfford in de Pougy's *Idylle saphique* (1901);Miss Flossie (the name by which she courted Liane de Pougy) in Colette's *Claudine s'en va* (1903); Vally and Lorély in Vivien's novel *Une Femme m'apparut* (1904 and 1905); Geraldine O'Brookmore in Ronald Firbank's *Inclinations* (1916); Amazone in Remy de Gourmont's *Lettres à l'Amazone* (1917); Valérie Seymour in Radclyffe Hall's *Well of Loneliness* (1928); Evangeline Musset in Djuna Barnes's *Ladies Almanack* (1928); Laurette in Lucie Delarue-Mardrus's *L'Ange et les pervers* (1930); and Miss Retchmore in Scott Fitzgerald's *Tender Is the Night* (1934). As Elaine Marks has pointed out, "only George Sand has been the imputed model for so many literary heroines."[16] All these novels testify not only to Barney's charisma, but also to her central role in the fantasies of lovers and friends. The variety of names bespeaks an odd consistency of character—all of them emphasize her cool confidence and sexual freedom. For her admirers Barney seemed not quite real until she was fiction.

Barney began directing private theatricals in 1902. Her plays, which mixed education and eroticism, entertained women friends, liberating them from the tradition that women's love for each other was a form of disembodied spirituality. Sappho's circle of lesbian friends was a favorite subject. For example, in *Équivoque (Ambiguity)*, performed in 1906, Barney gave a fresh twist to Sappho's putative suicide. The play opens with Sappho's followers saying good-bye, "Your life is your most beautiful poem; you are your own immortal masterpiece."[17] They assume she will leap into the sea because Phaon has decided to marry Timas. But Barney has Sappho leave a poem declaring that she always loved the beautiful Timas, played by Barney's oldest friend and former lover, the exquisite Eva Palmer. Timas, in a Vivienesque gesture, "clasps the pearls, the harp and the parchment that Sappho has left on the altar, and then takes the path which leads to the Sea."[18] The women are reunited in the ocean, the archetypal symbol of feminine pleasure. Barney's other political message was to seize the day. Before she dies Sappho insists to her disciples: "I sang for you, not for posterity. Fame for its own sake is vain, and what do I care for praise after death?" Unlike many gay male writers, Barney did not seek immortality in art. She felt no need to transfer her supposedly thwarted creativity from bearing a child into creating a work of art. The play or poem or epigram was a means to an end—to constructing a positive lesbian mythology, or to celebrating erotic pleasure, or to demonstrating to women how they could be fulfilled without men. It is no surprise that, living in the moment, Barney would turn a few years later to creating that most ephemeral of art forms, a salon.

Probably the most important theatrical influence on Barney was Sarah Bernhardt (1845–1923). The legendary Bernhardt had revolutionized the French theater in the 1870s and 1880s with her unconventional interpretations of the female leads in such famous French plays as *Phèdre, Hernani, La Dame aux camélias,* and *Théodora.* Bernhardt was a masterly fabricator of her own image, taking full advantage of the new technologies of photography, cinema, telegraphy, and electric lighting.[19] Her well-publicized slim beauty, personal extravagance, and sexual liaisons thrilled admirers everywhere. Photos, postcards (including pornographic versions of her most famous roles), card games, commemorative plates, and other mementos of the most famous actress of her time can still be found in antique markets. Bernhardt never feared controversy, publicly fighting with the Comédie Française, actively supporting Alfred Dreyfus, and openly praising the suffrage movement. She also included in her intimate circle the mannish artist Louise Abbéma.[20] In her fifties, at a time when most actresses retired or took supporting roles, Bernhardt shifted from her famous femmes fatales to portray a series of tragic male heroes. She chose her *travesti* roles carefully, specializing in men who had "a strong mind in a weak body," claiming that only an older woman was mature enough to interpret thought-wracked young men.[21] Unlike Charlotte Cushman she avoided roles such as Romeo, in which she might have to woo and kiss a woman on stage. Bernhardt's best-known roles, labeled after the color of their costumes, were her self-consciously lighthearted "black Hamlet" in Shakespeare's play (1899) and her vacillating, idealistic "white Hamlet," the title role in Edmond Rostand's *L'Aiglon* (1900). The tubercular Duke of Reichstadt, son of Napoleon Bonaparte, had died in his teens in Austria; his utterly blank life gave Rostand the opportunity to create a patriotic melodrama of failed revolt. French viewers, still smarting from the defeats suffered during the Franco-Prussian War, loved the play.

Why were lesbians so attracted to Bernhardt's irresolute heroes? The answer may be obvious: they liked her artificiality, her daring refusal to be who she was—an aging woman whose acting style and dramas were becoming outdated as the Ibsenite revolution swept Europe. Where else could a woman see such vivid enactments of forbidden emotions? Like Cushman Bernhardt seemed to release women to experience vicariously emotions they were afraid to express openly. The Duke of Reichstadt may have been the embodiment of thwarted patriotism for the mainstream theatergoer, but for lesbians he could be the ideal image of imprisoned desire. This doubling interpretive strategy underscores the difficulty of labeling the political stance of this generation of lesbians. Barney and her coterie took Bernhardt's tragic heroes and turned them into romantic exponents of their politics and love. After seeing Bernhardt in *L'Aiglon,* Barney addressed a troubadour-style poem to her. She published it, as well as a portrait of herself as a page, in a 1900 collection of her lesbian verse. Barney always insisted that war, central to male culture, was irrelevant to women.[22] The Duke of Reichstadt's failure to lead a rebellion against the Austro-Hungarian Empire became a refusal to accept the dictates of masculine political imperatives. Since Barney did not believe that lesbians were flawed men, she never felt compelled to identify with male ideals. Barney may also have learned from the great actress how to create and perpetuate her own legend. If Bernhardt could sustain her stardom into old age, then Barney too could aspire to a different kind of stardom, as the center of a group of like-minded friends.

The young Natalie Barney's courtship of Liane de Pougy, Paris's most famous courtesan, has all the ingredients of a popular melodrama starring Bernhardt. According to Barney's memoir, she was riding with a male suitor in the Bois de Boulogne when she noticed "a procession of open carriages in which a number of ravishing beauties displayed their charms."[23] She was "captivated" by de Pougy and her "angelic slenderness." Throughout her life Barney would favor tall, slim, small-breasted and narrow-hipped women. In her memoirs she insisted upon her youthful naïveté, claiming that she started the affair with de Pougy in order to save her from the life of a prostitute. But Barney probably wanted the privileges of a wealthy young man—to prove that she could rise above social taboos and have whatever she wanted. She certainly spent a good deal of money on de Pougy. She sent importuning notes, filled de Pougy's house with white lilies and iris, and came courting dressed as a page, with a lily embroidered over her heart. The twenty-two-year-old American could now test the effectiveness of her costuming as a form of lesbian courtship. Costume, Barney knew, drew the beloved's gaze toward one's body. De Pougy did not want to be saved, but she did fall in love. She permitted the lovely page to ride in her carriage, sitting at her feet, invisible to passersby. Whether the story is true or not, it has all the elements of a troubadour's tale, with the young boy/woman serving the cruel/kind mistress. But the younger Barney was already an experienced lover of women and took the lead in seducing the inexperienced (in matters of same-sex lovemaking) de Pougy. Barney never stayed for long in the role of adolescent supplicant; she preferred the posture of the confident lover, eager to experiment. Liane de Pougy may have taught her a thing or two. Accompanied by Vivien and another courtesan, the four women visited low-class brothels and probably engaged in all-female group sex.[24]

Liane de Pougy described her tumultuous affair with the young Barney in

a roman à clef, *Idylle saphique* (1901).[25] In one scene, drawn from their relationship, the two lovers watch Sarah Bernhardt play Hamlet. Rather than
falling in love with her Hamlet, as so many heterosexual women did, they
identify with him. The Natalie figure compares the frustrations of women
with Hamlet's impotent rage against tyranny: "For what is there for women
who feel the passion for action when pitiless Destiny holds them in chains?
Destiny made us women at a time when the law of men is the only law that is
recognized."[26] The staginess of the speech echoes Bernhardt's own grandiose
style of expression. But Barney did not see Hamlet only as a voice for her own
feminist yearnings. She also found his feminine masculinity, as portrayed by
Bernhardt, expressive of a desire that could not be identified as wholly male.
A beautiful actress playing an irresolute, feminized male represented lesbian
desire. Barney ordered a velvet suit similar in style to Bernhardt's Hamlet for
a series of self-portraits (fig. 19) that turned an indecisive adolescent boy into
the epitome of the self-confident lesbian. Her Hamlet includes a provocative
garter, as if to draw attention to the erotic nature of her costume.

The price of exposing real emotions on stage, as opposed to dramatizing
desire in privately circulated photos, was high. In January 1907 the writer
Colette and her lover, Missy (the Marquise of Belbeuf, born Mathilde de
Morny), appeared at the newly opened Moulin Rouge in a pantomime entitled *Rêve d'Égypte*. Colette played a beautiful mummy (fig. 20), and "Yssim"
(Missy backwards) played the male archeologist who discovers her and un-
winds her wrappings. At the culminating moment, the mummy embraces the
man who has brought her back to life. The management, probably with the
assistance of Colette's estranged husband, Willy (Henry Gauthier-Villars),
had shamelessly exploited the event. For days before the opening, the press
had virulently attacked the masculine-appearing Missy as a representative of
aristocratic degeneracy. Missy's family, furious that their name should appear
on a music-hall poster, came out in force with thugs to enforce their revenge.
Shouts, catcalls, noisemakers, and various missiles drowned out the music.
Pandemonium broke out when Missy kissed Colette. Willy and his mistress,
sitting in the balcony, were attacked, with the crowd chanting, "Cuckold."
The next day the prefect of police closed the show, but in a few days, the
management reopened, replacing Missy with a male pantomimist. Willy lost
his job as music critic of *L'Echo*, and Willy and Colette sued and countersued
each other for divorce.[27] In the months that followed, Colette and Missy
began their slow, seemingly inevitable descent into the demimonde of the
provincial music halls. Colette was a survivor who had flaunted her bisexual-
ity for years. But Missy, like others who took too seriously the possibilities of
theatrical self-revelation, as opposed to playful self-display, was ruthlessly
expelled by her family and excluded from good society; by the 1920s, in the

Fig. 19. Natalie Barney as Hamlet, ca. 1900. Courtesy of George Wickes.

words of the by-then respectably married de Pougy, "we gradually let our friendship with her drop."[28] She ended her life impoverished and alone.

IMPRESARIO OF LESBIANISM: NATALIE CLIFFORD BARNEY

Barney soon found that directing private theatricals was not a sufficient out-let for her talents. She decided to use her incomparable skills in conversation, wit, and "dressing up" to create a real, rather than imagined, community of women. After Liane de Pougy left her in 1901, she concluded that neither fashionable society nor the demimonde suited her: "I therefore have to find

Fig. 20. Colette in *Rêve d'Égypte,* 1907.

or found a milieu that fits my aspirations: a society composed of all those who seek to focus and improve their lives through an art that can give them pure presence. These are the only people with whom I can get along, and communicate and finally express myself openly among free spirits."[29] Like Charlotte Cushman in Rome over forty years earlier, Barney chose to "found a milieu" where she could make others like herself, or at least sympathetic to her values, feel comfortable. As Marie-Jo Bonnet has said, her salon was not only a cultural and social center in the tradition of the great eighteenth-century woman-led salons, but also a place for individual liberty.[30]

To chart Natalie Barney's Parisian career is to sum up more than a half-century of accomplishment. She began her famous theatricals in 1902, and her salon, for men and women, in 1909. In 1927 she organized the Académie des femmes to introduce French and Anglo-American women writers to each other and to provide a venue for novice writers to read their work to a sympathetic audience.[31] She also established the Renée Vivien prize to keep alive the name of her former lover. Finally, she held intimate women-only parties in her garden, in front of the small Greek-style Temple à l'amitié, featuring plays and readings with costumed friends and paid professionals. Barney held her salon every Friday for two months in the fall and two months in the late spring. She finally stopped the meetings in 1968, a few months after the famous May '68 uprising. The only interruption was during World War II, when she and Romaine Brooks lived in Italy. Barney's salon was unusually long-lived, courting not only scandal, but also dullness. As Meryle Secrest points out, Barney began as an outcast in 1910, was "fashionably smart" in 1925, and by 1950 had become an anachronism.[32] Numerous accounts of her salon survive in the form of oral histories, memoirs, and fiction. Each seems designed to show the author's distance or closeness to its legendary hostess; anecdotes reveal more about the author's relationship with lesbianism than the intellectual life of the salon. Barney's ability to ignore whatever went on in the streets or among ambitious social upstarts could be greatly freeing, but there is something bizarre about the ninety-two-year-old Barney waiting unmoved by the dangers her guests underwent to reach her salon during the May 1968 demonstrations.

Barney's Paris salon was based on different assumptions from Charlotte Cushman's all-woman family in Rome. The Victorian community was grounded in a metaphorical family, and the Modernist community in the metaphor of a network or web of friends, lovers, and ex-lovers. Cushman's group was more personal, more dependent upon her personality, and as a consequence, riven by jealousy; emotions ran deep and loyalties were long lasting. Barney despised jealousy as bourgeois and preferred a cool egalitarianism. She put enormous effort into maintaining her friendships, turning virtually every lover into a lifelong friend. Play, wit, and flirtation were the basis for Barney's salon. Barney's personality brought men and women together and kept them returning, but the salon's success depended upon her self-restraint. She let others reveal their ideas, ambitions, and hopes, while she parried with wit and sensitivity, never letting anyone be a bore. Her mannered formality gave participants room to grow. Both men and women have recorded their gratitude for the kindness and support that Barney offered without attempting to interfere with their choices. In addition to leading male writers and artists, she attracted lesbian and bisexual women whose self-confidence and style have become legendary. These included the portraitist Romaine Brooks (later Barney's longtime lover); Oscar Wilde's lesbian niece, Dolly Wilde; the novelists Radclyffe Hall, Gertrude Stein, Vita Sackville-West, Violet Trefusis, and Dorothy Bussy; and the French writers Colette, Rachilde, Adrienne Monnier, and Marguerite Yourcenar.[33] Barney had a genius for friendship, bringing together ex-lovers and exiles, including Eva Palmer, Winnaretta Singer de Polignac, Lucie Delarue-Mardus, and the Duchess of Clermont-Tonnerre. Over the years she created a salon where the lesbian was the privileged lover, friend, and advocate of sexual subjectivity.

Like an eighteenth-century aristocrat, Barney led much of her life in public, wearing the mask of good manners. Paradoxically, her open homosexuality and ready acceptance of all forms of sexual and emotional deviance created an open, but cool, distanced sociability. She was impersonal, rewarding each person, but always keeping her distance. Serenity was her secret, though others often felt they paid the price—both positive and negative—for her aloofness. This most famous of Parisian lesbians retained an aura of mystery. But she was a kindly female rake, who never willingly hurt her lovers, unlike, say, Cushman, who ruthlessly and painfully (for herself and others) pursued women. Barney's emotional inaccessibility was, in one sense, the natural result of her ideal of feminism: close family ties were emotionally suffocating for women; heterosexual marriage was disastrous for most women and men, so lesbians should not imitate it. In another sense her extreme sociability necessitated emotional distance. She could not have welcomed so wide a range of writers, artists, composers, intellectuals, and politicians, had she not been a deft giver of cursory attention. One and all received acknowledgment, but few called forth a distinctive response. Those whom she pursued must have recognized her penchant for wide-ranging sociability rather than pairings; each may have hoped she was unique, but she never was. Colette, who was very close to Barney after she left Willy, sadly concluded, "No serenity is as cruel as yours, Amazon."[34] If male libertines were hot and passionate, a liberated woman must be cool and rational.

Although Barney held many women-only events, she always liked men and turned to them for advice about her writings. In addition to her famous friendships with the authors Remy de Gourmont, Oscar Milosz, and Gabriele D'Annunzio, she collected now-forgotten writers and intellectuals. She did not care that many men came as voyeurs; she knew the pleasure of looking, as well as being looked at. Their attendance was at her pleasure; they had to accept her terms. Like George Sand she accepted the male gaze because she was free to look back—to unsettle and challenge their interpretation of life. Barney's open advocacy of lesbian sexual practices attracted disciples and adversaries; her offhand indifference toward the heated politics of the interwar period, as well as her open disdain for male privilege, fascinated and sometimes frightened participants. Barney, of course, could not control how her life might be interpreted. Those opposed to her open expression of nonnormative sexuality disparaged her and her salon. Edith Wharton considered Natalie Barney "something—appalling" and advised a younger friend, "You must never go near Mrs. Barney." But Wharton too moved with the times, and in 1926 she met Natalie at the home of her bisexual friend Walter Berry.[35]

In the 1920s a new generation of Americans arrived in Paris, many of whom envied Barney's elite sociability. Ezra Pound courted her friendship, critiqued her verse, advised her on politics—and asked her for money.[36] Other American men were determined to remain unimpressed. William Carlos Williams proudly remembered that he was unmoved by Barney's intelligence and wealth, but he compulsively paraded his phallic power: "She could tell a pickle from a clam any day. I admired her and her lovely garden. . . . Out of the corner of my eye I saw a small clique of [women] sneaking off together into a side room while casting surreptitious glances about them, hoping their exit had not been unnoticed. I went out and stood up to take a good piss."[37]

Brashness did not conceal his resentful anxiety, for he immediately added another (probably made-up) penis story, about a member of the Chamber of Deputies who watched women dancing with each other, and then "took out his tool and, shaking it right and left, yelled out in a rage, 'Have you never seen one of these?'" Class privilege protected Barney and her circle; rudeness and rumors could not affect her very real power in the French literary scene. Far more dangerous was a lack of self-confidence. Like jealousy, it was a social solecism. And Barney's serene self-assurance, likened to a lighthouse in a storm by Radclyffe Hall in The Well of Loneliness (1928), gave other lesbians the confidence to ignore rude Americans: "For Valérie, placid and self-assured, created an atmosphere of courage; everyone felt very normal and brave when they were gathered together at Valérie Seymour's."[38]

Although Barney had no political agenda for her salon, in a variety of ways she furthered her belief in lesbian superiority. Barney did not so much reject purity as redefine—misquote—its traditional meaning. An earlier generation of women had accepted the conventional belief that sex meant male penetration. But Barney countered this patriarchal definition with the notion of the virgin who avoided men in order to fulfill her own sexual desires in a more satisfying way. As Shari Benstock points out, all five of the plays that Barney published as Cinq petits dialogues grecs (1901) "praise virginity, suggesting that 'purity' and 'sensuality' need not be opposed constructions."[39] In both dramatic and ordinary ways, the Parisian Sapphists successfully played with the paradox of the sexually satisfied virgin, radically altering traditional beliefs about female purity. Barney, Vivien, and other women writers, by reinterpreting heterosexual virginity, may have drawn attention to its limited, even obsolete, meaning in the context of women who made love to other women. Virginity as a concept, moreover, was already under new pressures from influential sexologists, who would have considered the sexually fulfilled virgin a new type—a lesbian. By the mid-twentieth century, any sexual experience that came to orgasm might define the loss of virginity. Radclyffe Hall, for example, reminded her young lover in 1935: "I found you a virgin, I made you a lover. . . . I find that to take an innocent woman is quite unlike anything else in life."[40]

Purity, however, was more than the avoidance of penile penetration. For this generation it also included following the rules of one's true self with absolute honesty. Such radicalism, of course, was exclusionary: only those who were willing and able "to focus and improve their lives through an art that can give them pure presence" could be part of Barney's society of the free. In an autobiographical statement written late in life, Barney justified herself:

> I considered myself without shame: albinos aren't reproached for having pink eyes and whitish hair, why should they [society] hold it

against me for being a lesbian? It's a question of nature: my queerness isn't a vice, isn't "deliberate," and harms no one. . . . Let's be snobs, but in the opposite sense of our society which only accepts ready-made values; let's discover real values which alone can inspire us or make us comprehensible. I will submit to their much stricter laws than the social obligations which shield their egotistical inclinations.[41]

Barney and her circle were not anarchists; rather, they adhered to the "stricter laws" of "real values" embodied in a parallel society. To be born an invert was not a fate, but "a perilous advantage."[42] Barney, like Vernon Lee, was determined to offer women an alternative to a heterosexually defined identity. Whereas Lee believed that exceptional women would lead society out of its immoral ways, Barney believed that exceptional women should band together to form their own community. Barney embraced a special kind of purity—a purity of belief, of individual behavior, of self-defined sexual practices—to which she at least remained consistent throughout her long life.[43] Perhaps it was a life that only the self-confident and wealthy could live fully, but as a theatrical piece, it has never been equaled.

THE LESBIAN ANDROGYNE: RENÉE VIVIEN

In Barney's circle of wealthy lesbians, Renée Vivien was the most determined to embody her particular version of sexual desire. She transformed herself from the upper-class Anglo-American Pauline Tarn, to be *renée* or reborn as a French-writing lesbian. She wrote openly of lesbian desire in poems and fiction and gained cult status by her eccentric behavior. Whereas Barney chose drama to publicize lesbian love and courtship, Vivien preferred Decadent verse, derived from Baudelaire's exploration of moral perversity. The daughter of an English father and an American mother, Vivien hated her family and loved French culture. Pauline Tarn was a ward of the court until twenty-one, when she came into her inheritance, moved to Paris, and changed her name.[44] Born only a decade after the bourgeois, chaperoned Maggie Benson, Vivien took full advantage of being without family ties or money worries. In nine years she published over twenty volumes and twelve joint works (and produced six other books that were published posthumously), in spite of or perhaps because of increasing physical and mental debility . On her deathbed, from complications brought about by anorexia and alcoholism, she may have converted to Roman Catholicism.[45]

Renée Vivien believed in the androgynous woman as the better lesbian alternative to either mannishness or polymorphous pleasure; she was the perfect "misquotation," symbolizing an absolute refusal of heterosexuality.[46] Like Katharine Bradley and Edith Cooper, Vivien was determined to fashion a

new image of lesbian sexual subjectivity, but she replaced their sensual descriptions of Bacchic frolics with a series of erotic paradoxes that privileged
a cerebral sensuality. Her autobiographical ideal, the androgyne, would acknowledge the power of lesbian sex, but find her ultimate happiness in the
worship of the feminine in art. This unreal figure was preferable to a mannish
woman, who seemed to Vivien to be an imitation of the despised male. As the
Freudian critic Francette Pacteau has noted: "Androgyny cannot be circumscribed as belonging to some being; it is more a question of a relation between a look and an appearance. . . . I do not encounter an 'androgyne' in the
street; rather I encounter a figure whom I 'see as' androgynous."[47] Vivien did
not expect to "see" an androgyne on the street, but only in her imagination—
a world she inhabited more intensely with each passing year. Indeed she
prided herself on fashioning "imaginary landscapes, dream flowers, faces one
will never see in life."[48] In a remarkable body of work, Vivien created a complex Sapphic world utterly divorced from men and their mores.

During her brief life Vivien was both powerfully attracted to and deeply
revolted by the fullest and most varied lesbian sexual pleasures. She seems to
have alternated, according to her neighbor Colette, between "an immodest
consideration for 'the senses'" and an extreme ethereal disembodiment.[49]
Even though she idealized spiritual sisterhood as the best kind of lesbian
love, she never wavered in her exploration of sexual passion. For her that
meant the voluptuous pleasures of giving and receiving pain; love was always
a relationship of domination and submission. We do not know if she read the
Austrian philosopher Otto Weininger's *Sex and Character* (1906), but she
shares with him some of the same elements of a fashionable fin-de-siècle self-
hatred, including a Nietzschean belief in power and the will. In her final years
she refashioned her body, starving herself into a wraith-like representation of
spiritualized deviancy. Many years after Vivien's death, Barney wrote, "That
she wanted to lose herself so entirely in suffering tells me how necessary it
must have been to her poetic inspiration."[50] An alternative reading suggests
that Vivien put all of her resources into writing and into refashioning her
body, so that in both art and life she would represent the pleasures and ter-
rors of lesbian love. In the photograph presented earlier (fig. 18), dressed as
a mysteriously handsome page, Vivien refused to look at the camera; even in
costume she must avert the viewer's gaze. The attention Barney courted was
an anathema. Vivien will always evade our gaze. Too many private papers and
letters are missing, and she acted her androgyne role too well for anyone to
penetrate her costumed effect. All analyses, including mine, of Vivien's intensely personal writings and memories of her must be treated with caution.

Vivien, usually portrayed as a recluse, was as enamored with the theater as
all her contemporaries. Early in her career she held large parties, entertaining friends with women performers: her neighbor and friend Colette danced;

the actress Marguerite Moréno recited Vivien's poems; the opera singer Emma Calvé sang arias from *Carmen*; and professional musicians played. Colette danced nude if only women were present, and wore leather straps, transparent veils, and jewels if the audience was mixed. For a private tableau vivant at the Théâtre des Arts, Vivien played the imprisoned Jane Grey, and Colette's lover, Missy, played the executioner. Deeming herself too fat for the part, Vivien lost ten pounds, performed brilliantly, and then fainted back stage.[51] Louise Faure-Favier described Vivien as the "queen of poseurs," a title also given to Bernhardt. She recalled a visit to the cathedral at Chartres, when Vivien "swathed herself from head to foot—even her face—in thin veils the color of ashes, after the fashion of a priestess of antiquity." On another occasion Vivien met her dressed in "an empress's kimono and carrying a sheaf of roses in her arms, which she offered me by way of greeting."[52] According to contemporaries, she decorated her home as a theater set for her self-chosen lead role as a Decadent *femme damnée*. She drifted, "not so much clad as veiled in black or purple," through darkened rooms filled with rare objects.[53] Vivien's extraordinary behavior, like many of the extreme actions of women in public places, at first shocked and then led to contempt. Colette portrays a woman who could not distinguish between self-dramatization and madness or between sadomasochism and a ghoulish imagination.

Vivien's most concerted effort to create a lesbian androgyne was San Giovanni, the artist-hero of *A Woman Appeared to Me* (1904). The novella included an illustration of Leonardo da Vinci's androgynous *St. John the Baptist*, and each chapter began with a brief quotation from a musical work expressing love or grief. (Both Vernon Lee and Vivien believed that music could best express the inexpressible; one wrote long descriptions of the emotional power of music, and the other created tone poems.) The novella commemorates the death, in 1901, of Vivien's first love, the pious Violet Shilleto, or Ione, as well as the end of Vivien's passionate love affair with Natalie Barney, or Vally. Vivien divides herself into two characters, the narrator, whose "heart was full of hectic melancholy," and the androgynous, self-contained writer, San Giovanni. Written as a series of prose poems, each chapter encapsulates a stage in Vivien's tormented affair with Barney. Ione's illness and death are ignored under the spell of the charismatic but unfaithful Vally. Eva, who enters the novel as the affair is ending, offers the narrator the promise of future happiness. She is a composite of several women with whom Vivien had affairs, including Eva Palmer and the Baronne Hélène Van Zuylen de Nyevelt, who became Vivien's lover in 1901, following the first breakup with Barney.[54] Vivien threaded her way between spirituality and sexuality to create a stylized female world of profound sensuality.

Vivien's San Giovanni resembles the beautiful boy painted by Leonardo da Vinci and celebrated by many of her homosexual contemporaries, such as

Walter Pater and John Addington Symonds. Like the original John the Baptist, she is given prophetic powers that the other women reverentially heed;
Vivien leaves to our imagination who might be the lesbian Savior. San Giovanni admits that when she was younger, she considered dressing as a boy in
order to marry her first woman lover. All the women characters treat this idea
as a comic, adolescent aberration, inappropriate for those outside the bounds
of heterosexual courtship. Although the androgyne might be tempted to imitate society's norms, marriage, even same-sex marriage, is simply out of the
question. In all forms it is unnatural. Vivien underscores San Giovanni's special status as a mythic leader by identifying her as an ephebe and having her
compose poems about female cults, Sappho, and virginity, seated upon a
"worn slab" in a quiet cemetery, surrounded by "serpents, bats, tombs, solitude."[55] Her other subject matter, in a typical Vivien reversal, is the male prostitute, defined as the man who marries for money.

For Vivien women naturally love women but are obliged to follow society's dictates and marry men. Only the chosen few are committed to the sacred cause of same-sex love. They must bear the moral and creative burden
of fashioning a new lesbian artistic and literary tradition, Vivien came close
to endorsing the sexologists' dichotomy between the innate and the situational invert, but her construction of these types is radically different. She assumed that all women would be better off loving women, however difficult
and even painful individual relationships might be; thus, any self-respecting
woman would seek out women to love. But in her elitist vision, the woman
artist alone will sacrifice all to create a woman-centered world. Rare individuals, such as San Giovanni, willingly bore the burden of representing the superiority of same-sex love. Vivien believed she was among those who were
blessed and cursed with this responsibility. The veils, flowers, and thinness
that she wore in public made literal her visionary persona, the androgyne
who rejects all forms of masculinity. Everywhere she went she would be a
reminder to women that they had a prior duty to an all-female ideal, which
they had renounced by participating in heterosexual society. That most
women rejected her as eccentric confirmed her sense of being misunderstood
and reinforced a growing self-pity. Tama Lea Engelking has suggested that
only as Vivien lost confidence in her Sapphic vision did she focus on her fears
of being forgotten and misunderstood.[56]

Vivien's notion of what a new lesbian literature might be draws heavily on
the tropes of the Decadent and Symbolist movements. Style, rather than
plot, mattered, for she despised Victorian realism. Like Vernon Lee Vivien
used her horror stories and revised fairy tales to explore unnatural desires and
feelings. The unnatural was natural for the woman who refuses the heterosexual imperative. In *A Woman Appeared to Me,* Vally (Barney) and San Giovanni (Vivien) agree that "to be as different as possible from Nature is the true

function of Art." All experience must be constructed and shaped into art be-fore it can be understood. Vally has an instinctive love of the artificial; her lips were "long familiar with every verbal artifice," and she dresses in the cos-tume of a Venetian page or as a Greek shepherd, following "the music of the invisible pipes of Pan."[57] Mirrors, water, and lakes give Vivien an opportunity to accentuate the visible sameness, the self-reflexivity, of lesbian love. Karla Jay has drawn attention to Vivien's habitual misquoting of classical and Bib-lical sources, in which she turns such reviled female figures as Lilith and Vashti into heroines.[58] Vivien also reversed and reworked common symbols. Snakes, that most polymorphous of traditional symbols, are positive signs, as if to overturn Eve's sin. (Vernon Lee made similar reversals; her Prince Alberic willingly kisses his beloved snake.) San Giovanni describes finding a hermit in the Rockies who warns her that snakes can never be killed but always come back to haunt one. The boyish heroine is herself closely associated with snakes; on one occasion she is described as "glid[ing] over the carpet with a rustle of scales." Vivien sees the snake-temptress of Genesis as an embodi-ment of women's power, for "dead serpents come to life beneath the gaze of those who love them. The magic eyes of Lilith revive them as moonlight moves stagnant water."[59] Vivien's powerful image also reminds the reader of woman as avenger.

Vivien, like her male contemporaries, naturalizes homosexuality by de-naturalizing heterosexuality for those who were, in the language of the day, born inverts. Even though San Giovanni looks like a boy, we are never al-lowed to forget that she is an androgynous woman. Her privileged appear-ance is underscored by Vally's witticism: "Adolescent boys are beautiful only because they resemble women. [They].are still inferior to women, whom they do not equal either in grace of movement or harmony of form." An "oily" procurer, with "the air of a dirty pedlar who offers English tourists the ser-vices of untouched young boys," prophesies that the Androgyne will finish her "love-life in the arms of a man."[60] This statement is rebutted by Vally "in a profoundly shocked tone, 'That would be a crime against nature, sir. I have too much respect for our friend to believe her capable of an abnormal pas-sion.'" San Giovanni cuttingly responds, "I neither love nor hate men. . . . They are political adversaries whom I want to injure for the good of the cause. Off the battlefield of ideas, I know them little and am indifferent to them." In "The Charmer of Serpents," San Giovanni, "the ephebe," is warned to "guard against moderation as others guard against excess."[61] These rever-sals echo Natalie Barney's aphorisms, while setting a tone of insouciant sex-ual superiority.

Vivien's distrust of men and their deathlike ways led her toward a vision-ary all-female hiding place. She rewrote the tale of Prince Charming by having his cross-dressed sister court the waiting girl. Characteristically, they run away to a never-never land:

> They left for those blue shores where the desire of lovers runs out of patience. They were seen, the Divine Couple, with the eyelashes of one stroking the eyelids of the other. They were seen, lovingly and chastely intertwined, with her black hair spread over his [sic] blond hair. . . . They are hiding in the depths of a Venetian castle or of a Florentine mansion. And sometimes they are seen, as one sees a vision of ideal tenderness, lovingly and chastely intertwined.[62]

In the everyday world women's tender loving ways were destroyed by aggressive male sexuality; only in an unreal world can women achieve happiness. Louise Faure-Favier recounts how once when Vivien attended a wedding, she dressed as "a figure out of fairy land, crowned with lilies, trailing long scarves of glimmering white silk, in her arms a sheaf of lilies so immense it seemed to clothe her entirely."[63] She does not mention what the wedding guests thought about this egregious effort to upstage the bride, but presumably Vivien came out of her own special world in order to warn the bride. As a lesbian-androgyne, Vivien proudly wore white lilies, a symbol of the virginity that the bride will irrevocably sacrifice. As San Giovanni declared, "Virginal grace [is] barbarously violated" in heterosexual marriage.[64]

Female sensuality was best expressed through the rich garden imagery that suffuses Vivien's prose and poetry. Like Barney Vivien courted lovers and friends by sending them vast quantities of expensive flowers. After the death of Violet Shilleto, she increasingly identified with violets, a flower that was already a symbol of lesbian love. The moon, regularly compared to a lesbian lover, is always cold, always changing, as if Vivien could never find a woman who met her expectations. Her jungles, forests, rivers, and gardens do not exist in any real world, but are imagined spaces of danger, passion, and occasionally tranquility. But they are also always in excess. She juxtaposes "a vision of ideal tenderness" with acts of gratuitous violence, highlighting the voluptuous pleasures of pain. In her short stories the vengeful tigress bites the lips of the huntress, preventing her from crying out for help; men destroy or torture women without reason; the burning desert sun maddens; and monsters arise out of nowhere, within the breast of man or in a terrifying unnatural Nature.

Vivien explored erotic fulfillment more openly in her poems than her fiction. Sometimes happiness is the momentary merging of two selves: "Our lunar kisses have a pale sweetness / . . . And we can, when the belt comes undone, / Be at once both lovers and sisters."[65] But more often she longed for the bliss of assimilation into an oceanic hereafter. Vivien associated the ocean with an eroticized, deathlike loss of self: "For the sea and death, at last, restore me tonight," or "I will stay virgin like the moon. . . . Troubled by the long sigh of desire / For the ocean," or "I give my heart to the eternal ocean."[66] The crashing waves of the ocean, so frequently associated with a woman's multiple orgasms, were turned into an eager surrender to annihilation. Submission to oceanic dissolution was not associated with physical pain, unlike her vision of erotic love; rather it was a greater form of self-completion. Death and desire become one. For Vivien the living body was restrictive, so that death, literal, metaphoric, and sexual (as in *la petite mort* of orgasm), symbolized a highly desirable transformation into a condition without limits or boundaries.

Colette, who knew "Lesbos on the Seine" well, provides a penetrating portrait of Vivien. Writing in the late 1920s, at a juncture when she was half-regretting her lurid sexual past, she recalled asking "the listless" Renée if she was ill. To her surprise Renée began to describe "with the least ambiguous terms" her latest sexual encounters. The aghast Colette "caught a glimpse of 'Madame How-many-times' counting on her fingers, mentioning by name things and gestures."[67] In a classic case of displacement, as Sherry A. Dranch notes, Colette focused on Vivien's foul mouth, her obscene language, and the repulsive drinks she imbibed, living in fetid, airless rooms. Writing for a general audience, Colette could also safely shift her own sexual adventures over to a notoriously unconventional lesbian.[68] Although it is hard to believe that Colette could be shocked, the contrast between Vivien's conversation and her languorous behavior (and her poetry) was startling. Or was it? I would argue that Colette's surprise came less from Vivien's bawdy language and more from discovering Vivien's blunt pleasure in the more unsavory aspects of sexual power games.

Vivien did not differentiate between domination and submission, though she exhibits a special zest in describing the sadistic impulse lying just beneath the surface of erotic desire. In *A Woman Appeared to Me,* the narrator records her complex response to a young admirer: "She smiled at me, and I felt a sudden burning tenderness for this creature so like fruit and roses. I desired her like blue water at dawn. And then the cruel need to bite those lips naively offered for a kiss, to bruise that flesh like rosy eglantine, became so violent that I abruptly took my leave."[69] Vivien's narrator tells the naïve girl that hate is "as beautiful and as holy as love itself," and fantasizes torturing her for the "savage joy of seeing in those eyes the vivid intensity of some uncontrollable passion. To make that passive body tremble—with terror or love, what matter which?"[70] Several poems treat the delicious pleasure of submitting to unnamed torments that culminate in the orgasmic loss of self. For example, "Nocturne" opens with lines describing "carnal lips," "the calm perversity of your eyes," and "spreading out, alarming and savage, / The light reflections from your cruel nails." It ends, however, on a serene note of post-coital satisfaction:

I trace your body,—the eager lilies of your breasts,
   The pale gold under-arm,
Soft blossoming thighs, goddess legs,
The velvet belly and the curving of the loins.

The earth grows languid, weak, and the breeze,
Still warm from far away beds, comes to soften
   The ocean finally subdued . . .

Here is the night of love so long promised . . .
In the shadow I see you pale divinely.[71]

This is one of the few poems in which the ocean and its undifferentiated for-getfulness is held at bay by sexual completion. Like Vernon Lee's lush garden in the climactic moment of "Prince Alberic," the ocean captures a moment of deep sexual satisfaction. But Vivien preferred to describe sexual passion as a narrative of servitude and pain, in opposition to a longed-for oceanic disso-lution. In effect only death's embrace is tender.

Did Renée Vivien engage in sadomasochistic sexual dramas with Hélène van Zuylen, her principal lover after the breakup with Barney? A large force-ful woman with an unlimited fortune, van Zuylen was notorious for her im-perious treatment of her women lovers. Jean-Paul Goujon, Vivien's biogra-pher, argues that van Zuylen provided Vivien the kind of mothering she desperately needed, and that during the years of their relationship, Vivien wrote her best work.[72] Vivien told her Greek teacher that Mme. van Zuylen was "cet archange" (archangel), but to others she whispered of a jealous tyrant and a sadist who imprisoned her.[73] Barney, who despised the wealthy baroness, claimed that she kept her former lover in a "gilded cage." Colette hints of "English vices" and of having seen in Vivien's London apartment a room "full of whips, chains, and other sadomasochistic paraphernalia."[74] Vivien's well-known admiration for Algernon Swinburne may have had its roots in their shared interest in whipping. The bizarre tales of Vivien abruptly leaving her own dinner party, shaking with terror, called by a mys-terious She, may have had their basis in fact. Both contemporaries and her bi-ographers are divided on whether Vivien was in thrall to her mother-keeper or whether her "master" was the product of a diseased imagination. Colette recalled Vivien exclaiming, "She will kill me," but then adding, "With her I dare not pretend or lie, because at that moment she lays her ear over my heart."[75] Colette presents this incident and then suggests it might have been an alcoholic fantasy. But perhaps this frankest of women found it difficult to admit that her friend found the sources of her creativity within the deep well of sexual and emotional torture. Imprisonment and enslavement were psy-chic necessities for Vivien, but they betrayed her vision of lesbian love as

"ideal tenderness, lovingly and chastely intertwined." The evidence is fragmentary—perhaps Vivien was simply dramatizing her own self-inflicted
punishments—but violence and torture are repeated themes in her writings.
The sensual purity of the word could be achieved only when integrated with
sadomasochistic desires.

"MY INNER-SELF AND VALUE": ROMAINE BROOKS

Natalie Barney, according to her lifelong servant, had more than forty serious lovers and countless casual affairs, but after the death of Renée Vivien,
her most long-lasting and serious relationship was with Romaine Brooks
(1874–1970). She did not meet the American artist and expatriate until they
were both in their forties and had each arrived via separate paths at a similar
attitude toward lesbianism. Sometime around 1915 they became lovers; they
were partners for over forty-five years. Barney's advocacy of individualism
was congenial to Brooks because it confirmed her sense of being a misunderstood martyr. But she was less ready to interpret lesbian difference as a special opportunity. As a child Beatrice Romaine Godard had been physically
and mentally abused by her mother and her mentally ill brother. With great
perseverance she had educated herself and learned to paint. Then, in 1902,
her mother died, and Romaine and her sister were suddenly wealthy. She
married the homosexual John Ellingham Brooks on Capri in 1903, but immediately left him. Throughout her life, like Vivien (another neglected child),
Brooks was hypersensitive, enamored with suffering, and doubtful about the
pleasures of the flesh. She had been in love with the Italian patriot Gabriele
D'Annunzio, but her most profound attachments were to women. Her best
paintings were portraits of single, isolated figures placed in a desolate or loom-
ing background. Many were of friends or lovers, including the dancer and actress Ida Rubinstein, her lover during the years 1910–14. Brooks shared the
contemporary fascination with the stage, but by the early years of the twentieth century, she spurned the old-fashioned Bernhardt and favored the experimental drama and ballets in which Rubinstein was a pivotal figure.[76]
  An atmosphere of cool drama permeates Brooks's personal style. In reaction to the fussiness of *belle époque* styles, Brooks decorated her homes with the
same limited palette of grays, blacks, and whites as her paintings. She favored
black jackets with white, open-collared shirts and gray gloves, and was a
leader in the modern refashioning of the mannish style.[77] She may well have
seen her androgynous attire as a stylish updating of Vivien's and Barney's velvet page costumes, to be worn only on special occasions among other lesbians.[78] The deeply shy Brooks at once courted and rejected attention. In a
1923 letter to Barney, she described an evening at an underground lesbian
club in London and concluded: "Never have I had such a string of would-

be admirers, and all for my black curly hair and white collars. They like the dandy in me and are in no way interested in my inner-self and value."[79] For the suspicious Brooks, only Barney understood her real self. A defensive stance reinforced her reputation for originality and genius, but it also confirmed her acute sense of isolation. As the next chapter documents, she shared this feeling with the novelist Radclyffe Hall. Although neither woman ever lacked lovers, each posed as a lonely, misunderstood figure.

Brooks kept returning to the dramatic (in all senses) world of the 1900s and 1910s as a source of inspiration. The experimental fantasies she had witnessed on stage in those years may have helped her to visualize her personal drama of difference and solitude. Around 1930, when she had virtually given up oil painting, she completed some two hundred abstract drawings that have yet to receive critical attention.[80] Brooks exhibited some of them in Paris in 1931 and Chicago in 1935; all were titled, and some were given brief explanations. At nearly sixty she risked showing her private self to the public. She intended her drawings to be read as the product of her subconscious; the uninterrupted curving lines give an impression of continuous thought. Brooks placed herself at the edge of the paper or enveloped herself in swirls of mysterious forms. Either way, she cannot escape her destiny. In these drawings Brooks undermines the art of misquotation so characteristic of Barney, Vivien, and even her own earlier work. They reveal the demons that still possessed her. The tangled lines and carefully drawn eyes insist on the viewer's attention; Brooks defies Barney's cool disregard for public opinion and instead insists that her audience look directly at her private vision. She exposes her unresolved fears about boundary loss and merging in abstractions, just as Vivian did earlier in her numerous references to oceanic dissolution.

One of her drawings, Mummy, connects with a complex set of images, public and private (fig. 21). In 1930 the artistic fascination with ancient Egypt, launched by the discovery of Tutankhamen's tomb in 1922, was still in full flower. But Brooks may have had more personal "Egyptian" memories. She could not have missed the scandal following Colette's 1907 music-hall performance as the awakening mummy who unveiled her lesbian love life before a mixed audience. In 1909 Ida Rubinstein had played the title role in the Ballet Russe's production of Cléopâtre. She was carried on stage wrapped as a mummy inside a sarcophagus. In an elaborate dance her servants slowly unwound the strips of cloth so that she gradually emerged from swathes of swirling fabric.[81] Her tall, thin body was the personification of chic androgyny. The young homosexual writer and filmmaker Jean Cocteau found her "unforgettable." So did many lesbians. Rubinstein confirmed her cult status with homosexuals in 1911 when she starred in D'Annunzio's The Martyrdom of St. Sebastian. Just as gay actors would later play Sarah Bernhardt's signature travesti role in L'Aiglon, the bisexual Rubinstein played the quintessential gay

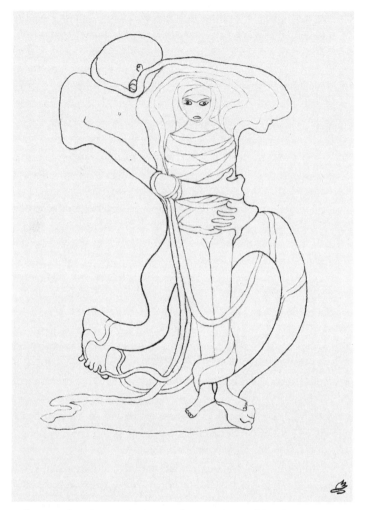

Fig. 21. Romaine Brooks's *Mummy* (1930). By permission of Smithsonian American Art Museum, gift of the artist.

icon of suffering and sacrifice.[82] Between 1911 and 1914 Brooks painted a series of full-length nude studies, as well as two portraits, of Rubinstein. Brooks's privileged gaze upon this famous new theatrical body disturbed viewers when the paintings were first exhibited. One critic wrote of her "exercises in morbidity," using the familiar code word for homosexuality.[83] This was homoeroticism that could not be concealed under the dandy's pose.

In her drawings twenty years later, Brooks returned to the exposed, sometimes naked or half-naked, woman. *Mummy* echoes Rubinstein's performance as Cleopatra, but alters the image from androgynous power to female vulnerability. In *Mummy*, unlike any of the other drawings, Brooks placed herself at the center of the paper, staring out at the viewer, demanding recognition. Nothing shades her eyes, which are drawn with pointed precision. The mummy's arms and breasts are still encased in bindings, as well as the tight embrace of her male savior, the archeologist. Or is the distorted figure behind the girl a ghostly double of herself, let loose by her resurrection? Why assume that the larger figure, tangled in the wrappings, is a man? The figure may be Brooks's mother, a "mummy" who smothers her vulnerable daughter. Brooks, as the staring mummy, seems to be defying her personal ghosts, as well as society; even stripped of her protective covering, she will remain true to her inner self. Where Vivien sought to lose herself in erotic submission, Brooks imagined absolute bodily integrity. The isolated lesbian, the *femme damnée*, stands defiant against all society. Her personal vision was a powerful alternative image that was distinctly against all that Natalie Barney stood for. The next chapter continues to examine the ideological and cultural roots of the early-twentieth-century suffering but transcendent lesbian in an English context.

8 *"A Love of Domination"*
THE MANNISH INVERT AND
SEXUAL DANGER

During the first quarter of the twentieth century, what purported to be a scientific language gradually replaced the equivocations and silences that had largely concealed women's passion from public view. In earlier chapters we saw how women privately constructed their sexual subjectivity, drawing on a variety of sources. Here I consider the interplay between this self-fashioning and the new formulations that privileged the binary homosexual/heterosexual rather than a series of gendered sexual roles and behaviors. In the first section I explore the impact of the pioneering sexologists, with particular reference to Havelock Ellis (1859–1939), the leading English writer to examine lesbian sexuality. In his book *Sexual Inversion*, Ellis built his theories of gender inversion upon traditional beliefs about the innately effeminate man and masculine woman. This wide-ranging study set the parameters for the discussion of homosexuality. Ellis argued that since the born invert could not change, society needed to accept her. Lesbians, educators, and social commentators all found compelling his construction of the "congenital invert," as well as his descriptions of "acquired inversion" in single-sex institutions. With the refinement of a scientific, nonpornographic vocabulary to describe sexual desires, however, the fluidity of cross-gender roles was gradually lost and replaced with the paradigm of an inborn nature.

The familiar cross-age prototype also changed. The nurturing mother-daughter tie, so important throughout the nineteenth century, was replaced with a negative model of pedagogic eros. What had been the most culturally acceptable form of same-sex love, the adolescent crush, was targeted as psychologically and socially dangerous. The identified deviant was the sexually independent and intellectually sophisticated older woman, often a teacher, who had no family responsibilities, but a distinct "love of domination." This seductive individual preyed upon vulnerable and naïve young women. Calls for expulsion, at least from schools, overwhelmed pleas for toleration.

The following sections examine two pivotal works that focus on the born invert, Clemence Dane's *Regiment of Women* (1917) and Radclyffe Hall's *The Well of Loneliness* (1928). Each novel explores cross-age and cross-class sexuality with greater depth and passion than any advice book or sexology tract. Dane's book belongs to that familiar genre, the schoolgirl story; it was quite influential in defining bourgeois fears of the independent unmarried woman during the interwar years. *The Well of Loneliness*, of course, is the most famous lesbian novel of the twentieth century; I concentrate on responses to the well-publicized trial for obscenity that it provoked and its aftermath. Where the dominant genres for self-fashioning among the Parisian lesbians discussed in chapter 7 were tragedy and comedy, in this chapter they are melodrama and romance. Barney's plays and Vivien's stories delivered their message aesthetically, preaching only to those who already sympathized with them. But Dane and Hall preferred the emotionalism of genres that could inspire outrage against or compassion for the mannish lesbian. Their works fixed in the popular imagination an image of the lesbian as a *femme damnée*. But this tortured character always had to share the stage with Barney's insouciant Hamlet, Vivien's mysterious San Giovanni, Lee's idealistic Prince Alberic, and the countless attractive teachers in Angela Brazil's ever-popular schoolgirl romances.

CONGENITAL AND ACQUIRED INVERSION

The sexologists writing around the turn of the century created elaborate taxonomies of sexual behaviors; they were collecting preexisting types and describing them to fellow experts. They trusted that their scientific vocabulary would place the discussion of difficult matters on a higher plane, excluding the prurient and phobic; this would alleviate the suffering of patients and add to the diagnostic repertoire of medical professionals. It is impossible to say how quickly or how thoroughly their publications were disseminated among the reading public, so we must be wary of assigning an excessive influence to them.[1] But they clearly had a wide audience among educated people who were curious and determined to understand their sexual desires and practices. Cosmopolitan inverts, for example, eagerly read early editions of sexology books and contributed to medical debates with further case studies.[2] Under their influence many sexologists came to believe that inversion was not a disease, but an innate biological and psychological anomaly. Ellis, for example, in *Sexual Inversion*, compared inversion to color-hearing, in which sounds are associated with colors; John Addington Symonds compared inversion to color-blindness. Both were groping to dissociate an "organic variation" from moral condemnation.[3] After World War I large numbers of advice books discussed sex and sexology, using a confusing and contradictory array of new labels. Their explanatory models ranged from the biological, innate, and hereditary to the psychological, cultural, and social. Newspapers and magazines, however, remained reticent, if not completely silent, about actual practices, thereby contributing a half-secretive atmosphere to the public discussion of the new sex theories and nonnormative sexual activities. Nevertheless, following the 1928 *Well of Loneliness* trial, Rebecca West could flatly state, "there are but few children old enough to read who are not in full possession of the essential facts regarding homosexuality."[4]

As several historians have noted, the most attractive feature of sexology was its new vocabulary for describing not only sex acts, but also sex types.[5] The available language for erotic love is still limited today—poetry, the Bible, and other traditional sources are not always helpful, especially in regard to deeply held personal feelings that have little public acceptance. Nineteenth-century women writers drew upon the rich traditions of Christianity and classicism, as well as nature, to create a metaphoric language for expressing female desire. But they did not explain or describe specific acts, and more especially, how these acts might relate to one's personal identity, beliefs, and emotions. For these reasons same-sex desire between women has generally been dated as beginning after the publication of the elaborate taxonomies of the sexologists, as if a direct, scientific vocabulary made sexual object choice "real." When the outspoken Socialist-feminist Stella Browne declared as late as 1915 that "the realities of women's sexual life have been greatly obscured by a lack of any sexual vocabulary," she had in mind the physical side of sex.[6] But in fact by then a scientific language of science was in place, alongside pornography and metaphor. During the interwar years, with surprising thoroughness, the specialized debates and descriptions of the sexologists moved into the intellectual discourse of Europe and America. The varied nomenclature and theories proved enabling to many lesbians seeking to understand their sexual desires.[7] But for some women, including Clemence Dane, the new psychology was debilitating because it oversexualized same-sex love and companionship. For others, such as Radclyffe Hall, it gave a rationale for a deeply held sense of self.

During the 1880s and 1890s, when the sexologists across all the major European countries were first gaining recognition, psychological ills were closely tied to somatic explanations: the body reflected one's mental state. Gradually a more sophisticated analysis developed, in which sexual characteristics and behaviors were partially separated from physical attributes. Sexologists concluded that homosexuality arose from a multitude of causes and could be identified through not only appearance but also temperament. Havelock Ellis reported that his lesbian wife "suffered much from neurasthenia" and "her love of domination."[8] Vernon Lee claimed that her mother's side was "acutely neuropathic and hysterical."[9] "Nerves," along with intelligence and artistic capability, were among the most prominent characteristics of the homosexual, male or female. But the question remained, was the neuropathic invert the product of her heredity or the product of the fast-paced, morally confusing intellectual life of the time. For most sexologists a minority of homosexuals were congenital inverts; the rest became inverts from a compound of nature and nurture.

A perplexing mixture of sex and gender reversals defined the congenital invert.[10] As we have seen in earlier chapters, throughout the nineteenth century a set of characteristics accrued around the figure of the masculine woman: she was strong-minded or intellectual, dressed unconventionally, suffered from "nerves" or even "hysteria," and seemed odd in countless small ways. Most of all she showed little interest in men and too much in women, especially pretty, younger women or older, maternal women. No one of these characteristics could identify a woman as an invert, but taken as a whole, they seemed to characterize someone whose identity was determined not simply by her erotic preference, but also by her entire manner of being. As Havelock Ellis said, "The brusque, energetic movements, the attitude of the arms, the direct speech, the inflexions of the voice, the masculine straightforwardness and sense of honor, and especially the attitude toward men, free from any suggestion either of shyness or audacity, will often suggest the underlying psychic abnormality to a keen observer."[11] He concluded, "Notwithstanding these tendencies, however, sexual inversion in a woman is, as a rule, not more obvious than in a man."[12] Gender inversion and sexual object choice were still confused, perhaps because it was hoped that the former made visible the latter—that if a woman looked mannish, then she might be identified as someone attracted to feminine members of her own sex. But even visible markers carried their own ambiguities. Ellis's wife was an "inborn invert," yet he defined her as "not really man at all in any degree, but always woman, boy and child, and these three it seemed in almost equal measure."[13] Many homosexuals found these confused and contradictory definitions, with their disarming imprecision, liberating. They could pick those parts that resonated with their own personalities and experiences and ignore the rest.

The assumption of inborn masculine (active) and feminine (passive) attributes was the starting point, and from our perspective the key weakness, in much of the early theorizing by sexologists. These binaries, deeply rooted in the Victorian age, worked against the development of a view of sexual behaviors apart from gendered characteristics. Ellis assumed that whoever took the initiative in a sexual encounter must be masculine, or at least masculinelike, because women were innately nonaggressive, or to use his term, modest. When a woman expressed her sexual desire, she inverted norms.[14] This left Ellis with no clear explanation for why some feminine women were attracted only to mannish women. Perhaps they belonged to the category of acquired or situational inversion, in which an early experience in a single-sex school, or a disappointment in heterosexual love, or a failure to meet men, led them to turn to women. Still seeking somatic identifiers, he concluded that these women were "the pick of the women whom the average man would pass by."[15] He, like most other sexologists, assumed that the "actively inverted woman" possessed "a more or less distinct trace of masculinity," but that the more feminine lover of women under the right circumstances might outgrow or revolt against same-sex love. The potential danger to society of the congenital invert was her masculine love of power, that of the acquired invert, her childlike impressionability. The great strength of the congenital invert was her strongly developed sense of honor and desire to protect weaker women; the great asset of the feminine invert was her "strongly affectionate nature." Although both feminine women and tomboys might acquire (and outgrow) inversion, masculine women were congenital inverts.

Havelock Ellis drew upon studies of boarding-school friendships and information from his wife and her friends (his six case studies in *Sexual Inversion*) to suggest that sexual acts grew out of idealized love between women. His informants eagerly emphasized their efforts to sublimate their love "to high mental and spiritual attainments."[16] Such a perspective was congruent with much feminist theorizing about women's sexual feelings.[17] Turn-of-the-century feminists such as Elizabeth Wolstenholme Elmy and Frances Swiney advocated higher heterosexual spirituality, along the lines espoused by Vernon Lee for women. Several of the women Ellis interviewed, however, insisted that their feelings for women were both spiritual *and* erotic. Edith Ellis, disguised as "Miss H., aged 30," claimed, "The effect on her of loving women is distinctly good . . . both spiritually and physically, while repression leads to morbidity and hysteria."[18] She believed that homosexual feelings per se were not morbid, but their repression was. Havelock Ellis concluded that "homosexual passion in women finds more or less complete expression in kissing, sleeping together, and close embraces. . . . One may also lie on the other's body, or there may be mutual masturbation. . . . The extreme gratification is . . . oral stimulation of the feminine sexual organs, not usually mutual, but practised by the more active and masculine partner."[19] He added in smaller type that sadism, masochism, and fetishism "may also arise in . . . inverted women, though, probably, not often in a very pronounced form."[20] Quite against his intentions, this suggestion of perversion became one of the defining characteristics of the power-loving invert in popular interwar advice books and in fiction.

In contrast to such trained medical men as Havelock Ellis, the Socialist and homosexual Edward Carpenter flatly denied the "morbidity" of "the homogenic type" and insisted on his or her healthy, active role in society. He rejected any sharp distinction concerning sexual preference and argued for the "immense diversity of human temperament and character in matters relating to sex."[21] He also expanded in positive ways on Ellis's proposition that the mannish woman might survive the hurly-burly of modern life better because of her masculine forthrightness.[22] Unlike most commentators, he did not see the adolescent as ignorant and innocent, but rather suggested special counseling for the born invert during the difficult transitional years to adulthood. If "the special affectional temperament of the 'Intermediate' is, as a rule, ineradicable," then social understanding of this "large class" was necessary: "We may point out how hard it is, especially for the young among them, that a veil of complete silence should be drawn over the subject, leading to the most painful misunderstandings, and perversions and confusions of mind; and that there should be no hint of guidance; nor any recognition of the solitary and really serious inner struggles they may have to face!"[23] Carpenter's commonsense suggestions are still controversial among educators; they were insupportable when male homosexuality was illegal and female homosexuality barely discussed. Because Carpenter was not a medical man, he was widely disparaged for his amateurishness. The *British Medical Journal* scoffed, "serious people in England might be spared the waste of time consumed in reading a low-priced book of no scientific or literary merit advocating the culture of unnatural and criminal practices."[24] Professionals feared accessible writings that presented the "intermediate sex" as equal to or even superior to the heterosexual.

The early sexologists did all they could to create a neutral, nonjudgmental atmosphere for the discussion of sex. They opposed the notion that schoolgirls were especially likely to be infected by lesbianism if they fell in love with an older student or a teacher. Ellis assured his readers that adolescent crushes were "a spurious kind of homosexuality, the often precocious play of the normal instinct." He assumed that in most cases, especially if the girl fell in love with a suitable young man, such feelings were of short duration; those few who continued their friendships in their twenties were "hypertrophied" because of an "unemployed sex instinct."[25] But among those who believed that lesbianism was contagious, Ellis's distinction between innate and acquired inversion seemed worthless. In 1927 Bernhard A. Bauer declared that acquired homosexuality was more common among women than men, and that the girls' boarding school was "a hot-bed of masturbation" and "seduction." He agreed with Ellis that "a great love passion for a man" would return a woman "to normality," but added, "it must not be forgotten that there is a possibility of relapse."[26] Once a woman had experienced "the voluptuous sensation" with another woman, she might always find penetrative sex less attractive.

Traditional arguments in favor of marriage as the most important goal in a woman's life were probably more influential than the new fears about attractive inverts. No one questioned the assumption that a man's fundamental

instinct was sexual and a woman's maternal. The sexologists themselves insisted that a woman's greatest erotic need, no less than her emotional need,
was to have a child. After World War I good mothering became a patriotic
duty. Feminists struggled with how large numbers of unmarried women, following the death of millions of young men, might deal with their sexual feelings. Most capitulated to the notion that a woman was not fully effective unless she was heterosexually fulfilled. A few radicals, such as Stella Browne and
Dora Russell, recommended an extramarital relationship. The Christian activist Maude Royden suggested that women "transmute the power of sex and
'create' in other ways" by using their maternal impulses to serve humanity.[27]
She and other feminists refused to blame women for remaining unmarried in
a postwar world they did not create, but they dressed up old solutions for new
problems. Others were less generous. Charlotte Haldane, in *Motherhood and
Its Enemies* (1928), warned against the power of virgins whose normal sex functions had atrophied or been deflected into "pseudo-masculinity" in the fields
of education and nursing. She considered single women dangerous, arguing
that "it can never for a moment be gainsaid that such individuals are of small
importance compared to those destined to carry on the race. To give such
females political and social power, to open all doors to them, may prove in
the end the means to inactivate or endanger those who must first of all be encouraged and protected."[28] Haldane's rationale led to one conclusion: the unmarried woman should be isolated from the main currents of society for failing to "carry on the race." A single woman's sexual options in the early
twentieth century were marriage, sublimation, heterosexual affairs, and
social expulsion. If she actively refused to marry, social and cultural forces
placed her at the edge of society, as a disreputable Bohemian or an embittered
spinster or a perverted invert.[29] The unstated alternative was a home with an
intimate friend. Perhaps it was too Victorian, too obvious—and potentially,
as we shall see with *The Well of Loneliness*, too contentious. How, then, could
society accept the single woman?

"INSPIRATION INCARNATE": THE
ABNORMAL SCHOOLTEACHER

During the most active period of the women's suffrage movement, 1903–13,
feminists effectively promulgated a blend of feminist politics, strong women's
communities, a call for premarital male chastity, and a positive ideology in
regard to female celibacy. But female political activism and sexual independence were a dangerous combination. A backlash was inevitable. Then the
wholesale slaughter of young men during the war reinforced demands that
women return to their homes and leave the public sphere to men. A girl's

education should be for marriage, not for a career. A new generation of reformers attacked women's single-sex schools for their antidomestic curricu-
lum and artificial, antifamily ethos under the leadership of single women.
The conservative eugenicist Arabella Kenealy spoke for many when she said,
"Young girls taken during the malleable phases of growth and development,
and forcibly shaped to masculine modes, become more or less irretrievably
male of trait and bent; losing all power to recover the womanly normal."[30]
The spinster schoolteacher was an easy target: she existed in large numbers,
had access to impressionable girls, and was independent from parents. Because teaching jobs were scarce during the interwar years, many local education committees passed regulations barring married women from continuing in their posts. Yet sex reformers emphatically condemned unmarried
schoolteachers for their narrow emotional lives and their negative influence
on adolescent girls.[31]

Advice books, whether directed at students or teachers, all recommended
vigilance in regard to teen-age crushes. Lilian Faithfull, head of the elite secondary school, Cheltenham Ladies College, represents the old guard responding to new uncertainties. In one of a series of "Saturday talks" for girls,
she worried about the "nervous unrest and mental instability" of the postwar
years, on account of which, she cautioned her charges, "it seems only too
likely that these ephemeral excitable forms of friendship may be more serious for you than they were for us."[32] She suggested "a good deal of self-
control" as the best cure. Her only advice to those "raved upon" was to warn
them against the pleasures of exercising power over a younger girl. Faithfull
carefully distinguished between "raves" and hero worship. She encouraged
the latter: "A really honest devotion to someone of fine character, who is
however rather remote from you, is healthy and natural."[33] Intimacy, left undefined, was unwholesome, but passion combined with distance was an in-
vigorating moral lesson for her upper-class girls. Faithfull trusted her pupils
to be responsible and did not blame the older girl, but instead urged the
younger girl to control her rave.

Most reformers, however, held teachers accountable for encouraging exaggerated emotional relations. Marie Stopes, the foremost popularizer of
sexual fulfillment within marriage, was especially outspoken. In a book aimed
at educators, *Sex and the Young* (1926), she spent several pages discussing the
homosexual teacher:

Such persons exist in a sufficient number to be an active danger in the
scholastic profession. Every head teacher should be eternally watchful
to see that no such member is on the staff. This abnormality is extremely difficult to detect, because very often the relation with the

younger pupils is built up with a protective tissue of romance and pseudo-chivalry which is exactly the type calculated to enlist every loyalty on the part of the pupil and to keep the relation absolutely secret.[34]

Like the sexologists, Stopes had no formula for identifying the deviant teacher; gender inversion was no longer sufficient. Although she chose not to go into detail, she went so far as to suggest that "solitary self-abuse" was less dangerous than mutual masturbation, which was "very apt to lead to grosser and more abominable vices . . . against which a warning is not superfluous in these days when a cult is being made of homosexual practices."[35] Stopes agitated not only for sex education and married teachers, but also for a mixed staff in all schools. Other reformers enforced this recommendation in a series of cautionary case studies. Nevertheless, coeducation did not become a widespread policy in Great Britain until the 1960s.[36]

The best-known novel documenting the damage done by cross-age love was by Winifred Ashton, writing under the pseudonym Clemence Dane. Her first novel, *Regiment of Women* (1917), centered on a teacher who rules by psychological manipulation the small empire of a girls school. The touching, caressing, and warmth of traditional Victorian school friendships are totally absent in the hard-pressed world of her fictional school. The moody, charismatic Clare Hartill selects a few intelligent girls each year to groom for examinations:

> Love of some sort was vital to her. . . . Clare, unconscious, had taught Clare, conscious, that there must be effort—constant, straining effort at cultivation of all her alluring qualities, at concealment of all in her that could repulse—effort that all appearances of complete success must never allow her to relax. She knew well the evanescent character of a schoolgirl's affection; so well that when her pupils left the school she seldom tried to retain her hold upon them.[37]

Adoring her, the girls push themselves too hard, but the outstanding examination results redound to the school's fame, so the aging head, Miss Marsham, does not interfere. Dane also admits to the value of such magnetism, "There are women today . . . who owe Clare Hartill the best things of their lives, their wide knowledge, their original ideals, their hopeful futures and happy memories: to whom she was inspiration incarnate."[38] Like Lillian Faithfull, Dane created a distinction difficult to maintain; hero worship was good, but adoration was bad.

Then Clare meets a new, enthusiastic teacher of eighteen, Alwynne Durand. Alwynne, brought up by her spinster aunt, is headstrong and susceptible; she comes from a modest background and is deeply impressed with Clare's glamour. Clare carefully grooms the naïve young teacher, described as childlike, to be her "wife." Alwynne, however, longs for an old-fashioned daughter-mother relationship; she cannot resist fantasizing about "a Clare beleaguered, with barriers down, a Clare with wide maternal arms, enclosing, comforting, sufficing . . ."[39] The impossibility of this positive form of womanly love is confirmed when we see Clare's cruel treatment of a brilliant, lonely thirteen-year-old pupil, Louise Denny. Clare Hart-ill, lacking all maternal instinct, ignores the child's emotional needs and instead promotes her prematurely into the advanced class. The child studies too hard and becomes exhausted and hysterical. Rejected by Clare after failing her exams, Louise commits suicide. The sadistic invert has destroyed one child and is about to destroy the childlike Alwynne.

Alwynne's motherly affection for the younger girls makes her a good and happy teacher. Then she suffers a breakdown, her psychic energy devoured by Clare's demanding love and her own guilt over the death of Louise. Aunt Elsbeth sends her to her cousins to recuperate; "the Dears" are middle-aged sisters modeled on a Victorian romantic-friendship couple. Living in an idyllic countryside, with plenty of fresh air and useful work, they lead contented, wholesome lives, bending to the rule of their beloved nephew, Roger. In a book that extols greater contact between the sexes, Roger, a stereotype of manliness, is the only male that readers meet. This lack of men reinforces the sense that women must discipline women. Inevitably, he rescues the innocent Alwynne, teaching her true passion. Dane hints at Clare's perverse sexual nature when Alwynne, in comparing her two lovers, concludes: "His kiss had been comforting too. She remembered the first of Clare's rare kisses—the thin fingers gripped her shoulders; the long, fierce pressure, mouth to mouth; the rough gestures that released her, flung her aside."[40]

A jealous Clare retaliates against Alwynne for staying in the country with the Dears (and Roger) for seven weeks. She knows she is being self-destructive, but as with so many sadists, her only pleasure is torturing the person she loves. Alwynne, still infatuated, cannot understand, "It's only that—that sometimes now you tease with needles—you used to tease with straws."[41] But when the thoroughly despicable Clare refuses Alwynne's birthday gift, a beautiful handmade nightgown, the young woman finally rejects her cruel sorceress. The intimate nature of the gift is left implicit, underscoring Alwynne's erotic innocence. Clare, however, is described as someone who knows, understands, and hates her desires. Dane clearly felt that Clare's cold intelligence and indifference to mothering were not enough to identify a dangerous congenital invert. She added to these perversions an additional abnormality, the quintessentially masculine love of power. Clare is possessed by an uncontrollable love of domination.

At first glance *Regiment of Women* is simply an exposé of the cruel lesbian schoolteacher. But on closer examination the plot centers on how difficult it is to lead a modern girl into marriage. Clare is so attractive that it takes three unmarried surrogate mothers and a man to push Alwynne into heterosexuality. Even though Alwynne is a young adult, everyone treats her as if she were still an unformed, adolescent in need of instruction to awaken her true feelings. Dane's spokesperson is the unsophisticated Aunt Elsbeth, who denounces Clare's "vampirism," which has already destroyed Louise. "And now you are to take Alwynne. And when she is squeezed dry and flung aside, who will the next victim be? And the next, and the next? You grow greedier as you grow older, I suppose. One day you'll be old. What will you do when your glamour's gone? I tell you, Clare Hartill, you'll die of hunger in the end."[42] Hunger is the key metaphor, echoing Sheridan LeFanu's *Carmilla* (1872), in which the vampire drank Laura's blood. Clare drinks the lifeblood of Alwynne, leaving her physically weakened and spiritually drained. In response to Clare's contempt for marriage, Elsbeth predicts a life of "work and loneliness—loneliness and work." In fiction no woman can stand in the way of heterosexual marriage. Dane, however, ends her novel with a lingering threat: Clare will be the next head of the school, replacing Miss Marsham's Victorian rule with her own distorted methods. Only coeducation, demonstrated by a rural school Alwynne visits, can eliminate power-hungry women such as Clare.

Even though the book was published in the third year of a bloody war, when one would think the reading public would take little interest in a seemingly minor matter, it was praised in *The Times* and the *Morning Post*, advertised in the weekly left-wing *Nation*, and generally admired. It sold well, going through several editions in the 1920s and 1930s. Dane's melodrama had struck a responsive chord among women seeking a nonscientific formulation of problematic sexual desires. As Alison Hennegan has noted, it also set a pattern, influencing such novels as Naomi Royde-Smith's *The Tortoise Shell-Cat* (1925), Rosamond Lehman's *Dusty Answer* (1927), Radclyffe Hall's *The Well of Loneliness* (1928), Molly Keane's *Devoted Ladies* (1934), and Dorothy Baker's *Trio* (1943).[43] The plot device of a handsome man rescuing an innocent woman from the clutches of an older woman was too good not to repeat in an age keenly aware of sexual theories. Interwar nonfiction about the dangers of lesbianism cited *Regiment of Women* as a brilliant real-life example.[44] Although Dane claimed she was revealing a preexisting problem, her work played a significant part in the creation and promotion of a problem.

Dane (fig. 22) based her plot on her experience as a boarding-school teacher, between working as an actress, painter, journalist, novelist, and playwright. During the interwar years she was a figure to reckon with in the theater world. Radclyffe Hall approached her to write a dramatic version of *The Well of Loneliness*. She lived first with Elsa Arnold, to whom she dedicated *Regiment of Women*, and then Olwen Brion-Davies.[45] Vita Sackville West and Violet Trefusis stayed with her in 1920 when they could neither give each other up nor leave their husbands.[46] Clearly Dane knew same-age lesbian relation-

Fig. 22. Clemence Dane, 1923. Courtesy of Mary Evans Picture Library, London (Graphic Photo).

ships well. At her express request no personal papers survive. She never spoke of her own relationships with women friends, but perhaps she had negotiated the newly available knowledge about the sexual roots of women's friendships by separating passion and friendship. Her stark portrayal of Clare Hartill conveys a deep unease about the unconscious and its power over our behavior.

Dane returned to the perverse teacher theme in a 1926 essay, "A Problem in Education." She recycles the arguments she had used in her novel for limiting the influence of women teachers over vulnerable pupils. She admitted that "in five cases out of ten" it remains a "mutually stimulating alliance," in which the teacher can derive "extraordinary pleasure" watching a young mind unfold. But "in the other five cases" the child starts to think as the teacher thinks and "rather enjoys the coercion." For Dane, "that sense of pleasure in a surrender of personality is not an attribute of friendship, but of love." The girl's health begins to fail, and "she becomes erratic, her manner is exaggerated, affected and jumpy. She grows extremely inconsiderate, and for a time really seems to feel very little affection for her own people. She loses all sense of proportion, becomes hyper-sensitive to praise and blame, is sentimental and silly; in short, she goes to pieces altogether."[47] Dane seems only vaguely aware that she might be describing virtually all adolescents, a point that the feminist journalist Vera Brittain made about the heroine of *The Well of Loneliness* only two years later.[48] How could parents identify to which half their daughter belonged—the 50 percent who found a "mutually stimulating alliance" or the 50 percent who lose all sense of proportion? Rather than addressing this insoluble question, Dane confessed the impossibility of stamping out adolescent crushes and focused her wrath on "vampire women" who overexcited defenseless pupils, leading to "an almost inconceivable state of tension and excitement and jealousy."[49] Lilian Faithfull seems far more sensible when she suggests that "some girls luxuriate in the excitement. . . . The fact is that they care more for the emotion of love, or what they are pleased to call love, than for the person loved."[50]

Possibly aware that she was overheated in her attack, Dane concludes her essay by claiming that,: "with most women the sex feeling is rather indirect and passive, that their active emotions are more maternal and spiritual than passionate."[51] A grave danger is abruptly reduced to Victorian clichés. But what of those women who were "imaginative and passionate"? Dane took very seriously the emotional depth of adolescent crushes. *Regiment of Women* does not portray women of "indirect and passive" sexual feeling: Aunt Elsbeth spends a sleepless night remembering her lost love of thirty years earlier; Clare is often up all night, tormented by a highly eroticized self-hatred; and Alwynne has repeated nightmares about Louise's suicide. These are women of extreme imagination and desire. The answer is segregation. The normal woman must be married, and the abnormal detached from society. Dane concluded that "the extra woman" should emigrate in order to fulfill "all the wholesome instincts of her age and sex"—a recommendation dating back to the 1860s and repudiated indignantly by feminists at the time. And for the unwholesome Clare Hartill, "If she didn't have these instincts, conscious or unconscious, we should draw away from her, instantly, instinctively, as if we were confronted with something abnormal, perverted, unnatural."[52]

The English schoolgirl novel is in marked contrast to the French. Colette's first-person, semi-autobiographical *Claudine at School* (1900) was a best-selling tale set in provincial France. Cast as a lighthearted account of schoolgirl cruelties, it recounts the amusing situation of female teachers in love with each other and male teachers fawning over the older girls. Readers were free to indulge in nostalgic memories or to peep into the psyche of a free-spirited adolescent girl. For Colette the most natural thing is erotically inspired sadism. Fifteen-year-old Claudine mocks the sexually starved teachers, exposes the budding love of a fellow student, and physically abuses a small girl who professes to love her. She openly admires her domination over them and expects the reader to agree. Colette's candid treatment of school savagery and her casual attitude toward cross-age single-sex love were excused because she presented Claudine as a guileful innocent and herself as a naïve writer.[53] Where Dane had portrayed the lesbian schoolteacher as driven by perverted desires, Colette sees all desire as amusing irrationality. But both recognized that the older woman, who ostensibly held such absolute power over her protégées, was ultimately the more vulnerable.

Claudine relishes watching the younger woman manipulate the older, needier woman. At the beginning of the new year, she surveys the school scene:

> The head-mistress . . . had her customary air of concentrated passion and reckless jealousy. Her Aimée, nonchalantly dictating problems in the next room, wandered back and forth, came and went, chatting always. There was no doubt of it, last year she hadn't this coquettish manner like that of a spoiled cat. Now she had become a pampered little pet, fondled, adored and tyrannical, for I saw Mlle. Sergeant's glances imploring her to find a pretext to come near her.[54]

Then, in a characteristic move, Colette withdraws Claudine's cruel gaze, closing the door on their private conduct: "They loved each other so utterly that I no longer dreamed of tormenting them, I almost envied them their delicious forgetfulness of all other things."[55] Contemporaries found the book delightfully amoral, but the real moral was, as Judith Thurman points out, the voracious selfishness of the adolescent girl.[56] As farfetched as it may seem, Claudine is closer to the real-life selfishness of someone like Ethel Smyth than to any English fictional character. Her curiosity, energy, and self-possession flower during a period of temporary independence. Ironically, in the next volume Claudine quickly marries an older, protective man. For a brief period, according to Colette, the girl was the center of attention and knew it. But in the more conventional world of English fiction, Alwynne's virtue rested upon being the center of attention and not knowing it. The adolescent girl in and out of love has uneasily oscillated between these two extremes in much twentieth-century literature.

"FLAWED IN THE MAKING": THE CONGENITAL INVERT

Radclyffe "John" Hall was a poet, a prizing-winning novelist, and a distinctive figure about town when she decided in 1926, with the encouragement of her partner, Una Lady Troubridge (1887–1963), to write an openly lesbian book (fig. 23). Hall was determined to show that one was born an invert but could be forced into perversion by a pitiless society. She took the coming-of-

Fig. 23. Radclyffe Hall and Una Troubridge, 1927. Courtesy of Hulton Archive by Getty Images, New York.

age story and transformed it into a melodramatic tale about the painful impossibility of same-sex love. She purposely placed her heroine at the far end of inversion, the categorically masculine woman. She kept her plot simple. After ten years of marriage, Sir Philip Gordon anticipates a male heir to complete his happiness. Instead his only child is "flawed in the making," for she is "a narrow-hipped, wide-shouldered little tadpole of a baby" daughter.[57] He insists on christening her after the first Christian martyr. Stephen, born in the shape of a mannish girl, is nurtured as a son. Hall's heroine possesses all the identified virtues of the abnormal, according to Havelock Ellis, Edward Carpenter, and other supporters of homosexuals. She is intelligent, high strung, courageous, and creative; her most manly quality is a keen sense of honor. She also suffers from the invert's "nerves" and hypersensitivity.

Hall insists on Stephen's absolute ignorance of her true nature until she discovers an annotated copy of Kraftt-Ebing's *Psychopathia Sexualis* in her father's study. Hall intended her novel to enlighten confused tomboys, as well as to garner sympathy from heterosexual readers. The love of a woman is never just an adolescent stage for Stephen, though she undergoes a masochistic initiation into idealized erotic love. The handsome young Stephen falls in love with a married neighbor, Angela Crossby, who then betrays her to cover her own heterosexual affair. Hall redefines "a passing phase" to mean a bored woman's flirtation with homosexuality, an interim dalliance until she finds the real thing, adultery. But Stephen's recently widowed mother, horrified by her daughter's masculinity and fearful of scandal, banishes her from Morton, her country home, forever. Leaving the estate symbolizes exclusion from normality, order, and established ethical standards.

Stephen finds a temporary purpose in life by joining the women's wartime ambulance corps. In this all-woman community she falls in love with a beautiful, poor girl, Mary Llewellyn. Mary resembles Alwynne. Some ten years younger than Stephen, she is "childish" and submissive to her masterful mentor. Hall includes the classic schoolgirl disciplinary scene. The head of the "Breakspeare Unit" warns Stephen: "I'm sure you'll agree with me, Miss Gordon, in thinking it our duty to discourage anything in the nature of an emotional friendship, such as I fancy Mary Llewellyn is on the verge of feeling for you. It's quite natural of course, a kind of reaction, but not wise—no, I cannot think it wise. It savours a little too much of the schoolroom and might lead to ridicule in the Unit."[58] The innocent young girl (Mary) is shorn of responsibility for (or understanding of) her behavior, and the older woman (Stephen) told to separate herself, even though their feelings are "quite natural," like any passing phase. The sensitive, honorable Stephen obeys her proto-headmistress. She alone must test her powers of self-control.

But Mary is no passive, infatuated adolescent; it is she, not Stephen, who makes all the sexual overtures before they finally consummate their love. Toward the end of the war, she tells Stephen: "All my life I've been waiting for something . . . I've been waiting for you, and it's seemed such a dreadful long time, Stephen."[59] Later, when Mary cannot understand Stephen's physical distancing from her, she forces Stephen to confess her inversion, as well as her fear that they will be social outcasts. Mary then precipitates the sexual consummation of their love: "'Can't you understand that all that I am belongs to you, Stephen?' Stephen bent down and kissed Mary's hands very humbly, for now she could find no words any more . . . And that night they were not divided." As Clare Hemmings points out, briefly the femme controls the narrative.[60] After this event the novel focuses exclusively on the emotional and moral conflicts Stephen must face.

At first it appears that Stephen might find a place—a new home—in Paris with her beloved Mary Llewellyn. Stephen settles down to her writing career, and Mary fills her time caring for their adopted dog and mending Stephen's male underwear. Mary and Stephen meet inverts suffering the consequences of Dane's recommendations, rejection from their homeland. Alcoholism, drug addiction, poverty, and despair undermine the creativity of their friends. After Mary suffers a series of social snubs, as well as depression brought on by her thwarted maternal instinct, Stephen believes that she must give Mary up. Only her old comrade, the nature-loving Martin Hallam, can give Mary "children, a home that the world would respect, ties of affection that the world would hold sacred, the blessèd security and the peace of being released from the world's persecution."[61] Stephen pretends to an affair with Valérie Seymour (based on Natalie Barney). Mary reluctantly falls into Martin's arms, and Stephen returns to her writing, determined to write on behalf of other inverts.

Lesbian readers have long puzzled about why Stephen must renounce Mary. Laura Doan has suggested an important radical reinterpretation: Martin as the understanding, sensitive male will procreate with the intense, boyish Mary, and they will create a new race of the intersexed.[62] But a less optimistic reading, consonant with the overall tone of melodramatic renunciation, foregrounds the inevitability of loneliness (the fate of the evil Clare). Stephen's decision also highlights Hall's conviction that there was an unbridgeable gap between the congenital masculine invert and other women, even those who loved inverts. Although Hall was by no means a slavish advocate for Havelock Ellis's views, she shared with him a profound respect for maternity as the true woman's greatest fulfillment. In a novel of sexual and gender contrasts, feminine women are innately nurturing. Inevitably they are less homosexual because their hunger for motherhood overrides their sexual desire. In *Regiment of Women* the old-fashioned spinsters are fulfilled mothering adopted children, but in the overtly homosexual subculture of the *Well*, the feminine women, Barbara and Mary, suffer from thwarted maternal feelings, and the masculine women, Jamie and Stephen, suffer from society's condemnation.

Hall knew that she would have difficulty getting her forthright novel published. She wrote to her editor at Cassell's, hoping to head off the problem:

> Hitherto the subject has either been treated as pornography, or introduced as an episode as in [Rosamond Lehmann's] *Dusty Answer*, or veiled as in [Clemence Dane's] *A Regiment of Women*. I have treated it as a fact of nature—a simple though, at present, tragic fact. I have written the

life of a woman who is a born invert, and have done so with what I believe to be sincerity and truth; and while I have refused to camouflage
in any way, I think I have avoided all unnecessary coarseness.[63]

Sincerity and truth could not overturn traditional attitudes. "A fact of nature,"
even when hedged in by reminders of the born invert's misery, proved to be
unacceptable in a popular novel. Lehmann and Dane had probably gone as
far as anyone could in their portrayals of school crushes. As long as same-sex
love was defined as a passing phase, or an unfortunate situational aberration,
it could be part of modern fiction. But when it became a way of life—a valid
alternative to heterosexuality—it was dangerous.

After Cassell's turned down the *Well*, Hall's agent shrewdly sent it to
Jonathan Cape, a new firm with a strong list of novels. Cape accepted the
work, but priced it at fifteen shillings, twice the normal cost of a novel, and a
familiar ploy for controversial books likely to attract police attention. For
three weeks all went well, and then James Douglas, editor of the *Sunday Express*, on 19 August 1928, used the book to attack "the decadent apostles of
the most hideous and most loathsome vices [who] no longer conceal their
degeneracy and their degradation":

> They do not shun publicity. On the contrary, they seek it, and they
> take delight in their flamboyant notoriety. The consequence is that this
> pestilence is devastating the younger generation. It is wrecking young
> lives. It is defiling young souls.
> I have seen the plague stalking shamelessly through great social as-
> semblies. I have heard it whispered about by young men and women
> who do not and cannot grasp its unutterable putrefaction. Both aspects
> of it are thrust upon healthy and innocent minds. The contagion can-
> not be escaped. It pervades our social life.[64]

For Douglas, as for Clemence Dane, homosexuality was a contagion that permanently warped the young. Douglas flaunted his knowledge of the sexologists' vocabulary but made no distinction between inversion and perversion.
Nor did he distinguish between predatory adults "wrecking young lives" and
the alluring "flamboyant notoriety" of adults that led young people to experiment among themselves. Perhaps he did not care, only wishing to cleanse
society "from the leprosy of these lepers, and making the air clean and wholesome once more." James Douglas knew his audience well when he launched
his attack on the "putrefaction" of Hall's novel. His readers were a broad
swathe of the prudish, provincial middle class that felt confused in the wake
of World War I. They were not the poor, whose crowded living conditions
ensured their sexual knowledge. Thanks to the popular press, the middle
class knew about and despised the sophisticates of London's literary world

and the effete aristocrats who had been educated at public schools where homosexuality flourished.

Cape sent the novel, the positive reviews, and Douglas's diatribe to the Home Secretary, asking him to rule on the book. It was a hopelessly misguided move. Sir William Joynson-Hicks, popularly known as Jix, was a self-appointed specialist in obscenity. His Christian fundamentalist principles were outraged by what he read. In the meantime the book was selling faster than Cape could reprint it. Under the Obscene Publications Act of 1857, the police raided Cape and a bookseller, confiscating all copies of the novel. Under the act the owners of a book and not its author were liable, so Hall could not testify at the subsequent trial. E. M. Forster and Virginia Woolf, both discreet homosexuals, led an effort to win support for freedom of expression, if not for homosexuality; they assembled an impressive array of potential witnesses. But the trial itself lasted barely a day, since the chief magistrate, Sir Chartres Biron, ruled out of order almost any discussion of the novel. As far as he was concerned, *The Well of Loneliness* was deeply immoral because of its positive portrayal of cross-age same-sex love. He devoted nearly half of his summing-up to Stephen's relationship with Mary, whom he described as "an innocent girl who has been debauched."[65] For him Stephen was a recognizable figure, encouraged by her all-female community (the ambulance corps) to lead a naïve girl astray. His opinion was not out of line with other judges. Hall never won wholehearted support for homosexuality as a natural, God-given state even among her fellow authors. Many hid behind the argument that the book was bad art.[66] Their vacillation and Hall's stubbornness broke useful friendships and literary connections. And her belief in the fundamental isolation of the invert was reconfirmed.

A middlebrow, popular novel about a forbidden subject could hardly have been more inflammatory. Hall could not expect much support from mainstream experts in medicine or the law. They longed for the good old days when sexual deviance was disguised or silent. Anticipating precisely these responses, early in the *Well*, Hall attacked those who wanted to banish or ignore all sexual difference: "The world hid its head in the sands of convention, so that seeing nothing it might avoid Truth. It said to itself: 'If seeing's believing, then I don't want to see—if silence is golden, it is also, in this case, very expedient.'"[67] *The Lancet*, Britain's leading medical journal, treated the novel as a poorly written case study: "The fallacy of the book lies in the failure to recognize that strong attachments between members of the same sex occur as a phase of normal development. Those who fail to outgrow this phase can be helped to divert their emotions into other channels. If their efforts are ineffectual their life must always be unhappy, for the race is bound to erect such barriers as will discourage the development of affinities dangerous to its existence."[68] "The race," heterosexual British citizens, needed to procreate and would therefore always understand same-sex love as a phase or as an aberration. This became the paradigmatic medical and legal position until the gay liberation movement of the 1970s.

The early reviews before Douglas's attack were generally respectful of Hall's book and her courage in openly discussing "a modern subject." One sympathetic reviewer pointed out: "The phenomenon has always existed and individual lives have been wrecked by the hostile attitude on the part of society towards inverts of either sex. We may pity the invert from the bottom of our hearts, but we cannot lighten the burden which Nature—in an unnatural mood—has laid upon them."[69] The feminist Vera Brittain argued that the book "convinces us that women of the type of Stephen Gordon, in so far as their abnormality is inherent and not merely the unnecessary cult of exotic erotics, deserve the fullest consideration and compassion from all who are fortunate enough to have escaped one of Nature's cruelest dispensations."[70] Hall's supporters all used the organic defect model of inversion to excuse without exonerating a practice most saw as immoral. Society need only change by tolerating, but never endorsing, the unfortunate invert. The invert born with a flawed nature became the dominant defense of the *Well* and of homosexuality in general until the post-Stonewall era.[71]

Arguments against the novel often worked by analogy, making all obscene art, visual, written, or aural, equivalent. Visual images of the deviant were especially important, as if readers needed further reinforcement in order to identify real-life Stephens. When Sir Chartres Biron disallowed the literary witnesses, he reminded them: "A book may be a fine piece of literature and yet obscene. Art and obscenity are not dissociated at all. There is a room at Naples to which visitors are not admitted as a rule, which contains fine bronzes and statues, all admirable works of art, but all grossly obscene."[72] How did Sir Chartres know about this room? If it was common knowledge among the educated classes, then possibly all kinds of perverted sexual practices were in danger of becoming known. Even the radical *New Statesman* refused its editorial sympathy: "Sir Chartres Biron was certainly right to exclude evidence as to the literary merit of the book, since that had nothing at all to do with the question. It would be easy to name books of considerable literary and artistic merit—a certain book, for example, by Aubrey Beardsley, published privately abroad—which are obscene in an extreme degree."[73] Why mention Beardsley's illustrations for *Lysistrata*, published in a limited edition in the 1890s? After all, Beardsley's muscular viragoes and effeminate men carrying penises taller than their bodies mocked heterosexual pretensions. Probably most *New Statesman* readers were more familiar with Beardsley as the onetime friend of that arch-deviant Oscar Wilde than they were with specific drawings from *Lysistrata*. But like the room in Naples, Beardsley's name summoned up images of sexual perversity. Lesbianism itself, in the ed-

ucated imagination, had virtually no literary or artistic cues, and so was identified by analogy to male homosexuality or other unnamed perversions. Sappho, the one exception, was never mentioned in connection with the *Well*.

A class-based double standard operated in the public discourse surrounding Hall's novel. References to classical art and literature were the shorthand
of the educated elite; newspapers used populist references. Traditionally
known as family reading, newspapers never used precise words, such as homosexuality or lesbianism, but instead referred to Wilde, Decadent art, degeneration, morbidity, and the like. Innuendo and allusion were more effective than outright speech in creating and sustaining various sexual scandals.
The educated were presumed to know and understand such matters and to be
inoculated against bad behavior. They could discuss sexual perversity without being harmed, whereas the semi-educated, like Mary Llewellyn, were
vulnerable. Once introduced to the "flamboyant notoriety" of homosexuality, they would be corrupted, just as she had been. At the heart of the public
debate about the *Well* was a fear that the Marys of the world were able and
willing to act on their own desires.

In spite of Douglas's trumpet call, most of the public debate was among
the literati. For sophisticated Londoners who knew all about homosexuality,
the novel's special pleading was offensive. Beresford Egan privately published
his Beardsleyesque illustrations in *The Sink of Solitude* (1928), a satire on all the
main personalities in the obscenity trial, for a coterie audience. Although he
claimed to be sickened by the vulgar rhetoric of James Douglas and the self-
righteous piety of Sir William Joynson Hicks, his principal target was Radclyffe Hall. Since female homosexuals, unlike their male counterparts, could
not be charged with a criminal offense, he found Stephen's martyrdom exaggerated.[74] The more candid reviewers agreed with him. Egan's best-known
illustration parodied Hall as a pseudo-Christ, hanging on a crucifix wearing
her signature Spanish sombrero (fig. 24). Egan drew upon a range of familiar
pornographic symbols of lesbian sexual practices in his illustrations, including not only enlarged pudenda and breasts, but also such phallic accessories
as elongated tongues, ties, cigarettes, scarves, and tails. Egan's friend Compton Mackenzie, in his spoof of English homosexual life on Capri, *Extraordinary Women* (1928), had mocked the large breasts of masculine women. Egan
took particular pleasure in doing the same, reminding his largely male viewers that nothing could turn these women into true men. His blasphemous
caricature solidified Hall's decision, as a devout convert to Roman Catholicism, to write an homage to Christ in her next novel.

The explicit torment portrayed in Egan's illustrations may seem far from
the moral high-mindedness of *The Well of Loneliness*. But suffering is fundamental to romantic love in both the novel and Radclyffe Hall's love letters.
The connection between pain and deviant love cannot be dismissed as a male

Fig. 24. Beresford Egan, *St. Stephen* (1928).

ploy, but was intrinsic to the twentieth-century construction of lesbianism.
Stephen and Mary fall into cruel love after they receive their first rejection
from Society, the withdrawal of an invitation to spend Christmas at a country house:

> That night Stephen took the girl roughly in her arms.
> "I love you—I love you so much . . ." she stammered; and she kissed Mary
> many times on the mouth, but cruelly so that her kisses were pain—
> the pain in her heart leapt out through her lips. "God! It's too terrible
> to love like this—it's hell—there are times when I can't endure it!"[75]

For Hall this episode is the world's "first real victory." Hall turns a rebuff that
Natalie Barney would have laughed at into a melodramatic turning point. But

rough sex cannot be blamed wholly on society in the *Well*. For Hall, as for Renée Vivien, love was always cruel, and she skillfully wove into the fabric of her novel images that combined her belief in the martyrdom of lesbian love, the necessity of suffering for the beloved, and the sexual attractiveness of romantic despair.

Wounds, lacerations, and self-inflicted torture pervade the *Well*, beginning with the child Stephen's desire "to bear all Collins' pain . . . to wash [the servant] Collins in my blood."[76] Stephen is "scourged" by her mother's rejection; when "tormented" by Angela Crossby, she carries a "wounded expression." After Angela's betrayal Stephen's "love lay bleeding, shamefully wounded." Her governess admits that inverts bear "the wound of existence." Mary is "wounded and utterly crushed" by society's rejection; only with Martin can she "sheathe her sword." Wounds and battle are also closely tied with sexual frustration. Many critics have referred to Stephen's war wound as her mark of Cain, but no one has mentioned that it resembles female genitalia. It is long, narrow, and red. We are told twice that Mary loves the wound and loves to kiss it.[77] At moments of intense sexual suffering, the wound swells and darkens, as if filled with genital desire. Stephen strains under the burden of sexual self-control: "With the terrible bonds of her dual nature, [Stephen] could bind Mary fast, and the pain would be sweetness, so that the girl would cry out for that sweetness, hugging her chains always closer to her. . . . Her face grew ominous, heavy and brooding; the fine line of her mouth was a little marred; her eyes were less clear, less the servants of her spirit than the slaves of her anxious and passionate body; the red scar on her cheek stood out like a wound."[78] Stephen's apotheosis occurs when she "wounds" Mary by denying her sex, and in the process she wounds herself, so that her writing is like blood drawn from her pen. In her final meeting with Martin, "The scar across Stephen's pale face stood out livid."[79] In the name of love, she hurts and is hurt. Sadomasochism, a perversion, is intrinsic to this novel of inversion.

At the very end of the *Well*, Stephen's creative talent is reborn through her suffering. As she is sitting alone at her desk, the downtrodden inverts of the world rise up, demanding that she be their voice. They torture her for failing them:

"You and your kind have stolen our birthright; you have taken our strength, and have given us your weakness!" They were pointing at her with white, shaking fingers.

Rockets of pain, burning rockets of pain—their pain, her pain, all welded together into one great consuming agony. Rockets of pain that shot up and burst, dropping scorching tears of fire on the spirit . . . In their madness to become articulate through her, they were tearing her to pieces, getting her under.[80]

Stephen turns her martyrdom into a new kind of spiritual fecundity unique to the invert: "They possessed her. Her barren womb became fruitful—it ached with her fearful and sterile burden." By masochistically accepting their pain, as well as her own, Stephen is fully empowered. She commands God to support her and others like her: "Acknowledge us, oh God, before the whole world. Give us also the right to our existence!" Stephen had to be a martyr if she was to be a great artist.

Hall's decision to steep her novel in religious symbolism evoked derision from not only Beresford Egan but also other contemporaries. Wyndham Lewis paraded his fascination with sadism and contempt for religiosity. *The Well of Loneliness* (and Compton Mackenzie's *Extraordinary Women*) are behind the savage portrayal of a lesbian artist in his 1930 novel, *Apes of God.* At one juncture in this inchoate, sprawling novel, the hapless hero, Dan Boleyn, agrees to pose nude for a woman artist. He enters the wrong studio, to be confronted by an aging man-woman wearing "a stiff Radcliffe-Hall [sic] collar, of antique masculine cut, suggestive of the masculine hey-day, when men were men." The woman, whose name we never learn, apes both men and artists. Her "cigarette-holder half a foot long protrud[ing] from a firm-set jaw" reminds the knowing reader of female oral sex. Dan is ordered to "peel," but he hesitates before "a large dog-whip." "The sight of this disciplinary instrument disturbed him extremely. In fancy he could see himself naked, in full flight, before this little hennaed white-collared huntress—her dog-throng cracking about his girl-white surfaces." The artist has Dan pose with the whip as a Roman soldier "threatening Our Saviour." He must stand in so twisted a posture that he faints. Regaining consciousness, he finds both the artist and her lover staring at him. "With an eel-like agility born of shame and terror . . . Dan regained the cover of the model's undressing screen. His 'vanish' was accompanied by two loud shouts of laughter from extraordinary woman No. 1—who, at his bashful exit, indulged in the coarsest mirth, pointing after him with her cigarette-holder to her sweetheart, who tittered sneeringly as the great white mass disappeared, like a rat into its hole."[81] Lewis vilifies both the effeminacy of Dan and the masculinity of the artist. He believed that no sterile deviant could be an authentic creative artist; the tormented lesbian in the *Well* is transformed into a harpy threatening to drain life out of men.

Djuna Barnes (1892–1982) also satirized lesbian love, but in a very different spirit from the misogynist Lewis. Her clever spoof of Renaissance courtly love, *Ladies Almanack* (1928), is an insider's view of lesbian life in Paris. Barnes, an itinerant American journalist, probably knew Barney's circle of friends better than did Hall, who spent little time in Paris and disapproved of their easy seductions and infidelities. Unlike Hall, who sought to maximize her audience, Barnes wrote for her friends. When her publisher refused to market the book, she met her expenses by selling it on the streets and in popular cafés.[82]

Interpretations of the *Ladies Almanack* vary, but Barnes surely intended it as a tribute to Natalie Barney, whom she calls Evangeline Musset. Although Barnes uses the word *lesbian* only once, she manages to celebrate and ridicule lesbian sexual practices through numerous references to female anatomy, including especially the tongue. Like Lewis, she reverses expectations, but in the name of comic rather than destructive satire. Barnes, for example, toys with the Renaissance conceit of calling sexual orgasm death. When Evangeline dies in December at the ripe age of ninety-nine, she is cremated, but her tongue "flamed, and would not suffer Ash, and it played about upon the handful that had been she indeed." The mourners pull up their skirts and rush to the urn, but "Señorita Fly-About came down upon that Urn first, and beatitude played and flickered upon her Face."[83] The month of March satirizes Radclyffe Hall, "Tilly-Tweed-in-Blood [who] sported a Stetson and believed in Marriage," and her partner, Una Troubridge, "Lady Buck-and-Balk [who] sported a Monocle and believed in Spirits." They self-righteously clamor for the legalization of same-sex matrimony and for "Straying [to] be nipped in the Bud," but Evangeline mocks their conventionality and exhorts them, "Love of Woman for Woman should increase Terror."[84]

Marital fidelity came to haunt Hall and Troubridge. When Troubridge left her husband for Hall in the middle of World War I, both women thought they were married for life. They shared a deep commitment to fidelity and to the public acknowledgment of their relation. During the humiliating publicity over the *Well*, Troubridge had been a rock of support. But by the early 1930s, Hall was bored with her partner's whims and illnesses. Less than six years after the trial, she fell in love with a White Russian refugee, Evguenia Souline. Through nine tumultuous years Hall pursued Souline. The terror of "Straying" was in full flower. But she never left Troubridge. Hall's letters to Souline alternate between extreme suffering and virtually sadistic demands for absolute loyalty. At one jealous juncture she destroyed everything in Souline's apartment, and then, in abject guilt, paid to replace it all.[85] Troubridge alternated between angry fury and masochistic altruism.

Hall's surviving letters to Souline echo her analysis of Stephen's state of mind when she was in love with Mary. They combine profound religious feeling and emotional pain mixed with intense physical desire: "I think that being deeply in love is the greatest pain & the greatest joy, and that these together make for beauty . . . Oh, you my torment, my most cruel desire—for surely you must know that desire is cruel?"[86] And later, flush with sexual satisfaction, she wrote: "When you look at people you can say to yourself in your heart—'I also has [sic] got a lover—I am loved until the love is a pain, as a scourge of whips on my lover's back, as a fire that torments and consumes my lover.' Blessed is the love that torments day and night, night & day, for it also illumines and sustains when the loved one is kind—be kind then, my Soulina."[87] Hall defined love as a complex alternation of giving and receiving, of master and slave, sadist and masochist. She played all these roles with Souline, attempting to retain mastery, but repeatedly acceding to her demands. Pain, religious ecstasy, and unrequited desire combine in Hall's moving letters; all of her creative energy went into them. The painful triangle of Hall, Souline, and Troubridge ended only in 1943 with Hall's death.

Sadomasochistic desire, much less its practice, is highly controversial within the women's movement. Today, more than twenty years after Pat Califia opened the subject in a series of articles in *The Advocate*,[88] it is still a matter of heated debate. As inheritors of Hall's tragic, morally superior heroine, many present-day lesbians are perhaps too inclined to see rough sex as a response to social pressures rather than a chosen practice. But in her life and her art, Hall, like Colette and Vivien, believed that pain and love were not easily separated. Just as the vulnerable headmistress in *Claudine at School* promised promotion and job security to her assistant in return for kisses and affection, the vulnerable Hall showered gifts and promises upon Souline, hoping to win compliance and fidelity. The active, mannish instigator of love is not always so simply defined as Clare Hartill, the charismatic sadist. *Regiment of Women* remains a period piece, but *The Well of Loneliness* still captures the imagination of critics. Yet supportive as Colette was, she was distressed that her "dear John" should insist on having her lesbian characters feel abnormal. Like the homosexuals who told Krafft-Ebing, Ellis, and Carpenter how much they liked who they were, Colette believed "an 'abnormal' man or woman must never have the feeling that he or she is abnormal."[89] She would have agreed with Djuna Barnes, who once defined depravity as "the ability to enjoy what others shudder at, and to shudder at what others enjoy."[90]

❄ The final two chapters examined two very different historical trajectories in the public recognition of same-sex love between women. Barney, Vivien, and Brooks actively fought against bourgeois family values and repudiated familial metaphors as characterizations of their relationships. They created imaginative and enduring myths of lesbian love, but limited their audience to those who agreed with them. Dane and Hall championed romance and marriage. Dane made sure her innocent heroine married an upright man. Hall created an honorable man-woman eager to settle into a homosexual marriage, if only society would let her. For both, in fiction, same-sex romance inevitably ended in melodramatic suffering. Although twentieth-century women who loved women might still speak in code or behind closed doors, just as Anne Lister and Charlotte Cushman had done, they now had a public discourse and a set of recognized stereotypes with which to shape their conversations. For many, the fictional characters created by Dane and Hall defined the lesbian. Clemence Dane and Radclyffe Hall, as well as Natalie Clifford Barney, Renée Vivien, Colette, Virginia Woolf, and other authors too numerous to mention, successfully created a complex, contradictory vocabulary about same-sex desire and love. But their greatest achievement may have been the creation of enduring myths that enrich and irritate those who came after them.

Conclusion

BEYOND THE FAMILY METAPHOR

From 1778, when the Ladies of Llangollen ran away from their families, to 1928, when *The Well of Loneliness* was banned, lesbian history did not move forward in any simple trajectory, from invisibility and secrecy to visibility and homophobia; nor was silence replaced by slang replaced by medical terms in how women described their relationships. Lives, and especially personal sexual feelings, are always more complicated than any historical model. Nevertheless, we see a sustained effort among women who loved women to construct a vocabulary and milieu suited to their sense of themselves as different from heterosexuals. Repeatedly individual women asserted that their intimate friendships were equal to, even better than, traditional social arrangements. Negotiating the invisible but palpable line between acceptable and suspect behavior, these women demanded respect for their intimate friendships and lesbian loves. As I have shown, women reworked family roles, adapting the husband-wife marriage, the mother-daughter bond, and the independent female rake for their own purposes. Even for those who deeply distrusted or disliked the nuclear family, it remained an important source for imagining and constructing same-sex intimacy. Yet by the 1920s the family metaphor had worn thin; marriage and family were themselves under new postwar pressures. The "bachelor girl" became the identified dangerous figure, accompanied by an assortment of new sexual labels. Greater personal autonomy, mass consumption, and new democratic ideas made obsolete notions of the exceptional genius, the privileged aristocrat, and the maternal spinster. A new vocabulary led to new models of familiar intimate relations. An analysis of these profound changes is the subject of another book.

In this conclusion I focus on the bedrock assumption of my study: the women I discuss here were erotically attracted to women, whatever their sexual practices. Women did not need the new, modern language to recognize their desires. Indeed, they fully understood the dangers of same-sex intimacy.

The adroitness with which these women used and deflected the public gaze upon their more private relations was extraordinary. They managed to be open and closed, to keep a secret and to tell it to anyone who might be listening. Their success has provided historians with an excuse to ignore or deny the depth of passion and commitment contained in women's intimate friendships. Many articles and books, including this one, have attempted to define and delineate the salient characteristics of a modern sexual identity, while admitting that women's sexual and erotic boundaries have always been both permeable and unstable. Anyone who studies women in the past knows that, however fragmentary the evidence, women have always loved women. It would be foolish and arrogant to assume that none of these women knew their own bodies well enough to practice sexual relations to orgasm with another woman. Because sex was usually defined as heterosexual penetration, women could describe their amative relations as chaste. But the pleasures of touching were well known. "Sex matters," in the words of one gay movement slogan.

Throughout the time period of this book, women struggled to accept their own desires as natural. Gender inversion remained the chief signifier of same-sex desire. Anne Lister frequently chopped logic when wooing a woman, claiming that her aggressively masculine sexual overtures were "natural" because she used no artificial devices. Edith Simcox reminded herself that she was instinctively "half-man" and not made for marriage. She resented George Eliot pushing her "to take a little more pains with her dress and drawing room conversation" in order to attract a man.[1] Clemence Dane's Clare Hartill "repels" men, but Radclyffe Hall's Stephen Gordon treats them as comrades. To ratify one's sexual self as natural is an immensely empowering act, but it also assumes that change is not possible. Eliza Lynn Linton and Dane seem to have feared this conclusion; each cordoned off the mannish deviant, even at the price of limiting her own emotional life. The sexologists' "congenital inversion" was a powerful explanatory tool, providing women with a language for their same-sex erotic desires, even if they never acted upon them. But contradictions remained. The sexologists had no explanation for what might seem an acquired passion. Women who refused to outgrow a phase could not always be labeled as gender inverts. Concepts such as natural, innate, and instinctive were dubious when applied to sexual feelings throughout the hundred and fifty years of this book. They remain slippery categories, inevitably placing the emphasis on "natural for *me* at this time in my life."

The use of family metaphors implies the creation of a home—a stable place where one can be oneself. In some cases this was an actual home, such as the rural retreats created by Lady Eleanor Butler and Sarah Ponsonby in Llangollen and Rosa Bonheur near Fontainebleau; for others it was a salon, such as that of Charlotte Cushman and Natalie Clifford Barney; and for still others it was an informal group of friends, such as Vernon Lee and Ethel

Smyth enjoyed. Since family obligations or economics prevented many women from living with another woman, a group of like-minded friends was crucial. Some women found a home among political or religious friends. Same-sex love was pervasive in the women's movement. Frances Power Cobbe, Bessie Rayner Parkes, and Emily Faithfull in the 1850s and 1860s were members of an extended network of feminists. By the early twentieth century, feminists had successfully propagated a positive image of the active, public-minded single woman. Suffragists believed profoundly in women's power and their separate communities; many were actively opposed to marriage and male privilege. Some also furthered the spiritual power of women's friendships. Although antifeminists raised the issue of lesbianism, the stereotype of the ugly spinster who could not catch a man was far more common.[2] For feminists the isolated lesbian was an inaccurate invention, created as part of the backlash against women's rights. But like many fictions, it also shaped the lives of individual women who sought new models of same-sex love.

The most sexually daring women were often indifferent to politics or hostile to feminism. Perhaps the decision to remain unmarried or to live with a woman was in itself so radical that women needed the security of tradition and order. Women who loved women generally accepted the beliefs of their social class. The Ladies of Llangollen remained Tory loyalists to the end, always pretending to a greater generosity to the poor than the reality. Lister ruthlessly expelled tenants who failed to vote as she commanded. Smyth loathed Lee's pacifism and condescended to all Roman Catholics. The casual anti-Semitism of wealthy lesbians like Radclyffe Hall (encouraged by Souline), Natalie Barney, and Romaine Brooks makes for unpleasant reading.[3] Shari Benstock has suggested that Barney and Gertrude Stein identified with the repressive masculinity of totalitarian political movements because they identified themselves with power.[4] Certainly Una Troubridge did so. Although wholesale generalizations cannot be made, generally class and economic privilege trumped sexual nonconformity. In their creation of metaphoric families, wealthy lesbians eschewed the figure of the father, but they firmly upheld patriarchy as the source of their social and economic status.

Obviously, in many of the cases discussed here, education, social class, and personal self-confidence were important determinants in sexual self-fashioning. Under the best of circumstances, this was not easy. It took a breakdown and years of spiritual discipline for Mary Benson to find herself; personal gossip helped to undermine the reputations of Linton and Lee; Lister never found the ideal wife after years of experimentation; Brooks became increasingly bitter against society in the 1930s, and spent the remaining forty years of her life writing and rewriting her unpublishable autobiography. For each of these women, an intimate friendship included a shadow adversary, perhaps a husband or a biological mother, judging and constraining sexual independence. These figures of righteousness were constant reminders: to love a woman was to risk social ostracism. Even though many of the women discussed here tolerated an uncertain social status and negative remarks in return for sexual freedom, respectability mattered. The lesbian enclaves in Rome, Paris, and London were always publicly circumspect. Even the unconventional Cushman carefully wove her highly erotic relationships into the conventional fabric of family and friendship. Barney confined her costume dramas to her private garden. Yet the women discussed in this book still insisted on the primacy of their relationships with other women. All were courageous and independent, and led emotionally rich, if conflicted, lives. They also considered their lives important enough to leave a record for future generations. Although they avoided using the word *lesbian*, they pioneered in creating lesbian images, narratives, and communities.

Over the course of the one hundred and fifty years, friendship, marriage, passion, and even love meant many different things. Expectations about a woman's personal happiness, social obligations, and family responsibilities varied. Not surprisingly, how women wrote and spoke about their own sexual pleasure also changed, and yet certain images and metaphors are evident throughout the period. Women who loved women did not invent a new language of love, but adapted the existing heterosexual tropes for their own purposes. As earlier chapters have documented, sexual consummation was less important than the acknowledgment of erotic love. Desire contained in memory or sublimated for a higher goal could be, in the minds of many women, a higher form of passion than felt by ordinary mortals. Classical restraint and male homoeroticism, as well as Christian celibacy and female sainthood, provided rich sources for alternative models to heterosexuality. These traditions glorified impassioned love, divorced from sex but not from the body. Women transformed these texts into narratives that reflected their own experiences of love, desire, and disappointment.

Sexual love and the functions of specific body parts were rarely described. A few women, in secret or more boldly, in public, might speak about their courtship of women, but rarely about their sexual activities. Before the twentieth century the most detailed accounts of women's lovemaking are Lister's candid diaries. She described, for example, her wooing of Maria Barlow:

[I] became rather excited. Felt her breasts & queer [genitals] a little. Tried to put my hand up her petticoats but she prevented. Touched her flesh just above the knee twice. I kissed her warmly & held her strongly. She said what a state I was putting myself into. . . . I felt her grow warm & she let me grubble [touch her genitals] & press her tightly with my left hand whilst I held her against the door with the other, all the while

putting my tongue into her mouth & kissing her passionately as to excite her not a little, I am sure.[5]

Barlow, "shedding a few tears, said 'You are used to these things. I am not.'"
Lister concluded her account, "Insinuated we had now gone too far to re-
tract."[6] Writing solely for her own pleasure, Lister reconstructed this and
similar events as examples of her erotic prowess. She bluntly credited herself
with skill, confidence, and a clear sexual goal. But even Lister quickly concluded her descriptions of grubbling, choosing only to enumerate the number of orgasms she and her partner had experienced. Few people in the past,
outside pornography, chose to describe the sex act in detail.

Surviving evidence suggests that most women in the nineteenth century
focused on feelings, rather than specific acts. They constructed same-sex intimacy as a narrative of romantic or spiritual discovery. Cushman encouraged
Emma Crow early in their relationship to "write to me as much & as often as
you will. All your love falls on ploughed ground & shall bring forth fruit," and
she signed her letters "your Faithful Ladie love."[7] Mary Benson breathlessly
wrote her friend Chat Bassett, "how I would lift up your head and heal your
heart, and fill you with that loving strength, the wholesome strength of His
right hand and charge your whole nature with Hope."[8] Falling in love was both
common and uncommon; each time, regardless of sex and object choice, the
woman felt swept up, unable to think of anything else, and yet also without
adequate words to recreate the experience. Vernon Lee, in her forties, described her unrequited love for Augustine Bulteau: "She had got hold of me
very completely, heart, imagination, nerves; and life seems oddly emptied of
all charm or purpose for the moment. The summer, particularly, & autumn,
without her in any part of it, seems as difficult to swallow as a handful of dry
flour. This is not her fault, but mine; for I should not have given myself away
so rashly & utterly."[9] Life without love, for Lee, was empty and dry, squeezed
of all meaning; life with love, as in her "Prince Alberic," was moist, green
fronds, and deep wells. None of these women has difficulty vividly expressing the pleasures and pains of loving another woman.

Erotic passion, however, was best left to calculated silences, metaphoric
language, and other linguistic flourishes. Given their strong public investment in chaste passion, nineteenth-century women-loving women elabo-
rated on the poetic metaphor of merging. Few women speak of the arrow of
love penetrating the heart. Most instead describe bosom-to-bosom love or
variations on two hearts beating as one. The pleasure of love is closeness,
touching, oneness, and a reciprocal feeling they believed was utterly lacking
in heterosexual relations. To speak of the ecstasy of being held close, of caressing and pressing heart to heart or breast to breast, signifies a very special
kind of intimacy, in which merging and oneness are treasured as signs of pas-

sionate love. Amidst the reserved, even hackneyed, phrases of love in Lady Eleanor Butler's Llangollen diary is the crossed-out note, "A Cottage August 13th [1788] The having but one Heart between my beloved and—"[10] The cottage, bedroom (or bed), and garden all liberate same-sex passion. Private enclosures act as metonymy for the pleasure they contain. Smyth used the image of tree roots entwined deep in the soil to describe the enduring love between herself and Lady Ponsonby. Mary Robinson wrote "Dear, dear Vernon" about "the nights I slept so securely in your arms," concluding, "I am always your Molly."[11] Renée Vivien's "Union" captures the glories of merging: "Our heart is the same in our woman's breast, / My dearest! Our body is made the same / . . . See, I am more than yours, I am you."[12] Sameness was a source of pleasure and power. We see little of the current lesbian fear of excessive merging; instead it is celebrated as superior to the obliteration of self women feared in a heterosexual relation.

For these writers metaphor and metonymy spoke for a passion that was better imagined than fully described. The unnamed cannot be censored. For early-twentieth-century Modernists, however, same-sex passion was both more present and more absent because it had been defined. In the 1920s and 1930s, sophisticated readers had a much clearer idea of lesbian sexuality, but both censorship laws and self-censorship led to a different kind of speech. In literary works same-sex passion, when not concealed by a heterosexual plot, was subject to a designedly obvious form of elision, the ellipsis. Writers encouraged flights of fantasy into unmentionable or unacceptable emotions and actions. The ellipsis contains the very act that cannot be described but can still be known. It begs for interpretation, yet resists it. Consider, for example, the original title of Colette's extended consideration of the "sad pleasures" of sex. *The Pure and the Impure* (1941) was *Ces plaisirs . . .* (1932), with dots to lure us into a text filled with more dots, for example, "Such things can't be explained. There are . . . subtleties . . . you have to feel them."[13] Colette relished drawing attention to the unspoken, underlining its implications to encourage her readers' imaginations. Renée Vivien, Clemence Dane, and Radclyffe Hall also employed ellipses with abandon, encouraging the reader to imagine passion outside the text. The unnamed desires of Clare Hartill could be sadistic cruelties, or reckless passion, or self-inflicted tortures—or nothing.

Yet only the daring felt free to employ ellipses. Far more common was drawing upon a tradition known as the "Language of Flowers." Flowers were both natural and bookish, for their meanings were derived from folklore and religious sources.[14] In the nineteenth century young men and women read flower books with elaborate explanations of what each flower or herb meant. Some flowers had obvious and long-standing connotations. A red rose, for example, began as Venus's flower, then became the Virgin Mary's, and then in secularized societies reverted to the flower of passionate love. Flower-courtship also fostered another kind of secrecy; flowers could speak for the lover without revealing a forbidden desire in words. Ed Madden has analyzed the ways in which homosexual men took the feminized language of flowers and turned it to their own purposes, to encode same-sex desire.[15] Women poets unselfconsciously used clichés such as unfolding buds, red petals of roses, vulva-shaped tulips, and sweet-scented violets to express female erotic pleasure. Renée Vivien associated the blond Natalie Clifford Barney with the white lily; its traditional associations with purity reinforced their shared belief in sensual purity. Vivien celebrated the heterosexual chastity of lesbian sexuality by flooding Barney and her poems with expensive white lilies, in season or out. Even the Modernist Virginia Woolf delicately describes Clarissa Dalloway's love for Sally Seton in startlingly familiar terms: "Sally stopped; picked a flower; kissed her on the lips. The whole world turned upside down! The others disappeared; there she was alone with Sally. She felt that she had been given a present, wrapped up, and told just to keep it, not to look at it— a diamond, something infinitely precious, wrapped up."[16]

Woolf here introduces an element that was typically linked to the language of flowers. Jewels, like flowers, spoke eloquently about what was known but could not be said openly; both included, as Paula Bennett has argued, a good deal of clitoral imagery.[17] Although Bennett focuses on American women writers, flower and gem imagery was crucial for women on both sides of the Atlantic as representations of the eroticized female body. Here I briefly examine the two body parts celebrated by lesbians, the breast and the clitoris. Each can stand for, directly or indirectly, female sexual subjectivity apart from and independent of the heterosexual imperative. By the late nineteenth century, lesbian poets wrote highly self-conscious poems praising the female body, including its most intimate parts. The clitoris is most often spoken about in symbolic ways, as a small bud, jewel, flower, pearl, or diamond. The breast, with its implicit reference to the heart, is more obviously a symbol of sexual maturity, and also more visibly an object to be admired. Fruits, the moon, and other luxurious objects stand in for the breast.

The breast, for lesbians, as yet has no recorded history.[18] It may seem like an odd choice for any discussion of lesbian sexuality, especially when we think of the lactating breast as a symbol of motherhood and the Western fixation on the breast as a source of male sexual arousal. Yet women too noticed breasts. Throughout the nineteenth century women wrote to each other about the pleasure of laying one's head upon the breast of a beloved friend; these references suggest both a regression to a childlike dependency and erotic satisfaction. The concealed breast was a source of private eroticism. The loose jacket worn by so many "mannish" women, from Harriet Hosmer to Romaine Brooks, prevented men from enjoying their "mature charms." The French writer Colette was always willing to speak of same-sex eroticism more openly than most of her early-twentieth-century English and American contemporaries. In her witty dissection of the Ladies of Llangollen, she asks her readers to define the difference between "patting a young cheek, fresh and warm and velvety as a peach" and "caressing and lightly weighing with the cupped hand a rosy breast shaped like a peach." She writes at length about the "indiscreet little breast," savoring such literary clichés as "pulpy fruit, rosy dawns, snowy landscapes."[19] Her indiscreet prose lays bare what had so long remained publicly concealed, namely, the powerful attraction for women of a woman's breast. Then she abruptly changes the subject by beginning her next paragraph, "The bedroom . . . our bed . . . " Dots once again avoid an explicit reference to female desire, while allowing her to hint broadly at the shift from foreplay—the gently cupped breasts—to the bed and orgasmic pleasure.

In a peroration against a journalist who denigrated women's breasts, Barney speculated, "Many women give themselves more willingly than they give their breasts—to avoid offering their breasts?" She recommends the superiority of a more subtle lovemaking, suggesting that "the breasts were more delicately connected with the center of sensation than the short-circuit of sexual climax." She concludes with a characteristic gesture, describing lesbian sexual practices in a series of richly evocative metaphors about the sexually responsive breast: "Flower of the senses, complex, dense, heavy with all your secrets, language, experience, throbbing perfumes, sight, touch; all sharpen to a point till this pre-eminence abdicates in favour of that excess which will extinguish it."[20] Barney joins a long tradition of women piling different sensory adjectives together—touch, smell, sight, even sound, combine to evoke sexual pleasure. At the same time, implicitly, the breast, like women, remains complex, dense, and secret. Only with the feminist movement and gay liberation in the 1970s do we again find such a candid description of the sensual pleasures of the breast.

Women were also willing, symbolically, to speak of even more intimate bodily pleasures. Unlike the breast, the clitoris short-circuits the maternal, going directly to pleasure. A flower in bud could be the blossoming of a new friendship, as Mary Benson declared to Chat Bassett, but it also could be the rising up of the clitoris, in response to that love. I earlier discussed Eliza Lynn Linton's description of her beloved as a diamond in a casket. Katharine Bradley wrote numerous poems describing pearls, iris, lilies, and roses as images of the clitoris or vagina. Inspired by Edith Cooper's gift of "a pot of golden, sweet-scented tulips," she united her niece's splendor with the tulips: "Wholly is your sweetness blent / With your beauty, as the scent / Of the golden tulip lies / Golden in the verdant leaves."[21] The golden vulva-shaped tulip, resting in green leaves, speaks of a closer intimacy that need not be explicit.

The day after Viginia Woolf attended a concert of Ethel Smyth's music, she wrote to "thank and praise" her new friend: "An image forms in my mind;

a quickset briar hedge, innumerably intricate and spiky and thorned; in the centre burns a rose. Miraculously, the rose is you; flushed pink, wearing pearls. The thorn hedge is the music; and I have to break my way through the violins, flutes, cymbals, voices to this red burning centre."[22] Well, yes, Smyth may have been the beautiful rose in the center of the music, but the image also conjures up the rosy beauty of the female genitals, surrounded by a hedge of hair. Surely Woolf must have been speaking of Smyth's *sexual* soul when she went on to compliment her for creating music drawn "from your centre" where "all the loves and ages you have been through" could be found. The two women had been delicately negotiating the nature of their relationship as they warmed to each other. But this letter burst forth with a vividly realized sense of the female body and its rich possibilities. In a characteristic move Woolf fuses creativity and feminine sexuality, suggesting their essential affiliation. Precisely because Smyth knows her sexual self so well, has plumbed to "this red burning centre," she can create powerful, moving music. With unerring instinct Woolf chose a vivid clitoral image to signal her sense of the lesbian roots of Smyth's genius.

Up to this point in this conclusion, I have drawn attention to the continuities over the span of a hundred and fifty years in imagery, metaphor, and metonymy among women writers who loved women. Yet I believe changes occurred, symbolized by the coy ellipses favored by Colette, Radclyffe Hall, and other twentieth-century writers. Woolf is more self-conscious than Lister, more keenly aware of the psychosexual implications of her friendship with Smyth. However, as long as they could use a literary language, women wrote with extraordinary ease and fullness about same-sex sexual pleasure. But as I discussed in chapter 8, a scientific vocabulary made the discussion of same-sex love both easier and more difficult. The obligation to know one's desires precisely, rather than to let them remain unnamed and unpredictable, was sometimes a frightening responsibility. I close with a representative example of the sheer difficulty of speaking about sex. Ethel Smyth was besotted with Virginia Woolf. Yet in her diary for 1933, trying to come to terms with her deep attraction to Woolf, the seventy-four-year-old Smyth could not define the nature of this love she felt for the fragile, brilliant author. Shorn of metaphor, how could she describe her passionate involvement with a woman whom she rarely touched, much less kissed. As she confided to her diary, "for many women, anyhow for me, passion is independent of the sex machine. Of course when you are young it will not be gainsaid—nor indeed did it cease to play any part—if I am frank—in my affections till all that should have been over & done with, going by things physical."[23] Smyth acknowledges the importance of sex as part of love, then denies its necessity in her old age, yet admits its continued power over her. Although the "sex machine" should not have persisted in playing a part in her love of women, it did, and perhaps because of this, she remained capable of the deep love she gave Woolf. Smyth's circumlocutions and awkward logic underscore the difficulty of writing plainly about sex. But she fully acknowledges the centrality of the erotic, if not the fully physical, to her love. Passionate desire was a compelling foundation for their friendship. And yet questions inevitably remain about Smyth's relationship with Woolf. Was this a lesbian friendship between women who had loved men but preferred women? Or a friendship between two aging geniuses, meeting at the right time and place? Or both? We are left to honor the mystery of intimate friendships, woven into a rich tapestry of words and images by so many women.

APPENDIX

THE PRINCIPAL INTIMATE FRIENDS

Anstruther-Thomson, Clementina (1857–1921): Friend of Vernon Lee, especially interested in bringing art to the working class. Later worked with the Girl Guides. Nickname Kit.

Ashburton, Lady Louisa (1827–1903): Born Louisa Caroline Stewart Mackenzie. Patron of the arts after the death of her husband, the second Baron Ashburton. Friend of Harriet Hosmer and Jane Carlyle.

Ashton, Winifred. *See* Dane, Clemence

Barney, Natalie Clifford (1876–1972): Wealthy heir of a railroad fortune. Bilingual American who ran a salon in Paris for nearly fifty years, attracting the avant-garde of Modernism. Wrote in French about women's same-sex desire; openly lesbian.

Benson, Margaret (1864–1916): Brilliant youngest daughter of Mary and Edward Benson. Egyptian archeologist and author of philosophical works. Suffered from poor physical health and was mentally ill from 1906 until her death. Called Maggie.

Benson, Mary Sidgwick (1842–1918): Married to Edward White Benson, who served as Archbishop of Canterbury from 1883 to 1896. Mother of six children, none of whom married. Offered assistance to women grappling with the loss of faith and with sexual problems.

Bonheur, Rosa (1822–99): Very successful French painter of animals, best known for *The Horsefair* (1853). After the death of her father, supported her two brothers and sister, all minor artists. Intimate friend of Nathalie Micas till Micas's death and then of Anna Klumpke.

Bradley, Katharine (1846–1914): Daughter of a Birmingham businessman. Coauthored poetry and plays with her niece, Edith Cooper, under the pseudonym Michael Field. Known as Michael among friends.

Brooks, Romaine (1874–1970): American painter and lover of Natalie Barney. Brought up by a mentally unstable mother. Painted the leading lesbians of the day. Distrusted the Paris socialite world that brought her fame.

Butler, Lady Eleanor (1739–1829): Member of an Irish Catholic aristocratic family; her brother converted to Protestantism to retrieve the family's political and economic powers. The older of the Ladies of Llangollen; lived with Sarah Ponsonby in Llangollen Vale, Wales, for 39 years in their home, Plas Newydd.

Carlyle, Jane Welsh (1801–66): Daughter of a prosperous Scottish doctor. Married the author Thomas Carlyle. Had no children and was wary of female sentimentality about domestic matters. A brilliant letter writer.

Codrington, Helen Smith (1828–?): Daughter of a gentleman. Brought up in Florence, Italy, where she married the naval officer Henry John Codrington in 1849, who sued her for divorce in 1863. Had two daughters. Friend of the feminist Emily Faithfull.

Colette, Sidonie-Gabrielle (1873–1954): Bisexual French writer, music hall performer, and lover of cats. Became famous for her Claudine series, about a young provincial girl who describes her sexual adventures with fresh candor.

Cooper, Edith (1862–1913): Lived with her aunt, Katharine Bradley, with whom she wrote under the pseudonym Michael Field. Known as Henry or Field.

Crow, Eliza. *See* Cushman, Eliza Crow

Cushman, Charlotte (1816–76): Became an actress when her father's business failed; supported her family. Known as America's first international star; high fees and shrewd investments made her wealthy. Her most important lovers were the poet Eliza Cook, the feminist writer Matilda Hays, the sculptor Emma Stebbins, and Emma Crow Cushman.

Cushman, Emma Crow (1839–1921). Daughter of the St. Louis, Missouri, businessman and philanthropist Wayman Crow. In 1861 married Edwin "Ned" Cushman, the adopted son of Charlotte Cushman; had five sons.

Dane, Clemence (1887–1965): Pen name for Winifred Ashton, a leading interwar playwright, film script writer, and journalist. Attacked schoolgirl friendships even though she was probably a lesbian herself.

Dods, Mary Diana (1791?–1830?): Illegitimate daughter of the fifteenth Earl of Morton. Wrote under male pseudonyms. As Walter Sholto Douglas, married Isabel Robinson, a pregnant friend. With the help of Mary Shelley, the couple moved to Paris, where Dods died in poverty.

Duclaux, Madame. *See* Robinson, A. Mary F.

Eliot, George (1819–80): Pseudonym of Mary Ann, later Marian, Evans. One of the greatest novelists of the Victorian age. Known for her penetrating psychological portraits and her agnosticism. Cohabited with George Henry Lewes and married John Cross after Lewes's death.

Faithfull, Emily (1835–95): Early feminist active in widening job opportunities for women; founder of the Victoria Press, employing women typesetters. Later moved to Manchester and continued her activities on behalf of women and suffrage.

Field, Michael. *See* Bradley, Katharine; Cooper, Edith

Hall, Radclyffe (1880–1943). Born Marguerite Radclyffe-Hall; known to her friends as John. Inherited her grandfather's fortune and supported her family all her life. Wrote the most famous openly lesbian novel of the 1920s, *The Well of Loneliness.*

von Herzogenberg, Elisabeth (1847–1892): Known as Lisl. Member of the aristocratic Austrian Stockhausen family. Married to a Leipzig composer; friend of the composer Johannes Brahms. First and most important mother-lover of the composer-writer Ethel Smyth.

Hosmer, Harriet (1830–1908): Daughter of a medical doctor. American neoclassical sculptor of international fame. Resided in Rome for many years, including seven years with Charlotte Cushman.

Jewsbury, Geraldine (1812–80): Daughter and sister of Manchester merchants. Author and reader of fiction manuscripts for the publishing firm of Richard Bentley. Deeply attracted to Charlotte Cushman and a lifelong friend of Jane Carlyle.

Ladies of Langollen. *See* Butler, Lady Eleanor; Ponsonby, Sarah

Lawton, Mariana Belcombe (1790–1868): Daughter and sister of York doctors. Friend and lover of Anne Lister; married Charles Lawton of Cheshire for economic reasons.

Lee, Vernon (1856–1935): Pseudonym of Violet Paget. Author of over forty books, encompassing fiction, horror stories, music and art criticism, aesthetics, history, and travel. Fluent in French, Italian, and German. Lived most of her life in Florence, Italy.

Linton, Eliza Lynn (1822–98): Daughter of a Cumberland clergyman. The first paid woman journalist. A controversial and prolific writer and novelist known principally for her antifeminism.

Lister, Anne (1791–1840): Yorkshire gentrywoman. Inherited the Lister estate upon the death of her uncle. Kept a diary recounting (in code) her many affairs with women; also recorded current events, her political and economic work in the Halifax area, and her travels to the continent.

Micas, Nathalie (1824–89): Lifelong intimate friend and support of the painter Rosa Bonheur; part-time inventor.

Paget, Violet. *See* Lee, Vernon

Pirie, Jane (1784–1821?): Daughter of a writer of religious books; granddaughter of a Presbyterian minister. Worked as a governess until she and Marianne Woods jointly opened a school for young ladies in 1809. Party, with Woods, to a lawsuit for libel in 1811. More pious and short-tempered than Woods.

Ponsonby, Lady Mary Bulteel (1832–1916): Married to Sir Henry Ponsonby, private secretary to Queen Victoria. Active in the movement for women's higher education and for women's trade unions. Spent her later years with women friends, including the composer and writer Ethel Smyth.

Ponsonby, Sarah (1755–1831): Orphaned daughter of a poor branch of a large Irish Protestant family. Lived with her partner, Lady Eleanor Butler, as the quieter, more domestic Lady of Llangollen.

Robinson, A. Mary F. (1857–1944): Poet, translator, and *femme des lettres*. Vernon Lee's first intimate friend. Later married two different Frenchmen. Held a literary salon for many years in Paris, where she was known as Madame Duclaux.

Simcox, Edith (1844–1901): Journalist, philosophical writer, co-owner of a shirtmaking cooperative. Active in the women's trade union movement and international socialism. In love with the novelist George Eliot.

Smyth, Ethel (1858–1943): Composer and writer who published nine memoirs about her passionate friendships with women, her relationship with the American aesthete Harry Brewster, and her efforts to get her music performed.

Tarn, Pauline. *See* Vivien, Renée

Troubridge, Una (1887–1963): Married an admiral, but formally separated after she began living with Radclyffe Hall. Supported Hall throughout *The Well of Loneliness* trial for obscenity and protected Hall's reputation after her death.

Vivien, Renée (1877–1909): Pseudonym of Pauline Tarn, a wealthy Anglo-American who wrote nonrealistic poetry and fiction in French exploring lesbian desire and its consequences. Died from alcoholism and anorexia. An early lover of Natalie Barney.

Walker, Ann (1803–54). Yorkshire heiress and neighbor of Anne Lister. Suffered from depression.

Woods, Marianne (1783–?): Niece of William Woods, comedy actor in Edinburgh. Taught rhetoric and elocution. Met Jane Pirie in 1802 and joined her in 1809 in opening a school for young ladies. With Pirie, sued Dame Cumming Gordon for libel in 1811.

NOTES

The following abbreviations have been used throughout the notes:

AA   Asburton Accession, Ashburton Collection, National Library of Scotland
BL   British Library
BRP   Bessie Rayner Parkes Papers, Girton College, Cambridge University
CC   Charlotte Cushman Papers, Cushman Collection, Manuscript Division, Library of Congress
DB   Mary Benson diary and letters, Deposit Benson, Bodleian Library, Oxford University
MW   *Miss Marianne Woods and Miss Jane Pirie against Dame Helen Cumming Gordon* (New York: Arno Press, 1975)
VLC   Vernon Lee Collection, Special Collections, Colby College

INTRODUCTION

1. William Rounseville Alger, *The Friendships of Women.* 10th ed. (Boston: Roberts Brothers, 1882), p. vi.

2. Ibid., p. viii.

3. For a discussion of Claire and Julie's friendship, see Janet Todd, *Women's Friendship in Literature* (New York: Columbia University Press, 1980), pp. 132–67.

4. Emma Donoghue, *Passions Between Women: British Lesbian Culture, 1668–1801* (London: Scarlet Press, 1993), pp. 183–219, discusses lesbians in pornography.

5. Anne Lister was exceptional in knowing Latin. She asked a friend if she had read the Sixth Satire of Juvenal to ascertain her knowledge of lesbian sexuality. Anna Clark, "Anne Lister's Construction of Lesbian Identity," *Journal of the History of Sexuality* 7 (1996): 39.

6. For attitudes toward female sexuality before and after the French Revolution, see Lynn Hunt, "The Many Bodies of Marie Antoinette: Political Pornography and the Problem of the Feminine in the French Revolution," in *Eroticism and the Body Politic,* ed. Lynn Hunt (Baltimore: Johns Hopkins University Press, 1991), pp. 108–30; Jeffrey Merrick, "The Marquis de Villette and Mademoiselle de Raucourt: Representations of Male and Female Sexual Deviance in Late Eighteenth Century France," and Elizabeth Colwill, "Pass as a Woman, Act Like a Man: Marie-Antoinette as Tribade in the Pornography of the French Revolution," in *Homosexuality in Modern France,* ed. Jef-

frey Merrick and Bryant T. Ragan, Jr. (New York: Oxford University Press, 1996), pp. 30–53, 54–79, respectively.

7. Susan S. Lanser, "Befriending the Body: Female Intimacies as Class Acts," *Eighteenth-Century Studies* 32 (Winter 1998–99): 192. See also Katherine Binhammer, "The Sex Panic of the 1790s," *Journal of the History of Sexuality* 6 (1996).

8. Alger, *Friendships of Women*, p. 4.

9. Harriette Andreadis, "Theorizing Early Modern Lesbianisms: Invisible Bodies, Ambiguous Demarcations," in *Virtual Gender: Fantasies of Subjectivity and Embodiment*, ed. Mary Ann O'Farrell and Lynne Vallone (Ann Arbor: University of Michigan Press, 1999), p. 144, n 29. See also pp. 131–34.

10. See Henry Abelove, "Some Speculations on the History of Sexual Intercourse During the Long Eighteenth Century," *Genders* 6 (Fall 1989): 125–30, for a discussion of "cross-genital intercourse (penis in vagina, vagina around penis, with seminal emission uninterrupted)."

11. Anne Lister, *I Know My Own Heart: The Diaries of Anne Lister (1791–1840)*, ed. Helena Whitbread (London: Virago, 1988), p. 145.

12. Mary Benson to Chat Bassett, 18 Feb. [1880], DB 3/28.

13. Benson diary, 1 Oct. 1896, 6 May 1898, St. Peter's Day 1898 entries, DB 1/78.

14. The needless homophobia of Anna Mary Wells, *Miss Marks and Miss Wooley* (Boston: Houghton Mifflin, 1978), started this debate.

15. Jennifer Terry, "Theorizing Deviant Historiography," *Differences* 3 (1991). See also Estelle Freedman, "'The Burning of Letters Continues': Elusive Identities and the Historical Construction of Sexuality," *Journal of Women's History* 9 (1998); and Jacquelyn Dowd Hall, "'To Widen the Reach of Our Love': Autobiography, History and Desire," *Feminist Studies* 26 (Spring 2000).

16. Randolph Trumbach, "London's Sapphists: From Three Sexes to Four Genders in the Making of Modern Culture," in *Body Guards: The Cultural Politics of Gender Ambiguity*, ed. Julia Epstein and Kristina Straub (New York: Routledge, 1991), p. 112.

17. Carroll Smith-Rosenberg, "Discourses of Sexuality and Subjectivity: The New Woman, 1870–1936," in *Hidden from History: Reclaiming the Gay and Lesbian Past*, ed. Martin Bauml Duberman, Martha Vicinus, and George Chauncey, Jr. (New York: New American Library, 1989), pp. 275–76.

18. Elizabeth Lapovsky Kennedy and Madeline D. Davis, *Boots of Leather and Slippers of Gold: The History of a Lesbian Community* (New York: Penguin, 1994), p. 3.

19. Judith M. Bennett, "'Lesbian-Like' and the Social History of Lesbianism," *Journal of the History of Sexuality* 9 (2000): 10.

20. Leila Rupp, "Toward a Global History of Same-Sex Sexuality," *Journal of the History of Sexuality* 10 (2001): 287–88.

21. John Stokes, *In the Nineties* (New York: Harvester Wheatsheaf, 1989), p. 27.

22. See Judith Butler, *Gender Trouble: Feminism and the Subversion of Identity* (New York: Routledge, 1990), as well as her response to critics in the introduction to *Bodies That Matter: On the Discursive Limits of "Sex"* (New York: Routledge, 1993), pp. x–xi.

23. For a discussion of the many different meanings of "effeminacy," see Tim Hitchcock and Michèle Cohen, introduction to *English Masculinities, 1660–1800* (London: Longman, 1999), pp. 5–6.

24. Judith Halberstam, *Female Masculinity* (Durham, N.C.: Duke University Press, 1998), p. 15.

25. Dianne Dugaw, *Warrior Women and Popular Balladry, 1650–1850* (Cambridge: Cambridge University Press, 1989).

26. Katherine Raymond, "Confessions of a Second-Generation . . . Dyke? Re-flections on Sexual Non-Identity," in *PoMoSexuals: Challenging Assumptions About Gender and Sexuality*, ed. Carol Queen and Lawrence Schimel (San Francisco: Cleis Press, 1997), pp. 53–54.

27. Ibid., p. 61.

28. See Judith M. Bennett, "Confronting Continuity," *Journal of Women's History* 9 (1997), for an important discussion of this issue.

29. Jeffrey Weeks, *Sex, Politics and Society: The Regulation of Sexuality Since 1800* (London: Longman, 1981), p. 105. Consider also the 1918 Maud Allan case, which turned on Allan's knowledge of the word *clitoris* in relation to lesbianism. Lucy Bland, "Trial by Sexology? Maud Allan, *Salome*, and the 'Cult of the Clitoris,'" in *Sexology in Culture: Labeling Bodies and Desires*, ed. Lucy Bland and Laura Doan (Chicago: University of Chicago Press, 1998).

30. Virginia Woolf, *A Room of One's Own* (New York: Harcourt, Brace & Jovanovich, 1957), p. 49.

31. Sheridan LeFanu, "Carmilla," in *Best Ghost Stories of J. S. LeFanu*, ed. E. F. Bleiler (New York: Dover, 1964), p. 307.

32. Carol Lasser, "'Let us be sisters evermore': The Sororal Model of Nineteenth-Century Female Friendship," *Signs* 14 (1988): 164–65.

33. Ibid.: 164, n 11.

34. See George Haggerty's analysis of erotic sister-love in Jane Austen's *Sense and Sensibility*, in *Unnatural Affections: Women and Fiction in the Later Eighteenth Century* (Bloomington: Indiana University Press, 1998), pp. 73–87.

35. "A Celebrated slang consarn, as chaunted at various lush cribs," *The Rummy Cove's Delight* [ca. 1833]., in *Nineteenth-Century Writings on Homosexuality: A Sourcebook*, ed. Chris White (London: Routledge, 1999), pp. 15–16.

36. *Octavia Wilberforce: The Autobiography of A Pioneer Doctor*, ed. Pat Jalland (London: Cassell, 1989), p. 38. Note how the first sentence mixes the receiving of love with the giving of love.

37. Ibid., pp. 73–74.

38. Lister, *I Know My Own Heart*, p. 136.

39. E. F. Benson, *Final Edition* (London: Longmans, Green, 1940), pp. 134–40. "For days, in the hot June weather, a bonfire flared or smouldered in the cherry orchard, and into it I cast everything which might make mischief if it fell into wrong hands— 'when in doubt burn' was the safer course—and all such papers (and seaweeds) as nobody would have regretted if they had been destroyed years before" (p. 139).

CHAPTER ONE

1. The details in this paragraph are taken from Elizabeth Mavor, *The Ladies of Llangollen: A Study in Romantic Friendship* (Harmondsworth, Eng.: Penguin, 1973), pp. 19–27. Lady Fownes knew Eleanor Butler's mother slightly and had asked her to keep an eye on her ward while she was in school; this responsibility soon became Butler's.

2. Sarah Tighe to Mrs. Lucy Goddard, 2 April 1778, in *The Hamwood Papers of the Ladies of Llangollen*, ed. Mrs. G. H. Bell (London: Macmillan, 1930), p. 27.

3. Lady Betty Fownes to Lucy Goddard, Monday [13 April 1778], quoted in Mavor, *Ladies*, p. 31. She does not specify who "they" are, but the reference may be to the Butler family.

4. Lucy Goddard's unpub. diary, Saturday, 2 May [1778], quoted in *The Hamwood Papers*, p. 38.

5. Judith Butler, "Imitation and Gender Insubordination," in *Inside/Out: Lesbian Theories, Gay Theories*, ed. Diana Fuss (New York: Routledge, 1991), focuses on the instability of the lesbian identity to counter "the framework that privileges heterosexuality as origin" and lesbianism as "bad copy" (p. 17).

6. Mary Benson to Mrs. Charlotte Mary Bassett, n.d., DB 3/28.

7. Lady Betty Fownes to Lucy Goddard, Monday [13 April 1778], quoted in Mavor, *Ladies*, p. 31.

8. Bridget Hill, *Women Alone: Spinsters in England, 1660–1850* (New Haven, Conn.: Yale University Press, 2001), pp. 81–93, discusses the animosities "learned ladies" aroused.

9. Amanda Vickery, *The Gentleman's Daughter: Women's Lives in Georgian England* (New Haven, Conn.: Yale University Press, 1998), pp. 82–83.

10. *Journals and Correspondence of Dr. Whalley*, ed. Wickham (1863), p. 247, quoted in Mavor, *Ladies*, p. 90.

11. Mavor, *Ladies*, pp. 87, 100.

12. Jill Liddington, "Anne Lister of Shibden Hall, Halifax (1791–1840): Her Diaries and the Historians," *History Workshop Journal* 35 (1993): 62. Eliza Raine wrote this diary entry in the same code that Lister used in her diary and with Mariana Lawton.

13. The actor Charles Mathews noted that the elderly couple, when seated, had "not one point to distinguish them from men. [The] dressing and powdering of the hair, their well-starched neckcloths, the upper part of their habits which they always wear, even at a dinner party, made them precisely like men's coats, and regular black beaver men's hats." Mavor, *Ladies*, p. 198.

14. Joseph Leach, *Bright Particular Star: The Life and Times of Charlotte Cushman* (New Haven, Conn.: Yale University Press, 1970), p. 188. The Quaker journalist Mary Howitt noted their identical tailored suits.

15. Julia Markus, *Dared and Done: The Marriage of Elizabeth Barrett and Robert Browning* (New York: Alfred Knopf, 1995), p. 256.

16. Diana Mulock Craik, *A Woman's Thoughts on Women* (London: Hurst & Blackett, [1858]), p. 179.

17. 4 Oct. 1820 entry, in Anne Lister, *I Know My Own Heart: The Diaries of Anne Lister*, ed. Helena Whitbread (London: Virago, 1988), p. 136.

18. Mavor, *Ladies*, p. 23.

19. Andrew Elfenbein, *Romantic Genius: The Prehistory of a Homosexual Role* (New York: Columbia University Press, 1999), pp. 1–7. I am indebted to Elfenbein, pp. 5–13, for drawing my attention to the importance of genius in regard to eccentric, masculine women.

20. Thrale Piozzi, 9 Dec.1795, in *Thraliana*, 2: 949, quoted in Emma Donoghue, *Passions Between Women: British Lesbian Culture, 1668–1801* (London: Scarlet Press, 1993), p. 266. Donoghue, pp. 149–50, explores Thrale Piozzi's "doublethink" about romantic friendships and their potential dangers. Liz Stanley, "Romantic Friendships? Some Issues in Researching Lesbian History and Biography," *Women's History Review* 1 (1992): 196, drawing on the unpublished diaries, notes that Piozzi privately thought the Ladies were Sapphists.

21. As Colette remarks about this phrase in *The Pure and the Impure*, tr. Herma Briffault (New York: Farrar, Straus & Giroux, 1966), it is words "fallen a hundred times from the pen of Lady Eleanor Butler and a hundred times stowed away like a sentimental bookmark between the pages of her Journal" (p. 114).

22. Mavor, *Ladies*, p. 138.

23. "Verses by Mrs. Grant, inscribed to Lady Eleanor Butler and Miss Ponsonby," n.d., quoted in ibid., p. 93.

24. Hester Thrale Piozzi to Penelope Sophia Pennington, 9 March 1800, in *The Piozzi Letters: Correspondence of Hester Lynch Piozzi, 1784–1821 (formerly Mrs. Thrale)*, ed. Edward A. Bloom and Lillian D. Bloom (Newark: University of Delaware Press, 1993), 3: 173.

25. John Hicklin, *The "Ladies of Llangollen" as sketched by Many Hands; with notices of Other Objects of Interest in "That Sweetest of Vales"* (Chester: Thomas Catherall, 1847), p. 27.

26. Frances Power Cobbe to Sarah Wister, 4 Oct. [1896], Wister Papers [1962], Historical Society of Pennsylvania: "We, 'The Ladies of Hengwrt' as undersigned— not to be confused with the Ladies of Llangollen—return hearty thanks for the large & wonderful box of grapes duly received from our kind friend of Butler Place." I am indebted to Sally Mitchell for sharing this reference with me.

27. Colette, *Pure and Impure*, pp. 121, 123. Ellipsis in the original.

28. *A Year with the Ladies of Llangollen*, comp. and ed. Elizabeth Mavor (Harmondsworth, Eng.: Penguin, 1986), p. 13. The excerpts are arranged by month, emphasizing the continuity of their lives, regardless of time passing.

29. *Memoirs of Charles Mathews the Elder*, ed. Yates (1860), p. 232, quoted in Mavor, *Ladies*, p. 182. I am indebted to Susan S. Lanser for discussions on the desexualizing of the Ladies.

30. 23 July 1822 entry, in Lister, *I Know My Own Heart*, p. 202.

31. Ibid., p. 204.

32. 3 Aug. 1822 entry, in ibid., p. 210. See also Lisa L. Moore, *Dangerous Intimacies: Toward a Sapphic History of the British Novel* (Durham, N.C.: Duke University Press, 1997), pp. 83–84.

33. Mavor, *Ladies*, p. 74. For a discussion of this news report and similar incidents, see Moore, *Dangerous Intimacies*, especially pp. 83–84.

34. Gretchen van Slyke, "Reinventing Matrimony: Rosa Bonheur, Her Mother, and Her Friends," *Women's Studies Quarterly* 19 (1991): 73.

35. Anna Klumpke, *Rosa Bonheur: The Artist's (Auto)biography*, tr. Gretchen van Slyke (Ann Arbor: University of Michigan Press, 1997), p. 127. As van Slyke notes, this account is the creation of Klumpke, based on Bonheur's conversations with her. Klumpke has so successfully conveyed the feel and voice of Bonheur that it is easy to forget Klumpke's role (pp. xiii–xiv).

36. van Slyke, "Reinventing Matrimony," p. 69.

37. Paul Chardin, quoting the "elder M. Passy," in *Reminiscences of Rosa Bonheur*, ed. Theodore Stanton (New York: Hacker Art Books, 1976 [1910]), p. 85. Micas wore red and black because of her Spanish heritage, even though friends thought the colors inappropriate for her sallow complexion.

38. Ibid., p. 102.

39. See Colette, *Pure and Impure*, pp. 122–27. Colette fantasizes, "Surely she would have confessed everything; now and then there would be the hint of a subtle and perhaps traitorous attraction, a wealth of sensual effusions" (p. 126). Gretchen van Slyke compares Nathalie Micas's relationship with Rosa Bonheur to that of Alice Toklas with Gertrude Stein. Klumpke, *Rosa Bonheur*, p. xxvi.

40. Rosa Bonheur to Mme. August Cain, 7 July 1889, in *Reminiscences*, pp. 102–3. She wrote this letter following Nathalie Micas's death.

41. Ibid., p. 103.

42. Klumpke, *Rosa Bonheur*, p. 72.

43. Anna Clark, "Anne Lister's Construction of Lesbian Identity," *Journal of the His-*

tory of Sexuality 7 (1996), traces how Lister, without access to a lesbian subculture, created a lesbian identity by "creatively put[ting] together the fragmentary cultural materials available to her to understand her desires for women" (p. 31). Clark argues that Lister found the passionate friendship modeled by the Ladies insufficiently sexual, but successfully read Juvenal, Martial, and Ovid against the grain to find positive images of same-sex love. Jennifer Frangoes, "'I love and only love the fairer sex': The Writing of a Lesbian Identity in the Diaries of Anne Lister (1791–1840)," in *Women's Life-Writing: Finding Voice/Building Community*, ed. Linda S. Coleman (Bowling Green: Bowling Green State University Popular Press, 1997), explores the ways in which "the diarist is not writing to 'find herself,' but rather to construct the very identity she wishes to assume" (p. 45). Judith Halberstam, *Female Masculinity* (Durham, N.C.: Duke University Press, 1998), pp. 66–73, focuses on Lister's self-construction in order to claim her as an early example of female masculinity and not a lesbian.

44. Lister's activities during the politically and economically turbulent 1830s, a period when her local power and income were at their greatest, are now well documented in Jill Liddington, *Female Fortune: Land, Gender, and Authority: The Anne Lister Diaries and Other Writings, 1833–36* (London: Rivers Oram, 1998). As Liddington points out, the authority of the Tory gentry was declining in the face of working-class radicalism and mercantile economic power.

45. 29 Jan. 1821 entry, in Lister, *I Know My Own Heart*, p. 145. Ellipsis in the original.

46. 30 June 1817 entry, in ibid., p. 15. Whitbread has transcribed Lawton's name as both Marianne and Marianna, but Liddington spells it Mariana. For consistency I have used the last spelling.

47. 18 Nov. 1819 entry, in ibid., p. 104.

48. Anne Lister, *No Priest But Love: The Journals of Anne Lister, 1824–1826*, ed. Helena Whitbread (New York: New York University Press, 1992), pp. 122–23.

49. Most of the ridicule she was subjected to came from lower-class men and boys, but some incidents were political, in response to Lister's Tory activism. See, for examples of the first, entries for 28 June, 17 Sept. 1818, and 25 July 1819, and for the second, 11 Jan. and 5 May 1820, in Lister, *I Know My Own Heart*, pp. 48–49, 64–65, 92, 113–14, 123–24. The *Leeds Mercury* ran a comic advertisement claiming that Lister sought a husband, and then an announcement that she had found one in Ann Walker. Cited in the entry for 29 Nov. 1819, p. 106. She also received importuning and/or mocking letters offering to marry her.

50. Liddington, *Female Fortune*, pp. 16–17.

51. 5, 20 Dec. 1820 entries, in Lister, *I Know My Own Heart*, pp. 139, 140–41.

52. John Gillis, *For Better, For Worse: British Marriages, 1600 to the Present* (New York: Oxford University Press, 1985), pp. 21–37, discusses the varieties of heterosexual, nonpenetrative sex practiced in the eighteenth century.

53. 20 Jan. 1824 entry, in Lister, *No Priest But Love*, p. 78.

54. 25 Oct. 1824 entry, in ibid., p. 36.

55. 25 Oct., 13 Nov. 1824 entries, in ibid., pp. 36, 49. According to Lister, Tib Norcliffe suggested in 1819 that she would "willingly marry me in disguise at the altar." *I Know My Own Heart*, p. 105.

56. 2, 23 Sept. 1825 entries, in Lister, *No Priest But Love*, pp. 124, 131. For the earlier exchange of rings, see Whitbread's description, p. 134, n 2.

57. 21 Sept. 1825 entry, in ibid., p. 131. A few days earlier Anne had admitted to Mariana that she had asked for and had received pubic hair from the "queer" of other

women, but had never given away any of her own. See also 12 Sept. 1825, p. 127. The word *queer* for genitals was uncommon before 1700, but slang variations on "crooked" for female genitals seem to have led to the usage by Lister's time.

58. 15 Jan. 1826 entry, in ibid., p. 154. Lister herself made a distinction between friendship and love on one occasion, lying to her friend Miss Pickford, "My manners might mislead you, but I don't, in reality, go beyond the utmost verge of friendship." 5 Aug. 1823 entry, in Lister, *I Know My Own Heart*, p. 273. Before their affair began, Lister had told Maria Barlow, "she went to the utmost extent of friendship, but that was enough." Clark, "Anne Lister's Construction," p. 40.

59. 15 Jan. 1826 entry, in Lister, *No Priest But Love*, p. 155.

60. 6 May 1834 entry, quoted in Liddington, *Female Fortune*, p. 103. Written in code; ellipses and emphasis in the original.

61. See Terry Castle, "Matters Not Fit to Be Mentioned: Fielding's The Female Husband," *ELH* 49 (Fall 1982). Consider also the intriguing "bachelor" Dr. James Barry (1795?–1865), who survived in the army by never drinking and keeping his distance from fellow officers. Isobel Rae, *The Strange Story of Dr. James Barry, Army Surgeon, Inspector-General of Hospitals, Discovered on Death to Be a Woman* (London: Longmans, 1958), discusses the known facts about Barry.

62. Betty T. Bennett, *Mary Diana Dods: A Gentleman and a Scholar* (New York: William Morrow, 1991). Unfortunately, Bennett writes her tale of discovery in the breathless style of an adventurer, always denying its homoerotic implications. See especially pp. 256–69.

63. [Eliza Rennie], *Traits of Character; Being Twenty-Five Years' Literary and Personal Recollections, By a Contemporary* (London: Hurst & Plackett, 1860), quoted in Bennett, *Mary Diana Dods*, p. 93, without page attribution.

64. Bennett, *Mary Diana Dods*, p. 156, quoting Mary Shelley's final *Journal* entry on the Douglases for November 1830. Most of Shelley's comments are about Isabella Robinson, leaving Dods a mysterious, perhaps misanthropic, figure.

65. Ibid., pp. 233–34.

66. Mavor, *Ladies*, pp. 53–72, provides details, including the 1788 account book showing an income of £289.3.01 and expenses of £444.13.02 (p. 64). The following year they began to receive a Civil List pension of £100. Throughout her life Anne Lister was equally meticulous in recording her income and expenditures.

67. 27 Sept., 14 Dec. 1832 entries, quoted in Liddington, "Anne Lister," pp. 69–70.

68. Liddington, *Female Fortune*, p. 250. See also Jill Liddington, "Beating the Inheritance Bounds: Anne Lister (1791–1840) and Her Dynastic Identity," *Gender & History* 7 (1995): 260–74.

69. Liddington, *Female Fortune*, pp. 95, 98. As Liddington notes, Lister's unusually confusing syntax leaves it unclear exactly who did what for whom.

70. Liddington discusses these difficulties in ibid., pp. 63–72. The Sutherlands were investigating a prospective suitor, Mr. Ainsworth, at the time Lister was courting Walker.

71. I am indebted to Liddington, ibid., p. 244, for reminding me of the significant differences in marital customs and behaviors between the 1830s and the present day.

72. Ibid., pp. 190–91.

73. 11 March 1824 entry, in Lister, *I Know My Own Heart*, p. 330.

74. 19 June 1824 entry, in ibid., p. 347. Radclyffe Hall's use of a "freak of nature" in describing her lesbian heroine, Stephen, is discussed in chap. 8.

75. Liddington, *Female Fortune*, p. 65.

76. *Year with the Ladies,* p. 205.

77. Rosa Bonheur, "Testamentary Letter of November 28, 1898," in Klumpke, *Rosa Bonheur,* p. 266. See also James M. Saslow "'Disagreeably Hidden': Construction and Constriction of the Lesbian Body in Rosa Bonheur's *Horse Fair,*" in *The Expanding Discourse: Feminism and Art History,* ed. Norma Braude and Mary D. Garrard (New York: HarperCollins, 1992).

78. van Slyke, "Reinventing Matrimony," p. 72.

79. My reading is the opposite of van Slyke's. She suggests that women such as Bonheur managed in their wills to subvert the law that banned female-female marriage, establishing "a transformed sense of matrimony: the transmission of property from woman to woman, bypassing the traditional father-son circuit and voiding the age-old prerogative of males in such matters." "Reinventing Matrimony," p. 72. See also Gretchen van Slyke, "Gynocentric Matrimony: The Fin-de-Siècle Alliance of Rosa Bonheur and Anna Klumpke," *Nineteenth-Century Contexts* 20 (1999).

CHAPTER TWO

1. For a full discussion of the appeal of the Mediterranean for male homosexuals, see Robert Aldrich, *The Seduction of the Mediterranean: Writing, Art and Homosexual Fantasy* (London: Routledge, 1993).

2. Jeffrey Weeks, *Sex, Politics, and Society: The Regulation of Sexuality Since 1800* (London: Longman, 1981), p. 116.

3. Entry for 5 Aug.1823, in Anne Lister, *I Know My Own Heart: The Diaries of Anne Lister,* ed. Helena Whitbread (London: Virago, 1988), p. 273.

4. John Pemble, *The Mediterranean Passion: Victorians and Edwardians in the South* (Oxford: Clarendon Press, 1987), p. 39.

5. See Henry James, *William Wetmore Story and His Friends* (Boston: Houghton Mifflin, 1903), 1: 257–62, 294–96, for a retrospective analysis of the women sculptors and the general artistic atmosphere of the times.

6. Charlotte Cushman to Emma Crow Cushman, 28 March 1863, CC Papers, vol. 2.

7. Frances Power Cobbe, *Italics: Brief Notes on Politics, People, and Places in Italy in 1864* (London: Trübner, 1864), p. 398.

8. Sally Mitchell, "'From Winter into Summer': The Italian Evolution of Frances Power Cobbe," *Women's Writing* 10 (2003): 347. See also Sarah Foose Parrott, "Networking in Italy: Charlotte Cushman and 'The White Marmorean Flock,'" *Women's Studies* 14 (1988): 307, on the same point.

9. Frances Power Cobbe, *Life of Frances Cobbe* (Boston: Houghton, Mifflin, 1894), 2: 358.

10. Mrs. Russell Barrington, *The Life, Letters, and Work of Frederic Leighton* (London: George Allen, 1906), 1: 146.

11. James, *William Wetmore Story,* 1: 254–55.

12. Dolly Sherwood, *Harriet Hosmer, American Sculptor, 1830–1908* (Columbia: University of Missouri Press, 1991), p. 118.

13. Cobbe, *Life,* 2: 358.

14. James, *William Wetmore Story,* 1: 255.

15. Lisa Merrill, *When Romeo Was a Woman: Charlotte Cushman and Her Circle of Female Spectators* (Ann Arbor: University of Michigan Press, 1999), pp. 110–30, 160–65, 181, documents Cushman's increasing fame on both sides of the Atlantic.

16. Lydia Maria Child wrote Hosmer in October 1859: "Mrs S[artois] in a letter

last week, in speaking of you, says, 'I love that child.' I don't know whether you like to have friends call you a child, I do." *Harriet Hosmer: Letters and Memories,* ed. Cornelia Carr (London: John Lane, 1913), p. 147. Hosmer was thirty-one at the time.

17. Fanny Kemble to Cornelia Carr, 8 Oct. [1853], Harriet Goodhue Hosmer Collection, Schlesinger Library, Harvard. Story makes similar, more negative comments. See James, *William Wetmore Story,* 1: 255.

18. 30 Dec. 1853, in *Elizabeth Barrett Browning: Letters to Her Sister, 1846–59,* ed. Leonard Huxley (London: John Murray, 1929), p. 196.

19. Grace Greenwood [Sara Lippincott], *Haps and Mishaps or A Tour of Europe* (Boston: Ticknor, Reed & Fields, 1865), pp. 217–18.

20. Matilda Hays, *Adrienne Hope: The Story of a Life* (London: T. Cautley Newby, 1866), 1: 45. Merrill, *When Romeo Was a Woman,* pp. 185–86, discusses how Hays embedded an attack on her former lover Charlotte Cushman into the heterosexual plot.

21. Judith Johnston, *Anna Jameson: Victorian, Feminist, Woman of Letters* (Aldershot, Eng.: Scolar Press, 1997), p. 233.

22. When rumors reached Hawthorne that Lander had been consorting with a man and earning money modeling, he cut her without making further inquiries. When she refused to participate in an informal court of inquiry, she was summarily dismissed from the Anglo-American circle. She returned to America to continue her career. See T. Walter Herbert, *Dearest Beloved: The Hawthornes and the Making of the Middle-Class Family* (Berkeley: University of California Press, 1993), p. 231.

23. Nathaniel Hawthorne, *The French and Italian Notebooks,* ed. Thomas Woodson (Columbus: Ohio State University Press, 1980), p. 158.

24. Mrs. E. F. Ellet [Elizabeth Fries], *Women Artists in All Ages and Countries* (New York: Harper & Brothers, 1859), p. 535. Matilda Hays wrote Cornelia Carr in April 1856, "she has developed a charming little waist and figure." Carr, *Harriet Hosmer,* p. 69.

25. William L. Vance, *America's Rome* (New Haven, Conn.: Yale University Press, 1989), 1: 211. Vance notes that since men were the main purchasers of sculptures, female nudes sold better than male nudes. See Joy S. Kasson, *Marble Queens and Captives: Women in Nineteenth-Century American Sculpture* (New Haven, Conn.: Yale University Press, 1990), p. 144, for a discussion of Hosmer's androgyny in the context of her statue *Zenobia.*

26. Hawthorne, *French and Italian Notebooks,* p. 158.

27. Geraldine Jewsbury to Emma Stebbins, 6 Feb. 1877, CC Papers, vol. 11. Emphasis in the original. She added, "the younger daughter was the mother's favourite."

28. Merrill, *When Romeo Was a Woman,* pp. 6, 9, 74.

29. Ibid., pp. 182–86, discusses how this "tussle before witnesses" revealed the deep erotic ties under romantic friendship. For Hays's later career as an editor of the *Englishwoman's Journal,* see Pam Hirsch, *Barbara Leigh Smith Bodichon (1827–1891): Feminist, Artist and Rebel* (London: Chatto & Windus, 1998), pp. 188–89, 196–200.

30. Rosalie Osborne Binstadt to Charlotte Cushman, [1868], quoted in Merrill, *When Romeo Was a Woman,* p. 196.

31. Charlotte Cushman to Emma Crow [Cushman], 27 April 1858, CC Papers, vol. 1. All the Cushman to Crow letters in the succeeding citations are from this volume of the papers unless otherwise noted.

32. Ibid., 30 June [1858], 3 May 1860. Similar comments are made frequently, along with reminders to Emma Crow to be careful about her letters.

33. Ibid., 3 Feb. 1858.

34. Ibid, [1858]. Emphasis in the original.

35. Ibid., 12 Aug.1858.

36. Ibid., 30 June 1860. Emphasis in the original.

37. Merrill, *When Romeo Was a Woman*, pp. 206–9.

38. Harriet Hosmer to Wayman Crow, 17 July 1858, quoted in ibid., p. 209. Ellipses Merrill's. For a different interpretation, see Sherwood, *Harriet Hosmer*, p. 167.

39. Harriet Hosmer to Wayman Crow, 22 Dec. 1858, quoted in Merrill, *When Romeo Was a Woman*, p. 209.

40. Charlotte Cushman to Emma Crow [Cushman], 9 March 1860.

41. Ibid., 4 April 1860.

42. Ibid., 3 May 1860. Emphasis in the original.

43. Ibid., 8 May 1860.

44. Ibid., 27 July 1860.

45. Charlotte Cushman to Emma Crow Cushman, 26 Jan. 1865, quoted in Merrill, *When Romeo Was a Woman*, p. 231. Emphasis in the original.

46. Ibid., p. 222.

47. Ibid., pp. 222, 235.

48. Charlotte Cushman to Emma Crow [Cushman], 24 June 1860.

49. Ibid., 20 June 1860.

50. Charlotte Cushman to Emma Crow Cushman, 8 Aug. 1861. Several letters in 1863 and 1864 speak of Stebbins's uncertain health.

51. Ibid., 11 May 1865, CC Papers, vol. 3. Emphasis in the original. Uncharacteristically, a letter addressed only to Emma ends addressed to both her and Ned.

52. Ibid.

53. Ibid. Emphasis in the original.

54. For details of their quarrel, see Sherwood, *Harriet Hosmer*, pp. 296–301.

55. Charlotte Cushman to Mary Lloyd, 23 Sept. 1874, quoted in Merrill, *When Romeo Was a Woman*, p. 239.

56. Charlotte Cushman to Emma Crow Cushman, 30 Jan. 1862, CC Papers, vol. 2. At the time women schoolteachers in Boston earned an average of $39 a month. See Carl F. Kaestle and Maris A. Vinovskis, *Education and Social Change in Nineteenth-Century Massachusetts* (Cambridge: Cambridge University Press, 1980), p. 263.

57. Harriet Hosmer to Wayman Crow, 12 Oct 1854, in Carr, *Harriet Hosmer*, pp. 32.

58. Sherwood, *Harriet Hosmer*, pp. 118–19.

59. Elizabeth Barrett Browning to Isa Blagden, 20 March [1860], quoted in ibid., p. 204. Charlotte Cushman also mentioned expensive gifts given to Hosmer in a letter to Emma Crow Cushman, 23 Nov. 1861, CC Papers, vol. 1.

60. Harriet Hosmer to Wayman Crow, 10 Aug. 1867, in Carr, *Harriet Hosmer*, p. 230.

61. Harriet Hosmer to Wayman Crow, 7 Aug. 1855,in Sherwood, *Harriet Hosmer*, p. 124. Sherwood sees Hosmer as fixated on older men and needing maternal, asexual comfort from women. She normalizes nineteenth-century female friendships as both asexual and wholly acceptable (pp. 169–71, 270–73).

62. Ibid., p. 270, quoting a February 1867 letter.

63. John Gibson to Harriet Hosmer, September 1858, quoted in Carr, *Harriet Hosmer*, p. 134. "Miss F—" probably refers to Margaret Foley, a Vermont-born cameo cutter, whom Cushman helped to obtain commissions.

64. Leach, *Bright Particular Star*, p. 258. See also Merrill, *When Romeo Was a Woman*, pp. 176–77.

65. Virginia Surtees, *The Ludovisi Goddess: The Life of Louisa, Lady Ashburton* (Salisbury: Michael Russell, 1984), p. 11.

66. Lady Walburga Ehrengarde Helena von Hohenthal Paget, *Embassies of Other Days* (London: Hutchinson, 1923), 1: 280–81.

67. Harriet Hosmer to Lady Ashburton, n.d., AA.11388/81. The succeeding citations of Hosmer's letters to Lady Asburton are from this file unless otherwise noted.

68. Surtees, *Ludovisi Goddess*, p. 161. Ellipses Surtees'. Surtees combines excerpts from several undated letters.

69. Hosmer to Ashburton, Saturday night [1875?].

70. Harriet Hosmer to Cornelia Carr, undated fragment [Dec. 1872?], in Sherwood, *Harriet Hosmer*, p. 272.

71. Hosmer to Lady Ashburton, Sat. Oct [1872?].

72. Ibid., Rome, Nov19 [1867]. Hosmer uses the slang "coze" to mean a long, cozy conversation.

73. Ibid., n.d. See AA 11388/10 for Hosmer's letters to Maysie Baring, virtually all of which are addressed to Twinniekins.

74. Hosmer to Lady Ashburton [Spring 1876?].

75. See Vance, *America's Rome*, 1: 184, 196–97, for American responses to the *Laocoön*. Nathaniel Hawthorne was fascinated with the statue. See, for example, *French and Italian Notebooks*, pp. 125, 138.

76. Surtees, *Ludovisi Goddess*, p. 161. Ellipses Surtees'.

77. For a discussion of *The Sleeping Faun*, its purchase by Sir Benjamin Guiness, and the extant replicas, see Kathryn Greenthal et al., *American Figurative Sculpture in the Museum of Fine Arts Boston* (Boston: Museum of Fine Arts, 1986), pp. 163–67. Cornelia Crow Carr offered the Museum of Fine Arts a copy of Hosmer's "best-seller," *Puck*, but the directors refused it (p. 167, n 18).

78. Carr, *Harriet Hosmer*, p. 223.

79. Frances Power Cobbe, "Ireland and Her Exhibition in 1865," *Fraser's Magazine*, 72 (July–Dec. 1865): 422. H. W., "Lady Artists in Rome," *The Art Journal*, 28 (June 1866): 177, speaks of the "perfect *abandon* of the figure." See also "The Dublin International Exhibition," *Illustrated London News*, Aug. 19, 1865, p. 165; and J. H. P. "The Fine Arts at the Dublin International Exhibition of 1865," *The Month*, August 1865: 186–93.

80. Andrea Marini, "Sleeping and Waking Fauns: Harriet Goodhue Hosmer's Experience of Italy, 1852–1870," in *The Italian Presence in American Art, 1760–1860*, ed.Irma B. Jaffe (New York: Fordham University Press, 1989), p.78. Marini places Hosmer's statue in the context of American responses to Italy as Arcadia.

81. Harriet Hosmer to Wayman Crow, Oct. 1866, quoted in Carr, *Harriet Hosmer*, p. 221.

82. Hosmer to Wayman Crow, Dec. 1867, quoted in ibid., p. 259.

83. Hosmer to Lady Ashburton, n.d., AA 11388/81. Sherwood, *Harriet Hosmer*, p. 311, says the *Pompeiian Sentinel* was exhibited in 1878, whereas Carr, *Harriet Hosmer*, pp. 246–49, sets the year as 1867. I have followed Carr.

84. Sidney Everett and his sister advanced Hosmer several thousand dollars for a statue of their father to be placed in Mt.Auburn Cemetery, Cambridge, Mass. Throughout the 1870s they wrote asking why the statue was not completed. See the correspondence of Charlotte Everett Wise, in Hosmer Collection, Schlesinger Library, A-162 (14).

85. See William Whitla, "Browning and the Ashburton Affair," *Browning Society Notes* 2 (July 1972).

86. Robert Browning to Emelyn Story, 4 April 1872, in *Robert Browning to His Amer-*

ican Friends: Letters Between the Brownings, Storys and James Russell Lowell, 1841–90, ed. Gertrude Reese Hudson (London: Bowes & Bowes, 1965), pp. 170–71.

87. See William Irvine and Park Honan, *The Book, the Ring, and the Poet* (New York: McGraw-Hill, 1974), pp. 444–54. The authors also emphasize the class difference between Browning and Lady Ashburton.

88. Maisie Ward, *Robert Browning and His World* (London: Cassell, 1969), 2: 297.

89. Henry James to Alice James, 10 Feb. 1873, in Henry James, *Letters,* ed. Leon Edel (Cambridge, Mass.: Belknap Press, 1974), 1: 339.

CHAPTER THREE

1. Lord Meadowlark, "Speeches of the Judges of the Second Division of the Court of Session," *Miss Marianne Woods and Miss Jane Pirie against Dame Helen Cumming Gordon* (New York: Arno, 1975), p. 2. Citations for this source, abbreviated as MW, are by section title (or a short form of it) and page number. In Scotland at this time a libel case went first to a hearing judge, the Lord Ordinary. If he felt that the case merited a hearing, as Lord Meadowbank had ruled in this instance, it went forward to the Lords of Session , a panel of seven judges. Each judge was expected to prepare a brief, explaining his decision, though all did not do so. There were no trials by jury.

2. See Martha Vicinus, "Lesbian History: All Theory and No Facts or All Facts and No Theory?" *Radical History Review* 60 (1994), for a discussion of the interpretive problems surrounding lesbian history.

3. Ed Cohen, *Talk on the Wilde Side: Toward a Genealogy of a Discourse on Male Sexualities* (New York: Routledge, 1993), especially pp. 4–5.

4. The trial is most readily available in Lillian Faderman's fictionalized *Scotch Verdict: Pirie and Woods v. Dame Cumming Gordon* (New York: Morrow, 1983). Faderman found a few details about Marianne Woods's aunt, Anne Quelch Woods, a minor actress married to a well-known local actor, who had died in 1802. She also includes information about the judges.

5. MW, "State of Process," pp. 70–71.

6. Ibid., p. 71.

7. Ibid., pp. 46–47.

8. Lord Gillies, MW, "Speeches of the Judges," p. 92.

9. MW, "State of Process," p. 139. Emphasis in the original.

10. MW, "Speeches of the Judges," p. 67. Emphasis in the original.

11. Faderman, *Scotch Verdict,* p. 107. Faderman also provides a believable reconstruction of these quarrels based on the economic uncertainty of the school and the intrusive aunt, Mrs. Woods (pp. 30–37).

12. Lord Woodhouselee, MW, "Speeches of the Judges," p. 81.

13. Lord Meadowbank, ibid., p. 7. Emphasis in the original.

14. Ibid., p. 8.

15. Cleland's *Memoirs of a Woman of Pleasure* was published at least thirteen times between 1800 and 1850. Lisa Z. Sigel, *Governing Pleasures: Pornography and Social Change in England, 1815–1914* (New Brunswick, N.J.: Rutgers University Press, 2002), p. 28.

16. MW, "Additional Petition," p. 25. Emphasis in the original.

17. MW, "State of the Process," p. 56.

18. Lord Woodhouselee, MW, "Speeches of the Judges," p. 69.

19. Lord Gillies, ibid., p. 92.

20. Lisa L. Moore, *Dangerous Intimacies: Toward a Sapphic History of the British Novel* (Durham, N.C.: Duke University Press, 1997), p. 79.

21. Lord Robertson, MW, "Notes of the Speeches," p. 4.

22. Ibid., p. 2.

23. Lord Woodhouselee, MW, "Speeches of the Judges," pp. 65, 66. Emphasis in the original.

24. Lord Gillies, ibid., pp. 92, 93.

25. MW, "State of the Process," p. 104.

26. Ibid., p. 108. Eliza Stirling's testimony corroborates that of Janet Munro (p. 48). Neither door to the drawing-room had a keyhole, but even if there had been one, the layout of the rooms proved that Whiffin could not have seen the couch through it (p. 158).

27. Ibid., Mary Brown's testimony corroborates that of Janet Munro (p. 48).

28. Lord Meadowbank, MW, "Speeches of the Judges," p. 37; Lord Robertson, MW, "Notes of the Speeches," p. 3.

29. See the retelling of the trial in William Roughead, *Bad Companions* (New York: Duffield & Green, 1941), pp. 111–46. Lillian Hellman based her play *The Children's Hour* (1934) on his version of events, but added a Freudian conclusion. See Mary Titus, "Murdering the Lesbian: Lillian Hellman's *The Children's Hour*," *Tulsa Studies in Women's Literature* 10.2 (1991): 215–32.

30. See Mary Poovey's discussion of Norton and the legislative efforts to broaden English divorce laws in *Uneven Developments: The Ideological Work of Gender in Mid-Victorian England* (Chicago: University of Chicago Press, 1988), pp. 51–88.

31. The details of the debates are analyzed by Mary Lyndon Shanley, *Feminism, Marriage, and the Law in Victorian England, 1850–1895* (Princeton, N.J.: Princeton University Press, 1989), pp. 22–48. See also Poovey, *Uneven Developments*, pp. 51–61.

32. The establishment of the Court for Divorce and Matrimonial Causes abolished the church courts' jurisdiction over the nullifying of marriages, vesting sole power in the new court to examine witnesses orally, to use a jury, to assign child custody, to order maintenance, and to assess costs. Collusion, connivance, and mutual guilt barred divorce. Deserted and judicially separated wives had their future earnings and property protected. The principals could not testify in court until 1869, and only an abbreviated court record was kept.

33. *Dictionary of National Biography*, ed. Sir Leslie Stephen and Sir Sidney Lee (Oxford: Oxford University Press, 1921–22), 4: 664.

34. *The Times*, 18 Nov. 1864: 9. See also the radical *Lloyd's Weekly London Newspaper*, 20 Nov. 1864: 7, which gives a more favorable version of Helen Codrington: "She was also artless, and the most guiltless and the most deceitless person who was ever placed in such a position. She talked rodomontade about her own affairs, being one of those persons who always use superlatives when they should use positives, and who were always endeavouring to create a sensation amongst themselves. There was no one better acquainted with that fact than her husband himself."

35. Jane Rendall, "Friendship and Politics: Barbara Leigh Smith Bodichon (1827–91) and Bessie Rayner Parkes (1829–1925)," in *Sexuality and Subordination*, ed. Susan Mendus and Jane Rendall (London: Routledge, 1989), p. 143.

36. Details about Faithfull's life are found in William E. Fredeman, "Emily Faithfull and the Victoria Press: An Experiment in Sociological Bibliography," *The Library* 29 (June 1974).

37. *The Times*, 21 Nov. 1864: 11.

38. Ibid., 30 July 1864: 10.

39. The colonel shared with the admiral a love of authority. The historian of An-

derson's regiment describes him as "one of the old school of British Officers [who] exercised an iron discipline which earned for him the title of one of the most stern but just Colonels in the Service." See Arthur Crookenden, *Twenty-Second Footsteps, 1849– 1914: An Account of the Life of the 22nd (Cheshire) Regiment in those years* (Chester, Eng.: privately published, 1956), p. 32.

40. Deposition filed on behalf of Helen Jane Codrington by Robert Few, her attorney. United Kingdom Public Record Office, XPO984CL J77/11/142.

41. Lady Bourchier, Henry's sister, obliquely justifies his unwillingness to accompany his wife to parties: "At moments he worked so hard, and so much at undue hours, that his health would quite have given way, if his doctor had not interfered and insisted on a change of system and of hours." Lady Bourchier, *Selections from the Letters of Sir Henry Codrington, Admiral of the Fleet* (London: Spottiswoode, 1880), p. 476.

42. *The Times*, 18 Nov. 1864: 9. The admiral "denied having used the least violence to her, but had admitted that he had removed her from his bedroom . . . one night after she had been dancing."

43. Ibid.: 8.

44. Ibid., 30 July 1864: 10.

45. Joseph Parkes to Bessie Rayner Parkes, 2 Aug. 1864, BRP 2/80. In contrast, see an earlier comment to his daughter, "Young English women will not believe, till older, in the natural distinctions of the two sexes; & that the Males will never allow the Females to wear men's clothes—much less to usurp their natural sexal [sic] superiority." 6 Oct. 1858, BRP, Ret 2/64. I am indebted to Kate Perry for checking these letters.

46. *The Times*, 1 Aug. 1864: 10. Deposition of Giovanni Battista Scichma, a boatman.

47. Ibid., 30 July 1864: 10.

48. Ibid., 21 Nov. 1864: 11.

49. Joseph Parkes to Bessie Rayner Parkes, 23 Jan. 1864, BRP 2/79. Emphasis in the original.

50. *Daily Telegraph*, 24 Nov. 1864: 4.

51. Joseph Parkes to Bessie Rayner Parkes, 23 Jan. 1864, BRP 2/79.

52. *The Law Journal Reports*, n.s. 34 (1864–65): 62.

53. Crookenden, *Twenty-Second Footsteps*, p. 32.

54. *Reynolds's Newspaper*, 27 Nov. 1864: 4.

55. Joseph Parkes to Bessie Rayner Parkes, 19 Nov. 1864, BRP 2/82.

56. Ibid., 23 Jan. 1864, BRP 2/79. There is no evidence that any customers broke their contracts with the Victoria Press.

57. Robert Browning to Isa Blagden, 19 Jan. 1865, in Edward C. McLeer, ed., *Dearest Isa: Robert Browning's Letters to Isabella Blagden* (Austin: University of Texas Press, 1951), p. 76. Browning incorrectly stated that the queen removed her "Royal Printership at once" from the Victoria Press; she never did so. Two years later he would write Blagden about the "not niceness" of Harriet Hosmer.

58. Eve Kosofsky Sedgwick, *Epistemology of the Closet* (Berkeley: University of California Press, 1990), pp. 3–5.

59. Emily Faithfull to Miss Phillips, 22 Feb. 1874. Fawcett Library Autograph Letter Collection, V12A, V12B, The Women's Library, London. Apparently the letter was forwarded to Hubbard for comment. Hubbard came from a wealthy merchant family; she could well afford to look down on a clergyman's daughter. I am indebted to Ellen Jordan for sharing this reference with me.

60. Emily Davies, "Family Chronicle," pp. 337–38, Girton College, Cambridge University. I am indebted to Barbara Caine for sharing this reference with me.

61. See Faithfull's comments on American divorces in *Three Visits to America* (Edinburgh: David Douglas, 1884), pp. 262–74.

62. Mrs. E. C. Wolstenholme Elmy to Harriet McIlquham, 30 Nov. 1898, unpub. correspondence, British Library add. mss. 47451/f.271. I am indebted to Barbara Caine for sharing this reference with me.

63. Emily Faithfull, *A Reed Shaken in the Wind: A Love Story* (New York: Adams, Victor, 1873), p. v. I have used this edition since the English edition is not easily available, but I have kept the book's original title, *Change upon Changes*, in the text.

64. Ibid., pp. 20, 39.

65. Ibid., p. 285.

66. Ibid., p. 286. Emphasis in the original.

67. Ibid., p. 61.

68. Ibid., p. 247.

69. Ibid., p. 251.

70. A second letter of Helen Codrington's was found in the stolen desk. Dated 1859, it was from an unidentified "Lillian" in Brighton, who teasingly mentioned "a scrape rushing into a man's room in your nightgown with your pretty naked feet" and added mockingly, "Thank God I have heard nothing of or from anything called Faithfull, and I am calming down, though I feel as if I should shoot out quills all over me at the sight of one." *The Times*, 30 July 1864: 10.

71. Ethyl Smyth to Harry Brewster, 6 Oct 1892, in Ethel Smyth, *As Time Went On . . .* (London: Longmans, Green, 1936), p. 156. Ellipsis in the original.

72. Harry Brewster to Ethel Smyth, 29 Oct. 1892, in ibid., p. 159.

73. Ethel Smyth, *What Happened Next* (London: Longmans Green, 1940), p. 252.

74. Ibid.

CHAPTER FOUR

1. Feminist historians have examined various aspects of Victorian women and religion. See *Religion in the Lives of English Women, 1760–1930*, the pioneering collection edited by Gail Malmgreen (Bloomington: Indiana University Press, 1986), as well as such recent collections as *Women of Faith in Victorian Culture: Reassessing "The Angel in the House,"* ed. Anne Hogan and Andrew Bradstock (London: Macmillan, 1998); *Women's Theology in Nineteenth-Century Britain: Transfiguring the Faith of Their Fathers*, ed. Julie Melnyk (New York: Garland, 1998); and *Women, Religion and Feminism in Britain, 1750–1900*, ed. Sue Morgan (London: Palgrave, 2002).

2. Benson retrospective diary describing the year 1864, DB 1/79. In addition to this retrospective work, a spiritual history written at the suggestion of Tan Mylne, Mary Benson kept a contemporaneous diary intermittently when under stress.

3. Linda Hunt Beckman, *Amy Levy: Her Life and Letters* (Athens: Ohio University Press, 2000), discusses Levy's complicated relationship to Judaism, as well as her infatuation with Vernon Lee.

4. Emma Donoghue, *We Are Michael Field* (Bath, Eng.: Absolute Press, 1998), p. 124. Donoghue mentions Radclyffe Hall and Una Troubridge, Renée Vivien and Violet Shilleto, "Tony" Atwood and Christopher St. John, and Alice B. Toklas.

5. Joanne Glasgow, "What's a Nice Lesbian Like You Doing in the Church of Torquemada? Radclyffe Hall and Other Catholic Converts," in *Lesbian Texts and Contexts: Radical Revisions*, ed. Karla Jay and Joanne Glasgow (New York: New York University Press, 1990), pp. 242–43. In the late twentieth century, religious homosexuals began vigorously claiming their place in mainstream churches. See, for example, Kathy Rudy,

Sex and the Church: Gender, Homosexuality, and the Transformation of Christian Ethics (Boston: Beacon Press, 1997); *The Lesbian and Gay Christian Movement: Campaigning for Justice, Truth and Love*, ed. Sean Gill (London: Cassell, 1998); and *Homosexuality and the Christian Community*, ed. Choon-Leong Seow (Louisville: Westminster John Knox Press, 1996).

6. Eliza Lynn Linton, *The Autobiography of Christopher Kirkland* (London: Richard Bentley, 1885), 1: 203.

7. Gordon S. Haight, *George Eliot: A Biography* (New York: Oxford University Press, 1968), pp. 450–55.

8. 3 Dec. 1878, in *A Monument to the Memory of George Eliot: Edith Simcox's "Autobiography of a Shirtmaker,"* ed. Constance M. Fulmer and Margaret E. Barfield (New York: Garland Press, 1998), p. 54.

9. There are fourteen references to Eliot as "Madonna" in *A Monument*. Men were more apt to call older women "teacher" than "mother."

10. Louisa Caroline Stewart Mackenzie, Lady Ashburton, to Jane Stirling, [June 1854?], AA 11388/95 #401.

11. Charlotte Brontë, *Jane Eyre* (Oxford: Oxford University Press, 1975), chap. 9, p. 287. She used much the same wording in a letter of 20 Feb. 1837 to Ellen Nussey: "Why are we to be divided? Surely, Ellen, it must be because we are in danger of loving each other too well—of losing sight of the *Creator* in idolatry of the *creature.*" *The Brontës: Their Lives, Friendships and Correspondence*, ed. Thomas J. Wise and J. Alexander Symington (Oxford: Blackwell, 1933), 1: 153. Emphasis in the original.

12. Margaret Coutts Trotter to Lady Louisa Ashburton, [1867?], AA 11388/98.

13. Benson retrospective diary, undated entry, DB 1/79.

14. During his years at Trinity College, Cambridge, Edward was the protégé of Francis Martin, who subsidized his education and continental holidays; Edward named his first-born Martin in honor of his benefactor. On the homoerotic attachment of Francis to the strongly heterosexual Edward, see David Williams, *Genesis and Exodus: A Portrait of the Benson Family* (London: Hamish Hamilton, 1979), pp. 8–10; and Mary's undated comment in her 1876 retrospective diary about their 1859 trip to the continent with Francis Martin: "Ed's feelings as to Mr. M's demonstrations—loving, I thought & think—quite wrong—but it was holiday weariness not yet recognised by him—it passed did Mr. M. ever know?" DB 1/79.

15. On the relationship between the private and public lives of the Benson men, see John Tosh, "Domesticity and Manliness in the Victorian Middle Class," in *Manful Assertions: Masculinity in Britain Since 1800*, ed. Michael Roper and John Tosh (London: Routledge, 1991).

16. See Benson's letter to Charlotte Mary Bassett ("Chat"), thanking her: "Your sweet & precious gift came last night—& I *love* it so! The two inextricably twined cords, the sweet knot, the dear symbol that will live near to my heart—The whole mixes into one dear touch from you to me—so *intensely* precious & loved—oh my own darling, *How* I love you!" Christmas eve 1882, DB 3/28. Emphasis in the original.

17. E. F. Benson, *Mother* (London: Hodder & Stoughton, 1925), p. 27.

18. Benson retrospective diary, undated entry, DB 1/79. Emphasis in the original.

19. Benson diary, 16 Jan. 1864, DB 1/73.

20. Williams, *Genesis*, quotes an 1869 letter from Edward to Mary indicating that she had been suffering depression for several years before her 1871 breakdown: "Do keep yourself well and strong that you may be a blessing always: if you were to have ill-health, what good would my life do me?" (p. 46).

21. Benson retrospective diary entry in regard to 1872, DB 1/79. Emphasis in the

original. An early letter (26 Sept. 1872) to Edward comments, "Miss Hall, the lady boarder is a *very* pleasant person—clever & bright & merry. . . . Says she has digestive problems and hints that she hopes it isn't pregnancy," DB 3/3. Emphasis in the original.

22. Benson retrospective diary entry in regard to 1874, DB 1/79. Emphasis in the original. As a note of thanks to Tan, Benson added, "oh, Thou keep me close to her—Friendship has its duties, like marriage—enable me to do mine, & make love ever grow & grow."

23. Virginia Woolf, *To the Lighthouse* (London: Hogarth Press, 1955), p. 35.

24. Kali Israel, *Names and Stories: Emilia Dilke and Victorian Culture* (New York: Oxford, 1999), pp. 110–18. See also the brief discussion of the friendships of married women in Joan Perkin, *Women and Marriage in Nineteenth-Century England* (London: Routledge, 1989), pp. 287–88.

25. Arthur Christopher Benson, *The Life of Edward White Benson, Sometime Archbishop of Canterbury* (London: Macmillan, 1899), 1: 397–98. Emphasis in the original.

26. Ibid., pp. 590–91.

27. Benson retrospective diary, Monday [1875], DB 1/79.

28. Benson retrospective diary entry describing an incident that occurred 12 June 1875, DB 1/79.

29. Ibid. Some historians have read Mary's handwriting incorrectly, seeing Mrs. Mylne's nickname as Tau.

30. Benson retrospective diary entry in regard to 1867, DB 1/79.

31. E. F. Benson, *Mother*, p. 26. See Arthur Benson's summary of his father's belief in the authority of the Church of England and its head, in *Life*, 1: 594–95, and 2: 764–65.

32. A. C. Benson, *The Trefoil: Wellington College, Lincoln, and Truro* (London: John Murray, 1925), p. 240. Arthur recounts an amusing anecdote. Her brother, "a friendly Major . . . with a roving eye and a big mouth full of jagged teeth," took the young Arthur through a garden maze to a summer house. On the table was a "big calf-bound volume, . . . lettered *Hymns of Faith and Love.*" But when a secret spring was touched, it opened to reveal "a little cavity containing cigarettes and matches" (pp. 242–43). Arthur disliked his mother's displays of religious faith and must have been amused at this secret indulgence by one of her special friends.

33. Mary Benson to Charlotte Bassett, undated fragment, ca. mid- November 1879, DB 3/28.

34. Ibid., 17 Feb [1879], DB, 3/28. Emphasis in the original.

35. The fundamental beliefs of Evangelicalism are discussed in D. W. Bebbington, *Evangelicalism in Modern Britain: A History from the 1730s to the 1980s* (London: Unwin Hyman, 1989), pp. 2–19. See also Boyd Hilton, *The Age of Atonement: The Influence of Evangelicalism on Social and Economic Thought, 1795–1865* (Oxford: Clarendon Press, 1988).

36. Mary Benson to Charlotte Bassett, 18 Feb. [1880], DB 3/28. Emphasis in the original.

37. Ibid., 24 Aug.1880, DB 3/28. Emphasis in the original.

38. Ibid., 4 Jan. [1881], DB 3/28. Emphasis in the original.

39. Williams, *Exodus*, for example, denies the sexual foundation of her friendships. Brian Masters, *The Life of E. F. Benson* (London: Chatto & Windus, 1991), agrees with him, but concludes (with Arthur) that Mary's friendships helped to destroy the family. Betty Askwith, *Two Victorian Families* (London: Chatto & Windus, 1971), admits that Mary's relationships "certainly transcended mere friendship" (p. 192), but she also insists: "It is not likely that Mrs. Benson ever had physical relations with any of these beloveds. She probably did not even know that such a thing was possible" (p. 134).

40. Mary Benson to Charlotte Bassett, 14 Jan. 1881, DB 3/28. Emphasis in the original.

41. E. F. Benson, *Final Edition* (London: Longmans, Green, 1940), p. 23.

42. Benson diary, 1 Oct. 1896, DB 1/77. The following prayer appears in Benson's diary entry for 17 Aug. 1896, DB 1/77, following her reading of Ethel Smyth's letters to the Bensons' now- deceased daughter Nellie: "O Merciful God, grant that the old Adam in me may be so buried that the new man may be raised up in me. / Grant that all carnal affections may die in me & that all things belonging to the Spirit may live and grow in me. / Grant that I may have power & struggle to have victory & to triumph against the devil, the world & the Flesh. Amen." Several entries also speak cryptically of "when I went to bed the fall came" and of excessive carnality. "Carnal affections" and "carnal stains" appear again in her 1898 diary entries for 6 May and St. Peter's Day, DB 1/78.

43. Ibid., 24 May 1875 entry DB 1/79. Emphasis in the original.

44. Ethel Smyth, *As Time Went On . . .* (London: Longmans, Green, 1936), p. 38.

45. Benson diary, 17 May [1876], DB 1/79. Emphasis in the original.

46. The details of the Benson children's lives are discussed in Williams, *Exodus;* and Masters, *Life*. See also David Newsome's selections from Arthur's voluminous diary, *On the Edge of Paradise: A. C. Benson, The Diarist* (London: John Murray, 1980); and the numerous biographical memoirs published by A. C. and E. F. Benson.

47. Masters, *Life*, p. 226, quoting from an undated and unattributed letter from A. C. Benson to E. F. Benson. Emphasis in the original. Arthur also called Maggie, who resembled her father temperamentally, a Puritan. A. C. Benson, *The Life and Letters of Maggie Benson* (London: Longmans, Green, 1917), p. 423.

48. Mary Benson to unidentified friend, 27 Dec. 1916, DB Additional Box 14. This is a typed excerpt from a letter, presumably selected by E. F. Benson after her death.

49. See Virginia Blain, "'Michael Field: The Two-headed Nightingale': Lesbian text as Palimpsest," *Women's History Review* 5 (1996): 249.

50. Mary Sturgeon, *Michael Field* (London: George G. Harrap, 1922), pp. 18–23. Sturgeon interviewed former friends for her biographical study of their poetry.

51. Although Bradley knew Greek, she and Cooper were probably inspired by the publication of Henry Thornton Wharton's translation of Sappho in 1885, which did not bowdlerize the same-sex poems by changing the female pronouns. For Michael Field's Sappho poems, see Yopie Prins, *Victorian Sappho* (Princeton, N.J.: Princeton University Press, 1999), pp. 74–111.

52. Critics have long noted that as soon as the joint authorship of an aunt and niece became widely known, the reviews became condescending and/or dismissive. See David J. Moriarty, "'Michael Field' (Edith Cooper and Katharine Bradley) and Their Male Critics," in *Nineteenth-Century Women Writers of the English-Speaking World*, ed. Rhoda B. Nathan (New York: Greenwood Press, 1986). At one juncture Bradley admitted to Havelock Ellis, "Want of due recognition is beginning its embittering, disintegrating work, and we will have in the end a cynic such as only a disillusioned Bacchante can become." Sturgeon, *Michael Field*, p. 30.

53. As well as the important work of Chris White and Virginia Blain, see Angela Leighton, *Victorian Women Poets: Writing Against the Heart* (Charlottesville: University of Virginia Press, 1992), pp. 202–43. For the best modern introduction to the work and lives of Bradley and Cooper, see Donoghue, *We Are Michael Field*.

54. See Bette London, *Writing Double: Women's Literary Partnerships* (Ithaca, N.Y.: Cornell University Press, 1999), pp. 63–74; and Holly A. Laird, *Women Coauthors* (Urbana: University of Illinois, 2000), pp. 81–96. For an illuminating analysis of their

masking, see Prins, *Victorian Sappho*, pp. 75–85. See also Hilary Fraser's important discussion of the continuities between their Dionysian and Catholic poetry, "The Religious Poetry of Michael Field," in *Athena's Shuttle: Myth, Religion, Ideology from Romanticism to Modernism*, ed. Franco Marucci and Emma Sdegno (Milan: Cisalpino, 2000).

55. See Yopie Prins, "Greek Maenads, Victorian Spinsters," in *Victorian Sexual Dissidence*, ed. Richard Dellamora (Chicago: University of Chicago Press, 1999), on the pervasive use of Dionysian and Bacchic imagery in regard to the New Woman.

56. Michael Field, *Wild Honey from Various Thyme* (London: T. Fisher Unwin, 1908), p. 58.

57. Edith Cooper was called Field until 1891. While she was recovering from scarlet fever in a Dresden hospital, her German nurse fell passionately in love with her. She called Cooper Heinrich, which soon became Henry. See entries for 19 Aug.–26 Sept. 1891, in "Works and Days: 1891," BL Add. 46779. Cooper's entries in their unpublished journal were transcribed for her by Katharine Bradley.

58. *Works and Days: From the Journal of Michael Field*, ed. T. and D. C. Sturge Moore (London: John Murray, 1933), p. 271.

59. Donoghue, *Passions Between Women*, p. 124.

60. Fr. Vincent McNab, O.P., preface to Michael Field, *The Wattlefold: Unpublished Poems*, comp. Emily C. Fortey (Oxford: Basil Blackwell, 1930), p. vi. See also Sturgeon, *Michael Field*, pp. 53–54, on the continuity of their interest in and enthusiasm for the ideal of sacrifice. The only full-scale analysis of the Catholic poems of Michael Field is M. Lynn Seitz, "Catholic Symbol and Ritual in Minor British Poetry of the Later Nineteenth Century," Ph.D. dissertation, Arizona State University, 1974, pp. 131–85.

61. T. & D. C. Sturge Moore, eds., *Works and Days*, p. 240.

62. These comments can be found throughout 1906 and 1907 as the two women came to terms with their changing religious affiliation and the profound effect it was having on their lives. See especially 22 Feb., 27 Oct. (Whym Chow's birthday), and 29 Dec., in "Works and Days: 1906," BL Add 46795.

63. Bradley, "Easter even (of the secret trinity) October 1st," ibid.

64. Cooper, 29 Jan. 1908, "Works and Days: 1908," BL Add. 46798.

65. Cooper, 31 Dec. 1909, "Works and Days: 1909," BL Add. 46799.

66. See, for example, "Venit Jesus (In the Confessional)," in Michael Field, *Poems of Adoration* (London: Sands, 1912), p. 89. All but two of these poems were written by Cooper, just as all but two of those in the companion volume, *Mystic Trees* (London: Eveleigh Nash, [1913]), were written by Bradley. Sturgeon, *Michael Field*, pp. 94–95. For a discussion of the Victorian Catholic Church's attitudes toward penance and physical suffering, see Mary Heimann, *Catholic Devotion in Victorian England* (Oxford: Clarendon Press, 1995), pp. 151–56.

67. Edith Cooper [Henry] to William Rothenstein, 8 June 1913, quoted in William Rothenstein, *Men and Memories* (New York: Coward-McCann, 1931), 1: 280.

68. Cooper, "Wednesday, May Day," "Works and Days: 1907," BL Add.46796.

69. Cooper, "Last day of the Year," "Works and Days: 1908," BL Add. 46798.

70. Cooper's copy of Katharine Bradley's October 1907 letter to the Rev. John Gray, in "Works and Days: 1907," BL Add 46796. For a fuller account of Father Gray's role in their lives, see Jerusha Hull McCormack, *John Gray* (Hanover, N.H.: University Press of New England, 1991), pp. 205–17.

71. Cooper, "Last day of the year," "Works and Days: 1907," BL Add. 46797.

72. Ivor C. Treby, *The Michael Field Catalogue: A Book of Lists* (London: De Blackland Press, 1998), p. 47, in regard to 22 April 1911.

73. T. & D. C. Sturge Moore, eds., *Works and Days*, pp. xix–xxx, imply that the two women consummated their love when they write that "the one [was] seventeen, the other thirty-two, [and] while making beds in their old house at Kenilworth, they had dedicated their lives to poetry." According to Blain, "Michael Field," p. 249, evidence from their letters suggests 1883, when Cooper was twenty-one and Bradley was thirty-six. Treby notes that the Cooper family had moved from Kenilworth in 1867, so the Sturge-Moores were mistaken about the place. Treby disagrees with my position in regard to the women's sexual life. See also Cooper's sexually knowing diary entries for Dresden in 1891 "Works and Days," BL Add 46779, noting how a German nurse made sexual advances to her.

74. Blain, "Michael Field," pp. 250–51.

75. See Donoghue, *We Are Michael Field*, p. 126. At the time Father Goscannon, her confessor, did not know they were published poets. Cooper was shocked when he thought she was trying to confess a heterosexual affair.

76. Cooper, "Last day of the year," Bradley and Cooper, "Works and Days: 1907," BL Add. 46797.

77. Treby, *Catalogue*, p. 46, suggests that after their conversion they never again wrote poetry jointly.

78. Field, *Wild Honey*, p. 173. Sturgeon, *Michael Field*, p. 81, attributes the poem to Bradley as an homage to Cooper. See also Michael Field, *Music and Silence: The Gamut of Michael Field*, chosen and annotated by Ivor C. Treby (London: De Blackland Press, 2000), p. 109.

79. Bradley's indignant comment about Robert Browning and his wife, Elizabeth Barrett Browning, has been noted by many critics: "these two poets, man and wife, wrote alone; each wrote, but did not bless or quicken one another at their work; *we are closer married.*" T. & D.C. Sturge Moore, eds., *Works and Days*, p. 16. Emphasis in the original.

80. "Imple Superna Gratia," in Field, *Poems of Adoration*, p. 92.

81. Katharine Bradley to Mary Berenson, [June 1912?], in Mary Berenson, Letters, I Tatti, Florence, Italy. Emphasis in the original.

82. Field, *The Wattlefold*, p. 191 (1912). Unlike the poems published in previous volumes, each poem in this posthumous volume is dated.

83. Michael Field, *Dedicated: An Early Work of Michael Field* (London: G. Bell & Sons, 1914), p. 123. Quoted also in T. & D. C. Sturge Moore, eds., *Works and Days*, p. 331; and Sturgeon, *Michael Field*, p. 58.

84. Blain, "Michael Field," p. 251.

CHAPTER FIVE

1. Frances Power Cobbe, *Life as told By Herself* (London: Swan Sonnenshein, 1904), p. 710.

2. Edith Simcox, "George Eliot," *Nineteenth Century* 9 (May 1881): 784–85.

3. Geraldine Jewsbury to Jane Carlyle, 15 June 1841, in *Selections from the Letters of Geraldine Endsor Jewsbury to Jane Welsh Carlyle*, ed. Mrs. Alexander Ireland (London: Longmans, Green, 1892), p. 16. Ireland does not always supply dates, nor does she indicate her editing of letters.

4. Geraldine Jewsbury to Jane Carlyle, 4 Aug. 1841, 19 Feb. 1842, 29 Oct. 1841, ibid., pp. 31, 55, 39.

5. Jane Welsh Carlyle to Thomas Carlyle, Friday [12 July 1844], in *The Collected Letters of Thomas Carlyle and Jane Welsh Carlyle*, gen. ed. Charles Richard Sanders (Durham, N.C.: Duke University Press, 1970–), 18: 131. Emphasis in the original.

6. Jane Welsh Carlyle to Helen Welsh, Friday [1 Dec. 1843], ibid., 17: 195. Emphasis in the original.

7. Norma Clarke, *Ambitious Heights: Writing, Friendship, Love—The Jewsbury Sisters, Felicia Hemans and Jane Welsh Carlyle* (London: Routledge, 1990), pp. 208–23. Aileen Christianson discusses Jane Carlyle's need to be at the center of any friendship, female or male, in "Jane Welsh Carlyle and Her Friendships with Women in the 1840s," *Prose Studies* 10 (1987).

8. Jane Welsh Carlyle to Thomas Carlyle, 15 April 1841, *Collected Letters*, 13: 101. Emphasis in the original.

9. Clarke, *Ambitious Heights*, p. 153. Emphasis in the original.

10. Jane Welsh Carlyle to Jeannie Welsh [18 or 19 Jan. 1843], *Collected Letters*, 16: 21. Emphasis in the original.

11. *Selections from the Letters of Geraldine Endsor Jewsbury*, p. 304.

12. Geraldine Jewsbury to Jane Carlyle, Sunday, May 1851, ibid., p. 397. The Jewsbury sisters had spent an idyllic summer in Wales in 1828 with the poet Felicia Hemans. See Susanne Howe, *Geraldine Jewsbury: Her Life and Errors* (London: George Allen & Unwin, 1935), pp. 13–14; and Clarke, *Ambitious Heights*, pp. 11–12.

13. Clarke, *Ambitious Heights*, p. 201.

14. Virginia Woolf, "Geraldine and Jane," in *The Second Common Reader* (New York: Harcourt Brace & World, 1932), pp. 178, 181.

15. Pauline Polkey usefully summarizes these responses in "Recuperating the Love-Passions of Edith Simcox," in *Women's Lives in Print: The Theory, Practice and Writing of Feminist Auto/Biography*, ed. Pauline Polkey (London: Macmillan, 1999), pp. 61–62.

16. Rosemarie Bodenheimer, *The Real Life of Mary Ann Evans: George Eliot, Her Letters and Fiction* (Ithaca, N.Y.: Cornell University Press, 1994), pp. 242–43, suggests that Lewes chafed at times as the manager of "a high-strung thoroughbred," and that he might have hoped for more time to write if the burden of care was picked up by young admirers. Frederick R. Karl, *George Eliot: Voice of a Century* (New York: W. W. Norton, 1995), pp. 376–77, discusses how Lewes benefited from isolating his wife.

17. Eliza Lynn Linton, *My Literary Life* (London: Hodder & Stoughton, 1899), p. 100.

18. Simcox, "George Eliot," p. 783.

19. Bodenheimer, *Real Life*, p. 243.

20. *Mary Ponsonby: A Memoir, Some Letters and a Journal*, ed. Magdalen Ponsonby (London: John Murray, 1927), p. 89. Mary Ponsonby felt that Eliot "shrank from the pessimistic consequences which might be the result of logically carrying out her theories" and instead meted them out "dealing absolution or damnation according to the faithfulness of the elect as rigidly as any fanatical priest" (p. 92).

21. Quoted from George Henry Lewes's diary in *The George Eliot Letters*, ed. Gordon S. Haight (New Haven, Conn.: Yale University Press, 1955), 6: 121. Emphasis in the original.

22. Edith Simcox to George Eliot, 26 March 1880 (draft), in *A Monument to the Memory of George Eliot: Edith Simcox's "Autobiography of a Shirtmaker,"* ed. Constance M. Fulmer and Margaret E. Barfield (New York: Garland, 1998), p. 120. Simcox called her unpublished diary (May 1876–January 1900) "Autobiography of a Shirtmaker" in honor of her work as head of a cooperative workshop, but as she admitted (26 May 1878), "This is *not* the autobiography of a shirtmaker, but a love so I need not speak of the Co-Operative Congress." *A Monument*, p. 32.

23. George Eliot to Sara Hennell, 21 April 1852, in *George Eliot Letters*, 2: 19: "[You] have been so generous and sympathetic, that if I did not heartily love you, I should feel deep gratitude—but love excludes gratitude."

24. Simcox diary, 29 Dec.1878 entry, in *A Monument*, p. 69.

25. John Kucich, *Repression in Victorian Fiction: Charlotte Brontë, George Eliot and Charles Dickens* (Berkeley: University of California Press, 1987), p. 119. Rosemarie Bodenheimer, "Autobiography in Fragments: The Elusive Life of Edith Simcox," *Victorian Studies* 44 (2002), points out that Simcox "went to George Eliot as a great writer who had led an unconventional women's life, and found herself battling instead with an icon who projected . . . 'the inexhaustible gospel of Renunciation.'" (p. 405).

26. Simcox diary, 9 March 1880 entry, in *A Monument*, p. 117. See also K. A. McKenzie, *Edith Simcox and George Eliot* (Oxford: Oxford University Press, 1961), p. 97.

27. Simcox diary, 18 Jan. 1881 entry, in *A Monument*, p. 146.

28. Simcox diary, 23 July 1881 entry, in *A Monument*, p. 159. Simcox, like Eliot, was not above a little flirtation. She admits that Miss Williams "went away a little hurt, though I rather wooed her at last. The only thing that checks my impulses of tenderness is the fear lest there is some flightiness and want of moral balance in her nature." Polkey, "Recuperating," pp. 71–74, identifies the woman as Caroline Williams, a fellow political activist and author of articles on various women's issues.

29. George Eliot, *Daniel Deronda* (New York: Penguin, 1995), p.735. I am indebted to Christopher Todd Matthews for pointing out this reference to me.

30. See, for example, *George Eliot Letters*, 1: 161, 223, 238, 239, 275, and 279. In one letter Eliot signs off, "Your loving wife" (1: 187), but her preferred signature was the semiandrogynous Pollian, a version of Polly Ann. Later Lewes often called her Polly.

31. Simcox diary, 16 Jan. 1881 entry, in *A Monument*, p. 146.

32. Rosemarie Bodenheimer, "Ambition and Its Audiences: George Eliot's Performing Figures," *Victorian Studies* 34 (Autumn 1990): 8.

33. Simcox, "George Eliot," p. 784.

34. Simcox diary, 24 April 1881 entry, in *A Monument*, p. 154.

35. The only modern biography to date is Louise Collis's unimaginative *Impetuous Heart: A Biography of Ethel Smyth* (London: William Kimber, 1984). See also, on the lesbian roots of Smyth's music, three articles by Elizabeth Wood: "Lesbian Fugue: Ethel Smyth's Contrapuntal Arts," in *Musicology and Difference: Gender and Sexuality in Music Scholarship*, ed. Ruth A. Solie (Berkeley: University of California Press, 1993); "Sapphonics," in *Queering the Pitch: The New Gay and Lesbian Musicology*, ed. Philip Brett, Elizabeth Wood, and Gary C. Thomas (New York: Routledge, 1994); and "The Lesbian in the Opera: Desire Unmasked in Smyth's *Fantasio* and *Fête Galante*," in *En Travesti: Women, Gender, Subversion, Opera* , ed. Corinne E. Blackmer and Patricia Juliana Smith (New York: Columbia University Press, 1995).

36. Ethel Smyth, *Impressions that Remained*. New York: DaCapo Press, 1981 [1919], pp. 179–80.

37. See Wood, "Lesbian Fugue," pp. 174–75.

38. Lisl von Herzogenberg to Ethel Smyth, 6 Jan. 1880, in Smyth, *Impressions*, pp. 280–81. Emphasis in the original.

39. Lisl von Herzogenberg to Ethel Smyth, 20 April 1880, in ibid., p. 284. See also 19 Oct. 1883: "And though I know—I *know*—the pedal-point is indestructible, in the meantime, what with your sorrow for a dead friend and your interest in a new living one I come off rather badly" (p. 358). Emphasis in the original.

40. Ibid., p. 246. Characteristically, Smyth found Baroness von Stockhausen's vi-

olence attractive, but after an initial meeting, Smyth was "implored to shun the house" whenever the baroness visited.

41. Lisl von Herzogenberg, Würzburg, to Ethel Smyth, March 1880, ibid., p. 282.

42. Lisl von Herzogenberg to Ethel Smyth, 19 Dec. 1887, quoted in Wood, "Lesbian Fugue," p. 176. Ellipses in the original.

43. Mary Benson to Ethel Smyth, 26 Jan. 1886, DB 3/38.

44. Smyth, *Impressions*, p. 422. Smyth called this period "In the Desert."

45. Ethel Smyth to Lady Mary Ponsonby, 1892, excerpted in Christopher St. John [Christabel Marshal], notebook 1, Special Collections, University of Michigan, Ann Arbor.

46. Ethel Smyth to Eleanor (Nellie) Benson, undated, excerpted in ibid.

47. Ethel and Harry had been corresponding off and on, and she had visited his sister in France. Christopher St. John, *Ethel Smyth: A Biography* (London: Longmans, Green, 1959), pp. 44–48.

48. Years later Smyth haughtily concluded that the Bensons showed "no great display of either understanding or loving-kindness. And over them, invisible but felt, hovers the tiresome spectre of the seventh Commandment." Ethel Smyth, *As Time Went On . . .* (London: Longmans Green, 1936), p. 67.

49. Wood, "Lesbian Fugue," p. 177.

50. Suzanne Raitt, "'The Tide of Ethel': Femininity as Narrative in the Friendship of Ethel Smyth and Virginia Woolf," *Critical Quarterly*, 30 (1988): 14. Clearly the 1928 *Well of Loneliness* trial for obscenity had an impact on Smyth.

51. Ethel Smyth to Lady Mary Ponsonby, 21 May 1898, in Ethel Smyth, *What Happened Next* (London: Longmans, 1940), p. 145. Emphasis in the original. In another, undated letter to Ponsonby, Smyth told her: "He has fallen in with my views & wishes in all things in a way that if you know of it all you would think unmanly and I know on what a profound knowledge of my nature & its possibilities as regards relations to men it is based & I am grateful to him as to a clever doctor who is the only minister to one's particular ailment." Excerpted in St. John, notebook 1.

52. Ethel Smyth to Virginia Woolf, 26 Dec. 1932., quoted in Raitt, "Tide of Ethel," p. 14.

53. See William M. Kuhn, *Henry and Mary Ponsonby: Life at the Court of Queen Victoria* (London: Duckworth, 2002), pp. 228–56. Kuhn records numerous intense friendships throughout Mary Ponsonby's life, as well as a pattern of tempestuous quarrels with her husband.

54. Smyth, *As Time Went On . . .* , p. 98.

55. Ethel Smyth to Lady Mary Ponsonby, June 1893, excerpted in St. John, notebook 1. Emphasis in the original.

56. Smyth, *Impressions*, p. 487.

57. Smyth, *As Time Went On . . .* , p. 15.

58. Ibid., pp. 99–100.

59. Ethel Smyth to Virginia Woolf, 2 May 1930, quoted in Raitt, "Tide of Ethel," p. 11.

60. Soon after her husband's death, Mary Benson recorded in her diary: "Fred was as tender as a child, as loving & strong as a husband & as sensitive as a woman. he only wanted not to disappoint me & he told me one evn'g he could never marry he loved me too much." 21 Nov. 1896, Paris, DB 1/77.

61. Mary Benson to Ethel Smyth, 8 Sept. 1889, DB 3/38.

62. Ibid., 26 Oct.1889. Emphasis in the original.

63. Ibid., 7 Nov. 1889. Emphasis in the original.

64. Virginia Woolf to Ethel Smyth., 15 Aug.1930, in *The Letters of Virginia Woolf*, ed. Nigel Nicolson and Joanne Trautmann (New York: Harcourt Brace & Jovanovich, 1978), 4: 200.

65. A. C. Benson, *The Life and Letters of Maggie Benson* (New York: Longmans, Green, 1917), pp. 48–49, 87, quoting Miss Beatrice Layman and Mrs. Lea.

66. Ibid., p. 144. See also Maggie's 1888 letter to her mother about a friend's "low" idea of friendships, defined as "of the good-fellowship sort" (p. 99).

67. Ibid., p. 122.

68. David Williams, *Genesis and Exodus: A Portrait of the Benson Family* (London: Hamish Hamilton, 1979), p. 112.

69. Mary Benson diary, 8 Nov. 1899 entry, DB 1/78. The following entries are all from the diary in this DB file.

70. 11 June 1898 entry. Emphasis and ellipses in the original.

71. 13 June 1898 entry.

72. 8 Nov.1899 entry. Emphasis in the original.

73. Ibid.

74. See Theresa de Lauretis's analysis of Benjamin's 1981 "A Desire of One's Own," in *The Practice of Love: Lesbian Sexuality and Perverse Desire* (Bloomington: Indiana University Press, 1994), p. 185.

75. Arthur Benson diary, 92 (April 22–Mary 18, 1907), p. 41, Pepys Library, Magdalene College, Cambridge University. Emphasis in the original.

76. Brian Masters, *The Life of E. F. Benson* (London: Chatto & Windus, 1971), pp. 164–70, based on Arthur's diary account of events. For a more circumspect version, see E. F. Benson, *Mother* (London: Hodder & Stoughton, 1925), pp. 222–29. Fred destroyed Maggie's diaries from this period, though Arthur had access to them for his memoir.

77. E. F. Benson, *Mother*, p. 245.

78. Masters, *Life*, pp. 194–99. See especially Arthur's comment, "One doesn't wonder at the idea of *possession*—indeed, the phenomenon has got to be explained for the credit of God. . . . The devilish nature of the things she says to Mamma is almost incredible" (p. 199).

79. Margaret Benson, *The Soul of a Cat and Other Stories* (London: William Heinemann, 1901), pp. 12, 15–16.

80. A. C. Benson, *Life and Letters*, p. 395.

81. St. John, *Ethel Smyth*, p. 77.

82. A. C. Benson, *Life and Letters*, p. 119.

CHAPTER SIX

1. Linton published a series of sensational essays on "The Girl of the Period" in the *Saturday Review* in 1867, followed by series on "The Shrieking Sisterhood" in the 1870s and on the "Wild Women" in the 1880s. Suffrage leaders responded vigorously to these attacks. But Mona Caird, in her 1892 essay "A Defense of So-Called Wild Women," admitted that some women had "made the mistake, as I think, of seeking to emphasise their demand for the liberty that men enjoy, by imitating men's habits and manners." Caird, *The Morality of Marriage and Other Essays on the Status and Destiny of Women* (London: George Redway, 1897), p. 164. These issues are discussed in Nancy Fix Anderson's definitive biography, *Woman Against Women in Victorian England: A Life of Eliza Lynn Linton* (Bloomington: Indiana University Press, 1987), pp. 117–35, 191–93.

2. Max Nordau, *Degeneration* (New York: Appleton, 1895), p. 24. Deborah T.

Meem, "Eliza Lynn Linton and the Rise of Lesbian Consciousness," *Journal of the History of Sexuality* 7 (1997), points out that as a Social Darwinist, Linton believed many of the ideas that were later consolidated by Nordau.

3. For summaries of Ulrichs's thinking, see James D. Steakley, *The Homosexual Emancipation Movement in Germany* (New York: Arno Press, 1975), pp. 1–19; and Hubert Kennedy, "Karl Heinrich Ulrichs, First Theorist of Homosexuality," in *Science and Homosexualities*, ed. Vernon A. Rosario (New York: Routledge, 1997). It is unlikely that Lee knew Ulrichs's writings, which were mostly privately published and circulated, but she did know of the work of later sexologists.

4. Vernon Lee to Mary Robinson, 12 Dec. 1883, Fonds Anglais 245, f 122, Bibliothèque Nationale.

5. George Somes Layard, *Mrs. Lynn Linton: Her Life, Letters, and Opinions* (London: Methuen, 1901), p. 21.

6. See F. B. Smith, *Radical Artisan: William James Linton, 1812–97* (Manchester: Manchester University Press, 1973), p. 133. Anderson, *Woman Against Women*, reaches the same conclusion: "it is indeed probable that Eliza, marrying in the spirit of self-sacrifice, did not extend her sense of duty to the bedroom" (p. 92).

7. Constance Harsh, "Eliza Lynn Linton as a New Woman Novelist," in Eliza Lynn Linton, *The Rebel of the Family*, ed. Deborah T. Meem (Peterborough, Ont.: Broadview Press, 2002), p. 459.

8. Anderson, *Woman Against Women*, p. 61. Andrea L. Broomfield analyzes Linton's career following the debacle of *Realities*. See her "Blending Journalism with Fiction: Eliza Lynn Linton and Her Rise to Fame as a Popular Novelist," in Linton, *Rebel of the Family*, pp. 442–50.

9. E. Lynn Linton, *Sowing the Wind: A Novel* (London: Tinsley Bros, 1867), p. 98.

10. Ibid., p. 185.

11. The *Athenaeum* review of *Sowing the Wind* is summarized and quoted by Anderson, *Woman Against Women*, p. 108.

12. Meem, "Eliza Lynn Linton," pp. 541–43.

13. Linton, *Rebel of the Family*, p. 173. Anderson, *Woman Against Women*, pp. 63–64, discusses Linton's flirtation with Lady Monson in the early 1850s. Monson became Matilda Hays's companion after she left Charlotte Cushman.

14. Linton, *Rebel of the Family*, p. 140.

15. Ibid., p. 174. See also Meem's discussion of this novel in "Eliza Lynn Linton."

16. Meem, "Eliza Lynn Linton," p. 540.

17. Eliza Lynn Linton to George Bentley, 21 Feb. 1885, quoted in Anderson, *Woman Against Women*, p. 11.

18. Publisher's reader, quoted in ibid., p. 179.

19. Mrs. Lynn Linton, *The Autobiography of Christopher Kirkland* (London: Richard Bentley, 1885), 3: 207.

20. Layard, *Mrs. Lynn Linton*, p. 189.

21. Anderson, *Woman Against Women*, p. 156.

22. Linton, *Christopher Kirkland*, 3: 216.

23. Ibid., p. 232.

24. Ibid., pp. 220, 224.

25. The young Vernon Lee wrote a friend: "We know rather a famous novelist here, Mrs. Lynn Linton . . . a terribly black and earnest woman, who takes things too grimly to be very pleasant." Vernon Lee to Mrs. Jenkin, 18 Dec. 1878, in *Vernon Lee's Letters*, ed. Irene Cooper Willis (London: Privately printed, 1937), p. 59.

26. Linton, *Christopher Kirkland*, 3: 240.

27. Ibid., pp. 241–42.

28. Layard, *Mrs. Lynn Linton*, p. 256.

29. Linton obituary, quoted in Anderson, *Woman Against Women*, p. 180.

30. Peter Gunn, *Vernon Lee/Violet Paget, 1856–1935* (London: Oxford University Press, 1964), p.17.

31. Linton, *Christopher Kirkland*, 1: iv–v.

32. Vernon Lee to Mary Robinson, 27 Feb. [1881], Fonds Anglais 244, f 120, Biblothèque Nationale.

33. These details come out in long letters to Mary Robinson, written following Mme. Meyer's death in December 1883. See ibid., 245, ff 120–36. See also Vineta Colby, *Vernon Lee: A Literary Biography* (Charlottesville: University of Virginia Press, 2003), pp. 52–53. According to Colby, Lee's cousin Adah Hughes thought that the vampish character Sacha Elaguine was based on gossip Lee had heard from her (p. 104).

34. Vernon Lee, *Miss Brown* (New York: Garland, 1978), 3: 149.

35. Ibid., 2: 234.

36. Ibid., 3: 280.

37. Ibid., 2: 307–8.

38. At the time Lee was a good friend of the aesthete and art historian Walter Pater, whose famous phrase concluding *The Renaissance* (1873), "to burn always with this hard gem-like flame," influenced a generation of young women and men.

39. John Addington Symonds mentored the young Mary Robinson and warned her against the masculine Lee. He revealed his own homosexuality only to close friends. His *A Problem in Modern Ethics* was published in 1896 in a limited edition of 100 copies. Lee, like other women of the time, may have seen little similarity between her situation and that of homosexual men.

40. Lee, *Miss Brown*, 2: 308–9.

41. Frances Power Cobbe, "Social Science Congresses and Women's Part in Them," in *Essays on the Pursuits of Women* (London: E. Faithfull, 1863), pp. 25–26. Emphasis in the original. In 1885 Cobbe wrote Lee praising *Miss Brown*. Colby, *Vernon Lee*, p. 344.

42. For Kathy Psomiades' important rereading of *Miss Brown*, see her, "'Still Burning from This Strangling Embrace': Vernon Lee on Desire and Aesthetics," in *Victorian Sexual Dissidence*, ed. Richard Dellamora (Chicago: University of Chicago Press, 1999), pp. 24–27.

43. Edward Carpenter, *Love's Coming-of-Age* (London: Methuen, 1906), p. 66.

44. Edward Carpenter, *Homogenic Love and its place in a free society* (London: Redundancy Press, 1980), p. 22.

45. Vernon Lee, undated journal, c. 1885, quoted in Burdett Gardner, *The Lesbian Imagination (Victorian Style): A Psychological and Critical Study of "Vernon Lee"* (New York: Garland, 1987, pp. 376–77.

46. Gunn, *Vernon Lee/Violet Paget*, pp. 104–5.

47. Vernon Lee to Matilda Paget, 30 Aug. 1887, VLC, #359. Neither Lee nor her brother believed that a Frenchman had the self-control to refrain from sex, and they strongly disapproved of birth control. See also *Vernon Lee's Letters*, p. 272. The editor of the *Letters*, Irene Cooper Willis, deleted the more damning comments about Darmsteter, as well as the proposal to keep the marriage unconsummated.

48. For a discussion of these variations on the unconsummated marriage, see Anne L. Ardis, *New Women, New Novels: Feminism and Early Modernism* (New Brunswick, N.J.: Rutgers University Press, 1990). Eugene Lee-Hamilton married the New Woman

novelist Annie Holdsworth in 1898. Lee also opposed that marriage on eugenic grounds. Gunn, *Vernon Lee/Violet Paget*, pp. 162–63.

49. Vernon Lee to Matilda Paget, 27 Sept. 1887, VLC, #372.

50. Madame Duclaux [A. Mary F. Robinson], "In Casa Paget: A Retrospect. In Memoriam Eugène Lee-Hamilton," *Country Life* 22 (Dec. 28, 1907): 936.

51. Vernon Lee, "A Wedding Chest," in *The Snake Lady and Other Stories*, ed. and intro. Horace Gregory (New York: Grove Press, 1954), pp. 75–85. Originally published in *Pope Jacynth and Other Fantastic Stories* (London: Grant Richards, 1904).

52. Lee, "A Wedding Chest," p. 85.

53. Gunn, *Vernon Lee/Violet Paget*, p. 91.

54. See Linton's exchange of letters with Mona Taylor in August 1904, in Gardner, *Lesbian Imagination*, pp. 304–5.

55. Vernon Lee to Matilda Paget, 24 July 1887, *Vernon Lee's Letters*, p. 261.

56. Vernon Lee, *Althea: A Second Book of Dialogues on Aspirations and Duties* (London: Osgood, McIlvaine, 1894), p. 31.

57. Ibid., pp. 7, 11.

58. See also Psomiades' discussion of the aesthetic relationship between Lee and Anstruther-Thomson in "Still Burning," pp. 34–36.

59. Vernon Lee, introduction to C. Anstruther-Thomson, *Art & Man: Essays & Fragments* (London: John Lane, 1924), pp. 7, 8.

60. For a full description of this aspect of their friendship, see Phyllis Manocchi, "Vernon Lee and Kit Anstruther-Thomson: A Study of Love and Collaboration Between Romantic Friends," *Women's Studies* 12 (1986); and Diana Maltz, "Engaging 'Delicate Brains': From Working-Class Enculturation to Upper-Class Lesbian Liberation in Vernon Lee and Kit Anstruther-Thomson's Psychological Aesthetics," in *Women and British Aestheticism*, ed. Talia Schaffer and Kathy Alexis Psomiades (Charlottesville: University Press of Virginia, 1999), pp. 211–29.

61. Vernon Lee to Mona Taylor, 17 March [18]99, VLC, #820. Mona Taylor penciled in, "I still think Kit loves the case more than *the person.*" Emphasis Taylor's.

62. Vernon Lee to Mona Taylor, 25 March 1899, VLC, #823.

63. Vernon Lee to Mrs. Christine Head, 10 April [1899], VLC, #824. This is a draft copy of the letter that was sent. Lee crossed out "must always live" and substituted "always must grow."

64. Vernon Lee to Mona Taylor, 12 Aug. 1900, VLC, #832.

65. See Bertha Harris's early essay "The More Profound Nationality of Their Lesbianism: Lesbian Society in the 1920's," in *Amazon Expedition*, ed. Phillis Birky et al. (New York: Times Change Press, 1974), pp. 77–88.

66. Judith Roof, *A Lure of Knowledge: Lesbian Sexuality and Theory* (New York: Columbia University Press, 1991), pp. 108–18.

67. Linton, *Christopher Kirkland*, 1: 174–75.

68. Ibid., p. 195.

69. Ibid, pp. 199–201.

70. Ibid, pp. 207–8.

71. Ibid., p. 209.

72. Edith Cooper, recuperating from scarlet fever in a Dresden hospital in August 1891, described a delirious fantasy: "I determine I will have as much pleasure as I can. I dance balls, I go to Operas, I am Mars & looking across at Sim's [Katharine Bradley] little bed I realise that she is a goddess hidden in her hair—Venus." Katharine Bradley and Edith Cooper, "Works and Days: 1891," BL Add. 46779.

73. Layard, *Mrs. Lynn Linton*, p. 41.

74. Vernon Lee, "Prince Alberic and the Snake Lady," in *Snake Lady*, p. 42. This story was originally published in *The Yellow Book* 10 (July 1896): 289–344, and reprinted in *Pope Jacynth and Other Fantastic Tales* (London: Grant Richards, 1904). The origin of the tale may be the famous French chivalric romance *Amadis de Gaule* (1540), in which the ideal knight encounters a series of monsters in service to his beloved Princess Oriana. Lee has completely altered that romance, which ends happily.

75. Lee, "Prince Alberic," p. 38.

76. Ibid., pp. 48, 51.

77. Ibid., p. 59. See Jane Hotchkiss's feminist psychoanalytic reading, "(P)revising Freud: Vernon Lee's Castration Phantasy," in *Seeing Double: Revisionary Edwardian and Modernist Literature*, ed. Carola M. Kaplan and Anne B. Simpson (New York: St. Martin's Press, 1996), p. 34. Hotchkiss does not focus on the lesbian implications of the story, but her reading confirms my argument that Lee's fiction repeatedly revises heterosexuality and creates lesbian narratives. See also Ruth Robbins, "Vernon Lee: Decadent Woman?," in *Fin de Siècle / Fin de Globe: Fears and Fantasies of the Late Nineteenth Century*, ed. John Stokes (New York: St. Martin's Press, 1992). Both readings usefully contest Gardner's reductive reading of the "perversity" of the story.

78. Lee, "Prince Alberic," p. 59. Lee wrote Robinson, "once at Siena . . . you said you had become mine, because you kissed me & I had held you tight." Vernon Lee to Mary Robinson, 27 Feb. 1881, Fonds Anglais 244, f 115, Biblothèque Nationale.

79. Lee, "Prince Alberic," p. 71.

80. Ibid., p. 72.

81. Gardner, *Lesbian Imagination*, p. 21.

82. Ibid., pp. 311–12. Gardner explains that the excerpt comes from pages "stuffed in an envelope which bears the label in Violet's hand, 'Some (slightly!) autobiographical notes, viz. A. M. in memoriam 1883, . . . preserved from the old notebooks sent to the Cartiena della Lima to make into new paper in March 1920'" (p. 307; ellipses Gardner's). Lee kept a picture of Anne Meyer over her bed her entire life.

83. Ibid., p. 311.

84. *The Academy*, 19 Feb. 1881, quoted in Linton, *Rebel of the Family*, p. 401.

85. Ethel Smyth believed that Lee "refused to face" the fact of her passionate feelings toward women, and instead pretended "that to her those friends were merely intellectual necessities." Ethel Smyth, *What Happened Next* (London: Longmans, Green, 1940), p. 28.

CHAPTER SEVEN

1. Public discussion of passing women coincides with the heyday of the female soldier, and with the beginning of what J. C. Flugel, in his classic study *The Psychology of Clothes* (London: Hogarth Press, 1930), called "The Great Masculine Renunciation" of flamboyant clothing (pp. 117–19). See also Valerie Steele, *Paris Fashion: A Cultural History* (New York: Oxford University Press, 1988), pp. 79–96; and Janet Wolff, "The Invisible Flâneuse: Women and the Literature of Modernity," *Theory, Culture and Society* 2.3 (1985). Wolff argues that modern man, symbolized by the premier Decadent poet, Charles Baudelaire, conceives of urban space as his, and in the process denies women subjectivity.

2. Karla Jay, introduction to *A Perilous Advantage: The Best of Natalie Clifford Barney*, ed. and tr. Anna Livia (Norwich, Vt: New Victoria Publishers, 1992), p. viii.

3. See, for example, Jill Dolan, "Gender Impersonation Onstage: Destroying or

Maintaining the Mirror of Gender Roles?" *Women and Performance: A Journal of Feminist Theory* 2.2 (1985); Sue-Ellen Case, *Performing Feminisms: Feminist Critical Theory and Theatre* (Baltimore: Johns Hopkins University Press, 1990); and Marjorie B. Garber, *Vested Interests: Cross-Dressing and Cultural Anxiety* (New York: Routledge, 1992).

4. Annette Kuhn, "Sexual Disguise in Cinema," in Kuhn, *The Power of the Image: Essays on Representation and Sexuality* (London: Routledge & Kegan Paul, 1985), p. 52.

5. Kaja Silverman, "Fragments of a Fashionable Discourse," in *Studies in Entertainment: Critical Approaches to Mass Culture*, ed. Tania Modleski (Bloomington: Indiana University Press, 1986), pp. 145–47.

6. Garber, *Vested Interests*, p. 9.

7. For the details of Barney's life, see George Wickes, *The Amazon of Letters: The Life and Loves of Natalie Barney* (New York: G. P. Putnam's Sons, 1976); Jean Chalon, *Portrait of a Seductress: The World of Natalie Barney*, tr. Carol Banko (New York: Crown, 1979); and Suzanne Rodriguez, *Wild Heart. A Life: Natalie Clifford Barney's Journey from Victorian America to Belle Époque Paris* (New York: HarperCollins, 2002).

8. Isabelle de Courtivon, "Weak Men and Fatal Women: The Sand Image," in *Homosexualities and French Literature: Cultural Contexts/Critical Texts*, ed. George Stambolian and Elaine Marks (Ithaca, N.Y.: Cornell University Press, 1979), discusses the attractions of the virile woman to nineteenth-century male writers.

9. Jean-Paul Goujon, *Tes blessures sont plus douces que leurs caresses: vie de Renée Vivien* (Paris: Régine Deforges, 1986), p. 84. Vivien wrote her own epitaph, which Barney translated into English.

10. I am indebted to Nancy Erber for the following list: *Deux amies* (1885), *La Comtesse de Lesbos* (1889), *Méphistophéla, roman contemporain* (1890), *Lesbia, maîtresse d'école* (1890), *Don Juan à Lesbos* (1892), *Les Deux Belles de nuit* (1893), *Voluptés bizarres, roman érotique* (1893), *Liqueurs et parfums des grand fabriques de Lesbos, Cythère et Gomorrhe* (1894), *Aphrodite* (1896), *Immortelle idole* (1900), *Monsieur de Phocas* (1901), *Journal d'un saphiste* (1902), *La Charmeuse des femmes* (1902), *Odette et Marine, histoire véridique de deux amies de pension jolies et passionnées* (1903), *Les Vicieuses de province par un journaliste du siècle dernier* (1907). This list excludes the three novels I discuss, Colette's *Claudine à l'école* (1900), Liane de Pougy's *Idylle saphique* (1901), and Renée Vivien's *Une Femme m'apparut* (1904). See also Jennifer Waelti-Walters, *Damned Women: Lesbians in French Novels* (Montreal: McGill-Queens University Press, 2000), pp. 49–94, for an examination of some of these novels.

11. Francesca Canadé Sautman, "Invisible Women: Lesbian Working-class Culture in France, 1880–1930," in *Homosexuality in Modern France*, ed. Jeffrey Merrick and Bryant T. Ragan, Jr. (New York: Oxford University Press, 1996).

12. Wickes, *Amazon of Letters*, pp. 88–99, and Rodriguez, *Wild Heart*, pp. 154–57, describe Barney's theatricals and the various participants.

13. Dolly Wilde to Natalie Barney, 1930s, quoted in Wickes, *Amazon of Letters*, p. 188.

14. The Barney circle's theatrical events are documented and illustrated in Chalon, *Portrait of a Seductress*, pp. 55–84, and Wickes, *Amazon of Letters*, pp. 53–77. Wickes's photographs are crucial to my interpretation of Barney and Vivien.

15. 27 July 1920 entry, in Liane de Pougy, *My Blue Notebooks*, tr. Diana Athill (London: André Deutsch, 1979), p. 111.

16. Elaine Marks, "Lesbian Intertextuality," in *Homosexualities and French Literature*, ed. George Stambolian and Elaine Marks (Ithaca, N.Y.: Cornell University Press, p. 355.

17. Wickes, *Amazon of Letters*, pp. 94–95. For a slightly different reading of Barney's plays, see Joan DeJean, *Fictions of Sappho, 1546–1937* (Chicago: University of Chicago

Press, 1989), pp. 281–84. She notes that *Cinq petits dialogues grecs* was dedicated to Pierre Louÿs.

18. Natalie Clifford Barney, "Équivoque," in *Actes et entr'actes* (Paris: Sansot, 1910), p. 81, quoted in Karla Jay, *The Amazon and the Page: Natalie Clifford Barney and Renée Vivien* (Bloomington: Indiana University Press), p. 68.

19. For a discussion of her private and public theatricality, see Heather McPherson, "Sarah Bernhardt: Portrait of the Actress as Spectacle," *Nineteenth-Century Contexts* 20 (1999): 409–54.

20. Gerda Tarnow, *Sarah Bernhardt: The Art Within the Legend* (Princeton, N.J.: Princeton University Press, 1972), p. 211. Biographies of Bernhardt are legion. In addition to Tarnow, see Arthur Gold and Robert Fizdale, *The Divine Sarah: The Life of Sarah Bernhardt* (New York: Alfred Knopf, 1991). For an analysis of her theatrical innovations and influence, see John Stokes, "Sarah Bernhardt," in *Bernhardt, Terry, Duse: The Actress in Her Time*, ed. John Stokes, Michael R. Booth, and Susan Basnett (Cambridge: Cambridge University Press, 1988).

21. Biographers detail contemporary critical responses to Bernhardt's numerous *travesti* roles. The best summary is Tarnow, *Sarah Bernhardt*, pp. 210–27. Bernhardt's description of her "Hamlets" as strong minds in weak bodies comes from her *The Art of the Theatre*, tr. H. J. Stenning (London: Geoffrey Bles, 1924), p. 141.

22. A full discussion of the political attitudes of the Parisian lesbians is not possible here. For an introduction to their complex political and economic beliefs, see Shari Benstock, "Paris Lesbianism and the Politics of Reaction, 1900–1940," in *Hidden from History: Reclaiming the Gay and Lesbian*, ed. Martin Bauml Duberman, Martha Vicinus, and George Chauncey, Jr. (New York: New American Library, 1989); and Anna Livia, "The Trouble with Heroines," in *A Perilous Advantage*, pp. 181–93.

23. Wickes, *Amazon of Letters*, p. 37.

24. Claude Francis and Fernande Gontier, *Creating Colette*, vol. 1: *From Ingenue to Libertine, 1873–1913* (South Royalton, Vt: Steerforth Press, 1998), p.189. Sautman, "Invisible Woman," pp. 185–95, discusses the seamier side of these excursions in her analysis of lesbian sex workers.

25. The only full consideration of the novel is Melanie Hawthorne, "The Seduction of Terror: Annhine's Annihilation in Liane de Pougy's *Idylle saphique*," in *Articulations of Difference: Gender Studies and Writing in French*, ed. Dominique D. Fisher and Lawrence R. Schehr (Stanford, Calif.: Stanford University Press, 1997).

26. Wickes, *Amazon of Letters*, p. 40. Wickes's translation.

27. The events surrounding *Rêve d'Égypte* are recounted in Francis and Gontier, *Creating Colette*, 1: 249–59. They emphasize the way in which Willy and Colette had played with fire for years in their increasingly libidinous stage productions, accompanied by well-orchestrated publicity.

28. de Pougy, *Blue Notebooks*, p. 110.

29. Chalon, *Portrait of a Seductress*, pp. 47–48. These and the previous comments were made in old age; at the time she may not have been so clear about her plans.

30. Marie-Jo Bonnet, *Les Relations amoureuses entre les femmes du XVI au XX siècle: essai historique* (Paris: Odile Jacob, 1995), p. 260. See also the list of the women who attended on p. 263.

31. For a brief description of her académie, see the comments by Aurel and Lucie Delarue-Mardrus, in Natalie Clifford Barney, "An Academy of Women: Forward," *Adventures of the Mind*, tr. John Spalding Gatton (New York: New York University Press, 1992), pp. 133–40.

32. Meryle Secrest, *Between Me and Life: A Biography of Romaine Brooks* (London: Macdonald & Jane's, 1976), p. 366.

33. See Shari Benstock, *Women of the Left Bank: Paris, 1900–1940* (Austin: University of Texas Press, 1986), pp. 37–64; and Lillian Faderman, *Surpassing the Love of Men: Romantic Friendship and Love Between Women from the Renaissance to the Present* (New York: William Morrow, 1981), pp. 369–73.

34. Secrest, *Between Me and Life*, p. 267.

35. Robert A. Martin and Linda Wagner-Martin, "The Salons of Wharton's Fiction: Wharton and Fitzgerald, Hemingway, Faulkner, and Stein," in *Wretched Exotic: Essays on Edith Wharton in Europe*, ed. Katherine Joslin and Alan Price (New York: Peter Lang, 1993), p. 106.

36. See "Ezra Pound: Letters to Natalie Barney" (ed. Richard Sieburth), *Paideuma* 5 (Fall 1976).

37. *The Autobiography of William Carlos Williams* (New York: New Directions, 1967), p. 229. See also Hemingway's brutal account of overhearing the lovemaking of Alice B. Toklas and Gertrude Stein in *A Moveable Feast* (New York: Charles Scribner's Sons, 1964), pp. 117–19.

38. Radclyffe Hall, *The Well of Loneliness* (New York: Doubleday, 1956), p. 352.

39. Benstock, *Women of the Left Bank*, p. 289.

40. Radclyffe Hall to Evguenia Souline, 7 June 1935, quoted in Sally Cline, *Radclyffe Hall: A Woman Called John* (Woodstock, N.Y.: Overlook Press, 1998), p. 338.

41. Chalon, *Portrait of a Seductress*, pp. 47–48.

42. "Being other than normal is a perilous advantage," foreword to *Souvenirs indiscrets*, epigraph on the title page of *A Perilous Advantage*.

43. Barney's extreme individualism in regard to her sexuality is succinctly summarized in "Illicit Love Defended" and "Predestined for Free Choice," in *A Perilous Advantage*, pp. 85–94.

44. Goujon, *Tes blessures*, pp. 36–42, suggests that Mrs. Tarn did not like having an eligible daughter because it drew attention to her own age; she also tried to commit her daughter to a mental institution in order to maintain control over her inheritance (John Tarn had died in 1886). Goujon works hard to normalize all of his heroine's sexual relations and practices.

45. Vivien's life remains shrouded in mystery. For the available details, see Goujon, *Tes blessures*; Paul Lorenz, *Sapho 1900: Renée Vivien* (Paris: Julliard, 1977); and Jay, *Amazon and Page*.

46. For the definitive account of this figure, see A. J. L. Busst, "The Image of the Androgyne in the Nineteenth Century," in *Romantic Mythologies*, ed. Ian Fletcher (London: Routledge & Kegan Paul, 1967).

47. Francette Pacteau, "The Androgyne," in *Formations of Fantasy*, ed. Victor Burgin, James Donald, and Cora Kaplan (London: Methuen, 1986), p. 62.

48. Renée Vivien, *A Woman Appeared to Me*, tr. Jeannette H. Foster (Reno, Nev.: Naiad Press, 1976), p. 14. On Vivien's attempt to create a Lesbos out of time and place in her poetry, see Elyse Blankley, "Return to Mytilène: Renée Vivien and the City of Women," in *Women Writers and the City: Essays in Feminist Literary Criticism*, ed. Susan Merrill Squier (Knoxville: University of Tennessee Press, 1984).

49. Colette, *The Pure and the Impure*, tr. Herma Briffault (New York: Farrar, Straus & Giroux, 1967), p. 98. Colette published her essay on Vivien in 1928 (an *annus mirabilis* for lesbian fiction in Britain, as documented in chap. 8).

50. Natalie Barney, "Renée Vivien," in *A Perilous Advantage*, p. 25. From Barney's

Souvenirs indiscrets (1960). In actuality, Barney's memoirs are very discreet; for example, she never mentions her rival, the Baroness van Zuylen, by name.

51. Colette, *Pure and Impure*, pp. 93–94; Francis and Gontier, *Creating Colette*, 1: 223–24, 238.

52. Louise Faure-Favier, "The Muse of Violets" (1953), tr. Jeannette H. Foster, in Renée Vivien, *The Muse of Violets*, tr. Margaret Porter and Catharine Kroger ([Bates City, Mo.: Naiad Press, 1977), pp. 9, 17.

53. Colette, *Pure and Impure*, pp. 87–88, 90. Colette could not resist pointing out that this Decadent role was out of date by the early twentieth century. Goujon, *Tes blessures*, pp. 229–33, summarizes other contemporary descriptions.

54. The details about Vivien's life in this paragraph are from Gayle Rubin's introduction to Vivien, *A Woman Appeared to Me*, p. xiii. See also the lengthy description of her relationship with Barney in Rodriguez, *Wild Heart*, pp. 105–36, 164–69, 198–225.

55. Vivien, *A Woman Appeared to Me*, p. 19.

56. Tama Lea Engelking, "Renée Vivien's Sapphic Legacy: Remembering the 'House of Muses,'" *Atlantis* 18 (1992–93): 130.

57. Vivien, *A Woman Appeared to Me*, pp. 9, 14.

58. Jay, introduction to *A Perilous Advantage*, pp. ii, v–vii.

59. Vivien, *A Woman Appeared to Me*, p. 62. McPherson, "Sarah Bernhardt," p. 415, discusses the association of Bernhardt with the serpentine form and actions.

60. Vivien, *A Woman Appeared to Me*, pp. 7, 8, 1. Vivien's characterization of Petrus the procurer betrays the casual anti-Semitism of this generation, as well as her dislike of homosexual men. San Giovanni, the moral center of the novel, describes him as "congenitally obscene, like all Levantines. When he leaves, one feels the need to open the windows and shake the hangings" (p. 7).

61. Ibid., p. 1.

62. Renée Vivien, *The Woman of the Wolf and Other Stories*, tr. Karla Jay and Yvonne M. Klein (New York: Gay Presses, 1983), pp. 27–28.

63. Faure-Favier, *Muse of Violets*, pp. 17–18.

64. Vivien, *A Woman Appeared to Me*, p. 54.

65. "Sappho Lives Again," in Renée Vivien, *At the Sweet Hour of Hand in Hand*, tr. Sandia Belgrade ([Weatherby Lake, Mo.]: Naiad Press, 1979), p. 3.

66. "Departure," "I shall be always virgin," and "Let a Wave Take It," in Vivien, *Muse of the Violets*, pp. 32, 63, 70. Lucie Delarue-Mardrus also developed the association between femininity and the sea in a series of poems titled "L'Âme et la mer" in *Occident* (1901).

67. Colette, *Pure and Impure*, pp. 98–99. Colette goes on to say, "I put an end to the indiscretion of those young half-conscious lips, and not very tactfully." According to Francis and Gontier, *Creating Colette*, 1: 107–8, Colette had shocked Paris with her crude language.

68. Sherry A. Dranch, "Reading Through the Veiled Text: Colette's *The Pure and the Impure*," *Contemporary Literature* 24 (1983). Dranch focuses on Colette's use of circumlocutions and ellipses to leave unsaid certain lesbian sexual practices, while still conveying them to the reader.

69. Vivien, *A Woman Appeared to Me*, p. 47.

70. Ibid., p. 50.

71. "Nocturne," in Vivien, *Muse of the Violets*, tr. Catharine Kroger, p. 54. Suspension points in the original.

72. Goujon, *Tes blessures*, pp. 187–202. Goujon contends that Vivien probably

wrote numerous poems to van Zuylen that have been lost, along with her letters, when van Zuylen (born a Rothschild) had to flee France in 1940. He also claims that Vivien may have written van Zuylen's ten publications, as well as their numerous putatively coauthored works published under the pseudonym Paule Riversdale.

73. Ibid., p. 190.

74. Colette, *Pure and Impure*, p. 101; Goujon, *Tes blessures*, p. 191; Francis and Gontier, *Creating Colette*, 1: 223.

75. Colette, *Pure and Impure*, p. 101.

76. The biographical information in this paragraph is drawn from Secrest, *Between Me and Life;* and Wickes, *Amazon of Letters*, pp. 163–71.

77. Laura Doan, *Fashioning Sapphism: The Origins of a Modern Lesbian Culture* (New York: Columbia University Press, 2001), pp. 110–25, discusses how this mannish style of dress became the height of fashion for modern Englishwomen in the early 1920s. For another discussion of the fashionable lesbian styles of the decade, see Katrina Rolley, "Cutting a Dash: The Dress of Radclyffe Hall and Una Troubridge" *Feminist Review* 35 (Summer 1990).

78. I am indebted to Melanie Hawthorne for the suggestion that Brooks reserved her mannish outfits for lesbian gatherings. Group photos in Secrest's biography show Brooks dressed simply as a stylish woman.

79. Romaine Brooks to Natalie Clifford Barney, 23 June 1923, quoted by Joe Lucchesi, "'The Dandy in Me': Romaine Brooks's 1923 Portraits," in Susan Fillin-Yeh, ed., *Dandies: Fashion and Finesse in Art and Culture* (New York: New York University Press, 2001), p. 153. The dandy was an important figure for lesbians before the 1920s. See Martha Vicinus, "Turn of the Century Male Impersonation: Rewriting the Romance Plot," in *Sexualities in Victorian Britain*, ed. Andrew H. Miller and James Eli Adams (Bloomington: Indiana University Press, 1996).

80. Catherine McNickle Chastain, "Romaine Brooks: A New Look at Her Drawings," *Woman's Art Journal*, 17.2 (Fall 1996–Winter 1997), discusses the drawings in terms of Brooks's unpublished autobiography.

81. For the best description of the *Cleopâtre* performance, see Joe Lucchesi, "'An Apparition in Black Flowing Cloak': Romaine Brooks's Portraits of Ida Rubinstein," in *Amazons in the Drawing Room: The Art of Romaine Brooks*, ed. Whitney Chadwick (Berkeley: University of California Press, 2000), p. 73.

82. Michel de Cossart, *Ida Rubinstein, 1886–1960: A Theatrical Life* (Liverpool: Liverpool University Press, 1987), pp. 15–43, for descriptions of her roles as Cleopatra and St. Sebastian. Rubinstein also played Sheherazade and Salomé, confirming a popular fin-de-siècle image of the vampiric woman.

83. Lucchesi, "An Apparition," p. 83.

CHAPTER EIGHT

1. The early sexologists came under feminist fire in the late twentieth century for "morbidifying" same-sex relations. See Lillian Faderman, *Surpassing the Love of Men: Romantic Friendship and Love Between Women from the Renaissance to the Present* (New York: William Morrow, 1981), pp. 314–31; Sheila Jeffreys, *The Spinster and Her Enemies: Feminism and Sexuality, 1880–1930* (London: Pandora, 1985); and Margaret Jackson, *The Real Facts of Life: Feminism and the Politics of Sexuality, ca. 1850–1940* (London: Taylor & Francis, 1994). Responses to this perspective show a far more complex and nuanced view. See the authors cited below, especially Bland, Doan, and Oosterhuis.

2. The inverts' interest in sexology books is discussed in Harry Oosterhuis, *Step-*

children of Nature: Krafft-Ebing, Psychiatry and the Making of Sexual Identity (Chicago: University of Chicago Press, 2000), pp. 139–84; and Laura Doan, *Fashioning Sapphism: The Origins of a Modern English Lesbian Culture* (New York: Columbia University Press, 2001), pp. 126–63.

3. Havelock Ellis, *Sexual Inversion*, in Ellis, *Studies in the Psychology of Sex* (New York: Random House, 1936)., Originally published in 1897, this book was withdrawn from publication in Britain. The seven volumes that make up *Studies in Psychology* were completed by 1909; they were reprinted in two volumes in the United States in 1936.

4. Rebecca West, "A Jixless Errand," *Time and Tide*, 15 March 1929: 282.

5. See, for example, Lucy Bland, *Banishing the Beast: Sexuality and the Early Feminists* (New York: The New Press, 1995), pp. 273–83; and Jeffrey Weeks, *Sexuality and Its Discontents: Meanings, Myths and Modern Sexualities* (London: Routledge & Kegan Paul, 1985), pp. 65–69.

6. Stella Browne, "The Sexual Variety and Variability Among Women," *British Society for the Study of Sex Psychology* 3 (1916), quoted in Bland, *Banishing*, p. 274. Browne's paper was originally presented to the British Society for the Study of Sex Psychology in October 1915.

7. Doan, *Fashioning Sapphism*, pp. 126–44.

8. Ellis, *Sexual Inversion*, pp. 225, 226, in regard to Miss H, known to be Edith Ellis. See Jo-Ann Wallace, "The Case of Edith Ellis," in *Modern Sexualities*, ed. Hugh Stephens and Caroline Howlett (Manchester: Manchester University Press, 2000), pp. 22–23.

9. Vernon Lee to Carlo Placci, 1894, quoted in Vineta Colby, *Vernon Lee: A Literary Biography* (Charlottesville: University of Virginia Press, 2003), p. 134.

10. George Chauncey, Jr, "From Sexual Inversion to Homosexuality: Medicine and the Changing Conceptualization of Female Deviance," *Salmagundi* 58–59 (Fall 1982-Winter 1983), discusses the contradictions of American sexologists.

11. Ellis, *Sexual Inversion*, p. 250.

12. Ibid., p. 257.

13. Havelock Ellis, *My Life* (Boston: Houghton Mifflin, 1939), p. 263. See also Chris White, "'She was not really man at all': The Lesbian Practice and Politics of Edith Ellis," in *What Lesbians Do in Books*, ed. Elaine Hobby and Chris White (London: The Women's Press, 1991), pp. 68–85.

14. See Bland, *Banishing*, pp. 258–62, as well as the American examples in Christina Simmons, "Companionate Marriage and the Lesbian Threat," *Frontiers* 4.3. (1979).

15. All quotations in this paragraph are from Ellis, *Sexual Inverstion*, p. 222.

16. Ibid.

17. As Bland, *Banishing*, pp. 40–42, documents, women did not so much undermine the vested belief in heterosexuality as mankind's goal as suggest alternative forms that privileged sexual self-control.

18. Ellis, *Sexual Inversion*, p. 226.

19. Ibid, pp. 257–58.

20. Ibid, pp. 200–201. See Lisa Duggan's discussion of Ellis in connection with the 1892 Alice Mitchell murder of her lover, Freda Ward, in *Sapphic Slashers: Sex, Violence and American Modernity* (Durham, N.C.: Duke University Press, 2000), pp. 174–79.

21. Edward Carpenter, *The Intermediate Sex: A Study of Some Transitional Types of Men and Women* (London: George Allen & Unwin, 1908), p. 19. See also Ruth Brandon, *The New Women and the Old Men: Love, Sex and the Woman Question* (London: Secker & Warburg,

1990), pp. 245–48, for a discussion of how lesbian women turned to Carpenter for advice and comfort.

22. Margaret Gibson, "The Masculine Degenerate: American Doctors' Portrayals of the Lesbian Intellect, 1880–1949," *Journal of Women's History* 9 (Winter 1998): 78–103, discusses the inconsistent attitudes of American experts toward the presumed male intellect of the lesbian.

23. Carpenter, *Intermediate Sex*, p. 26.

24. *British Medical Journal*, 29 June 1909, quoted in Laura Doan, "'The Outcast of One Age Is the Hero of Another': Radclyffe Hall, Edward Carpenter and the Intermediate Sex," in *Palatable Poison: Critical Perspectives on 'The Well of Loneliness,'* ed. Laura Doan and Jay Prosser (New York: Columbia University Press, 2001), p. 165.

25. Ellis, *Sexual Inversion*, pp. 216–17, 220.

26. Bernhard A. Bauer, *Woman and Love*, tr. Eden and Cedar Paul (New York: Liverwright, 1927), 1: 260–61. Bauer places great responsibility on men to meet their wives' sexual needs.

27. Susan Kingsley Kent, *Making Peace: The Reconstruction of Gender in Interwar Britain* (Princeton, N.J.: Princeton University Press, 1993), p. 129.

28. Charlotte Haldane, *Motherhood and Its Enemies* (Garden City, N.Y.: Doubleday, Doran, 1928), p. 154. See also p. 150, where she speaks approvingly of Clemence Dane's *Regiment of Women*. In contrast to the many pages Haldane spends discussing the problem of "intersexed women," she dismisses homosexual men in a few sentences, concluding, "Men with slightly abnormal sex lives continue, as we know, to play useful and often even heroic parts in social and political spheres" (p. 144).

29. The classic analysis of these female types remains Carroll Smith-Rosenberg, "Discourses of Sexuality and Subjectivity: The New Woman, 1870–1936," in *Hidden from History: Reclaiming the Gay and Lesbian Past*, ed. Martin Bauml Duberman, Martha Vicinus, and George Chauncey, Jr. (New York: New American Library, 1989), pp. 272–73.

30. Arabella Kenealy, *Feminism and Sex-Extinction* (London: T. Fisher Unwin, 1920), p. 203.

31. See Alison Oram's analysis of the difficulties faced by unmarried schoolteachers in *Women Teachers and Feminist Politics, 1900–1939* (Manchester: University of Manchester Press, 1996), pp. 185–212.

32. Lilian M. Faithfull, *You and I; Saturday Talks at Cheltenham* (London: Chatto &Windus, 1927), p. 112.

33. Ibid., p. 119.

34. Marie Carmichael Stopes, *Sex and the Young* (London: G. P. Putnam's Sons, 1926), p. 54. Stopes's chief source of information on homosexuality was Bauer, *Woman and Love*.

35. Stopes, *Sex and the Young*, p. 44.

36. See Annabel Faraday, "Lessoning Lesbians: Girls' Schools, Coeducation and Anti-lesbianism Between the Wars," in *Learning Our Lives: Sexuality and Social Control in Education*, ed. Pat Mahony and Carol Jones (London: The Women's Press, 1989).

37. Clemence Dane, *Regiment of Women* (London: Virago, 1995), p. 30. Positive portraits of schoolgirl crushes continued into the 1950s, according to Rosemary Auchmuty, *The World of Girls* (London: The Women's Press, 1992), but she also traces "an ever declining ration of expressed love between women" from the 1930s (p.174).

38. Dane, *Regiment of Women*, p. 31.

39. Ibid., p. 325. Ellipsis in the original. Dane repeatedly uses ellipses for emphasis, as well as to indicate her characters' thought processes.

40. Ibid., p. 300. Clare's kisses are mentioned only one other time, when Alwynne promises to disobey her aunt and visit her on Christmas. As she leaves Clare's flat, "Carefully Clare deposited her candlestick on the stair above. Leaning over the banisters, she put her arms round Alwynne and kissed her passionately and repeatedly" (p. 70).

41. Ibid., p. 327.

42. Ibid, p. 337. See Gay Wachman's comments on the Gothic intensity of Elsbeth's attack on Clare, in *Lesbian Empire: Radical Crosswriting in the Twenties* (New Brunswick, N.J.: Rutgers University Press, 2001), p. 61.

43. Alison Hennegan, introduction to Dane, *Regiment of Women*, p. xiii. See also Henry Handel Richardson, *The Getting of Wisdom* (1910); D. H. Lawrence's banned *The Rainbow* (1915); Virginia Woolf, *Mrs. Dalloway* (1925); Dorothy Sayers, *Unnatural Death* (1927); Rosalind Wade, *Children, Be Happy* (1931); Christa Winsloe, *The Child Manuela* (1934, in German); Brett Young, *White Ladies* (1935); and after World War II, Muriel Spark, *The Prime of Miss Jean Brodie* (1961). Dane's enterprising American publisher reprinted her novel in the 1930s to capitalize on the widespread publicity for Winsloe's novel and film.

44. See, for example, Mary Scharlieb, *The Bachelor Woman and her Problems* (London: Williams & Norgate, 1929); and Mary Chadwick, *Adolescent Girlhood* (London: George Allen & Unwin, 1932). Chadwick warns against "the component instinct *sadism*" in teachers (p. 237). I am indebted to Alison Oram for suggesting these references.

45. Nicky Hallett, *Lesbian Lives: Identity and Auto/Biography in the Twentieth Century* (London: Pluto Press, 1999), p. 19, identifies the person. in the dedicatory poem to *Regiment of Women* (p. iv) as Dane's lover of many years, Elsa Arnold: "To E. A. / Here's Our Book / As it grew. / But it's Your Book! / For, but for you, / Who'd look / At My Book? / C.D." At the height of her fame, two autobiographical pieces appeared, "Personalities and Powers: Clemence Dane," *Time and Tide*, Jan. 19, 1923: 55–56; and St. John Adcock, *The Glory that was Grub Street: Impressions of Contemporary Authors* (London: Low, Marston, [1928]), pp. 33–42. On Dane's career in the theater, see Maggie B. Gale, "From Fame to Obscurity: In Search of Clemence Dane," in *Women, Theatre and Performance: New Histories, New Historiographies*, ed. Maggie B. Gale and Viv Gardner (Manchester: Manchester University Press, 2000).

46. Victoria Glendinning, *Vita: A Biography of Vita Sackville West* (New York: Quill, 1983), p. 110. For the events leading up to Trefusis and Sackville West's stay with Dane, see Nigel Nicolson, *Portrait of a Marriage* (New York: Atheneum, 1973), pp. 118–44.

47. Winifred Ashton [Clemence Dane], *The Women's Side* (Freeport, N.Y.: Books for Libraries Press, 1970, pp. 59–60.

48. "We feel that, in describing the supposedly sinister predilections of the child Stephen Gordon, much ado is often made about nothing; so many of them appear to be the quite usual preferences of any vigorous young female who happens to possess more vitality and intelligence than her fellows." "New Fiction: Facing Facts," *Time and Tide*, 10 Aug. 1928: 765.

49. Ashton/Dane, *The Women's Side*, pp. 64–65.

50. L. Faithfull, *You and I*, pp. 112–13.

51. Ashton/Dane, *The Women's Side*, p. 73.

52. Ibid., p. 128.

53. From their first publication, critics have been intrigued with the autobiographical elements in the Claudine novels. See Claude Francis and Fernande Gontier, *Creating Colette* (South Royalton, Vt: Steerforth Press, 1998), 1: 161–69.

54. Colette [and Willy], *Claudine at School*, tr. Antonia White (New York: Albert & Charles Boni, 1930), p. 123.

55. Ibid., p. 161.

56. Judith Thurman, *Secrets of the Flesh: A Life of Colette* (New York: Alfred A. Knopf, 1999), p. 114.

57. Radclyffe Hall, *The Well of Loneliness* (New York: Doubleday, 1956), pp. 204, 13.

58. Ibid., p. 289.

59. Ibid., p. 294.

60. Ibid., p. 313. I discuss the importance of ellipses in my conclusion. Clare Hemmings discusses the "banishment of the feminine from the masculine narrative" in "'All My Life I've Been Waiting for Something . . . ': Theorizing Femme Narrative in *The Well of Loneliness*," in *Palatable Poison*, ed. Laura Doan and Jay Prosser (New York: Columbia University Press, 2001), pp. 189–92.

61. Hall, *Well of Loneliness*, p. 430.

62. Doan, *Fashioning Sapphism*, pp. 156–59.

63. Radclyffe Hall to Newman Flower (Hall's editor at Cassell's), 16 April 1928, quoted in Sally Cline, *Radclyffe Hall : A Woman Called John* (Woodstock, N.Y.: Overlook Press, 1998), p. 235.

64. James Douglas, "A Book That Must Be Suppressed," *Sunday Express*, 19 Aug. 1928, quoted in *Palatable Poison*, ed. Laura Doan and Jay Prosser (New York: Columbia University Press, 2001), p. 37.

65. Sir Chartres Biron, chief magistrate, "Judgment" 1928, in ibid., p. 47. See also Adam Parkes, "Lesbianism, History, and Censorship: *The Well of Loneliness* and the SUPPRESSED RANDINESS of Virginia Woolf's *Orlando*," *Twentieth-Century Literature* 40 (1994): 434–60. For full details of the trial, see Cline, *Radclyffe Hall*, pp. 234–67.

66. Rebecca West, in an American review, declared: "The book constantly gives us a sense of fictitious values, of 'Cry, damn you, cry,' hokum. Hence considerable dismay is being felt by those who are compelled by their belief in a free press to wrestle with the authorities over the suppression of this book, but who realize perfectly well that this is the kind of book they have denounced again and again in the course of other tussles with censorship." "Concerning Censorship," in West, *Ending in Earnest: A Literary Log* (Garden City, N.Y.: Doubleday Doran, 1931), p. 9. W. R. Gordon, Cyril Connolly, and *Life and Letters* also attacked the novel's special pleading. See *Palatable Poison*, ed. Laura Doan and Jay Prosser (New York: Columbia University Press, 2001), pp. 65–69, 71–72.

67. Hall, *Well of Loneliness* , p. 123.

68. *Lancet*, 1 Sept. 1928, quoted in *Palatable Poison*, ed. Laura Doan and Jay Prosser (New York: Columbia University Press, 2001), p. 71.

69. A. M. A., "Books of the Week: The Modern Amazon," *Liverpool Post and Mercury*, 15 Aug. 1928.

70. Vera Brittain, *Radclyffe Hall: A Case of Obscenity?* (London: Femina Books, 1968), p. 765.

71. See, for example, ibid., p. 60: "Forty years ago, except for a scientific few, the psychological variation known to us today as homosexuality was classified as sin, wanton and unashamed. Almost no one realised that its origins lay in glandular abnormalities."

72. Ibid., p. 91. Compton Mackenzie, in *Extraordinary Women* (London: Hogarth Press, 1986), p. 66, mocks this fear of the "special room" at Naples. When sixteen-year-old Lulu first kisses a woman, she remembers an afternoon when she was twelve,

"in the museum at Naples and [she] had discovered in a remote room a young faun whose marble lips she had climbed up to kiss. . . . The impulse had been nothing more than a surrender to a childish delight in that debonair nudity—a display of premature sensuality perhaps in acknowledgement of the beauty which had roused it without her knowing why."

73. *New Statesman*, 24 Nov. 1928, quoted in Brittain, *Radclyffe Hall*, p. 115.

74. In a letter to Michael Baker (a Hall biographer), Egan admitted that he had been furious when a mannish lesbian had "made amorous advances to his wife." Michael Baker, *Our Three Selves: The Life of Radclyffe Hall* (New York: William Morrow, 1985), p. 257. Egan dedicated his *The Sink of Solitude* (London: Hermes Press, 1928) "To Compton Mackenzie's Extraordinary Women."

75. Hall, *Well of Loneliness*, p. 371. When Stephen's affair with Angela Crossby is winding down "there would be something crude, almost cruel in their kisses; a restless, dissatisfied hungry thing—their lips seemed bent on scourging their bodies" (p. 189).

76. Ibid., p. 20.

77. Ibid., pp. 343, 421. For a discussion of the frequent metaphors of battle, war, and wounding throughout the novel in the context of postwar wounded masculinity, see Susan Kingsley Kent, "*The Well of Loneliness* as War Novel," in *Palatable Poison*, ed. Laura Doan and Jay Prosser (New York: Columbia University Press, 2001), pp. 220–21.

78. Hall, *Well of Loneliness*, p. 300. See also p. 396, describing Jamie's "nerves vibrating" and her "unreasoning anger" from "sex frustration" when her beloved Barbara becomes too ill for sexual relations.

79. Ibid., pp. 428, 431, 432.

80. Ibid., p. 437.

81. Wyndham Lewis, *Apes of God* (New York: Robert M. McBride, 1932), pp. 222, 224–25, 229, 232. The chapter is titled "Lesbian Ape."

82. See John Glassco, *Memoirs of Montparnasse* (Toronto: Oxford University Press, 1970), pp. 40–41. Glassco comments: "The women were passing around the page-proofs of a book that was later to cause a small sensation in literary and lesbian circles. I remember being taken by the style, at once sprightly and spinsterish."

83. Djuna Barnes, *Ladies Almanack* (New York: New York University Press, 1992), p. 84.

84. Ibid., pp. 18, 20.

85. Cline, *Radclyffe Hall*, p. 337. See also Baker, *Our Three Selves*, pp. 298–337.

86. Radclyffe Hall to Evguenia Souline, 7 Sept. 1934, in *Your John: The Love Letters of Radclyffe Hall*, ed. Joanne Glasgow (New York: New York University Press, 1997), p. 55.

87. Radclyffe Hall to Evguenia Souline, 24 Oct. 1934, in ibid., p. 79. At first Hall used the feminine Russian form, Soulina, rather than her first name, but she later reverted to calling her Souline.

88. See Pat Califia, *Sapphistry* (Tallahassee, Fla.: Naiad Press, 1981). For two analyses of the "porn" debates, see Lisa Henderson, "Lesbian Pornography: Cultural Transgression and Sexual Demystification," in *New Lesbian Criticism: Literary and Cultural Readings*, ed. Sally Munt (New York: Columbia University Press, 1992); and Heather Findlay, "Freud's 'Fetishism' and the Lesbian Dildo Debates," in *Lesbian Subjects: A 'Feminist Studies' Reader*, ed. Martha Vicinus (Bloomington: Indiana University Press, 1996), pp. 151–66. See also *Lesbian Erotics*, ed. Karla Jay (New York: New York University Press, 1995.

89. Colette to Radclyffe Hall, quoted without citation in Francis and Gontier, *Creating Colette*, 2:137.

90. Susan Sniader Lanser, "Speaking in Tongues: *Ladies Almanack* and the Discourse of Desire," in *Silence and Power: A Reevaluation of Djuna Barnes*, ed. Mary Lynn Broe (Carbondale: Southern Illinois University Press, 1991), p. 167.

CONCLUSION

1. Edith Simcox journal, 13 June 1880 entry, in *A Monument to the Memory of George Eliot: Edith Simcox's 'Autobiography of a Shirtmaker,'* ed. Constance M. Fulmer and Margaret E. Barfield (New York: Garland, 1998), p. 125

2. I discuss the figure of the ugly spinster in "Fin-de-Siècle Theatrics: Male Impersonation and Lesbian Desire," in *Borderlines: Genders and Identities in War and Peace, 1870–1930*, ed. Billie Melman (New York: Routledge, 1998), pp. 180–86.

3. Natalie Clifford Barney's anti-Semitism and pro-Mussolini stance during World War II are discussed by Anna Livia, "The Trouble with Heroines: Natalie Clifford Barney and Anti-Semitism," in *A Perilous Advantage: The Best of Natalie Clifford Barney*, ed. and tr. Anna Livia (Norwich, Vt: New Victoria Publishers, 1992).

4. Shari Benstock, "Paris Lesbianism and the Politics of Reaction, 1900–1940," in *Hidden from History: Reclaiming the Gay and Lesbian Past*, ed. Martin Duberman, Martha Vicinus, and George Chauncey, Jr. (New York: New American Library, 1989), p. 336. See also pp. 340–42 for Benstock's discussion of Stein's reconfiguration of the patriarchal bourgeois family in her relationship with Alice B. Toklas. The few wealthy lesbians who fought for racial equality and feminist principles, such as Nancy Cunard and Winifred Bryher, became active anti-Fascists as well.

5. Lister diary, 14 Nov. 1824 entry, in *No Priest But Love: Excerpts from the Diaries of Anne Lister, 1824–1826*, ed. Helena Whitbread (New York: New York University Press, 1992), p. 50.

6. Ibid., pp. 50, 51.

7. Charlotte Cushman to Emma Crow [Cushman], 30 June 1858, CC Papers, vol. 1.

8. Mary Benson to Charlotte Bassett, 1 June [1880], DB 3/28.

9. Vernon Lee to Clementina Anstruther-Thomson, 7 April 1904, VLC, unnumbered.

10. Elizabeth Mavor, *The Ladies of Llangollen: A Study in Romantic Friendship* (Harmondsworth, Eng.: Penguin, 1971), p. 99.

11. A. Mary F. Robinson to Vernon Lee, 30 Sept. [1886?], Fonds Anglais, 243, f 106, Bibliothèque Nationale.

12. Renée Vivien, "Union," in *The Muse of Violets*, tr. Margaret Porter and Catharine Kroger ([Bates City, Mo.]: Naiad Press, 1977), p. 73.

13. Colette, *The Pure and the Impure*, tr. Herma Briffault (London: Farrar, Straus & Giroux, 1966), p. 105. In her introduction to *A Perilous Advantage*, Karla Jay says of the ellipsis, "yes, it may be the primary signifier of female desire that dare not speak its name, and Barney, one of its primary devotees" (p. ix).

14. For a full analysis of the different meanings of flowers, see Beverly Seaton, *The Language of Flowers: A History* (Charlottesville: University of Virginia Press, 1995).

15. Ed Madden, "Say It with Flowers: The Poetry of Marc-André Raffalovich," *College Literature*, 24.1 (1997).

16. Virginia Woolf, *Mrs. Dalloway* (London: The Hogarth Press, 1954), p. 40.

17. Paula Bennett, "Critical Clitoridectomy: Female Sexual Imagery and Feminist Pscyhoanalytic Theory," *Signs* 18.2 (1993).

18. Marilyn Yalom, *A History of the Breast* (New York: Knopf, 1997), a survey of 2,500 years of Western history, does include a few references to same-sex passion. On

pp. 74–75 she briefly analyzes the late-sixteenth-century painting of Gabrielle d'Estrées and one of her sisters, who is tweaking her nipples.

19. Colette, *Pure and Impure*, p. 125.

20. Natalie Clifford Barney, "Breasts," in *A Perilous Advantage*, p. 73.

21. Katharine Bradley, untitled poem (1899), in *Music and Silence: The Gamut of Michael Field*, chosen and annotated by Ivor C. Treby (London: De Blackland Press, 2000), p. 115.

22. Virginia Woolf to Ethel Smyth, 26 May 1930, in *The Letters of Virginia Woolf*, ed. Nigel Nicolson and Joanne Trautmann (New York: Harcourt Brace & Jovanovich, 1978), 4: 171.

23. Ethel Smyth diary, 30 Jan. 1933 entry, Diary 4 (31 [sic] Jan. 1933– 16 July 1936), Ethel Smyth Collection, Special Collections, University of Michigan, Ann Arbor. This comes from the opening paragraph to a long description of her love for Virginia Woolf. See also Suzanne Raitt, "'The Tide of Ethel': Femininity as Narrative in the Friendship of Ethel Smyth and Virginia Woolf," *Critical Quarterly*, 30.4 (Winter 1988).

SELECTED BIBLIOGRAPHY

Primary and secondary sources are listed separately in this bibliography. In both, unsigned (or only initialed) newspaper and journal articles have been omitted, but their full citations can be found in the notes. Several secondary works that either bear only tangentially on the subject matter or are onetime references have also been omitted from this bibliography.

PRIMARY SOURCES

Adcock, St. John, *The Glory that was Grub Street.* London: Low, Marston, [1928].

Alger, William Rounseville. *The Friendships of Women.* 10th ed. Boston: Roberts Brothers, 1882.

Ansthruther-Thomson, Clementina. *Art and Man: Essays and Fragments.* Intro. Vernon Lee. London: John Lane, 1924.

Ashburton, Lady Louisa. Letters. Ashburton Collection, National Library of Scotland, Edinburgh.

Barnes, Djuna. *Ladies Almanack* Intro Susan Sniader Lanser. New York: New York University Press, 1992 [1928].

Barney, Natalie Clifford. *Adventures of the Mind,* tr. John Spalding Gatton. New York: New York University Press, 1992.

―――. *Cinq petits dialogues grecs.* Paris: Éditions de la Plume, 1902.

―――. "Équivoque." In Barney, *Actes et entr'actes.* Paris: Sansot, 1910.

―――. *A Perilous Advantage: The Best of Natalie Clifford Barney,* ed. and tr. Anna Livia. Intro. Karla Jay. Norwich, Vt.: New Victoria Publishers, 1992.

―――. *Selected Writings.* Ed. and intro. Miron Grindea. London: Adam Books, 1963.

―――. *Souvenirs indiscrets.* Paris: Flammarion, 1960.

Barrington, Mrs. Russell. *The Life, Letters, and Work of Frederic Leighton.* London: George Allen, 1906.

Bauer, Bernhard A. *Woman and Love,* vol. 1, tr. Eden and Cedar Paul. New York: Liverwright, 1927.

Benson, Arthur Christopher. Diaries. Pepys Library. Magdalene College, Cambridge University, Cambridge, Eng.

―――. *The Life and Letters of Maggie Benson.* New York: Longmans, Green, 1917.

―――. *The Life of Edward White Benson, Sometime Archbishop of Canterbury.* 2 vols. London: Macmillan, 1899.

―――. *Memories and Friends.* New York: Putnam's, 1924.

―――. *The Trefoil: Wellington College, Lincoln, and Truro.* London: John Murray, 1925.

Benson, E. F. *Dodo: A Detail of the Day.* 2 vols. London: Methuen, 1893.

―――. *Final Edition.* London: Longmans, Green, 1940.

―――. *Mother.* London: Hodder & Stoughton, 1925.

Benson, Margaret. *The Soul of a Cat and Other Stories.* London: William Heinemann, 1901.

―――. *The Venture of Rational Faith.* London: Macmillan, 1908.

Benson, Mary. Diary and letters. Deposit Benson, Bodleian Library, University of Oxford, Oxford, Eng.

Berenson, Mary. Papers. I Tatti, Renaissance Center, Harvard University, Florence, Italy.

Bernhardt, Sarah. *The Art of the Theatre,* tr. H. J. Stenning. London: Geoffrey Bles, 1924.

Bradley, Katharine, and Edith Cooper. Journal, "Works and Days: 1868–1914." Manuscript Collection, British Library, London.

―――. Letters. I Tatti, Renaissance Center, Harvard University, Florence, Italy.

Brittain, Vera. "New Fiction: Facing Facts," *Time and Tide,* 10 Aug. 1928: 765–66.

Browning, Elizabeth Barrett. *Elizabeth Barrett Browning: Letters to Her Sister, 1846–59,* ed. Leonard Huxley. London: John Murray, 1929.

Browning, Robert. *Dearest Isa: Robert Browning's Letters to Isabella Blagden,* ed. Edward C. McLeer. Austin: University of Texas Press, 1951.

―――. *Robert Browning to His American Friends: Letters Between the Brownings, Storys and James Russell Lowell, 1841–90,* ed. Gertrude Reese Hudson. London: Bowes & Bowes, 1965.

Caird, Mona. "A Defense of So-Called Wild Women." In Caird, *The Morality of Marriage and Other Essays on the Status and Destiny of Women,* 157–91. London: George Redway, 1897.

Carlyle, Jane Welsh, and Thomas Carlyle. *The Collected Letters of Thomas Carlyle and Jane Welsh Carlyle,* gen. ed. Charles Richard Sanders, vols. 13, 17–19. Durham, N.C.: Duke University Press, 1970–.

Carpenter, Edward. Edward Carpenter Collection, Sheffield Public Archives, Sheffield, Eng.

―――. *Homogenic Love and its place in a free society.* London: Redundancy Press, 1980 [1895].

―――. *The Intermediate Sex: A Study of Some Transitional Types of Men and Women.* London: George Allen & Unwin, 1908.

―――. *Love's Coming-of-Age.* London: Methuen, 1906 [1896].

Chadwick, Mary. *Adolescent Girlhood.* London: George Allen & Unwin, 1932.

Cleland, John. *Memoirs of a Woman of Pleasure.* London: G. Fenton, 1749.

Cobbe, Frances Power. "Ireland and Her Exhibition in 1865," *Fraser's Magazine* 72 (July-Dec. 1865): 422.

―――. *Italics: Brief Notes on Politics, People, and Places in Italy in 1864.* London: Trübner, 1864.

―――. *Life as Told by Herself.* London: Swan Sonnenschein, 1904.

―――. *Life of Frances Cobbe.* 2 vols. Boston: Houghton, Mifflin, 1894.

―――. "Social Science Congresses and Women's Part in Them." In Cobbe, *Essays on the Pursuits of Women.* London: E. Faithfull, 1863.

―――. "What Shall We Do with Our Old Maids?" *Fraser's Magazine* 66 (1862): 594–610.

Codrington, Henry. *Adm. Henry Codrington against Helen Smith Codrington and Col. David Anderson.* XPO984CL J77/11/142, United Kingdom Public Record Office, London.

―――. *Selections from the Letters of Sir Henry Codrington, Admiral of the Fleet,* ed. Lady [Jane Barbara (Codrington)] Bourchier. London: Spottiswoode, 1880.

Colette. *Claudine at School,* tr. Antonia White. New York: Albert & Charles Boni, 1930. [Her husband Willy is listed by law on the title page.]

———. *My Apprenticeships, and Music-Hall Sidelights,* tr. Helen Beauclerk. London: Secker & Warburg, 1957.

———. *The Pure and the Impure,* tr. Herma Briffault. New York: Farrar, Straus & Giroux, 1967.

Craik, Dinah Mulock. *A Woman's Thoughts on Women.* London: Hurst & Blackett [1858].

Cushman, Charlotte. Cushman Collection, Manuscript Division, Library of Congress, Washington, D.C.

Dane, Clemence [Winifred Ashton]. *Regiment of Women.* London: Virago, 1995 [1917].

———. *The Women's Side.* Freeport, N.Y.: Books for Libraries Press, 1970 [1926].

Davies, Emily. "Family Chronicle." Girton College, Cambridge University, Cambridge, Eng.

Delarue-Mardrus, Lucie. *The Angel and the Perverts,* tr. Anna Livia. New York: New York University Press, 1995 [1930].

Egan, Beresford. *The Sink of Solitude.* London: Hermes Press, 1928.

Eliot, George. *The George Eliot Letters,* ed. Gordon S. Haight. 9 vols. New Haven, Conn.: Yale University, 1954–78.

Ellet, Mrs. E. F. [Elizabeth Fries]. *Women Artists in All Ages and Countries.* New York: Harper & Brothers, 1859.

Ellis, Havelock. *My Life.* Boston: Houghton Mifflin, 1939.

———. *Sexual Inversion.* In Ellis, *Studies in the Psychology of Sex,* vol. 1. New York: Random House, 1936. [Originally published in England in 1897.]

———. *Studies in the Psychology of Sex.* 2 vols. New York: Random House, 1936.

Ernst, Morris. Papers. Harry Ransom Humanities Research Center, University of Texas, Austin.

Faithfull, Emily. *A Reed Shaken in the Wind: A Love Story.* New York: Adams, Victor, 1873. [Originally published in England as *Changes upon Changes.*]

———. *Three Visits to America.* Edinburgh: David Douglas, 1884.

Faithfull, Lilian M. *You and I; Saturday Talks at Cheltenham.* London: Chatto & Windus, 1927.

Faure-Favier, Louise. "The Muse of Violets," tr. Jeannette H. Foster. In Renée Vivien, *The Muse of the Violets,* tr. Margaret Porter and Catharine Kroger, 7–20. [Bates City, Mo.]: Naiad Press, 1977 [1953].

Field, Michael [Katharine Bradley and Edith Cooper]. *Dedicated: An Early Work of Michael Field.* London: G. Bell & Sons, 1914.

———. *Music and Silence: The Gamut of Michael Field,* chosen and annotated by Ivor C. Treby. London: De Blackland Press, 2000.

———. *Mystic Trees.* London: Eveleigh Nash, [1913].

———. *Poems of Adoration.* London: Sands, 1912.

———. *A Shorter Shîrazâd: 101 Poems of Michael Field,* chosen and annotated by Ivor C. Treby. London: De Blackland Press, 1999.

———. *The Wattlefold: Unpublished Poems,* comp. Emily C. Fortey. Oxford: Basil Blackwell, 1930.

———. *Wild Honey from Various Thyme.* London: T. Fisher Unwin, 1908.

———. "Works and Days: 1868–1914." British Library, London.

———. *Works and Days: From the Journal of Michael Field,* ed. T. and D. C. Sturge Moore. London: John Murray, 1933.

Gordon, W. R. "Miss Radclyffe Hall's Strange Story," *The Daily News and Westminster Gazette,* 23 Aug. 1928.

Greenwood, Grace [Sara Lippincott]. *Haps and Mishaps or a Tour of Europe.* Boston: Ticknor, Reed & Fields, 1865.

Haldane, Charlotte. *Motherhood and Its Enemies.* Garden City, N.Y.: Doubleday, Doran, 1928.

Hall, Radclyffe. *The Master of the House.* London: Falcon Press, 1952 [1932].

———. *The Unlit Lamp.* London: Jonathan Cape, 1933 [1924].

———. *The Well of Loneliness.* New York: Doubleday, 1956 [1928].

———. *Your John: The Love Letters of Radclyffe Hall,* ed. Joanne Glasgow. New York: New York University Press, 1997.

The Hamwood Papers of the Ladies of Llangollen, ed. Mrs. G. H. Bell. London: Macmillan, 1930.

Hawthorne, Nathaniel. *The French and Italian Notebooks,* ed. Thomas Woodson. Columbus: Ohio State University Press, 1980.

Hays, Matilda. *Adrienne Hope: The Story of a Life.* 2 vols. London: T. Cautley Newby, 1866.

Hicklin, John. *The "Ladies of Llangollen" as sketched by Many Hands; with notices of Other Objects of Interest in "That Sweetest of Vales."* Chester, Eng.: Thomas Catherall, 1847.

Hosmer, Harriet. *Harriet Hosmer: Letters and Memories,* ed. Cornelia Carr. London: John Lane, 1913.

———. Harriet Goodhue Hosmer Papers. Schlesinger Library, Radcliffe Institute, Harvard University, Cambridge, Mass.

Ives, George. George Ives Collection, Harry Ransom Humanities Research Center, University of Texas, Austin.

James, Henry. *Henry James: Letters.* Vol. 1: *1843–1875,* ed. Leon Edel. Cambridge, Mass.: Belknap Press, 1974.

———. *William Wetmore Story and His Friends.* 2 vols. Boston: Houghton Mifflin, 1903.

Jewsbury, Geraldine Endsor. *The Half-Sisters.* 8th ed. London: Chapman & Hall, 1854.

———. *Selections from the Letters of Geraldine Endsor Jewsbury to Jane Welsh Carlyle,* ed. Mrs. Alexander Ireland. London: Longmans, Green, 1892.

———. *Zoe: The History of Two Lives.* 3 vols. London: Chapman & Hall, 1845.

Kenealy, Arabella. *Feminism and Sex-Extinction.* London: T. Fisher Unwin, 1920.

Klumpke, Anna. *Rosa Bonheur: The Artist's (Auto)biography,* tr. Gretchen van Slyke. Ann Arbor: University of Michigan Press, 1997.

Krafft-Ebing, R. [Richard] von. *Psychopathia Sexualis.* Philadelphia: F. A. Davis, 1893 [1886].

Layard, George Somes. *Mrs. Lynn Linton: Her Life, Letters, and Opinions.* London: Methuen, 1901.

Lee, Vernon [Violet Paget]. *Althea: A Second Book of Dialogues on Aspirations and Duties.* London: Osgood, McIlvaine, 1894.

———. Introduction to Clementina Anstruther-Thomson, *Art and Man: Essays and Fragments.* London: John Lane, 1924.

———. *Laurus Nobilis: Chapters on Art and Life.* London: John Lane, 1909.

———. Letters to and from A. Mary F. Robinson. Biblothèque Nationale, Paris.

———. *Miss Brown.* 3 vols. New York: Garland, 1978 [1884].

———. *The Snake Lady and Other Stories,* ed. and intro. Horace Gregory. New York: Grove Press, 1954.

———. Vernon Lee Collection, Special Collections, Colby College, Waterville, Maine.

———. *Vernon Lee's Letters,* ed. Irene Cooper Willis. [London]: Privately printed, 1937.

Lee, Vernon, and C. Ansthruther-Thomson. "Beauty and Ugliness," *Contemporary Review,* 2 parts: 72 (Oct., Nov. 1897): 544–69; 669–88.

LeFanu, Sheridan. "Carmilla." In *Best Ghost Stories of J. S. LeFanu*, ed. E. F. Bleiler, 274–339. New York: Dover, 1964.

Lewis, Wyndham. *Apes of God.* New York: Robert M. McBride, 1932.

Linton, E. Lynn [Elizabeth Lynn]. *The Autobiography of Christopher Kirkland.* 3 vols. London: Richard Bentley, 1885.

———. *My Literary Life.* London: Hodder & Stoughton, 1899.

———. *Realities: A Tale.* 3 vols. London: Saunders & Otley, 1851.

———. *The Rebel of the Family,* ed. Deborah T. Meem. Peterborough, Ont.: Broadview Press, 2002.

———. *The Second Youth of Theodora Desanges.* London: Hutchinson, 1900.

———. *Sowing the Wind: A Novel.* London: Tinsley Bros, 1867.

Lister, Anne. *I Know My Own Heart: The Diaries of Anne Lister (1791–1840),* ed. Helena Whitbread. London: Virago, 1988.

———. *No Priest But Love: Excerpts from the Diaries of Anne Lister, 1824–1826,* ed. Helena Whitbread. New York: New York University Press, 1992.

Mackenzie, Compton. *Extraordinary Women.* London: Hogarth Press, 1986 [1928].

Miss Marianne Woods and Miss Jane Pirie against Dame Helen Cumming Gordon. New York: Arno Press, 1975.

Nordau, Max. *Degeneration.* New York: Appleton, 1895.

Paget, Lady Walpurga Ehrengarde Helena von Hohenthal. *Embassies of Other Days.* 2 vols. London: Hutchinson, 1923.

Parkes, Joseph. Letters. Girton College, Cambridge University. Cambridge, Eng.

Pearson, Karl. "Variation in Man and Woman." In Pearson, *The Chances of Death and Other Studies in Evolution,* vol. 1, 356–77. London: Edward Arnold, 1897.

———. "The Woman's Question." In Pearson, *The Ethic of Freethought and Other Addresses and Essays,* 354–78. London: Adam & Charles Black, 1901 [1888].

Piozzi, Hester Thrale. *The Piozzi Letters: Correspondence of Hester Lynch Piozzi, 1784–1821 (formerly Mrs. Thrale),* ed. Edward A. Bloom and Lillian D. Bloom. 5 vols. Newark: University of Delaware Press, 1993.

Ponsonby, Mary Elizabeth. *Mary Elizabeth Ponsonby: A Memoir, Some Letters and a Journal,* ed. Magdalen Ponsonby. London: John Murray, 1927.

Pougy, Liane de. *Idylle saphique.* Paris: Jean-Claude Lattès, 1979 [1901].

———. *My Blue Notebooks,* tr. Diana Athill. London: André Deutsch, 1979.

Robinson, A. Mary F. [Madame Duclaux]. *The Collected Poems: Lyrical and Narrative.* London: T. Fisher Unwin, 1902.

———. "In Casa Paget: A Retrospect. In Memoriam: Eugène Lee-Hamilton," *Country Life* 22 (28 Dec. 1907): 935–37.

Rousseau, Jean-Jacques. *Julie, or The New Heloise,* tr. and annotated by Philip Stewart and Jean Vaché. Hanover, N.H.: University Press of New England, 1997.

Scharlieb, Mary. *The Bachelor Woman and her Problems.* London: Williams & Norgate, 1929.

Schreiner, Olive. *Women and Labour.* New York: Frederick A. Stokes, 1911.

Seward, Anna. *The Swan of Litchfield: Being a Selection from the correspondence of Anna Seward,* Ed. Hesketh Pearson. London: H. Hamilton, 1936.

Shelley, Mary. *The Letters of Mary Wollstonecraft Shelley,* ed. Betty T. Bennett. 3 vols. Baltimore: Johns Hopkins University Press, 1980–88.

Simcox, Edith. "George Eliot," *Nineteenth Century* 9 (May 1881): 778–801.

———. *A Monument to the Memory of George Eliot: Edith Simcox's "Autobiography of a Shirtmaker,"* ed. Constance M. Fulmer and Margaret E. Barfield. New York: Garland Press, 1998.

Smyth, Ethel. *As Time Went On . . .* London: Longmans, Green, 1936.
———. Diaries. Special Collections, University of Michigan, Ann Arbor.
———. *Impressions that Remained.* New York: DaCapo Press, 1981 [1919].
———. *Inordinate Affection: A Story for Dog Lovers.* London: The Cresset Press, 1936.
———. Letters. Deposit Benson, Bodleian Library, University of Oxford, Oxford, Eng.
———. Letters. Vernon Lee Collection, Miller Library, Colby College, Waterville, Maine.
———. Letters. University Archives and Manuscripts, Walter Clinton Jackson Library, University of North Carolina at Greensboro.
———. *Streaks of Life.* London: Longmans, Green, 1921.
———. *What Happened Next.* London: Longmans, Green, 1940.
St. John, Christopher [Christabel Marshal]. Notebooks. Special Collections, University of Michigan, Ann Arbor.
Stanton, Theodore, ed. *Reminiscences of Rosa Bonheur.* New York: Hacker Art Books, 1976 [1910].
Stebbins, Emma. *Charlotte Cushman: Her Letters and Memories of Her Life.* Boston: Houghton, Osgood, 1878.
Stopes, Marie Carmichael. *Sex and the Young.* London: G. P. Putnam's Sons, 1926.
Symonds, John Addington. *A Problem in Moden Ethics.* London, 1896.
Vivien, Renée. *At the Sweet Hour of Hand in Hand,* tr. Sandia Belgrade. [Weatherby Lake, Mo.]: Naiad Press, 1979.
———. *The Muse of the Violets,* tr. Margaret Porter and Catharine Kroger. [Bates City, Mo.]: Naiad Press, 1977.
———. *A Woman Appeared to Me,* tr. Jeannette H. Foster. Intro. Gayle Rubin. Reno: Nev.: Naiad Press, 1976.
———. *The Woman of the Wolf and Other Stories,* tr. Karla Jay and Yvonne M. Klein. New York: Gay Presses of New York, 1983.
West, Rebecca. "Concerning Censorship." In West, *Ending in Earnest: A Literary Log,* 6–12. Garden City, N.Y.: Doubleday Doran, 1931.
———. "A Jixless Errand." *Time and Tide,* 15 March 1929: 282–86.
Wilberforce, Octavia. *Octavia Wilberforce: The Autobiography of A Pioneer Doctor,* ed. Pat Jalland. London: Cassell, 1989.
Woolf, Virginia. "Geraldine and Jane." In Woolf, *The Second Common Reader,* 186–201. New York: Harcourt Brace & World, 1932.
———. *The Letters of Virginia Woolf,* ed. Nigel Nicolson and Joanne Trautmann. 6 vols. New York: Harcourt Brace & Jovanovich, 1975–80.
———. *Mrs. Dalloway.* London: Hogarth Press, 1954 [1925].
———. *A Room of One's Own.* New York: Harcourt Brace & Jovanovich, 1957 [1928].
———. *To the Lighthouse.* London: Hogarth Press, 1955 [1927].

SECONDARY SOURCES
Abelove, Henry. "Some Speculations on the History of Sexual Intercourse During the Long Eighteenth Century," *Genders* 6 (Fall 1989): 125–30.
Aldrich, Robert. *The Seduction of the Mediterranean: Writing, Art and Homosexual Fantasy.* London: Routledge, 1993.
Anderson, Nancy Fix. *Woman Against Women in Victorian England: A Life of Eliza Lynn Linton.* Bloomington: Indiana University Press, 1987.
Andreadis, Harriette. "Theorizing Early Modern Lesbianisms: Invisible Bodies, Ambiguous Demarcations." In *Virtual Gender: Fantasies of Subjectivity and Embodiment,* ed.

Mary Ann O'Farrell and Lynne Vallone, 125–46. Ann Arbor: University of Michigan Press, 1999.

Askwith, Betty. *Two Victorian Families*. London: Chatto & Windus, 1971.

Auchmuty, Rosemary. *The World of Girls*. London: The Women's Press, 1992.

Baker, Michael. *Our Three Selves: The Life of Radclyffe Hall*. New York: William Morrow, 1985.

Barbedette, Gilles, and Michel Carassou. *Paris Gay 1925*. Paris: Presses de la Renaissance, 1981.

Bebbington, D. W. *Evangelicalism in Modern Britain: A History from the 1730s to the 1980s*. London: Unwin Hyman, 1989.

Beckman, Linda Hunt. *Amy Levy: Her Life and Letters*. Athens: Ohio University Press, 2000.

Bennett, Betty T. *Mary Diana Dods: A Gentleman and a Scholar*. New York: William Morrow, 1991.

Bennett, Judith M. "Confronting Continuity," *Journal of Women's History* 9 (1997): 73–84.

———. "'Lesbian-Like' and the Social History of Lesbianism," *Journal of the History of Sexuality* 9 (2000): 1–24.

Bennett, Paula. "Critical Clitoridectomy: Female Sexual Imagery and Feminist Psychoanalytic Theory." *Signs* 18 (1993): 235–59.

Benstock, Shari. "Paris Lesbianism and the Politics of Reaction, 1900–1940." In *Hidden from History: Reclaiming the Gay and Lesbian Past*, ed. Martin Bauml Duberman, Martha Vicinus, and George Chauncey, Jr., 332–46. New York: New American Library, 1989.

———. *Women of the Left Bank: Paris, 1900–1940*. Austin: University of Texas Press, 1986.

Binhammer, Katherine. "The Sex Panic of the 1790s." *Journal of the History of Sexuality* 6 (1996): 409–34.

Blain, Virginia. "'Michael Field: The Two-headed Nightingale': Lesbian Text as Palimpsest." *Women's History Review* 5 (1996): 239–57.

Bland, Lucy. *Banishing the Beast: Sexuality and the Early Feminists*. New York: The New Press, 1995.

———. "Trial by Sexology? Maud Allan, *Salome* and the 'Cult of the Clitoris.'" In *Sexology in Culture: Labeling Bodies and Desires*, ed. Lucy Bland and Laura Doan, 183–98. Chicago: University of Chicago Press, 1998.

Blankley, Elyse. "Return to Mytilène: Renée Vivien and the City of Women." In *Women Writers and the City: Essays in Feminist Literary Criticism*, ed. Susan Merrill Squier, 45–67. Knoxville: University of Tennessee Press, 1984.

Bodenheimer, Rosemarie. "Ambition and Its Audiences: George Eliot's Performing Figures." *Victorian Studies* 34 (Autumn 1990): 7–33.

———. "Autobiography in Fragments: The Elusive Life of Edith Simcox." *Victorian Studies* 44 (2002): 399–419.

———. *The Real Life of Mary Ann Evans: George Eliot, Her Letters and Fiction*. Ithaca, N.Y.: Cornell University Press, 1994.

Bonnet, Marie-Jo. *Les Relations amoureuses entre les femmes du XVIe au XXe siècle: essai historique*. Paris: Odile Jacob, 1995.

Bray, Alan. "Homosexuality and the Signs of Male Friendship." *History Workshop: A Journal of Socialist and Feminist Historians* 29 (1990): 1–19.

Brittain, Vera. *Radclyffe Hall: A Case of Obscenity?* London: Femina Books, 1968.

Broomfield, Andrea. "Blending Journalism with Fiction: Eliza Lynn Linton and Her Rise to Fame as a Popular Novelist." In Eliza Lynn Linton, *The Rebel of the Family*, ed. Deborah T. Meem, 441–55. Peterborough, Ont.: Broadview Press, 2002.

Brown, Irene Q. "Domesticity, Feminism, and Friendship: Female Aristocratic Culture and Marriage in England, 1660–1760." *Journal of Family History* 7 (1982): 406–24.

Busst, A. J. L. "The Image of the Androgyne in the Nineteenth Century." In *Romantic Mythologies*, ed. Ian Fletcher, 1–95. London: Routledge & Kegan Paul, 1967.

Butler, Judith. *Bodies That Matter: On the Discursive Limits of "Sex."* New York: Routledge, 1993.

———. *Gender Trouble: Feminism and the Subversion of Identity*. New York: Routledge, 1990.

———. "Imitation and Gender Insubordination." In *Inside/Out: Lesbian Theories, Gay Theories*, ed. Diana Fuss, 13–31. New York: Routledge, 1991.

Case, Sue-Ellen. *Performing Feminisms: Feminist Critical Theory and Theatre*. Baltimore: Johns Hopkins University Press, 1990.

Castle, Terry. *The Apparitional Lesbian: Female Homosexuality and Modern Culture*. New York: Columbia University Press, 1993.

———. *Masquerade and Civilization: The Carnivalesque in Eighteenth-Century English Culture and Fiction*. Stanford, Calif.: Stanford University Press, 1986.

———. "Matters Not Fit to Be Mentioned: Fielding's The Female Husband." *ELH* 49 (Fall 1982): 602–22.

Chadwick, Whitney. *Amazons in the Drawing Room: The Art of Romaine Brooks*. Berkeley: University of California Press, 2000.

Chalon, Jean. *Portrait of a Seductress: The World of Natalie Barney*, tr. Carol Banko. New York: Crown, 1979.

Chastain, Catherine McNickle. "Romaine Brooks: A New Look at Her Drawings." *Woman's Art Journal* 17.2 (Fall 1996-Winter 1997): 9–14.

Chauncey, George, Jr. "From Sexual Inversion to Homosexuality: Medicine and the Changing Conceptualization of Female Deviance." *Salmagundi* 58–59 (1982–83): 114–46.

Chodorow, Nancy. *The Reproduction of Mothering: Psychoanalysis and the Sociology of Gender*. Berkeley: University of California Press, 1978.

Christianson, Aileen. "Jane Welsh Carlyle and Her Friendships with Women in the 1840s." *Prose Studies* 10 (1987): 283–95.

Clark, Anna. "Anne Lister's Construction of Lesbian Identity." *Journal of the History of Sexuality* 7 (July 1996): 23–50.

Clarke, Norma. *Ambitious Heights: Writing, Friendship, Love—The Jewsbury Sisters, Felicia Hemans and Jane Welsh Carlyle*. London: Routledge, 1990.

Cline, Sally. *Radclyffe Hall: A Woman Called John*. Woodstock, N.Y.: Overlook Press, 1998.

Cohen, Ed. *Talk on the Wilde Side: Toward a Genealogy of a Discourse on Male Sexualities*. New York: Routledge, 1993.

Colby, Vineta. *Vernon Lee: A Literary Biography*. Charlottesville: University of Virginia Press, 2003.

Collis, Louise. *Impetuous Heart: A Biography of Ethel Smyth*. London: William Kimber, 1984.

Colwill, Elizabeth. "Pass as a Woman, Act Like a Man: Marie-Antoinette as Tribade in the Pornography of the French Revolution." In *Homosexuality in Modern France*, ed. Jeffrey Merrick and Bryant T. Ragan, Jr., 54–79. New York: Oxford University Press, 1996.

de Courtivon, Isabelle. "Weak Men and Fatal Women: The Sand Image." In *Homosexualities and French Literature: Cultural Contexts/Critical Texts*, ed. George Stambolian and Elaine Marks, 210–27. Ithaca, N.Y.: Cornell University Press, 1979.

de Lauretis, Teresa. *The Practice of Love: Lesbian Sexuality and Perverse Desire*. Bloomington: Indiana University Press, 1994.

Doan, Laura. *Fashioning Sapphism: The Origins of a Modern English Lesbian Culture.* New York: Columbia University Press, 2001.

———. "'The Outcast of One Age Is the Hero of Another': Radclyffe Hall, Edward Carpenter, and the Intermediate Sex." In *Palatable Poison,* ed. Laura Doan and Jay Prosser, 162–78. New York: Columbia University Press, 2001.

Doan, Laura, and Jay Prosser, eds. *Palatable Poison: Critical Perspectives on 'The Well of Loneliness.'* New York: Columbia University Press, 2001.

Dolan, Jill. "Gender Impersonation Onstage: Destroying or Maintaining the Mirror of Gender Roles?" *Women and Performance: A Journal of Feminist Theory* 2.2 (1985): 5–11.

Donoghue, Emma. *Passions Between Women: British Lesbian Culture, 1668–1801* London: Scarlet Press, 1993.

———. *We Are Michael Field.* Bath, Eng.: Absolute Press, 1998.

Dranch, Sherry A. "Reading Through the Veiled Text: Colette's *The Pure and the Impure.*" *Contemporary Literature* 24 (1983): 176–89.

Dugaw, Dianne. *Warrior Women and Popular Balladry, 1650–1850.* New York: Cambridge University Press, 1989.

Duggan, Lisa. *Sapphic Slashers: Sex, Violence and American Modernity.* Durham, N.C.: Duke University Press, 2000.

Elfenbein, Andrew. *Romantic Genius: The Prehistory of a Homosexual Role.* New York: Columbia University Press, 1999.

Engelking, Tama Lee. "Renée Vivien's Sapphic Legacy: Remembering the 'House of Muses.'" *Atlantis* 18 (1992–93): 125–41.

Faderman, Lillian. *Scotch Verdict: Pirie and Woods v. Dame Cumming Gordon.* New York: William Morrow, 1983.

———. *Surpassing the Love of Men: Romantic Friendship Between Women from the Renaissance to the Present.* New York: William Morrow, 1981.

Faraday, Annabel. "Lessoning Lesbians: Girls' Schools, Coeducation and Anti-lesbianism Between the Wars." In *Learning Our Lines: Sexuality and Social Control in Education,* ed. Pat Mahony and Carol Jones, 23–45. London: The Women's Press, 1989.

Faxon, Alicia. "Images of Women in the Sculpture of Harriet Hosmer." *Women's Art Journal* 2 (Spring-Summer 1981): 25–29.

Flugel, J. C. *The Psychology of Clothes.* London: Hogarth Press, 1930.

Forster, Margaret. *Elizabeth Barrett Browning: A Biography.* London: Chatto & Windus, 1988.

Foster, Jeannette H. *Sex Variant Women in Literature: A Historical and Quantitative Survey.* New York: Vantage Press, 1956.

Foucault, Michel. *The History of Sexuality: Introduction,* tr. Robert Hurley. New York: Random House, 1978.

Francis, Claude, and Fernande Gontier. *Creating Colette.* 2 vols. South Royalton, Vt.: Steerforth Press, 1998.

Frangoes, Jennifer. "'I love and only love the fair sex': The Writing of a Lesbian Identity in the Diaries of Anne Lister (1791–1840)." In *Women's Life-Writing: Finding a Voice/Building a Community,* ed. Linda S. Coleman, 43–61. Bowling Green, Ohio: Bowling Green State University Popular Press, 1997.

Fraser, Hilary. "The Religious Poetry of Michael Field." In *Athena's Shuttle: Myth, Religion, Ideology from Romanticism to Modernism,* ed. Franco Marucci and Emma Sdegno, 127–42. Milan: Cisalpino, 2000.

Fredeman, William E. "Emily Faithfull and the Victoria Press: An Experiment in Sociological Bibliography." *The Library* 29 (June 1974): 139–64.

Freedman, Estelle. "'The Burning of Letters Continues': Elusive Identities and the Historical Construction of Sexuality." *Journal of Women's History* 9 (1998): 181–200.

Friedli, Lynne. "'Passing Women': A Study of Gender Boundaries in the Eighteenth Century." In *Sexual Underworlds of the Enlightenment*, ed. G. S. Rousseau and Roy Porter, 234–60. Chapel Hill: University of North Carolina Press, 1988.

Gale, Maggie B. "From Fame to Obscurity: In Search of Clemence Dane." In *Women, Theatre and Performance: New Histories, New Historiographies*, ed. Maggie B. Gale and Viv Gardner, 21–41. Manchester: Manchester University Press, 2000.

Garber, Marjorie. *Vested Interests: Cross-Dressing and Cultural Anxiety.* New York: Routledge, 1992.

Gardner, Burdett. *The Lesbian Imagination (Victorian Style): A Psychological and Critical Study of "Vernon Lee."* New York: Garland, 1987.

Gillis, John. *For Better, For Worse: British Marriages, 1600 to the Present.* New York: Oxford University Press, 1985.

Glasgow, Joanne. "What's a Nice Lesbian Like You Doing in the Church of Torquemada? Radclyffe Hall and Other Catholic Converts." In *Lesbian Texts and Contexts: Radical Revisions*, ed. Karla Jay and Joanne Glasgow, 241–54. New York: New York University Press, 1990.

Glassco, John. *Memoirs of Montparnasse.* Toronto: Oxford University Press, 1970.

Glendinning, Victoria. *Vita: A Biography of Vita Sackville West.* New York: Quill, 1983.

Gold, Arthur, and Robert Fizdale. *The Divine Sarah: The Life of Sarah Bernhardt.* New York: Alfred Knopf, 1991

Goujon, Jean-Paul. *Tes blessures sont plus douces que leur caresses: vie de Renée Vivien.* Paris: Régine Deforges, 1986.

Greenthal, Kathryn, Paula M. Kozol, and Jan Seidler Ramirez. *American Figurative Sculpture in the Museum of Fine Arts Boston.* Boston: Museum of Fine Arts, 1986.

Grosskurth, Phyllis. *Havelock Ellis: A Biography.* New York: Alfred Knopf, 1980.

Gunn, Peter. *Vernon Lee / Violet Paget, 1856–1935.* London: Oxford University Press, 1964.

Haggerty, George. *Unnatural Affections: Women and Fiction in the Later Eighteenth Century.* Bloomington: Indiana University Press, 1998.

Haight, Gordon S. *George Eliot: A Biography.* New York: Oxford University Press, 1968.

Halberstam, Judith. *Female Masculinity.* Durham, N.C.: Duke University Press, 1998.

Hall, Jacquelyn Dowd. "'To Widen the Reach of Our Love': Autobiography, History and Desire." *Feminist Studies* 26 (Spring 2000): 231–47.

Hallett, Nicky. *Lesbian Lives: Identity and Auto/Biography in the Twentieth Century.* London: Pluto Press, 1999.

Harris, Bertha. "The More Profound Nationality of Their Lesbianism: Lesbian Society in the 1920's." In *Amazon Expedition*, ed. Phillis Birkey et al., 77–88. New York: Times Change Press, 1974.

Harsh, Constance. "Eliza Lynn Linton as a New Woman Novelist." In Eliza Lynn Linton, *The Rebel of the Family*, ed. Deborah T. Meem, 456–74. Peterborough, Ont.: Broadview Press, 2002.

Hauser, Renate. "Krafft-Ebing's Psychological Understanding of Sexual Behaviour." In *Sexual Knowledge, Sexual Science: The History of Attitudes to Sexuality*, ed. Roy Porter and Mikuláš Teich, 210–27. Cambridge: Cambridge University Press, 1994.

Hawthorne, Melanie. "The Seduction of Terror: Annhine's Annhilation in Liane de Pougy's *Idylle saphique.*" In *Articulations of Difference: Gender Studies and Writing in French*, ed. Dominique Fisher and Lawrence R. Schrehr, 136–54. Stanford, Calif.: Stanford University Press, 1997.

Heimann, Mary. *Catholic Devotion in Victorian England.* Oxford: Clarendon Press, 1995.

Henderson, Lisa. "Lesbian Pornography: Cultural Transgression and Sexual Demystification." In *New Lesbian Criticism: Literary and Cultural Readings,* ed. Sally Munt, 173–92. New York: Columbia University Press, 1992.

Herbert, T. Walter. *Dearest Beloved: The Hawthornes and the Making of the Middle-Class Family.* Berkeley: University of California Press, 1993.

Herrmann, Anne. "Imitations of Marriage: Crossdressed Couples in Contemporary Lesbian Fiction." In *Lesbian Subjects: A 'Feminist Studies' Reader,* ed. Martha Vicinus, 102–15. Bloomington: Indiana University Press, 1996.

Hill, Bridget. *Women Alone: Spinsters in England, 1660–1850.* New Haven, Conn.: Yale University Press, 2001.

Hill, Marylu. *Mothering Modernity: Feminism, Modernism and the Maternal Muse.* New York: Garland, 2000.

Hilton, Boyd. *The Age of Atonement: The Influence of Evangelicalism on Social and Economic Thought, 1795–1865.* Oxford: Clarendon Press, 1988.

Hirsch, Pam. *Barbara Leigh Smith Bodichon, 1827–1891: Feminist, Artist and Rebel.* London: Chatto & Windus, 1998.

Hitchcock, Tim, and Michèle Cohen, eds. *English Masculinities, 1660–1800.* London: Longman, 1999.

Hogan, Anne, and Andrew Bradstock, eds. *Women of Faith in Victorian Culture: Reassessing "The Angel in the House."* London: Macmillan, 1998.

Holden, Katherine. "'Nature takes no notice of Morality': Singleness and Married Love in Interwar Britain." *Women's History Review* 11 (2002): 481–503.

Hotchkiss, Jane. "(P)revising Freud: Vernon Lee's Castration Phantasy." In *Seeing Double: Revisionary Edwardian and Modernist Literature,* ed. Carola M. Kaplan and Anne B. Simpson, 21–38. New York: St. Martin's Press, 1996.

Howe, Susanne. *Geraldine Jewsbury: Her Life and Errors.* London: George Allen & Unwin, 1935.

Hunt, Lynn. "The Many Bodies of Marie Antoinette: Political Pornography and the Problem of the Feminine in the French Revolution." In *Eroticism and the Body Politic,* ed. Lynn Hunt, 108–30. Baltimore: Johns Hopkins University Press, 1991.

Irvine, William, and Park Honan. *The Book, the Ring, and the Poet.* New York: McGraw-Hill, 1974.

Jay, Karla. *The Amazon and the Page: Natalie Clifford Barney and Renée Vivien.* Bloomington: Indiana University Press, 1988.

———. Introduction to *A Perilous Advantage: The Best of Natalie Clifford Barney,* ed. and tr. Anna Livia, i–xiv. Norwich, Vt.: New Victoria Publishers, 1992.

———, ed. *Lesbian Erotics.* New York: New York University Press, 1995.

Jeffreys, Sheila. *The Spinster and Her Enemies: Feminism and Sexuality, 1880–1930.* London: Pandora, 1985.

Johnston, Judith. *Anna Jameson: Victorian, Feminist, Woman of Letters.* Aldershot, Eng.: Scolar Press, 1997.

Karl, Frederick R. *George Eliot: Voice of a Century.* New York: W. W. Norton, 1995.

Kasson, Joy S. *Marble Queens and Captives: Women in Nineteenth-Century American Sculpture.* New Haven, Conn.: Yale University Press, 1990.

Kennedy, Elizabeth Lapovsky, and Madeline D. Davis. *Boots of Leather and Slippers of Gold: The History of a Lesbian Community.* New York: Penguin, 1994.

Kennedy, Hubert. "Karl Heinrich Ulrichs, First Theorist of Homosexuality." In *Science and Homosexualities,* ed. Vernon A. Rosario, 26–45. New York: Routledge, 1997.

Kent, Susan Kingsley. *Making Peace: The Reconstruction of Gender in Interwar Britain.* Princeton, N.J.: Princeton University Press, 1993.

———. "*The Well of Loneliness* as War Novel." In *Palatable Poison: Critical Perspectives on 'The Well of Loneliness,'* ed. Laura Doan and Jay Prosser, 216–31. New York: Columbia University Press, 2001.

Kucich, John. *Repression in Victorian Fiction: Charlotte Brontë, George Eliot, and Charles Dickens.* Berkeley: University of California Press, 1987.

Kuhn, Annette. "Sexual Disguise in Cinema." In *The Power of the Image: Essays on Representation and Sexuality,* ed. Annette Kuhn, 48–73. London: Routledge & Kegan Paul, 1985.

Kuhn, William M. *Henry and Mary Ponsonby: Life at the Court of Queen Victoria.* London: Duckworth, 2002.

Laird, Holly A. "Contradictory Legacies: Michael Field and Feminist Restoration," *Victorian Poetry* 33 (Spring 1995): 111–28.

———. *Women Coauthors.* Urbana: University of Illinois, 2000.

Lanser, Susan Sniader. "Befriending the Body: Female Intimacies as Class Acts." *Eighteenth Century Studies* 32 (Winter 1998–99): 179–98.

———. "Speaking in Tongues: *Ladies Almanack* and the Discourse of Desire." In *Silence and Power: A Reevaluation of Djuna Barnes,* ed. Mary Lynn Broe, 156–69. Carbondale: Southern Illinois University Press, 1991.

Lasser, Carol. "'Let us be sisters evermore': The Sororal Model of Nineteenth-Century Female Friendship." *Signs* 14 (Autumn 1988): 158–81.

Leach, Joseph. *Bright Particular Star: The Life and Times of Charlotte Cushman.* New Haven, Conn.: Yale University Press, 1970.

Leighton, Angela. *Victorian Women Poets: Writing Against the Heart.* Charlottesville: University of Virginia Press, 1992.

Lewis, Jane. *The Politics of Motherhood: Child and Maternal Welfare in England, 1900–1939.* London: Croom Helm, 1980.

Liddington, Jill. "Anne Lister of Shibden Hall, Halifax (1791–1840): Her Diaries and the Historians." *History Workshop Journal* 35 (1993): 45–77.

———. "Beating the Inheritance Bounds: Anne Lister (1791–1840) and Her Dynastic Identity." *Gender & History,* 7 (1995): 260–74.

———. *Female Fortune: Land, Gender and Authority: The Anne Lister Diaries and Other Writings, 1833–36.* London: Rivers Oram Press, 1998.

Livia, Anna. "The Trouble with Heroines: Natalie Clifford Barney and Anti-Semitism." In *A Perilous Advantage: The Best of Natalie Clifford Barney,* ed. and tr. Anna Livia, 181–93. Norwich, Vt: New Victoria, 1992.

London, Bette. *Writing Double: Women's Literary Partnerships.* Ithaca, N.Y.: Cornell University Press, 1999.

Lorenz, Paul. *Sapho 1900: Renée Vivien.* Paris: Julliard, 1977.

Lucchesi, Joe. "'An Apparition in Black Flowing Cloak': Romaine Brooks's Portraits of Ida Rubinstein." In *Amazons in the Drawing Room: The Art of Romaine Brooks,* ed. Whitney Chadwick, 73–87. Berkeley: University of California Press, 2000.

———. "'The Dandy in Me': Romaine Brooks's 1923 Portraits." In *Dandies: Fashion and Finesse in Art and Culture,* ed. Susan Fillin-Yeh, 153–84. New York: New York University Press, 2001.

Madden, Ed. "Say It with Flowers: The Poetry of Marc-André Raffalovich." *College Literature* 24 (1997): 11–27.

Malmgreen, Gail, ed. *Religion in the Lives of English Women, 1760–1930.* Bloomington: Indiana University Press, 1986.

Maltz, Diana. "Engaging 'Delicate Brains': From Working-Class Enculturation to Upper-Class Lesbian Liberation in Vernon Lee and Kit Anstruther-Thomson's Psychological Aesthetics." In *Women and British Aestheticism*, ed. Talia Schaffer and Kathy Alexis Psomiades, 211–29. Charlottesville: University Press of Virginia, 1999.

Manocchi, Phyllis. "Vernon Lee and Kit Anstruther-Thomson: A Study of Love and Collaboration Between Romantic Friends." *Women's Studies* 12 (1986): 129–48.

Marini, Andrea. "Sleeping and Waking Fauns: Harriet Goodhue Hosmer's Experience of Italy, 1852–1870." In *The Italian Presence in American Art, 1760–1860*, ed. Irma B. Jaffe, 66–81. New York: Fordham University Press, 1989.

Marks, Elaine. "Lesbian Intertextuality." In *Homosexualities and French Literature: Cultural Contexts/Critical Texts*, ed. George Stambolian and Elaine Marks, 353–77. Ithaca, N.Y.: Cornell University Press, 1979.

Markus, Julia. *Dared and Done: The Marriage of Elizabeth Barrett and Robert Browning*. New York: Alfred Knopf, 1995.

Masters, Brian. *The Life of E. F. Benson*. London: Chatto &Windus, 1991.

Mavor, Elizabeth. *The Ladies of Llangollen: A Study in Romantic Friendship*. Harmondsworth, Eng.: Penguin, 1971.

———, ed. *A Year with the Ladies of Llangollen*. Harmondsworth, Eng.: Penguin, 1986.

McCormack, Jerusha Hull. *John Gray*. Hanover, N.H.: University Press of New England, 1991.

McKenzie, K. A. *Edith Simcox and George Eliot*. Oxford: Oxford University Press, 1961.

McPherson, Heather. "Sarah Bernhardt: Portrait of the Actress as Spectacle." *Nineteenth-Century Contexts* 20 (1999): 409–54.

Meem, Deborah T. "Eliza Lynn Linton and the Rise of Lesbian Consciousness." *Journal of the History of Sexuality* 7 (1997): 537–60.

Meijer, Maaike. "Pious and Learned Female Bosom Friends in Holland in the Eighteenth Century." Paper delivered at the Among Men, Among Women conference, Amsterdam, June 1983.

Melnyk, Julie, ed. *Women's Theology in Nineteenth-Century Britain: Transfiguring the Faith of Their Fathers*. New York: Garland, 1998.

Merrick, Jeffrey. "The Marquis de Villette and Mademoiselle de Raucourt: Representations of Male and Female Sexual Deviance in Late Eighteenth Century France." In Jeffrey Merrick and Bryant T. Ragan, Jr., eds., *Homosexuality in Modern France*, 30–53. New York: Oxford University Press, 1996.

Merrill, Lisa. *When Romeo Was a Woman: Charlotte Cushman and Her Circle of Female Spectators*. Ann Arbor: University of Michigan Press, 1999.

Mitchell, Sally. "'From Winter into Summer': The Italian Evolution of Frances Power Cobbe." *Women's Writing* 10 (2003): 342–52.

Moore, Lisa L. *Dangerous Intimacies: Toward a Sapphic History of the British Novel*. Durham, N.C.: Duke University Press, 1997.

Morgan, Sue, ed. *Women, Religion and Feminism in Britain, 1750–1900*. London: Palgrave, 2002.

Moriarty, David J. "'Michael Field' (Edith Cooper and Katharine Bradley) and Their Male Critics." In *Nineteenth-Century Women Writers of the English-speaking World*, ed. Rhoda B. Nathan, 121–42. New York: Greenwood Press, 1986.

Newsome, David. *Edwardian Excursions: From the Diaries of A. C. Benson, 1898–1904*. London: John Murray, 1981.

———. *On the Edge of Paradise: A. C. Benson, the Diarist*. London: John Murray, 1980.

Newton, Esther. "The Mythic Mannish Lesbian." In *Hidden from History: Reclaiming the*

Gay and Lesbian Past, ed. Martin Bauml Duberman, Martha Vicinus, and George Chauncey, Jr., 281–93. New York: New American Library, 1989.

Nicolson, Nigel. *Portrait of a Marriage.* New York: Atheneum, 1973.

Oosterhuis, Harry. "Richard von Krafft-Ebing's 'Step-Children of Nature': Psychiatry and the Making of Homosexual Identity." In *Science and Homosexualities,* ed. Vernon Rosario, 67–88. New York: Routledge, 1997.

———. *Stepchildren of Nature: Krafft-Ebing, Psychiatry and the Making of Sexual Identity.* Chicago: University of Chicago Press, 2000.

Oram, Alison. *Women Teachers and Feminist Politics, 1900–1939.* Manchester: University of Manchester Press, 1996.

Orenstein, Gloria Feman. "The Salon of Natalie Clifford Barney: An Interview with Berthe Cleyregue." *Signs* 4 (1979): 484–96.

Origo, Iris. "The Carlyles and the Ashburtons: A Victorian Friendship." *Cornhill Magazine* 984 (Autumn 1950): 441–83.

Pacteau, Francette. "The Androgyne." In *Formations of Fantasy,* ed. Victor Burgin, James Donald, and Cora Kaplan, 62–84. London: Methuen, 1986.

Parkes, Adam. "Lesbianism, History, and Censorship: *The Well of Loneliness* and the SUPPRESSED RANDINESS of Virginia Woolf's *Orlando.*" *Twentieth-Century Literature* 40 (1994): 434–60.

———. *Modernism and the Theater of Censorship.* New York: Oxford University Press, 1996.

Parrott, Sarah Foose. "Networking in Italy: Charlotte Cushman and 'The White Marmorean Flock.'" *Women's Studies* 14 (1988): 305–38.

Pemble, John. *The Mediterranean Passion: Victorians and Edwardians in the South.* Oxford: Clarendon Press, 1987.

Perkin, Joan. *Women and Marriage in Nineteenth-Century England.* London: Routledge, 1989.

Polkey, Pauline. "Recuperating the Love-Passions of Edith Simcox." In *Women's Lives in Print: The Theory, Practice and Writing of Feminist Auto/Biography,* ed. Pauline Polkey, 61–79. London: Macmillan, 1999.

Poovey, Mary. *Uneven Developments: The Ideological Work of Gender in Mid-Victorian England.* Chicago: University of Chicago Press, 1988.

Prins, Yopie. "Greek Maenads, Victorian Spinsters." In *Victorian Sexual Dissidence,* ed. Richard Dellamora, 43–81. Chicago: University of Chicago Press, 1999.

———. *Victorian Sappho.* Princeton, N.J.: Princeton University Press, 1999.

Psomiades, Kathy. "'Still Burning from This Strangling Embrace': Vernon Lee on Desire and Aesthetics." In *Victorian Sexual Dissidence,* ed. Richard Dellamora, 21–41. Chicago: University of Chicago Press, 1999.

Rae, Isobel. *The Strange Story of Dr. James Barry, Army Surgeon, Inspector-General of Hospitals, Discovered on Death to Be a Woman.* London: Longmans, 1958.

Raitt, Suzanne. "'The Tide of Ethel': Femininity as Narrative in the Friendship of Ethel Smyth and Virginia Woolf." *Critical Quarterly* 30 (Winter 1988): 3–21.

Raymond, Katherine. "Confessions of a Second-Generation . . . Dyke? Reflections on Sexual Non-Identity." In *PoMoSexuals: Challenging Assumptions About Gender and Sexuality,* ed. Carol Queen and Lawrence Schimel, 53–61. San Francisco: Cleis Press, 1997.

Rendall, Jane. "Friendship and Politics: Barbara Leigh Smith Bodichon (1827–91) and Bessie Rayner Parkes (1829–1925)." In *Sexuality and Subordination,* ed. Susan Mendus and Jane Rendall, 136–70. London: Routledge, 1989.

Rich, Adrienne. "Compulsory Heterosexuality and Lesbian Existence." *Signs* 5 (1980): 631–60

Robbins, Ruth. "Vernon Lee: Decadent Woman?" In *Fin de Siècle/Fin de Globe: Fears and Fantasies of the Late Nineteenth Century*, ed. John Stokes, 139–61. New York: St. Martin's Press, 1992.

Roberts, Mary Louise. *Civilization Without Sexes: Reconstructing Gender in Postwar France, 1917–1927*. Chicago: University of Chicago Press, 1994.

Rodriguez, Suzanne. *Wild Heart: A Life. Natalie Clifford Barney's Journey from Victorian America to Belle Époque Paris*. New York: HarperCollins, 2002.

Rogers, Pat. "The Breeches Part." In *Sexuality in 18th-Century Britain*, ed. Paul Gabriel Boucé, 244–56. Manchester: Manchester University Press, 1983.

Rolley, Katrina. "Cutting a Dash: The Dress of Radclyffe Hall and Una Troubridge." *Feminist Review* 35 (Summer 1990): 54–66.

Roof, Judith. *A Lure of Knowledge: Lesbian Sexuality and Theory*. New York: Columbia University Press, 1991.

Rothenstein, William. *Men and Memories*. 3 vols. New York: Coward-McCann, 1931–40.

Roughead, William. *Bad Companions*. New York: Duffield & Green, 1941.

Rowbotham, Sheila, and Jeffrey Weeks. *Socialism and the New Life: The Personal and Sexual Politics of Edward Carpenter and Havelock Ellis*. London: Pluto Press, 1977.

Rubin, Gayle. Introduction to Renée Vivien, *A Woman Appeared to Me*, tr. Jeannette H. Foster, iii–xli. Reno, Nev.: Naiad Press, 1976.

Rupp, Leila. "Toward a Global History of Same-Sex Sexuality." *Journal of the History of Sexuality* 10 (2001): 287–302.

Saslow, James M. "'Disagreeably Hidden': Construction and Constriction of the Lesbian Body in Rosa Bonheur's *Horse Fair*." In *The Expanding Discourse: Feminism and Art History*, ed. Norma Braude and Mary D. Garrard, 186–205. New York: HarperCollins, 1992.

Sautman, Francesca Canadé. "Invisible Women: Lesbian Working-class Culture in France, 1880–1930." In *Homosexuality in Modern France*, ed. Jeffrey Merrick and Bryant T. Ragan, Jr., 177–201. New York: Oxford University Press, 1996.

Seaton, Beverly. *The Language of Flowers: A History*. Charlottesville: University of Virginia Press, 1995.

Secrest, Meryle. *Between Me and Life: A Biography of Romaine Brooks*. London: Macdonald & Jane's, 1976.

Sedgwick, Eve Kosofsky. *Epistemology of the Closet*. Berkeley: University of California Press, 1990.

Seitz, M. Lynn. "Catholic Symbol and Ritual in Minor British Poetry of the Later Nineteenth Century." Ph.D. dissertation, Arizona State University, 1974.

Shanley, Mary Lyndon. *Feminism, Marriage, and the Law in Victorian England, 1850–1895*. Princeton, N.J.: Princeton University Press, 1989.

Sherwood, Dolly. *Harriet Hosmer, American Sculptor, 1830–1908*. Columbia: University of Missouri Press, 1991.

Sieburth, Richard, ed. "Ezra Pound: Letters to Natalie Barney." *Paideuma* 5 (1976): 279–95.

Sigel, Lisa Z. *Governing Pleasures: Pornography and Social Change in England, 1815–1914*. New Brunswick, N.J.: Rutgers University Press, 2002.

Silverman, Kaja. "Fragments of a Fashionable Discourse." In *Studies in Entertainment: Critical Approaches to Mass Culture*, ed. Tania Modleski, 139–52. Bloomington: Indiana University Press, 1986.

Simmons, Christina. "Companionate Marriage and the Lesbian Threat." *Frontiers* 4 (1979): 54–59.

Smith, F. B. *Radical Artisan: William James Linton, 1812–97.* Manchester: Manchester University Press, 1973.

Smith-Rosenberg, Carroll. "Discourses of Sexuality and Subjectivity: The New Woman, 1870–1936." In *Hidden from History: Reclaiming the Gay and Lesbian Past,* ed. Martin Bauml Duberman, Martha Vicinus, and George Chauncey, Jr., 264–80. New York: New American Library, 1989.

———. "The Female World of Love and Friendship." In Smith-Rosenberg, *Disorderly Conduct: Visions of Gender in Victorian America,* 53–76. New York: Knopf, 1985.

Souhami, Diane. *The Trials of Radclyffe Hall.* London: Weidenfeld & Nicolson, 1998.

St. John, Christopher [Christabel Marshal]. *Ethel Smyth: A Biography.* London: Longmans, Green, 1959.

Steakley, James D. *The Homosexual Emancipation Movement in Germany.* New York: Arno Press, 1975.

Steele, Valerie. *Paris Fashion: A Cultural History.* New York: Oxford University Press, 1988.

Stokes, John. *In the Nineties.* New York: Harvester Wheatsheaf, 1989.

———. "Sarah Bernhardt." In *Bernhardt, Terry, Duse: The Actress in Her Time,* ed. John Stokes, Michael R. Booth, and Susan Bassnett, 13–63. Cambridge: Cambridge University Press, 1988.

Sturgeon, Mary. *Michael Field.* London: George G. Harrap, 1922.

Super, R. H. "Landor's 'Dear Daughter,' Eliza Lynn Linton." *PMLA* 59 (Dec. 1944): 1059–85.

Surtees, Virginia. *The Ludovisi Goddess: The Life of Louisa Lady Ashburton.* Salisbury: Michael Russell, 1984.

Tarnow, Gerda. *Sarah Bernhardt: The Art Within the Legend.* Princeton, N.J.: Princeton University Press, 1972.

Terry, Jennifer. "Theorizing Deviant Historiography." *Differences* 3 (1991): 55–74.

Thurman, Judith. *Secrets of the Flesh: A Life of Colette.* New York: Alfred A. Knopf, 1999.

Todd, Janet. *Women's Friendship in Literature.* New York: Columbia University Press, 1980.

Tosh, John. "Domesticity and Manliness in the Victorian Middle Class." In *Manful Assertions: Masculinity in Britain Since 1800,* ed. Michael Roper and John Tosh, 44–73. London: Routledge, 1991.

Treby, Ivor C. *The Michael Field Catalogue: A Book of Lists.* London: De Blackland Press, 1998.

Trumbach, Randolph. "London's Sapphists: From Three Sexes to Four Genders in the Making of Modern Culture." In *Body Guards: The Cultural Politics of Gender Ambiguity,* ed. Julia Epstein and Kristina Straub, 112–41. New York: Routledge, 1991.

van der Meer, Theo. "Tribades on Trial: Female Same-Sex Offenders in Late Eighteenth-Century Amsterdam." *Journal of the History of Sexuality* 1 (1991): 424–45.

van Slyke, Gretchen. "Gynocentric Matrimony: The Fin-de-Siècle Alliance of Rosa Bonheur and Anna Klumpke." *Nineteenth-Century Contexts* 20 (1999), 489–502.

———. "Reinventing Matrimony: Rosa Bonheur, Her Mother, and Her Friends." *Women's Studies Quarterly* 19 (1991): 59–77.

Vance, William L. *America's Rome.* 2 vols. New Haven, Conn.: Yale University Press, 1989.

Vanita, Ruth. *Sappho and the Virgin Mary: Same-Sex Love and the English Literary Imagination.* New York: Columbia University Press, 1996.

Vicinus, Martha. "The Adolescent Boy: Fin-de-Siècle Femme Fatale?" *Journal of the History of Sexuality* 5 (1994): 90–114.

———. "Distance and Desire: English Boarding School Friendships, 1870–1920." In *Hidden from History: Reclaiming the Gay and Lesbian Past,* ed. Martin Bauml Duberman,

Martha Vicinus, and George Chauncey, Jr., 212–29. New York: New American Library, 1989.

———. "Fin-de-Siècle Theatrics: Male Impersonation and Lesbian Desire." In *Borderlines: Genders and Identities in War and Peace, 1870–1930*, ed. Billie Melman, 163–92. New York: Routledge, 1998.

———. *Independent Women: Work and Community for Single Women, 1850–1920.* Chicago: University of Chicago Press, 1985.

———. "Lesbian History: All Theory and No Facts or All Facts and No Theory?" *Radical History Review* 60 (1994): 57–75.

———. "Turn of the Century Male Impersonation: Rewriting the Romance Plot." In *Sexualities in Victorian Britain*, ed. Andrew H. Miller and James Eli Adams, 187–213. Bloomington: Indiana University Press, 1996.

———, ed. *Lesbian Subjects: A 'Feminist Studies' Reader.* Bloomington: Indiana University Press, 1996.

Vickery, Amanda. *The Gentleman's Daughter: Women's Lives in Georgian England.* New Haven, Conn.: Yale University Press, 1998.

Wachman, Gay. *Lesbian Empire: Radical Crosswriting in the Twenties.* New Brunswick, N.J.: Rutgers University Press, 2001.

Walkowitz, Judith R. *Prostitution and Victorian Society: Women, Class and the State.* Cambridge: Cambridge University Press, 1980.

Waller, Susan. "The Artist, the Writer, and the Queen: Hosmer, Jameson, and Zenobia." *Women's Art Journal* 4 (Spring-Summer 1983): 21–28.

Ward, Maisie. *Robert Browning and His World.* 2 vols. London: Cassell, 1967–69.

Weeks, Jeffrey. *Sex, Politics, and Society: The Regulation of Sexuality Since 1800.* London: Longman, 1981.

———. *Sexuality and Its Discontents: Meanings, Myths, and Modern Sexualities.* London: Routledge & Kegan Paul, 1985.

White, Chris. "Flesh and Roses: Michael Field's Metaphors of Pleasure and Desire." *Women's Writing* 3 (1996): 47–62.

———. "Poets and Lovers Evermore: Interpreting Female Love in the Poetry and Journals of Michael Field." *Textual Practice* 4 (1990): 197–212.

———. "The Tiresian Poet: Michael Field." In *Victorian Women Poets: A Critical Reader*, ed, Angela Leighton, 148–61. Oxford: Blackwell, 1996.

White, Patricia. "Female Spectator, Lesbian Specter: The Haunting." In *Inside/Out: Lesbian Theories, Gay Theories*, ed. Diana Fuss, 142–72. New York: Routledge, 1991.

Whitla, William. "Browning and the Ashburton Affair." *Browning Society Notes* 2 (July 1972): 12–41.

Wickes, George. *The Amazon of Letters: The Life and Loves of Natalie Barney.* New York: G. P. Putnam's Sons, 1976.

Williams, David. *Genesis and Exodus: A Portrait of the Benson Family.* London: Hamish Hamilton, 1979.

Wise, Thomas J., and J. Alexander Symington, eds. *The Brontës: Their Lives, Friendships and Correspondence.* 4 vols. Oxford: Blackwell, 1933.

Wolff, Janet. "The Invisible Flâneuse: Women and the Literature of Modernity." *Theory, Culture and Society* 2.3 (1985): 37–46.

Wood, Elizabeth. "Lesbian Fugue: Ethel Smyth's Contrapuntal Arts." In *Musicology and Difference: Gender and Sexuality in Music Scholarship*, ed. Ruth A. Solie, 164–83. Berkeley: University of California Press, 1993.

————. "The Lesbian in the Opera: Desire Unmasked in Smyth's *Fantasio* and *Fête Galante.*" In *En Travesti: Women, Gender, Subversion, Opera,* ed. Corinne E. Blackmer and Patricia Juliana Smith, 285–305. New York: Columbia University Press, 1995.

————. "Sapphonics." In *Queering the Pitch: The New Gay and Lesbian Musicology,* ed. Philip Brett, Elizabeth Wood, and Gary C. Thomas, 27–66. New York: Routledge, 1994.

Yalom, Marilyn. *A History of the Breast.* New York: Knopf, 1997.

Zimmerman, Bonnie. "'The Dark Eye Beaming': Female Friendships in George Eliot's Fictions." In *Lesbian Texts and Contexts: Radical Revisions,* ed. Karla Jay and Joanne Glasgow, 126–44. New York: New York University Press, 1990.

INDEX